Norman Fischer – 1998 Abbot   Shunryu Suzuki –
                                          Founder 1971

Willam Malten – informer, bakery   Mel Weitsman – 5th Abbot
                                     Linda Cutts 2000 Abbot
Reb – Richard's heir   7 or 8

Richard Baker 1971 Abbot
    Virginia – wife
    Anna – girlfriend –
    Paul Hawkins ↖ Anna's husband
    John Bailes – friend

SHOES OUTSIDE THE DOOR

Also by Michael Downing

Michael Downing

SHOES OUTSIDE

THE DOOR

Desire, Devotion, and Excess at

San Francisco Zen Center

COUNTERPOINT

WASHINGTON, D.C.

Library of Congress Cataloging-in-Publication Data
Downing, Michael.
Shoes outside the door : desire, devotion, and excess at San Francisco
Zen Center / Michael Downing.
p. cm.
ISBN 1-58243-113-2 (alk. paper)
1. San Francisco Zen Center. 2. Baker, Richard, 1936– 3. Suzuki,
Shunryā, 1904– I. Title
BQ6377.S362 S363 2001
294.3'927'0979461—dc21   2001028895

FIRST PRINTING

Jacket and text design by David Bullen

Printed in the United States of America on acid-free paper
that meets the American National Standards Institute
Z39-48 Standard.

COUNTERPOINT
P.O. Box 65793
Washington, D.C. 20035-5793

Counterpoint is a member of the Perseus Books Group

10 9 8 7 6 5 4 3 2 1

for Jack Shoemaker

ACKNOWLEDGMENTS This
book is based on the words, work, advice, impressions, and generosity of
many people. I am especially grateful for the contributions and kindness
of Robert Aitken, Steve Allen, John Bailes, Marie-Louise Baker, Richard
Baker, Butch Baluyut, Frank Barron, Joe Beckett, Frederique Botermans,
Stewart Brand, Ed Brown, Mayor Jerry Brown, the brown-sugar priest,
Tim Buckley, the red buddha, Lucy Calhoun, David Chadwick, Darlene
Cohen, Peter Coyote, Linda Cutts, Renée des Tombe, Diane, Paul Discoe,
Mike Dixon, Rick Fields, Norman Fischer, Therese Fitzgerald, Nelson Fos-
ter, George, Karin Gjording, Della Goertz, Blanche Hartman, Lynn Hen-
nelly, Jane Hirshfield, Brian Hopping, Leslie James, Jeremy & Meg, Joan,
Wendy Johnson, Jonathan, KJM, Kathy, Les Kaye, Ken, Carole Koda, Bar-
bara Kohn, Arnie Kotler, Bill Kwong, Paul Lee, Pat Leonetti, Tom Lip-
scomb, Deborah Madison, Willem Malten, Marilyn, MB, Patrick McFar-
lin, Michael Murphy, David Padwa, Tony Patchell, Julian Todd Pennington,
Grahame Petchey, Pat Phelan, Hilary Rand, Yvonne Rand, Bill Redican,
Lewis Richmond, Gib Robinson, Peter Rudnick, Jeffrey Schneider, Kath-
erine Shields, Gary Snyder, Annie Somerville, Brother David Steindl-
Rast, Teah Strozer, Terry, Katherine Thanas, Bill Tolliver, DeWayne Tully,
Helen Tworkov, Sim Van der Ryn, Mel Van Dusen, Ingrid Vollnhofer,
Betty Warren, Steve Weintraub, Mel Weitsman, Dan Welch, Michael
Wenger, Celeste West, Philip Whalen, and Solange Zanetti.

To the women and men who asked me to remember their stories and
forget their names, I remember you.

To the people whose names I have forgotten without reason or request,
I beg your pardon.

For forty years, students and staff at Zen Center produced *Wind Bell* and several other newsletters, and their steady work made this work possible. I am also indebted to everyone at Zen Center over the years who took legible notes during meetings; kept ledgers; typed and mimeographed and photocopied proposals, announcements, letters, and memoranda; filed documents and memorabilia; and everyone who didn't throw away or lose whatever it was.

At every stage of the book-making process, this book was made better by the work done at Counterpoint Press by Jack Shoemaker, Trish Hoard, Heather McLeod, John McLeod, and Keltie Hawkins—and they always lifted my spirits. For the care and intelligence of his copyediting, I thank Norman MacAfee.

Finally, I am ever grateful to Jonathan Matson, Jane Vandenburgh, Jeanne Heifetz, Mary Ann Matthews, and, of course, Peter Bryant, for reasons beyond reason.

These songs that are here and gone,
here and gone,
to purify our ears.

Gary Snyder

INTRODUCTION. This is the story of Americans who did something original. They just sat down.

I am the wrong person to write this story, and this seems to make sense to everyone. Early in 1998, I met Norman Fischer, then Abbot of Zen Center, and I told him I did not have a Zen practice, was not even an aspiring Buddhist, had never meditated, ate more than my share of meat, and basically knew nothing.

"Knowing nothing is a great place for you to begin," Norman said. "I hope you end up there."

Since then, I've often been in a room with a bald person in a black robe who says things like, "It's not this, and it's not that; and it's not *not* this, and it's not *not* that." In those moments, in those rooms, the nature of *it*—whether we are talking about rice, compassion, or sex—seems perfectly clear and true. Later, sometimes as soon as the door closes behind me, *it* is a little murky, and soon enough I find myself in the dark again, where I waste a lot of time trying to articulate the difference between a monk and a priest, or a priest and a layperson, or a monastery and a madhouse.

Such distinctions—the detritus of dualistic thinking, according to a young Zen student I met during my first visit to the San Francisco Zen Center in 1997—don't matter, of course. Will the man I am to meet today wear robes or street clothes? Immaterial. Will we sit on chairs or cushions on the floor? No difference. Is that incense burning behind me or tea brewing? Doesn't matter. Is Zen a religion? Is Zen Center a cult? Don't think about it.

That's the situation every time I sit down to talk with somebody associated with the San Francisco Zen Center, somebody with a long history of just sitting still for hours every day in cross-legged, mind-emptying, mantraless, motionless *zazen*, the no-point meditation that is the unspeakable truth of this story.

The first time I spent a day at the San Francisco Zen Center, I wasn't in San Francisco, and I didn't know I was at Zen Center. I'd been invited to join a small group of writers and editors, including Wendell Berry, who was giving an afternoon talk at Green Gulch Farm. Just about twenty miles north of San Francisco, in a hilly, coastal stretch of Marin County, the farm is a rich green secret stretch of land that slips down from Highway 1 to the ocean. It is also the home of the Green Dragon Temple, one of the San Francisco Zen Center's three splendidly sited residential training temples.

It was the autumn of 1997. I was in the Bay Area for a week to promote a novel I'd written, in which the American Shakers figure prominently. The Shakers had organized themselves as a collective of self-supporting residential farms, so a day at Green Gulch Farm, and the few facts I picked up about the larger Zen Center project, were enough to make me think I should read a book about the place.

Most of the people I asked in San Francisco had heard about Zen Center, and more than a few had visited or practiced there, but no one knew of a book to recommend. The history of Zen Center has been summarized and analyzed in chapters of books dedicated to the broader topic of Buddhism in the West, and the development of Buddhist thought and practice in America. There was no full account of the people who had built Zen Center, I was told, but had I eaten at Greens restaurant overlooking the Golden Gate Bridge? Greens, the home of haute vegetarian cuisine, was a Zen Center invention. Many of the longtime teachers at Zen Center have written or contributed to books about spiritual practice in the last ten years, and they and their community are well-represented in the periodicals devoted to the widening circle of Buddhist practice in America. And did I like to bake? The *Tassajara Bread Book* was written by a Zen Center priest. Had I ever taken a summer vacation at the Tassajara hot springs resort? Owned and operated by Zen Center. A few people also recalled some newspaper articles about Zen Center—most of them in the 1980s, and most of them not good news. I learned that novelist David Chadwick was completing *Crooked Cucumber* (1999), a biography of Shunryu Suzuki, the Japanese Zen Buddhist who founded Zen Center and who died in 1971. Did I know that Zen Center was the home of the first Buddhist monastery established outside of Asia in the history of the world?

I knew nothing, but it was soon apparent that in the 1970s and early 1980s, Zen Center's reputation and influence as a center of spiritual, cultural, and entrepreneurial innovation were profound. I began to ask some people who might know about the story, and why it had not been written.

"Not much of what we did or what happened at Zen Center has been written down," said Mel Weitsman, the fifth Abbot of Zen Center, the first time I spoke to him. "It's too bad. There is *Wind Bell*, which does tell the story, or a story." *Wind Bell* was a monthly newsletter that developed into a biannual magazine for members and supporters, though only a single issue of *Wind Bell* was published from 1977 through mid-1983. "You'll have to talk to people," said Mel.

Thousands of books have been written by Buddhists and about Buddhism, and after a couple of years of reading nothing but, I did suffer the recurring delusion that I had read most of them. None was more useful than *How the Swans Came to the Lake*, Rick Fields's narrative history of Buddhism's arrival in the West over the course of the twentieth century. Before he died in 1999, Rick Fields, who was familiar with the Zen Center story and its place in the history of the early communal efforts to cultivate Buddhist practice in America, gave me some advice. If you want to know what happened, he said, don't ask too many questions. Ask people what led them to Zen Center; ask people who visited once or twice, and people who stayed for a year and thirty years. In one conversation, I asked Rick a number of questions, all of which he pointedly did not answer. He did say I could talk to plenty of people who'd explain to me why things happened as they did at Zen Center, but it might be more interesting to talk to some people who actually knew what had happened.

What had happened, I thought initially, happened mostly in the 1970s, which was the period that interested me most. In effect, Zen Center had translated its spiritual practice into cultural, retail, and social experiences that made it possible for a few hundred devoted Zen Buddhists to transmit the ancient teaching of the Buddha, the dharma, to countless Americans who might not be ready or willing to meditate or bow nine times at four or five in the morning. The Shakers had successfully influenced the material culture of America with their beautiful chairs, their architecture, and their famous food and hospitality, but the degree to which Shaker practice and principles penetrated the hearts and minds of their customers is debatable; some would say it was negligible. Had Zen Center had better luck?

All I really knew when I first wrote letters to current and former members of Zen Center was that their story was not widely known. I learned quickly that 1983 was a troubling year. More than half of the people to whom I spoke specifically suggested or stipulated that we not discuss 1983 or the events that led up to that hard year; however, no one did not speak about 1983, and most people's personal recollections were organized around that year—Before and After stories. I was never less than fascinated by anyone's recollection of the details of the 1983 crisis and its effects. For more than two years, however, I remained convinced that it was not only *not* the story, but it was not even central to the story. This took some doing on my part. I ignored some obvious hints. First, that everyone talked about it. Second, that many would only speak about it "off the record" (especially current students). In early 1998, a former Zen Center student responded to my initial letter with an enthusiastic telephone call, made immediate arrangements to clear several hours in a complex and busy schedule, and then told me that everything had to be "deeply off the record; when you tell whatever stories you tell, I never existed." I did begin to get the sense that something of consequence had happened. There were other hints; for instance, Linda Cutts, who was installed as Abbess of Zen Center in 2000, refers to 1983 as the Apocalypse.

My reluctance was not noble. It was, in part, an unwillingness to give up the story I had invented for them. But it was more than that, I think; many of the accounts I'd heard were disheartening, and the elements seemed somehow too ordinary or familiar for a story about people whose fundamental life choices I considered admirably inventive and not a little exotic.

Tens of thousands of people can tell you a story of Zen Center. I didn't speak to all of them. Zen Center had only two Abbots in its first two decades (from 1962 through 1983), and yet in the year 2000, its eighth Abbot was installed. I spoke to six of the seven living Abbots. I also spent a lot of time in the Zen Center archives trying to round out the story line that is, as Mel had told me it was, traced out in forty years of *Wind Bell* articles and announcements. Still, hundreds of people have held positions of responsibility within the community—elected and appointed—for one or for many three-month terms; some have remained in a single position for five or ten years, or more. How many stories are sufficient to stand in for all of the stories?

A longtime community resident and leader, who was also a former Treasurer, speculated that after talking to "ten or twenty-five or fifty people with very different profiles in the community" I might see that "most of us were trying to tell the same story; we were trying to learn to say, *Yes. Just sit with it.*" I interviewed more than eighty people, spoke to many more, and I think he was right. As he was when he added, "You could also say that what happened broke the bounds of what any of the mortals at the time were able to sit through."

Remember, I was told time and again, *it was a voluntary thing.* I always knew this was true; no one told me a tale of being snatched from home and deposited at Zen Center, and I heard not a single account of a person who spent time at Zen Center in shackles. Many practitioners remember being told they could leave at any time, that the door was always open.

For a couple of years, I used this fact to discredit or at least dilute the stories I had been told. If people were suffering and disappointed and unhappy, why didn't they just leave? It's interesting because I am accustomed to being impressed by people whose occupations occasion physical, psychological, and emotional hardships, and the cultural reward of money or fame or prestige answers any question I might have about their determination to keep at it. Spiritual awakening and devotion, or simple hopefulness, are less compelling currencies.

Finally, I stopped telling myself that they didn't *have* to be there and tried to remember that these were the people who *were* there. And that seemed as good a reason as any to listen to what they had to say.

Some people volunteered to tell their stories. Some spoke for an hour; others spoke for ten hours or more. I transcribed the audiotapes and notes

I'd made, and read them many times. What I heard, time and again, defeated my fragile sense of the sequence of events. The frame I had assembled while reading and thinking and spending time in the archives was way too small—so way too small that it was nothing.

Most of the material here was neither reviewed nor revised by the people to whom it is attributed. Their stories were edited only by my selection; I've tried to make even small changes to their diction obvious. My only prepared question was my first: *What led you to Zen Center?* In the course of these conversations, I did not ask many questions. Rarely did I ask the same question of two people, and only rarely did anyone ask what others had told me. Before and after we met, many people gave me additional documents and dug up old letters and files they thought might be useful, or directed me to essays and books they had written, which I read.

There is nothing definitive here. Even the budget figures for a given year or the time people actually were awakened for morning meditation when checked against ten sources—paper and people, included—aren't fixed. Numbers in a ledger, a memorable conversation with a spiritual teacher, the meaning of it all—these are stories someone once told. I sat with the stories and the documentary evidence, and what emerged was not indisputable, but it was overwhelming.

If you spend time at any of Zen Center's three residential temples, you will see that even if you've invested nothing but an afternoon, it is hard to leave. You'll see this when you drop in for a lecture, an introductory zazen period, or if you spend a week as a guest student, practicing and working with the community for half of every day and behaving like a guest for the rest of the day. After many days and many nights at each of the three temples, I think my initial impressions of Zen Center were true and not.

Green Gulch still seems like a folk song of a farm. It makes you want to wear overalls and forget to shave, and maybe it's just me, but I suspect the setting will always be at odds with black robes and polished pates. Maybe that's the point; maybe we are all at odds with where we live. Rich soil, clean water, and cool air nurture a landscape's wild and ramshackle nature. Why should human nature be immune? A body's just a building; it's impermanent, and before it disappears, it gets older and stops looking like it used to, and it cracks and bends and hunches over. Sometimes at Green

Gulch, it seems easy to bear that in mind, and sometimes it is not. In the mid-1990s, a former Zen Center resident brought a group of veterans to Green Gulch for a day of meditation and writing practice. There was some disturbance because a few of the veterans didn't want to take off their shoes to enter the meditation hall in the Japanese way. "The head of the meditation hall was aghast with this breach of protocol," remembers the group's leader. "I proceeded to explain that for at least two of the veterans, their shoes *were* their feet. It was a thunderous moment for me, but, alas, I didn't see much realization in the eyes of the head of the meditation hall."

We're not—but you could say we are—all homeless. You could say our shoes are our feet. Take off your feet. Leave yourself outside the door. We're all going away. Even the elegant and expensive structures erected in the 1980s—an octagonal guest house for conference attendees and a magnificent little ceremonial teahouse—will tilt and sag and recede into the earth.

You can see all of this and more at the farm.

Most people who visit Green Gulch for a morning or a week probably don't catch all the finer points of crop rotation or water-saving irrigation strategies or every bend in Buddhism's Eightfold Path, but many of them spend at least a few hours weeding and setting seeds or eating a muffin made by human hands, and they can take away a head of lettuce and a bunch of beets and a way of sitting—all unimproved, unaltered, unenhanced, and all the better for it.

The spirit of the place is not *not* friendly. Meals begin in silence; once everyone is seated, someone slaps the wooden clackers and leads a little chant. The food is often amazingly good, and despite the growing number of vegans in the ranks, heaps of delicious cheese are often melted and sprinkled and layered into the hot things that come out of the kitchen. At breakfast, watch the very senior people deal with rice gruel, and you'll know enough to spike yours with brown sugar and stir in some whole milk or cream, and you could do much worse on a morning in March. ("You can't change your karma, but you can sweeten your cereal," whispered an elderly priest when I nobly and foolishly added nothing to that blob in my bowl during my first stay at the farm.) Once eating is under way, the common dining room looks rather like a high school cafeteria; there are insider and outsider tables, and it is often easy to spot the new students and short-term guests—they're a few minutes late because they haven't memorized the schedule; they're smiling bravely, wielding their dinner trays like steering wheels, weaving around, desperately looking for a public parking space, hoping someone will wave or smile or otherwise signal them to safety. I asked a practice leader about this, and she said she knew it was hard but people have to get over their self-consciousness; for some newcomers, she said, that's zazen, that's their meditative practice. I think that's what I mean by not *not* friendly.

The residents-only feeling is not pervasive; it's not there during meditation, or a lecture or a class, or even on a work crew. And that's the most of your day. But something else happens in the interstices, in the gaps, when the force of activity does not bind an outsider to the insiders. "I don't feel unwelcome," said a funny woman visiting Green Gulch for a week from the Midwest, "but I do feel like the only person walking around without a badge."

The atmosphere at Zen Center's residential temple in San Francisco is not so different, but it is not so surprising there, because the big, handsome brick City Center building is all interiors, and to get anywhere, you have to travel through the low-wattage hush of hallways, as you might in a convent or a fancy convalescent home, and this keeps your social expectations in the right range. Also, City Center is equipped with a safety valve—its door opens to the city. 300 Page Street is in the Western Addition neighborhood, a few blocks from Haight-Ashbury, the Fillmore, Hayes Valley, Market Street, and the Castro. If you do begin to feel sad or self-conscious at the City Center temple, you can drop the truss of neo-Japanese manners, which you've probably got on backwards anyway, open the door, walk outside, and wave at a passerby, or yell, "Hello. How are you?" to someone sitting on a neighboring stoop, or smile at a stranger, and that makes all the difference in the world.

"The first time I went into the *zendo* [meditation hall] at City Center I'd had no instruction," recalled Pat Leonetti, a public health nurse who has lived at Zen Center for almost twenty years. "I went in and sat down and watched what people did. At the end of the meditation period, when I got up, I stood up on the *tan* [a two-foot-high platform on which people sit in meditation; it extends along the perimeter of the room, like a generous bench]. I had never seen the proper form." This is akin to visiting a Christian church and kneeling on a bench and facing away from the altar. "As soon as you make a mistake like that, you can see it. I mean, I saw that everyone else was standing on the floor." Pat is not tall, and she is laughing as she remembers her moment of towering above everyone else. "And this is what amazed me—no one batted an eyelash. No one corrected me. No one smiled. They let me notice I had made a mistake, correct it myself, and I stood down and joined them. I felt like a boulder had dropped into the room, but there was not a ripple. In my heart, I thought, Who are these people?"

That's also what I mean by not *not* friendly.

I should say, too, that I made fast friends from the start at the farm and in the city, not because I lack self-consciousness or do well by manners, but because I am a smoker, and at Green Gulch, as at City Center, there is a little outdoor den of iniquity for the weak, where people behave like humbled people everywhere—they offer you a chair; they might nod or bow slightly in greeting, but when their faces bob back into sight, they are reliably smiling; and they take turns running to the kitchen to get all the cold smokers a cup of hot tea.

"Uh-huh," said the brown-sugar priest when I explained to him how I'd made myself feel at home. He was not impressed. He was smiling and slurping soup. I was slurping but not smiling. I thought he'd sort of missed the point. Then he told me what one of the strictest ceremonial Japanese priests ever to spend time at Zen Center had to say on the subject thirty years ago: "Tatsugami-roshi said smoking is zazen."

And then there's Tassajara, the Zen Center monastery, deep in a profound wilderness valley 150 miles south of San Francisco, at the end of an unpaved fourteen-mile mountain road apparently designed to make sure you don't get there. If you do get there, you pass through a gate that marks the official end of the journey, and you feel you are swimming in . . . something. It was not, for me, a familiar feeling, and it was not foreign. It was like a transfusion, as if some essential fuel had been leaking out of me for a long time and my tank was suddenly refilled. *Oh*, I remember thinking, *so this is how I feel when I feel like myself*. I spent a few days feeling so completely like myself that I started to feel I owed myself an introduction, and after a while, I wasn't even sure I really liked myself, though I couldn't come up with any compelling reasons not to, so I took another dunk in the creek. What is it? Of course, it is the old land and the cold creek and the hot springs; it is the distance you have traveled; it is the way other people feel who have also found their way there; if you are not a resident of Zen Center, it is the summer; this is the guest season, and Tassajara is a resort, a retreat, a way to spend time at a deep remove; but it is also something in the way the Zen students don't stiffen their backs before they bow to a passing priest; it is the crusty and plentiful bread; it is feeling that early morning meditation is compensatory, not compulsory. What is it? It is knowing that Tassajara is really no one's home—it is seasonal; students and priests practice in the autumn and winter, sometimes for several years, but even they cannot stay; everyone must leave Tassajara, as we must leave our very lives. What is it? It is in the air. What is it? "The heart practice," says Dan Welch, who was among the first Zen students to live at Tassajara. What is it? Ed Brown, author of the *Tassajara Bread Book*, says, "It's lineage." Whatever its ingredients, this stuff—you could say it is *sangha*, the community itself—does sort of stick with people who have cared for Tassajara, who have sat there in the winter while the rest of us didn't. I don't suppose it is unique to them, but it is something about them. What is it? It's as if they once got through a long, dark winter by setting their hair on fire and burning up their egos. What is it? It's something like the way wood smoke makes your old clothes smell good. What is it? It's nothing. It's just a sense.

Remember, I was told, *it was a voluntary thing.*

I can't seem to forget it.

SHOES OUTSIDE THE DOOR

1.

AT SOME POINT DURING THE LATE SPRING OF 1983, Richard Baker realized he was in a pickle. He wasn't alone. Hundreds of people were stewing in the same juice. But Richard was an enlightened Zen master. He was the Chief Priest of the San Francisco Zen Center, the most influential Buddhist training and teaching center in the country. He was Abbot of the first Buddhist monastery established outside of Asia in the history of the world. Even people who didn't particularly like him or his flamboyant style conceded that he was an intuitive genius, reliably able to anticipate cultural trends and to dream up events and enterprises to exploit them. So it surprised a lot of people in and around Zen Center that Richard hadn't smelled trouble sooner.

"I was at Tassajara during the Peace Conference," says John Bailes, who was Richard's student for more than a decade. "And you had to wonder, Is this guy this stupid?"

It had been going on for years, says Paul Discoe, a carpenter and ordained priest, but "most people didn't want to see anything."

One of Richard's personal attendants remembers how he told himself the story of his teacher's behavior until that weekend. "I thought, I wish I could say to [Richard] Baker-roshi, 'I know that nothing is wrong, that it is all aboveboard, but you should be careful of appearances as well.'" He shrugs. "I did not know his history."

He was not alone. After Richard was installed as Abbot in 1971, dozens of Zen students rotated through his three residences, earning their room and board and tiny monthly stipends as household staff. Most of them saw nothing that unsettled their faith in their teacher; within the year, most Zen Center students—the largest and most seasoned community of

Buddhist practitioners in America—terminated their relationships with Richard in the aftermath of the revelations, accusations, and hijinks referred to by Abbess Linda Cutts as "the Apocalypse."

This apocalypse was not occasioned by a sudden, eye-opening moment of *satori*, the instantaneous enlightenment that incited so many Americans in the fifties and sixties to explore Buddhism and other yogic cultural practices. Whether they were busy contemplating their navels or trying to come up with a passably irrational response to a question about the sound of one hand clapping, those early enlightenment groupies wanted to be splashed with the cold, clear waters of awakening.

The San Francisco Zen Center Buddhists are descended from the Japanese Soto Zen tradition. They like to wake up to their Buddha nature softly, gradually, slowly; they're sleepers who are reluctant to get out of bed, just like the rest of us. This may explain why so many of them didn't respond to the many alarms they heard in the years before 1983. Who hasn't hit the snooze button a few times?

So, it was not an insight into the nature of all things that attracted their attention one sunny weekend in March of 1983. It was a dusty pair of women's slip-on shoes. The shoes were spotted at several different times outside the door of Richard's cabin at Tassajara, an old hot springs resort 150 miles south of San Francisco.

Richard was in one of the little wooden cabins. He had first visited the resort in the early 1960s with his wife, Virginia, and even then "I thought it was great," he remembers, though "it looked pretty run down—the kind of place you bring your girlfriend or boyfriend, to be away from your spouse or job or something. It was pretty tacky, but beautiful." By 1983, when Richard invited his friend Anna and her children to join him there for a long weekend, the buildings and landscape at Tassajara had been subtly and thoroughly transformed. A pearl had been polished.

The Esselen people and other Native Americans visited the Tassajara hot springs for centuries before the first white settlers arrived in the 1860s. These settlers named the place Tassajara, a coinage that probably derives from the Esselen phrase denoting "the place where dried meat is hung." Tassajara acquired its basic shape as a rustic resort in the early years of the twentieth century, long after the anonymous Chinese laborers cleared and dug the road, and long before one of Joan Crawford's husbands bought it and, like almost every other owner, could not manage to make it pay. It's not a gold mine. Even today, after thirty years of extensive renovation by the current owners, including a few new residential buildings and some low-cost improvements to a couple of saggy old barns (where they stick the kitchen and cleanup crews during the summer guest season), Tassajara can only accommodate about seventy overnight guests.

Tassajara is far from anywhere. On a map, it is about ten sky miles east of Big Sur. When you look inland from California's central coast, you see the outskirts of the two-million-acre Los Padres National Forest. Near its center is the Ventana Wilderness—200,000 acres of rugged and profound sanctuary. It is ringed by a snaggle-toothed grin of granite peaks more than a mile high; inside, the sloping land is dense with stands of conifer that give way to sudden, almost purely vertical ridges. A single dirt road winds slowly upward for more than ten miles and plunges down the last four toward Tassajara Creek in a series of switchbacks that sometimes will spare a car's transmission (if a recent rain hasn't washed a lot of trees and rock into the road) though often at the cost of the brakes, which go mushy and can melt under constant pressure in summertime temperatures of 110 degrees.

The road ends—it just ends. You're almost there. It's a short walk down a soft hill to the valley floor, where the little village spreads out along the creek. A central stand of long, low buildings houses the kitchen and dining room, a large deck overlooking the creek, and an administrative office. There is one telephone (sometimes), and four giant propane tanks provide fuel for cooking and hot water for cleaning up, but the guest rooms are not electrified, and every night the paths and cabins are lit by kerosene lamps. This keeps the nightly fire-watch crew alert, as wildfires have more than once nearly burned Tassajara out of existence.

Follow the dusty footpath to the right, and you pass a short string of pine and stone rooms set along the banks of the creek. Only one building project—a large concrete bathhouse—was ever completed across the creek, where a steep piece of ridge intrudes almost into the water. It is now in ruins. Erosion has turned the big old bunker into a temporary retaining wall. It'll be gone soon. The path winds through the narrow valley floor—you're at the bottom of an ancient gorge, and the land rises so precipitously from the creek basin that direct sunlight slips inside for only a couple of hours every day, even in the summer. A few hundred yards further on, you pass the new Japanese-style wood-and-tile hot-bath complex, and then you head into deeper woods, where land begins to rise toward the ridge and the path dwindles away and you are hiking out of the gorge on a narrow trail.

If you head left from the central courtyard and dining room along the footpath, you pass painted wooden huts clinging to the creek's edge, and then the men's and women's "dormitories"—two little rustic motels for solo travelers willing to share one of the five twin-bedded rooms with a stranger. The valley floor is a little more generous over here. There is room enough for a few big public buildings, a neighborly cluster of eight-by-ten cold-water cabins, a flower and vegetable garden, one strange cylindrical cabin with a deck that is bigger and much less charming than anything else on the property, a couple of refitted barns where students live, and a swimming pool filled with a temperate blend of creek and hot-spring waters.

Every night there is nothing but the unsteady amber glow of glass lanterns lined up like jarred fireflies along the path, an embarrassment of stars overhead, and the creek water smooth-talking its way around a lot of rocks.

Richard's wife Virginia and their two children had decided not to join him at Tassajara that weekend in March of 1983. Anna and her kids had their own cabin, but the neighbors—most of them not more than ten feet away—figured those dusty shoes outside Richard's door were Anna's. "They were," Richard says, years later, nodding. Several people also remember Richard and Anna holding hands as they walked along the path toward a trail into the woods. When he hears this, he looks genuinely confused. "Could've been," he says, and then he smiles briefly, as if he wishes he had held Anna's hand. "I actually don't think so, but it could've looked like it. It was impossible to hide what we were feeling."

Hiding? Who said anything about hiding?

No one in this story supposed that Richard and Anna had traveled to Tassajara for a clandestine rendezvous. Just for starters, Richard is six-foot-two, with dark eyes, a big Roman nose, and he shaves his head. He attracts attention. Anna was lithe, blonde, and "so beautiful"—according to a young female Zen student who remembers the first time she saw Anna on Zen Center property—"so beautiful that I didn't ask her if she needed help, even though she looked lost. I immediately thought, She must be here visiting [Richard] Baker-roshi. No way he doesn't know this woman."

On the merits of their appearance and behavior alone, Richard and Anna might reasonably have expected to excite passing glances no matter where they were that weekend. And secrecy was not served by their selection of a resort with one public byway, a communal dining room, and sleeping arrangements only slightly more private than bunk beds. Also, Richard sort of owned the place.

Since 1967, the Tassajara hot springs resort has been owned and operated as a summer-season business by the San Francisco Zen Center, a nonprofit corporation sole at the time, with Richard as its legally designated Chief Priest. Tassajara is also Zen Center's monastery. Here, for the first time in the 2,500-year history of Buddhism, Zen priests and monks were trained and ordained in the West. And though the guest season was still a few months away and Tassajara typically is closed to all visitors from September until May for intense monastic practice periods, that spring weekend in 1983, Richard had invited the most eminent Buddhist teachers, scholars, and poets in the Western world to the first Buddhist Peace Conference. Thich Nhat Hanh, spiritual pioneer of the Buddhist Mindfulness communities, was at Tassajara, along with poet Gary Snyder, American Zen master and founder of the Diamond Sangha Robert Aitken, Esalen cofounder Michael Murphy, former California governor Jerry Brown, and most of the senior priests of Zen Center. Richard was spending the weekend at the one place on earth where every sentient being he passed was bound to recognize him—and to miss him when he wasn't around. "He and Anna didn't make it to most of Thich Nhat Hanh's talks," a former Zen Center Board member recalls. "Of course, by then, Paul was there."

Richard had invited Paul Hawken to the conference, too. Paul was Richard's friend. Paul was Anna's husband. Paul had recently turned over to Zen Center 200 shares of stock in his new business enterprise, the Smith and Hawken garden-tool catalog company. He and Anna had also made a recent donation—$25,000 in cash and a $20,000 loan—to Zen Center in exchange for a home that had been built for them on the Zen Center farm and practice center in Marin County, twenty miles north of San Francisco, where Richard's wife and two children lived most of the year.

And yet, everyone who lived through the Apocalypse will tell you, as more than eighty of them have told me, it was not about sex.

Okay; but it was not *not* about sex.

"How could these people not have known there were other women in his life?" Frederique Botermans had spent several years at Tassajara and was on her way back from a stay in Japan when she heard the news. "I was shocked by the community more than Richard. Did they think he was perfect?"

By 1983, John Bailes was not looking for perfection. "I didn't care who Dick slept with," he says. "I did care that he cared who I slept with and told me who I could or couldn't. That he did." John had taken a leave of absence from college in 1972; it was not until February of 1984 that he left Zen Center and returned to Harvard to complete his undergraduate degree. Fifteen years later, John is a married investment advisor, and he is training to spend the year 2000 as a crew member ("one of seventeen in a seventy-two-foot boat," he says) in a sailing race around the world. "I like situations," John explains. "That's why I like Zen."

John remembers Richard, at his best, challenging and pressing people to exceed their own perceived limits, "and people rarely do that." John says, "The relationship with Dick was always one of love, and it made me strong." He smiles and rakes his big hands through his curly brown hair. John is taller and more obviously muscular than Richard, but as a young Zen student, "I used to feel I had gone fifteen rounds with Muhammad Ali. As my practice matured," says John, "well. . . I think it was difficult for [Richard] to acknowledge the growth of his students. He couldn't do it." After several years as Richard's student, "there was always this confusion: Is this Zen practice, or is this just a power trip?"

John attended a public lecture in San Francisco given by the Vietnamese monk Thich Nhat Hanh during his stay at Zen Center in early 1983. "I remember sitting in the back of the theater. [A lot of us] had worked to get Thich Nhat Hanh here. Dick introduced him. And I realized I was fed up," says John. "I thought this had Nobel Peace Prize written across it—everything people imagine Harvard is about, not Zen." John is one of several Zen students who were "shocked and not" in March of 1983. "Dick stated, before the Hawken affair—I heard him say—'The shit is going to hit the fan.' As far as Dick could make a plea, he was making a plea," explains John. "But he couldn't give anyone an opportunity to help him."

2.

"BEFORE THIS ALL HAPPENED, BEFORE this whole gathering at Tassajara, you would see a lonely man walking around like a crazy person—Reb Anderson—frequenting the holy altars and doing secretive practice having to do with his Transmission," remembers Willem Malten. "The [Transmission] ceremony asks you to profess oneness with the teacher, the intent of the teacher. We understood that as a mystical union—that you become a master."

Willem runs the popular Cloud Cliff Bakery and Café, which he started in a garage in Santa Fe in 1984. He is in his early forties now, but when he is especially excited, or amused, or intent—as he often is, often at the same time—you see the face of the blond, blue-eyed, young Dutchman who turned up at Zen Center in the late seventies during his first trip to America.

Like most of the students who managed and staffed the multimillion-dollar not-for-profit retail businesses that fueled Zen Center's phenomenal growth in the seventies, Willem never met Shunryu Suzuki, the Japanese Zen monk who emigrated to America in 1959 and, in 1962, founded the San Francisco Zen Center. (By the mid-1960s, students at Zen Center called their teacher Suzuki-roshi. The title *roshi* traditionally was accorded only to a few venerable Zen masters in Japan; however, in the West, it became customary to refer to all Zen teachers who receive Transmission as roshis.) Suzuki-roshi was a legend by the time Willem arrived, and everyone in the Buddhist world knew that Richard was the Japanese master's only American dharma heir. Suzuki-roshi had thousands of American students, but he had only one American heir.

As Willem saw it from the start, "Richard was the indisputable leader.

You can't believe how charismatic he was. When the Clinton story started to unravel, I thought, I have seen this before. Magnetic. They make you feel special, in the first place. They're hilariously funny. And he was always right there; very aware." From the first, Willem believed that "Richard had the vision. And maybe he was right. Maybe America wasn't ready to support a Buddhist community the way it was traditionally done, by begging on the street and by performing ceremonies—weddings and funerals. But there was something else in the businesses and the conferences," says Willem. "There was his personal ego. The structure of Zen Center was an S Corp [Corporation Sole], as I have now with Cloud Cliff. You can do whatever you want. This made it hard to depose him. He could change the rules. And he did what he wanted and legitimized it with the mantle of practice."

Suzuki-roshi's historic Transmission of the dharma to one and only one American man haunts everything that ever happened at Zen Center. And it only got spookier when, in 1983, Richard publicly identified his own first dharma heir.

The job of a Zen master is to transmit the dharma.

The word *dharma* is a cognate of the Pali word for carrying. The dharma that is passed from teacher to student involves the essential teachings of the Buddha and the spirit of living those truths. *Transmission* is applied both to the ritual identification and acknowledgment of a particular student as the legitimate successor, or dharma heir, of a Zen master, and to the ordinary, daily interactions between the teacher and all students.

Transmit is an oddly technical verb, and the analogies it occasions are oddly useful. If you imagine the dharma as an electrical current arcing across a distance from one conductive wire to another, you get the basic idea. However, if you have even a rudimentary grasp of physics, you know that the power of an electrical charge decreases as it travels this way. This is precisely what is not supposed to happen to the dharma as it passes from master to disciple. A dharma heir is meant to be someone whose enlightenment or understanding equals or, preferably, surpasses that of the master.

It may be more useful to imagine a teacher as a radio station. Anyone nearby with a radio can catch the news. The challenge for the Zen student is to develop the equipment to catch the signal and become a broadcaster. A student who has the equipment and skill to take the dharma signals and make a more powerful, or more skillfully modulated, broadcast than the master transmitted is a legitimate dharma heir. After a protracted series of private ceremonies and ritual tests, the heir's name is added to the master's lineage chart, which constitutes a genealogy of the dharma. A teacher might have one dharma heir or dozens, and some teachers receive ceremonial Transmission from more than one master (sometimes from different schools or sects), but if you trace any strand of this tangled web of teachers' names, it will lead you back to the Buddha.

Personal encounters between teacher and student are especially significant as Zen is transmitted without regard to orthodoxy or sacred scriptures. The dharma is passed, essentially unworded, from the teacher's "heart-mind" to the student's "heart-mind." In Soto Zen, the aim is not accumulation of insights or ideas but the realization of one's essential nature, Buddha nature, which has no boundaries and no form. It is an awakening to what you are not.

Even to a relative newcomer like Willem, it was evident that "Reb was first in line for Transmission. Then the master fell down from his pedestal, and where did that leave Reb, who had just professed oneness with Richard? Reb faced an existential dilemma," says Willem. "Was he going to say, 'Look, I will stick up for Richard and be with him. If you throw him out, I will go with him and serve him to the end of my days'?"

What Reb said in July of 1983 was recorded in the notes of a meeting of the Outside Financial Advisory Board (OFAB). "Zen Center has entered a new phase—it is like these flowers," he said, pointing to a centerpiece on the table. "When the petals fall off, the seeds are left. We would not have chosen this particular catalyst, of course. Fortunately, our meditation practice helps us retain some level of calm. An expansive period has just ended for Zen Center, and a contractive, solidifying period has begun. We don't want to overdo it and get too withdrawn, but the changes we are undertaking are actually two years overdue."

This speech was perfectly pitched to discredit and dismiss his teacher. But if that was his intent, his method was indirect. Indeed, in the records of this and other meetings, Reb's mannered tone and diction often make him seem somewhat remote from the business at hand, typified by his reference to the flowers. Robert Aitken, who was called in to consult at various stages of the long-running Zen Center crisis, characterizes this quality of voice as "a cultivated habit of making enigmatic, Zen-ish proc-lamations." Reb's implication is clear enough. As Darlene Cohen, a Zen priest whose speech is never robed or pious, explains, "It was all inevitable earlier than almost anyone could have known. It became inevitable when Richard gave Reb dharma Transmission. Then, we were valid without Richard; he was dispensable for the first time. We turn a corner at that moment." Reb had become an acknowledged master two months before the Apocalypse.

In July of 1983, Richard was still the Abbot; however, he had begun a year's leave of absence and no one ever seemed to know exactly where he was. Reb's meditation-induced calm at the center of this storm certainly distinguished him; most of the rest of the community was spending more time in meetings large and small than in meditation. "Most people just stopped keeping the schedule," a senior priest remembers. Often, at the first morning period, there were fewer than a dozen people in the *zendo*, or meditation hall. "We were used to it being full—fifty or sixty people, at least—with latecomers seated on cushions in the hall outside." By mid-1983, in fact, Zen Center had spent thousands of dollars on group-process consultants and psychological counselors, who were hired to bat relief for the exhausted lineup of Buddhist big-hitters who'd stepped up to the plate in the immediate aftermath of the crisis. And this was just the beginning; it would be three years before Zen Center installed a new Abbot.

What Reb described as a "solidifying period," others recall as "a com-munity-wide nervous breakdown," "a witch hunt," and the beginning of "fifteen years of total reaction" (this is Darlene again), "dead as a door-nail, no energy. Everything that was visionary and bright and shining—Oh! [Richard] Baker-roshi would have done that. And that was the end of it. Fifteen years dead as a doornail."

It was no exaggeration for Reb to call the seventies an expansive period or to highlight the dire need for fiscal restraint. At this same OFAB meet-ing, the Treasurer reported that Zen Center had just finished two years of deficit spending (at least $155,000 in the red) with a $100,000 deficit projected for the year ahead. In the same period, the "Abbot's department budget" (which had come to mean, "Richard's lifestyle expenses") had grown from $130,000 to $180,000 to $215,000. And most people in the room considered these figures to be fractional estimates of Richard's annual spending. In these same years, Deborah Madison, the head chef at Greens, Zen Center's celebrated vegetarian restaurant, was sharing a monthly stipend of $300 with her husband. "And that was considered a lot of money, something other people in the community might resent," Deborah recalls.

As a result, there was a lot of discussion that summer about the affordability of a full-scale audit of Zen Center's finances as the accusations about Richard and his use of Zen Center funds quickly escalated from grandiosity toward graver, criminal charges.

"There are fanciful stories around about money," laments Richard. "That's one of the things I hate. I hate that people say I stole money from Zen Center. The opposite is true, as far as I'm concerned. All of [my wife] Ginny's resources went into it. You can draw a line, what was personal and what was not—and I don't think I practically have a personal life—and I drew the line maybe differently from the way other people did."

This sentiment doesn't surprise Willem. When Willem first arrived at Zen Center from the Netherlands, Richard told him that before he became Abbot, he was ambivalent about the material and ceremonial aspects of Zen. This tallies with the questions and concerns expressed in letters Richard wrote to his teacher, Suzuki-roshi, and to the Board of Zen Center during his first trip to the monasteries in Japan during the late sixties. "But he really grew into the ceremonial role," says Willem, smiling and looking suddenly very young. "Richard would go into Japantown [in San Francisco], into exclusive antique stores, and order antique, certified Zen master robes for thousands of dollars apiece. He developed a powerful combination of sincerity and theatrics." This is one of several stories about the ceremonial robes Richard wore as Abbot of Zen Center. More than a decade after the Apocalypse, the provenance, cost, and ownership of the robes were still in dispute.

But even more serious in the minds and memories of almost everyone who spoke about this period was the quality of Richard's remorse. He did apologize—repeatedly. But his expressions of responsibility and remorse for having caused harm did not register as sincere within the community. Almost overnight, Richard's performance in the role of Abbot lost its authority. Why, after twelve years, was his audience unwilling to suspend its disbelief?

Do not harm. This is the first precept, or obligatory rule for behavior, given to a Zen Buddhist during lay ordination, a ceremony that marks a period of sincere practice, typically a year, with a teacher and other practitioners. If the first precept was not clear to the Abbot, what had been transmitted to him from the ancient lineage of dharma teachers? It was an alarming question for everyone at Zen Center, and it became a question about Reb, who was Richard's heir.

The precept is literally a prohibition against killing, but it is understood as a proscription against all words or actions that will add to suffering in the world. (Our doctors operate under the Greek version of this wisdom, of course. They take the Hippocratic oath, and then they pick up their scalpels.) The founder of Zen Center, Suzuki-roshi, had repeatedly reminded his young students that the easiest way to do no harm was to "just sit."

And though Zen eschews comparative judgments, most of the priests and lay practitioners point to one person as Zen Center's best sitter. "Reb is a rock in the zendo," says a longtime student, aptly summarizing the opinion of her former colleagues. "His presence during practice [sitting meditation] is total." For many, the stillness and discipline of Reb's practice invites comparison to the legendary Japanese samurai, the warriors who trained in medieval Zen monasteries. Reb's magnetism is more purely physical than Richard's charisma. Reb is not a big man—5' 10" and 155 pounds. He is fit; he shaves his head; he moves and doesn't move with a genuine, economical grace. His eyes are blue, and his gaze unsettles a lot of people. One of his young students said that whenever Reb looks right at her she has an impulse to ask him what he's looking at.

What do people see when they see Reb? They see a boxer. He was—and this is typically the first fact repeated about Reb—a Golden Gloves boxer in his youth.

It was not irrelevant training, and when the bell for Round One was rung at the conclusion of the 1983 Buddhist Peace Conference, Reb was the first to step into the ring. As recorded by Willem in his voluminous ringside journals, Reb hammered away at the first precept, but he also whacked himself upside the head a couple of times, a dramatic demonstration of the sincerity of his own remorse.

> The room fell silent. Reb Anderson was about to speak. People were still filing into the dining room at Tassajara. It was the night after we had been told. Hadn't Reb just finished the Transmission ceremony with Richard that would make him technically not only an equal to Baker but, as far as intention is concerned, an identical clone to Baker-roshi? As students, we must accept that Reb's word is of authority, even though it is the same authority that has just been drawn into complete question. How can it be? These were the kind of paradoxes that stared us in the face with urgency, like life-sized koans that were not just to be studied while meditating, but called for instantaneous authenticity, which was in scarce supply. Caught. No way out. No longer any room for denial.
>
> Reb was facing a huge dilemma. By doing the Transmission ceremony together with Baker-roshi, Reb had freshly and publicly expressed his oneness with Baker. The question thus became how to keep his own leadership position while Baker was tumbling down. From this almost impossible position, Reb came up with a solution worthy of Machiavelli. Being the next in line to speak, he began his performance by hyperventilating as if frantically trying to suck in all of the attention that had just focused on him. Like a child throwing the worst temper tantrum, his head swelled up until it was purple and almost featureless, just his nose sticking out. He was holding on to his seat as he finally burst out and screamed in anguish

at the top of his lungs that actually everybody had perceived it all wrong. It was Reb Anderson! It was Reb Anderson, not Baker-roshi who was actually responsible for the whole mess at the Zen Center! And he felt terribly bad and sorry that he had let Baker-roshi do what he did for such a long time before correcting the situation. And he begged the whole community for forgiveness.

Like a good fundamentalist preacher of hell and condemnation, he actually shed tears of repentance and denounced his own evil ways. Then he asked the whole community for forgiveness, before sinking back into his chair like a hot air balloon, which was suddenly deflated.

He pressed his point once more. Everybody present could count on his repentance.

He repeated this crafty, high-strung performance before audiences not just at Tassajara but also at the Green Gulch Farm and the San Francisco City Center. It left Reb wounded, but he retained his power base.

"I realize," wrote Willem after some reflection, "that I am caught in the world of judgments. And that all of this must be, in essence, superfluous, but I did have a bad taste in my mouth after Reb finished speaking. If these words had been the mark of enlightenment, I was disappointed . . . this was about as far away as one could get from what I take to be mystical understanding."

It is a commonplace among Americans that every person has his own reality, his own truth, his own valid account of anything he has seen, heard, felt, or otherwise experienced. Willem was young and disillusioned, and he was still closely allied with Richard as a teacher and friend when Reb spoke. All the more significant, then, that his deep discouragement was not singular.

"I backed Reb," Paul Discoe told me. "Reb was my dharma brother. And I thought we needed leadership and that Reb would be willing to lead." Paul's a stout, brusque man who finds a lot to laugh about. You also quickly get the sense that he thinks most people are full of shit. He doesn't like to listen to himself talk, so he doesn't say much. The legacy of Paul's work as head carpenter includes the elegant, enduring temple-style architecture he learned in Japan and taught to the young Zen students who worked on his crews. The only American equivalent of this craftsmanship is the style invented and perfected by the Shakers.

Paul was also one of Suzuki-roshi's early disciples at Zen Center, and he eventually received Transmission from Reb. But in 1983, "I kept saying, 'Lead, Lead. Lead.' And, no, he wouldn't do it." Paul remembers Reb ceding authority to a community more interested in democracy than singular authority. "Reb tries to put on a macho front, but it's not there, really. He was a Golden Gloves champ, but all that means is that he is dogged. It means that he is determined and dogged."

3. "I REMEMBER PEOPLE WOULD COME UP and say to me, 'You're no longer the roshi.' I always thought that was weird. To me *roshi* meant that your teacher had confidence in you." Richard shrugs.

Richard is constantly saying something so apparently simple and reasonable that you begin to share his consternation about the confusion that engulfed him in 1983. Why didn't everyone else get it? As Richard explains it, Transmission happens outside the limits of identity and ego. The fact that an acknowledged master acknowledges you as a Zen master means "you are no longer a Buddhist; what you do is Buddhism. You might be a lousy form of Buddhism. As Suzuki-roshi would say, 'We are always showing people what kind of Buddha we are.'"

Richard wasn't perfect. But it wasn't exactly Richard who was kicked out of Zen Center; it was Buddha, Buddhism, and Suzuki-roshi, whose confidence in Richard, warts and all, is a matter of public and ecclesiastical record.

Is that what he said?

"I felt this had not done Buddhism any good. It hadn't done people's practice any good," says Richard, who saw Erik Erikson for therapy. After several sessions, he recalls Erikson saying, "Well, you understand what has happened; now, you just have to survive it." Richard's close friend and advisor, Esalen's Michael Murphy, told Richard that "the whole alternative movement was crippled by what happened at Zen Center. He always felt we should put it back together." First, though, Richard had to get away. After the Buddhist Peace Conference, while Richard was holed up in his house on Page Street in San Francisco (next door to the big brick Zen Center city residence and temple), several women students accused Richard of "sexualizing" his relationship with them. His erstwhile best friend, Paul Hawken, had a lawyer and had spoken to the Board about his legal options regarding Zen Center and its Chief Priest. Senior priests were testifying at public meetings about physical and psychological abuse Richard had perpetrated. And word was leaking out to Laurance Rockefeller, Fidelity Investments CEO Ned Johnson, and the worldwide network of patrons Richard had cultivated on behalf of Zen Center. "It was pretty hard going through it," says Richard, and then he reconsiders. "Hard? I went through—I walked to Tassajara."

Did he say he walked 150 miles from San Francisco to Tassajara?

"He did this famous walk to Tassajara," Lew Richmond told me. Lew was one of the handful of senior priests at Zen Center who composed the Abbot's inner circle, the people often credited and blamed for Richard's demise. "I actually think he did want to do a dramatic act of penance, that he wanted to demonstrate in all sincerity that he felt very badly about all of this. He told people that he spent a lot of time walking down Route One crying."

Richard dismisses this interpretation. "People thought it was a walk for penance. I never walked for penance at all."

This was news to Mel Weitsman, then head of the Berkeley Zen Center, who remembers trying to help Richard figure out what he should do. "At that time, he was planning to take a walk to Tassajara as a kind of pilgrimage or something. I talked to him about it. I told him, 'What I think would be the best thing is for you to make a public confession about everything you have done, and apologize, and ask for forgiveness. Come clean, and turn yourself over. If you do that, we will have a big repentance ceremony, and we will all do this with you. We can all do this together.'"

Yvonne Rand, the only woman in Richard's inner circle of senior priests, says flatly, "Dick didn't really walk to Tassajara as he promised."

Did Richard announce that he was taking a penitential walk? "Absolutely not. Absolutely not. Never. No, in fact, I didn't discuss it with anybody except [my wife] Ginny. And then I planned it maybe a week or two before. Pretty much I decided on the spur of the moment. And when I camped, I would make a little fire. Playing at being alive."

"Well," says Lew, "he *did* say it, no matter what he says now. Probably his idea of doing it was different from everybody else's, too."

"I started out at eight at night," Richard remembers. He had a knapsack with two Buddhas and some camping gear. "I'd always wanted to walk to Tassajara, and [poet and Zen practitioner] Gary Snyder and I had talked about finding a walking path to have students go down there. I started walking, and I got down to—I think to a certain point toward the airport, and I stopped to call Earl [McGrath, one of Richard's best friends] in New York. I said, 'I decided to walk to Tassajara.'" Earl persuaded Richard to interrupt his walk, and he offered Richard his Los Angeles home as a place to rest.

So did Richard walk to Tassajara?

Yvonne says, "The description of the walk and the actuality of the walk are like everything else—press releases. He would walk, and then he'd get a ride, and then he'd stay at someone's house and get distracted."

An indignant friend of Richard's later assured me that he'd found Richard on the side of the road, many miles south of San Francisco, with blistered, black-and-blue feet.

Richard later told me that his wife and daughters joined him at Earl's house in Los Angeles. There, Linda Ronstadt took Richard and his family to Disneyland, and Richard found himself with Linda Ronstadt on the roller coaster. Linda was biting his hand. Disneyland is approximately 400 miles south of San Francisco.

What was the question?

4

No one is allowed to live in Golden Gate Park. It is half a mile wide and three miles long, and its twisty roads and trails are dotted with handsome old museums, a couple of windmills, America's first Japanese-style garden, and no end of deep, fragrant shade. It is a refuge from ordinary life. An exception to the occupancy rule was made after the 1906 earthquake and fire. Almost 200,000 homeless citizens were sheltered in Golden Gate Park; about 40,000 stayed long enough to establish a tent city of temporary homes and schools and private garden plots. It was a natural response to a natural disaster. Today, however, the citizens of San Francisco pay police to make sure the city's 15,000 homeless residents don't drag their plastic-bagged belongings into the park's Japanese Tea Gardens and set up camp in the sweet little wooden gazebos beside the ponds and bamboo groves. You're not supposed to sleep anywhere in the park, never mind die there. It's a refuge from ordinary life.

It wasn't always there. Stretching from the Pacific Ocean to the edge of San Francisco's Haight-Ashbury neighborhood, Golden Gate Park was a thousand-acre spill of sand dunes until 1870. Of course, you'd never know that by looking at it.

This is one of the principal reasons people seek out spiritual teachers. They figure there is more to most things than meets the eye.

In 1983 (no one is sure exactly when this happened; more than one of Richard's supporters date it to the moment of Richard's leave of absence or his resignation), a white man in a dark sweat suit jogged through the greenery of Golden Gate Park. (No one saw this happen. Until 1987, almost no one knew that this *had* happened.) Can you see the man jogging? His head is shaved smooth. His eyes are blue. His gaze is riveting and wary. He is five-feet ten-inches tall, lean and fit. He is forty-three. Time has not diminished his adolescent physical confidence. As he runs, he holds his torso straight and still. Like a deer, his composure is fierce and fragile. Like a darting boxer, he is not there when you look again. He knows how to erase himself.

As he runs, he becomes aware of something in the bushes beside the path, a familiar form in an unlikely place.

He stops. The form is human. He approaches. It is the body of a man. He sits down. The man is dead.

For some time, he sits on the ground beside the body of the dead man, legs crossed, spine erect, eyes half-closed. He is sitting zazen, the no-point, no-mantra, no-focus meditation that is the heart of this story.

Apparently no one among the thousands of other people in Golden Gate Park that spring day in 1983 noticed the body in the bushes. And if any of them saw Reb meditating with a cadaver, the sighting went unreported. Maybe the dead man didn't look so dead with a live man sitting still beside him. Or perhaps by 1983, every passerby could interpret the meaning of the Lotus meditation posture: Do Not Disturb. Important Spiritual Work Under Way.

Sometime later, Reb stands up and runs away along the path. He does not ask any of the not-dead people in the park for help or advice, as if they are not there. He runs. He does not stop to call the police and alert them to the presence of a corpse in a public place, as if it is not there. He runs. Later that day, he does not tell his colleagues that he sat zazen beside an unidentified man with a bullet hole in his head, as if he wasn't really there.

You could say nothing happened, but you would have to say that nothing happened the next day, and the next, because Reb ran back to the body several times. He took a woman priest-in-training with him once, but she didn't mention it to anyone, either. On the third day, or maybe the fourth—the scant public record varies; let's just say, during one of his alfresco meditation sessions—Reb discovered a gun near the corpse. A moment of enlightenment? Or was he disturbing a crime scene? No one knows. Reb ran the loaded gun back to Zen Center, emptied the chamber, and stashed the bullets and the gun in a trunk. ("I never saw a gun," the female priest assured her friends, years later.)

Whether a passerby, someone at Zen Center, or a routine patrol first alerted authorities to the presence of the body in the bushes is not clear. The body was gone. What did Reb's ritual in the park signify? For four years, no one really knew. He did not mention the body or the gun during any of his meetings with the members of the Outside Financial Advisory Board or the many other boards and councils at Zen Center, where, as far as almost everyone knew until 1987, nothing had happened.

No harm done?

5.

ZEN IS SIMPLE. JUST SIT.

It is the form of Buddhism shaped most by the ideal of enlightenment, as opposed to scriptures, personal salvation, or the Tantric wisdom of a guru. Zen took root in Japan in the twelfth and thirteenth centuries. It was imported from China, where Buddhism had been imported much earlier from India. The word *Zen* is an abbreviation of the Japanese word *zenna*, which is a transliteration of the Chinese word *chan-na* (which is usually shortened to *chan*), which is a transliteration of *dhyana*, a Sanskrit word that means meditation, or the utter and unadorned wakefulness achieved through meditation.

Just sit.

Two principal schools of Zen—Rinzai and Soto—developed in Japan. Rinzai Zen stresses the study of koans, or teaching paradoxes. A teacher assigns the student a koan, and the student meditates on it. (One of the hundreds of codified koans is the infamous question "What is the sound of one hand clapping?") During a private interview, *dokusan,* with the teacher, the student has an opportunity to demonstrate understanding of the koan and move on to the next.

Soto Zen is especially simple. It does not exclude the koans, but they are not studied systematically. Students practice the wordless, mantraless form of sitting meditation, or *zazen,* taught by Japan's preeminent master, Dogen Zenji (1200–1253). The pure and unadorned form of zazen advocated by Dogen is nothing but sitting.

This is what the prince Gautama Siddhartha did after he saw the suffering of the world outside the palace walls. He sat, and at the age of thirty-five, he was enlightened and thereafter was known as the Buddha—

literally, the awakened one. This happened in 525 B.C.E. It took nearly 1,700 years for the story of the man who sat down to reach Japan, and by then the Buddha's teachings had been culturally elaborated and ritualized throughout much of Asia.

Zen is Buddhism made simple again. The robes worn by Zen priests are plain black affairs (unlike the colorful getups favored by the Tibetans and their other Buddhist cousins), and even after receiving Transmission, the Zen master's daily dress is a dull brown robe. You can sit anywhere; Dogen Zenji said that the heart is the real zendo. This informs temple architecture. Plainness here is neither false humility nor a façade. It is true to the bone. Skeletal beams and rafters are seamlessly joined; they are not nailed or screwed into place; they are made to fit together. Inside a zendo, there is mostly open space, dimly lit, with a small central altar and a *tan*, a two-foot-high wooden platform built around the perimeter, where meditators sit on plain black cushions, facing the wall. There are few ceremonial objects—the teacher's staff, a stick of incense burning in a bowl— and it is rare to run into more than one or two bronze or wooden Buddhas. Zen rituals are spare, too. Music is reduced to an isolated ding or bong of a bell, the flat report of a mallet tapped against a slab of wood, and a thrumming bang from a giant bass drum. Even the chanting is monochromatic; students pitch their voices toward the deep, dark end of the register and grumble in unison.

Zen Buddhists cultivate nondiscriminating habits of mind. They eschew dualistic thinking—the codifying, categorizing, and comparing that characterize the Western world's traditions of logic and rational thought. Sitting still, you cultivate Way-seeking mind, or Big Mind, which promotes awareness of the allness and nothingness of each moment, which is every moment. Thus, in the formulation from the *Heart Sutra* that they chant daily, "form is emptiness; emptiness is form."

According to them, this makes perfect sense in Japan and throughout most of Asia. Which is not to say it does not *not* make sense here.

To practice zazen, Suzuki-roshi often reminded his students, is to study the self. By 1983, the senior priests at Zen Center had logged a lot of hours in the study hall. The work and meditation schedule they kept was famous for its rigor. Typically, they sat for almost two hours every morning, beginning at five, attended a midday service, and sat again for an hour or two in the evening until nine. During the two annual Practice Periods, the daily meditation periods were extended. Once a month, they sat for twelve or fourteen hours—a one-day *sesshin* (intensive retreat). At the end of each Practice Period, they sat a seven-day sesshin—twelve to fourteen hours a day for seven straight days, during which they took their meager meals in the zendo, and slept on their cushions. In fifteen years, Reb, Yvonne, Lew, and the other senior students who'd kept the daily schedule had each sat zazen for at least 10,000 to 15,000 hours.

And yet, by any common-sense standard, the most seasoned meditators at Zen Center repeatedly flunked simple tests of self-awareness. "I wonder," wrote a former Zen Center student in a letter to Yvonne in 1987, "if in some cases doing zazen doesn't augment or aggravate the dissociative process—as if in some way it cauterizes the personality and seals it off, encapsulates it, widens the breach between heart and mind."

In 1983, Reb Anderson was sitting in that breach, apparently waiting for an opportunity to exert a spiritual authority he had inherited from a teacher he did not respect or trust.

Yvonne Rand was sitting with the stories of several women who had been students at Zen Center and had sexual relationships with Richard. It was a fundamental breach of ethics for a teacher, and Yvonne sat with the knowledge for a long time. "[Richard] kept saying—and none of us believed him—'I don't know how to teach.' He wanted a lot of activity to keep people around. He had a sense of what was possible if you had a stable community over the long haul," says Yvonne, whose diction is always clear and unmannered. She has short hair, a strong, solid physical presence, and a very steady gaze—which often gives way to a half-smile, as if there is more to say. "One of the weaknesses was that those of us who were close to him didn't believe he couldn't teach. I heard it. I didn't entirely understand why he would say it. And only after I had separated from him emotionally did I realize he had been right."

Lew Richmond had the unenviable task of reconciling the breach. He was the treasurer in the early days. Lew is a tall, lithe, vigorous man with short graying hair and an incongruously youthful face. Fifteen years after he left, he still speaks with an infectious ardor about the creativity and controversies that shaped Zen Center. "Dick drew a small salary," says Lew, "but he had unlimited expense accounts. He could spend money on, quote, *Zen Center things* that were for him. In a time when we had very little money, he thought nothing of spending $20,000 on a statue that he happened to like. He loved objects. He was like an art collector, somebody who would die to get that thing, go to the auction and bid it up. He liked objects in the way someone else likes a man or a woman—he got erotically charged about things." In the early days, says Lew, "it was inconceivable to me why he would spend all of our hard-earned money on a statue, but to him it was more important than anything. The Zen Center collection [of art and artifacts] was worth hundreds of thousands. One Gandharan stone statue," which Lew says is one of the finest examples in the world of the celebrated sculpture from the Gandhara region of India, "he bought for 10K and it's—well, it's priceless. Compare it to those in museums. Dick knew a bargain when he saw one," says Lew, who admires the statue and Richard's aesthetics, but says, "I was against it. I was the money man. It was one of the first times he and I disagreed. I was against the purchase of Green Gulch Farm, too. I thought it was too expensive. But it wasn't as simple as his asking and getting advice or approval—there was always an elaborate spin that made it seem this was essential to our practice. It took a long time for it to dawn on us that maybe there was another way to look at this."

Richard had been sitting zazen, studying himself, for almost twenty years. He, too, managed to misinterpret or ignore many wake-up calls from his students. One of the most poignant came during a meeting with students at Green Gulch Farm. Lew remembers that the mood in the room was relaxed. "Then one of the students said, 'Baker-roshi, we want you to not sit in the Abbot's seat but to come down on the floor and sit with us.' Richard didn't do it. He couldn't do it. He really did not see himself like he saw the rest of us."

Richard maintains that too often he sees others exactly as he sees himself. "I have no interest in status. That's not Buddhism. Really." As a result, "I have a blind spot when it comes to people's ambitions. Like they'd rather have this slightly different position in an office? I don't know what the hell they're talking about." In this way, Richard explains, he is like Philip Whalen, the Beat poet who became Richard's student and, eventually, one of Richard's dharma heirs. "I always think everyone is like Philip. We don't give a shit about all that stuff, but you have to do it."

He concedes that he has never been able to account for his impact on people. He calls it a defect. A patron of Zen Center used to chastise him about taking up too much space. When you enter a room, she told him, you change everything. Richard's response? "How am I supposed to know that? I wasn't in the room before, when it was different." Even after 1983, after he left Zen Center and spent much of his time in Europe, he struggled "to figure out this strange person I occupy. For the most part, nobody knew I was a Zen teacher. Many times, I was just hanging out. People would fall in love with me—and by that time I began to notice it. People would want me to do this, or they'd want me to talk them, and so I found myself very sought after—not because I was the Abbot or anything. I don't know. I look convincing? I don't know what I do. I had to deal with that."

It's not clear that Richard believes any of this is a satisfactory explanation for his performance at Zen Center. It is clear that he believes the perception of him and his behavior was distorted by students' projections. "I am practicing at Zen Center, and I'm trying to learn what impact I have on people as the teacher, and it was two or three years before I got the first glimmer that you have a big impact on people as their teacher. I just didn't get it. Teachers never had a big impact on me—I didn't give a damn about my teachers at Harvard. Maybe I'm just too self-centered or self-motivated or self-something. Projection? As far as I know, I've never projected onto anybody. Intellectually, I understand projection. But the fact that people were projecting on to me? [His wife] Ginny used to say, 'You don't know, you don't know.'"

He didn't know.

He didn't know?

"I realize now," muses Richard, as if it were a subtle point, "that being the landlord, the employer, the teacher, and the manager / president of the businesses, I had a tremendous influence on people's lives. I decided where they lived, worked, practiced, and what salaries they got. I didn't see it, then."

For most people who lived through Richard's reign, this is simply not credible. Of course, it is also incredible that Richard was the last to wake up to the crisis occasioned by Anna's shoes.

And in 1983, everyone's credibility was at issue because almost every so-called revelation, every serious offense with which Richard was charged, had involved the participation of a practicing member of the community who, at some point long before the Apocalypse, had informed other practitioners about the incident. Richard's access to funds had been subject to the approval of the Board; plans and budgets for major capital projects were reviewed by the Board, as well as a council of advisors.

"This was a smart bunch of people," says Gary Snyder. "Without Suzuki-roshi, it could not have happened. Their behavior was the legacy of their profound respect for him. Many of them thought, Suzuki-roshi made Dick the teacher, so I guess it is all okay." Gary was an infrequent visitor to Zen Center; however, in the minds and hearts of the practitioners, he has been an enduring, almost heroic presence by virtue of his celebrated poetry, and his lifelong study of Zen and Asian languages and cultures. And he and Richard have been friends for thirty-five years. "Dick was carrying out something big. I remember feeling this at the time—they were building Zen in America. It was exciting, and people wanted to be there and be part of it. So serving dinner to him and his guests or getting up at four in the morning to drive him to Tassajara— you can make that normal in your mind." Gary smiles. "And Dick carried himself well. There was an enormous energy around the place, bigger than Dick by far. He was just an agent of that and, in some senses, its victim."

Richard met Suzuki-roshi in 1961, and he was elected Treasurer when the dozen or so regular meditators incorporated themselves as the San Francisco Zen Center the following year. At that time, practitioners did not live at Zen Center; everyone who sat zazen in the morning and evening was on the way to or from a job in the city. The annual budget— principally, a small contribution to their teacher—was $2,000. The budget grew modestly with the organization until the purchase of Tassajara, which Richard negotiated on behalf of the members.

"I just think things are possible," Richard explains, recalling Suzuki-roshi's enthusiasm when he first saw the Tassajara property. "My question was, 'Do you want it?' Suzuki-roshi said, 'Can we afford it?' I said, 'Do you want it?' Suzuki-roshi said, 'How will we be able to—?' And I said, 'Do you want it?'" The asking price was $300,000. "When I represented it to Zen Center, everyone said, 'We can't possibly do that. We only have a budget of $6,000.' And I said, 'Then what do we have to lose? We can't lose more than that. What's the problem?'"

"I completely believed in Richard's vision—his picture of the world and of Buddhism," says Yvonne, "—and I trusted him. I believed in what he was trying to do, and I still think that the creative energy and force that he came up with—the dream of a Buddhist community, and the activity that grew out of meditation that was directed at social change—is viable and exciting. Dick had a vision about the whole network of work activities that would make it possible for people to stay in a practice environment for a long time. It took me a long time to realize that the description did not fit my experience."

It was supposed to be simple. The practice of Buddhism is the practice of taking refuge. The individual renews this awareness by chanting the threefold refuge: *I take refuge in the Buddha. I take refuge in the dharma [the teaching]. I take refuge in the sangha [the spiritual community].*

Buddha, dharma, sangha: these are the three treasures of Buddhism.

In 1983, more than 350 full-time practitioners and thousands of part-time students and occasional visitors were taking refuge at Zen Center. And the refuge was threefold. Zen Center comprised three separate temples and residential practice centers—three treasures of California real estate.

Tassajara was a year-round monastery, and the monks managed and staffed a summer guest season that not only funded the stipends and scholarships for students and staff at the monastery but by 1980 contributed more than $100,000 in profits to the annual budget. City Center, which was initially a single large brick residence and temple on the corner of Page and Laguna Streets in San Francisco, had extended its reach across the street and around the block. By 1983, Zen Center owned several neighboring apartment buildings and townhouses in the Western Addition neighborhood between Hayes Valley and Haight-Ashbury, including a two-story home for the Abbot and a separate Guest House. During the

1970s, the Guest House was so frequently occupied by Jerry Brown that the *San Francisco Chronicle* and the *Los Angeles Times* ran front-page exposés of "the Zen Center connection" and its influence on the governor's political appointments. City Center also served as administrative headquarters for the $4 million operation, including retail and service businesses developed, owned, and staffed by Zen Center in locations across the city—Tassajara Bread Bakery (serving 1,000 customers a day); Alaya Stitchery (makers of futons, meditation cushions, and clothing); Cole Valley Graphics; the Whole Earth Bookstore; the Greengrocer's organic-produce market; and Greens restaurant, which opened to praise for its food and design from *Gourmet, Interiors,* and the *International Herald Tribune.*

As if this were not enough, within a year of becoming Abbot in 1971, Richard had launched "a semi-monastic experiment in developing a practice for men and women and families." Seventeen miles north of San Francisco, in Marin County, Zen Center students were transforming 115 acres of ranch land on the Pacific Coast into Green Gulch, a practice, retreat, and conference center, as well as an organic farm and garden. In a 1982 letter to donors, Richard summarized a decade of work, which had included "laying of tens of thousands of feet of line for drinking water, irrigation, sewage, gray water, fire protection, electrical conduit, and telephones," as well as "composting acres of former pasture" and securing housing for thirty single students and fifteen families. Each Sunday, 300 people from the Bay Area attended Sunday dharma lecture at Green Gulch, and by 1983, work was nearing completion on the $300,000 Lindisfarne Hall guest house—an octagonal post-and-beam and plaster structure whose design specifications required aged and custom-milled lumber and the participation of three craftsmen from Japan, who used fiberglass and wheat straw to approximate the traditional pliant plaster used to finish the walls and ceilings.

What was the problem?

"I didn't know what the issues were at Zen Center," explains John Bailes, who was nineteen when he met Richard, "but I would say things like, Why am I living in a barn?" Other unlucky students and families at Green Gulch were living in trailers. "'Oh, that's practice,' I was told. Practice? Well, I've got a problem with that." John dropped out of Harvard and found his way to Zen Center in 1972. "I'm a guy who loves Dick," he says, but "Green Gulch Farm was total, utmost torture. You were on display every Sunday. The visitors loved Sunday lecture—as if that was what Zen was about. Meanwhile you're digging your guts out, and trying to sleep in a barn. There was no way for me to socialize with the larger world that came to look. Okay, I would think, you're nice, you're rich, you live in Marin—Fuck you. I was something to look at, someone doing Zen. Baker was there now and again, but God knows where he lived. In cars and airplanes mostly, I think."

Richard took well to travel—Japan, the Adirondacks, the Soviet Union, England, and at least once to the Netherlands, to visit his young student Willem Malten, who had gone home for a year to complete his undergraduate thesis. Willem doesn't know exactly why Richard came to visit him. "I filled a void, I guess. I was an attractive young punk. What was required of me from the sangha side [the spiritual community of Zen Center]—well, they saw me as a flunkie. They made it clear that they had gone through a lot of shit to get to where they were, and if I wanted any position, I would have to go through all the same shit. Wash the floor. And don't think you are anybody. I was willing to do that. So, I was harmless." Willem was pleased and surprised when Richard arrived in the Netherlands with Michael Murphy. "And there, at home, I could see who Richard was—his sexuality," says Willem. "And he would buy everything in threes—one book for himself, and one for the city, and one for Tassajara or Marin [Green Gulch]. And he knew how to rationalize his purchases and his privileges."

"Richard Baker had a duplicate library in three places," says Yvonne in her matter-of-fact way. "He had a full-time assistant in each of those places—cooking, cleaning, tending, and doing laundry. He and his family went out to dinner [often]. And it was all paid for by Zen Center." Yvonne was not living in a barn, but neither did she have a household staff or an expense account. And unlike the Abbot, she and the other practitioners with college-aged children did not receive tuition bonuses. What distinguishes Yvonne from many of the senior priests is her willingness to acknowledge the material benefits that accrued to the Abbot's intimates.

"There was a very real hierarchy, with an inner and outer group. Our trips to Japan with an entourage—all paid for by Zen Center. The inner group got special things that cost money. There was a real disparity in how people lived. I don't think any of it quite reads coherently unless you look at it through the lens of abuse of authority. The financial inequalities might not be malfeasance, technically, but it is a hair-thin line."

"I suppose I invented the role of being Abbot," says Richard, who was thirty-six when he was suddenly elevated to the position in 1971. He had been studying in Japan, and it had become clear to everyone at Zen Center that Suzuki-roshi, who was only sixty-seven, was dying of pancreatic cancer. "When I first came in the room where Suzuki-roshi was in bed, I sat with him. He said, 'I am very sorry for what I am about to do to you.' And he started to cry."

The recollection makes Richard weep.

Gary Snyder remembers, "Dick quoted that to me himself, not knowing quite what it meant."

"I wasn't going to think about what it meant," says Richard. "I knew I didn't have the capacity, but I just knew I was going to do it. I didn't think, Can I do it? I didn't think about it. I had one thought—I will do it. That's all." He looks genuinely curious when he adds, "What could I do?"

"Look at what he *did* do that should have disaffected people," says Gary. "Like having them all stand in rows and bow as he drove away from Tassajara. Which he did. I was there for that peace conference. I didn't know he was having an affair with Anna Hawken. What offended me was that Dick was turning it into an imperial presidency. That offended me personally. I don't like that style, and I don't like to see it in Buddhism. He had become the Dick Nixon of Zen."

6. "DOZENS OF STUDENTS STANDING IN black robes and bowing to a white BMW—you can say that's megalomania, or you can say that Richard had become a masterful manipulator of the symbology of Zen." Willem shrugs. "It made him larger than life."

It's a hard picture to read from outside of Zen Center. Bowing to the teacher was not bothersome for most practitioners; it tallied with many students' sense of the egoless ideal of Zen Buddhism. In effect, they were bowing to the dharma. More troubling was the knowledge that they had bowed to that car.

The picture finally came clear to Richard in the aftermath of the Apocalypse, though not without the help of an eminent theologian. "William Sloane Coffin said to me, 'That BMW was a mistake.' He couldn't understand it," says Richard, still sounding a note of incredulity. "It just didn't occur to me that people were so involved in such things, the status of things. I loved it because of the way it drove; it didn't mean anything to me as status. Now I know."

It was 1979 when, according to Yvonne, "Richard did that craziness with the BMW, which was a flagrant violation of the will of the Board. It happened at the time of Greens, and that was the point at which Dick stopped listening."

Greens restaurant was the most ambitious of the student-operated businesses, which were essential to Richard's vision of a self-sustaining Buddhist community. No one had anticipated the numbers involved. Zen Center had started the restaurant from scratch, in an empty military warehouse in the abandoned Fort Mason waterfront complex, which was being redeveloped by the National Parks Service. From construction and wiring to learning to brew espresso and resolving menu controversies (should a Buddhist business serve wine?), the project required so many students that staffers were almost daily dragged away from other Zen Center businesses and from administrative posts at the three temples. And the number of hours in an average restaurant worker's day made it impossible for the students employed at Greens to observe the meditation schedule.

"The project was a very heady, visionary idea," says Steve Weintraub, a psychotherapist who is married to Linda, the current Abbess. In 1979, he was Treasurer of Zen Center. "Buddhism has a long history [in matters of financial support]. There was the Indian way, which was monks begging. And then there was the Chinese way, which was working and self-sufficiency. And now there was an American way. And that's how Richard Baker thought. In grand historical terms. I think the name of the project was how to integrate business into spiritual practice. But down on the ground, among the people working, it was less clear. Richard was into micromanagement before they ever coined the term. So, you had no authority and tremendous responsibilities. I was producing all the numbers toward the end of that period [of expanding retail business], when things became more abusive, or more obviously so. The corker was when Richard wanted to buy a BMW."

"It was fantastic to drive," says Richard. "One of my feelings about the car was—and this wasn't just justification—I spent," Richard calculates his time spent in cars and the total is "three months each year driving. And [the BMW] just made it better. Let people give me a break. People attacked me for the amount of gas it used. I used to say, Look, we've got to get rid of this gasoline anyway; I am going to burn it up as fast as I can! They didn't like my remarks like that. "

When Willem asked his teacher about the necessity for such an expensive car, "he told me that the BMW was safer to drive, and who would take care of Zen Center if he was hurt?"

"It *was* safe," says Richard, recalling a ride to Tassajara when his assistant, Arnie Kotler, lost control of the car. "I was asleep, and Arnie fell asleep. We bounced over three lanes, and basically the car saved us. So that justified it in my mind. And I knew I could raise money from friends for the car. Anyway," he concedes, "it was an issue, and it was a mistake, and I wouldn't do it again."

Why has a $25,000 car become legendary? At the time, a high-end Volvo cost about $15,000, and Richard speculates that there would have been no problem if he'd bought two Volvos. Michael Murphy of Esalen dismisses the controversy, reasoning, "In retrospect, he should've gotten a Toyota, but he got a BMW. It's hilarious what that became."

It was harder, presumably, to have a sense of humor about it if you were a student on stipend. Monthly stipends in 1979 ranged from $75 to $300; these were the salaries students earned in addition to room and board and bonuses for travel and medical emergencies. (Unlike the Abbot, students and their families weren't provided with any health-insurance benefits.) According to notes from the April 1979 meeting of the Abbot's Council at which the BMW purchase was considered, the average student stipend was $115 per month—and that stipend represented 80 to 85 percent of the total reimbursements each student received. The bonuses were not big.

It gets funnier.

Richard's reasons for buying a BMW were not as simple as they might seem. He had other motives in mind. "Suzuki-roshi was really committed to there being lay practice. So I decided I would try to prove that you could be fully a layperson and a monk, and that was part of my thing," he explains. "That was a big part of the BMW. I thought, okay, I'll drive a nice car, and I'll have girlfriends, and I'll go to dinner, which I had basically never done. And I did all these things to see if I could also practice. I wanted to be like a layperson. And I don't think I was an exaggerated layperson. I was trying an all-fronts experiment."

Peter Rudnick was helping to run Green Gulch Farm at the time. He feels the car was consistent with the fine-art and real-estate purchases Richard made. "He could not differentiate. He said everything he did was practice. I was a little disappointed in him."

Perhaps the purchase of the BMW was not entirely a spiritual maneuver, Richard admits. In fact, practical considerations drove the decision. "I thought I ought to look at a BMW because I thought, Here's a good car that isn't ostentatious—that's exactly what I thought. I went and looked at the small ones, and I can't sit in the small ones. I can't sit up straight. I like to drive in zazen posture." The newly introduced 700 series BMW afforded more sitting room than the earlier models; however, even the new 700 did not fit him properly, so he had to have the driver's seat torn out and refitted to suit his frame.

Zazen posture?

In the end, even Richard doesn't really buy this logic. "It was on the edge, but who cared? Most of the people I knew—Werner Erhard [founder of est], for instance—I mean, chauffeurs, a huge Mercedes. [Tibetan teacher] Trungpa Rimpoche went around in huge cars with flags. I thought, compared to my sort of peers, I'm being pretty modest. But it was just sheer indulgence. I mean, I had finished Greens. It hadn't opened yet, and I intuitively knew it was going to be a huge success. I don't know how I knew, but I knew. So I was feeling my Cheerios, I guess. And I thought, We're kind of on a roll. And I was in love with Mayumi [a painter with whom he was then having an affair], and so I thought I should buy a car."

At its April meeting, the Abbot's Council asked Richard to leave the room while it debated the purchase. By 1979, this group of senior priests hand-picked by the Abbot had effectively displaced the legally empowered Board of Directors in administrative decision making. This is especially odd because so many members of the Council—including Reb, Lew Richmond, Yvonne, and Steve Weintraub—were still voting members of the Board.

The minutes of the Council meeting record some resistance. "The car is very expensive and Zen Center cannot afford it. The purchase of this car will cause problems for some of the students." In its favor? The Council considered it "a very safe car," and it was not a Mercedes-Benz. "After a very long discussion, the Council decided to go along with the purchase of the BMW that Roshi had found for $25,000."

Richard was on a roll.

The Council also approved a 20 percent increase in monthly stipends; Richard may have "finished Greens," but for the students who had actually done the work of building Greens and training a staff to run it, the workload was about to increase dramatically. However, a petition for vacation pay for students was turned down. "Vacations should come out of the twice yearly bonuses," reasoned the Council, though just the year before, one of the two anticipated student bonuses had been cut from the budget to realize savings of $18,800—almost enough to pay for the Abbot's car.

Twenty years later, the BMW is still a matter of contention and confusion. Richard does remember that the Board didn't think the BMW was a good idea, but he doesn't remember that the Board absolutely refused to endorse the purchase. It was paradoxical to think he could defy Zen Center, he says, because "I could make the decisions."

Not exactly. Under the terms of the Corporation Sole, Richard shared such authority with the Board. In the case of unresolved disputes between the Chief Priest and the Board, issues were to be resolved by a vote of the membership. There was no vote of the membership about the BMW because there was no official dispute between the Chief Priest and the Board. In this limited sense, Richard is right.

Yvonne was Chair of the Board. She remembers how the BMW decision was made. "The Board actually said, 'We don't want you to buy this.' But he'd already bought it. And what I can't believe is that we said, 'Oh, well, then there's nothing we can do about it.' Isn't that amazing?"

7.

"I USED TO WONDER, HOW CAN THIS PERSON be the Abbot of Zen Center?" Ed Brown had been assigned many different jobs at Greens by 1983. "Whenever Dick came to the restaurant, he refused to acknowledge me. That was a teaching. I was supposed to decide that he was my teacher anyway and let go of trying to get anything— even recognition—from him. Especially recognition. He *would* acknowledge me when I was his waiter."

In 1966, Ed was the cook at the Tassajara hot springs resort. When Zen Center purchased the property, he became a disciple of Suzuki-roshi almost immediately and worked as the cook at the monastery. In 1970, a year before Suzuki-roshi died and Richard became Abbot, Ed collected the recipes he'd been using and wrote the first of his best-selling cookbooks, *The Tassajara Bread Book.* By 1985, nearly 500,000 copies of the bread book had been sold; another 250,000 copies of Ed's second book, *Tassajara Cooking,* had been sold; and at least 90 percent of the considerable profits had gone directly into the coffers of Zen Center.

In 1979, Ed was living in an apartment on Page Street owned by Zen Center. He put in a request to have the interior repainted, which was turned down. "Our Abbot was remodeling his home right across from me on Page Street. He had been at the renovations for months. He'd hired a Japanese carpenter to build hand-planed bookshelves. Someone on a scaffold was painting white clouds on the blue ceilings. He had a marble fireplace mantle installed, and then he didn't like it, so he had it taken out and another one was installed—and that happened one more time. He designed etched-glass windows and had them made and installed as room dividers. And he'd bought carpet and furniture. He'd spent $70,000—and he wasn't finished." Ed shakes his head, then exhales, expiating something.

It's often hard to tell if Ed is happy or sad. He is a compact man with dark hair and dark eyes, and his halting conversation is a patchwork of light and dark memories that he lays down side by side, sometimes stitching them together with laughter, sometimes with silent tears, and sometimes he just lets them sit there, unassimilated fragments of a complicated life. "One day, in dokusan"—a private interview between student and teacher—"I said to our Abbot, 'There is something I don't understand. How can Zen Center afford $70,000 to remodel your apartment when it cannot afford $700 to paint mine?' And Dick said, 'Oh, Ed, we're in the same boat.' My mouth dropped open. Then he said to me, 'My apartment isn't finished, you know. You can't finish your apartment. I can't finish mine. Zen Center wants to do this for me. Maybe someday Zen Center will want to do this kind of thing for you.'"

Ed smiles. "Zen Center had hundreds of thousands of dollars from my book." He exhales again. "A friend of mine said it best: I give thanks to Dick Baker every day for fucking up so incredibly well that it gave me my life back, because I had given it to him.'"

What was the event that prompted Ed to retake control of his life? He says unequivocally, "The affair was not the problem as far as I was concerned." However, it was about to become the problem as far as Richard was concerned. Indeed, the affair—the problem that every senior priest refers to as *not the problem*—proved to be the solution. As Ed says, "The affair brought us all together." It was the glue that the fractured Board used to paste itself back together.

Like many of his senior colleagues, in 1983 Ed was not *not* on the Board, but he was not attending meetings. He was working at Greens, and soon after the peace conference at Tassajara, he received a phone call. The full Board of Directors was being convened. "You were supposed to be on the Board for life, but if you weren't reliably with Dick on everything, he would have you go on sabbatical. At least five of us were not going to meetings by then, because we were on the outs. We were invited not to go.

And none of us knew how to challenge him. Over the years, he had cultivated our obedience by marginalizing people. In effect, we shunned people. He marginalized Yvonne."

"That happened in 1981," says Yvonne.

In August of 1981, a young student with whom Richard had conducted
a sexual relationship for several years had confided the details of the affair
to Nancy Wilson Ross, a very important friend to Richard and a beloved
patron and mentor at Zen Center. Nancy Wilson Ross wrote a letter to
Yvonne about the student's confession. It was not news to Yvonne, who
had helped the student leave Zen Center, but it was the opportunity
Yvonne took to disclose her own sexual experience with Richard to
Nancy.

This does not begin to account for the complicated role played by
Nancy in Richard's rise and fall. But in 1981, "there was a big Zen Center
Board meeting—four days." Yvonne was on the board of another national
organization, which had an overlapping meeting, "so I excused myself to
go to the other board meeting. And when I came back, a few days later,
none of the Zen Center Board members would look at me or talk to me.
And after a couple of days, I realized that something had happened. I went
to Reb and asked him. Reb said that Dick had gone through a tirade about
me—saying I was crazy, I wasn't really practicing, that Dick had tolerated
my staying at Zen Center all of these years out of mercy for my suffering,
that I actually never really practiced. That I was basically a basket case."

According to Reb and people who subsequently talked to Yvonne, no
one said anything in her defense at the meeting. "Reb's theory was that
no one was talking to me because no one wanted to be reminded about
how terrible they felt. It was very freeing for me." Richard had inadvertently awakened Yvonne. "Dick had done the one thing I was afraid he
would do, which was to destroy me in the community. I had given my life
to the community. These were my closest friends. And I was still breathing. I felt liberated. My fear of him left at that point."

Richard's damaging speech about Yvonne in 1981 impressed Ed, who
was at the table when the Abbot disposed of the most influential woman
in the community and her reputation. "Dick said, 'Well, Yvonne's not
going to be coming to the meetings for a while. She's having some diffi-

culties. She'll have to take care of them; she's not so stable these days. And you know, everyone in America knows this—all the Buddhist teachers realize that Yvonne has these kinds of problems. You know, she picks up strays all the time, cats and dogs, and she does this with people, and she doesn't always make such good choices.'"

As if the literal text of what Richard said was not damaging enough, there was a clear subtext for Yvonne to read. She had become one of Richard's discarded, discredited women. She knew it could happen. In the late sixties, when Richard and his wife were living in Japan, "Dick wrote to [a young woman he'd met in the States] about how he would leave Virginia, that this girl was the love of his life, and he would marry her. She didn't cook any of this up. It was all there in the letters. And she went to Japan," says Yvonne. "What [Richard] said is, She made it all up and she's completely crazy." After Suzuki-roshi died, Yvonne remembers the young woman "hanging around Zen Center, kind of trying to figure out what happened." Yvonne nods. "And she's fragile enough so she did get unhinged."

If Suzuki-roshi witnessed this kind of craziness, why did he choose Richard as his heir? Yvonne believes "Suzuki-roshi made a giant mistake, but pathology doesn't read across cultures." Many of Suzuki-roshi's disciples and admirers offer similar explanations to dispose of this troubling question. The cross-cultural logic, which exempts the founder from responsibility for his choice, is undercut by the fact that so many Americans embraced Richard as the legitimate successor. As Willem said of his time with Richard in the Netherlands, "I saw who that man was." Like his superiors, who were in positions to see exactly who Richard was almost daily, Willem continued to seek spiritual guidance from Richard.

Why didn't the troubles at Zen Center trouble its admirers and supporters? Richard's lifestyle was no secret; his assistants charged most of his purchases on a Zen Center credit card, and there were other clues. The BMW, for instance. Many of the scholars, poets, celebrities, and social activists who accepted invitations to Tassajara or to dinner at Richard's home at Green Gulch were aware of Richard's extramarital affairs and often dined with his mistresses. They enjoyed elaborate, innovative vegetarian food prepared and served by adult students who did not speak unless spoken to by the Abbot. In the same year that Yvonne was publicly shunned, a major capital campaign was launched. In a letter distributed to potential donors, no less an expert in human behavior and culture than Robert Bellah, Ford Professor of Sociology and Comparative Studies at UC Berkeley, wrote, "At a time when radical individualism threatens virtually all social commitments in our society, Zen Center has been helping thousands of Americans become more responsible, sensitive, and caring individuals and has given an example of how a community can at the same time respect individuality and work harmoniously together for the greater good." Of all the Buddhist communities Bellah had studied, "none has been more important or has made a greater impact on the environing society than the San Francisco Zen Center."

It must have been very rough going at those other communities.

It is not lost on Yvonne that she was living with mature adults whose fundamental religious precepts were wisdom and compassion. Their practice of meditation was meant to be an expression of their intention to wake up. "Years later, one of the puzzles for me was, What did I do with what I saw? I just suspended judgment," she says. When the young woman who had fallen in love with Richard returned to Zen Center, Yvonne "tried to accept that here was somebody who was suffering whom Dick had asked me to take care of. I isolated the real cruelty. I put that in a box and didn't deal with it. I supported Richard and enabled him to do a lot of harm to a lot of people. Of course, it was not at all my intention. But it *is* what happened out of my own ignorance and being asleep myself."

And yet the Abbot's power was not effectively challenged until Anna's shoes were spotted outside his cabin door. "I knew that he had been attracted to Anna Hawken, who was beginning to be a real student at Zen Center," explains Yvonne. "I remember going to a public talk in San Francisco that Thich Nhat Hanh gave and watching Dick come in with Anna, and I thought, Another one. This happened the week after the big conference and retreat with Thich Nhat Hahn that March, at Tassajara, to which I was definitely not invited. I had decided by then that this situation would not change until what was happening at Zen Center with Dick began to matter to the men in the community. Dan Welch called me about Dick's affair with Anna. Paul Hawken called me. Three or four other senior men called me to discuss Dick's affair with Anna. They told me Paul was suffering terribly. I think that seeing the fallout for Paul woke the men up." It was the first time Yvonne believed that enough people were sufficiently upset to do something. "I was still Chairman of the Board—weird, huh?" She called a meeting of the Board and the most senior members of the community. "At the meeting, I told them everything I knew. I told them the whole miserable story. And other people told what they knew."

Leslie James was on the Board in 1983. One of the few senior teachers at Zen Center today who has not been ordained as a priest, Leslie first practiced at Zen Center in 1971 with her husband, Keith, with whom she has raised two children. She was appointed to a leadership position because "Richard had certain people who were close to him join the Board." Of the meeting called by Yvonne, Leslie says, "It was a shock." Leslie was shocked by the litany of her teacher's sexual involvements. "I'd heard about it, but people who were friends of mine had spoken directly to Richard, and he had told them it wasn't happening. And then we heard about the most difficult ones—one with a student that I'd had no idea about." Leslie and her husband and two children had lived and practiced at Tassajara for six years before moving back to the city to practice in the early 1980s. In the aftermath of the Apocalypse, she emerged as the President of Zen Center, a position she held until 1990. She still practices and lives with her family at Tassajara. So, it is significant—if somewhat enigmatic—when Leslie says, "Immediately, it was wider than the sexual behavior. I never felt that Richard did things we didn't allow him to do. We totally participated."

This notion of shared culpability is often voiced at Zen Center today. But the senior students didn't lose their homes. Richard and his family did.

"He was left out on the street," says Steve Allen, who succeeded Steve Weintraub as Treasurer. "I figured, If you want to fire this guy, you should take care of him. I didn't think he should have nothing. It made no sense to me. The Board wanted me to go out and tell everyone how Richard had screwed everything up. It wasn't true. The community had remarkable resources." Steve was not quite a senior student; he'd never been assigned a position of administrative responsibility before he became Treasurer. He was constantly astonished by the behavior of the Abbot and his colleagues. "Sensible people were acting like idiots. I worked with every director, every manager, setting up budgets, preparing monthly reports, but none of them wanted to take any responsibility. They always figured someone else should take care of the money. And this is not to say that Richard was a good manager. He wasn't. I was living on $150 a month. He had a $200,000 budget. His phone bill for the year was $24,000. I had people who'd been in the community for twelve years coming into my office to ask for $25 to buy a pair of pants for their kids."

Steve Allen is a mild man with thin, shaggy brown hair and a scraggly beard to match. He speaks slowly and quietly, and even when he says alarming things, his affect is pacific, like a proper hippie philosopher. And he has an exacting intelligence. Steve remained loyal to his teacher throughout the crisis and, with a few other Zen Center students, eventually followed Richard to Santa Fe. His faith in the practice was not shaken in 1983. "Curiously enough, the inner teaching and the institutional teaching can be maintained in any society under any circumstances," he says. Steve credits an "inner structure" for safeguarding the integrity of the dharma. "Zen practice survived for years with fascism in Japan. It is like an individual maintaining a life outside of a family."

Steve's loyalty to his teacher was not blind, nor was it rewarded. "In December of 1982, when it was clear we needed to make a lot of administrative changes, we reviewed everything, and we accounted for every business, how everything would have to be changed to make it work. During the meeting, Richard started to change every plan. And I turned to him, and I said, 'Why are you trying to destroy what we are doing here?' I was taken aside by a senior member and told, 'Don't you realize this is Richard's place?' I didn't realize it. It had never occurred to me because Richard was never there. We were all working twelve hours a day and it was clear who was keeping it together—it was this group of people. But they didn't have the sense that they were doing it. Their sense was clear—it was Richard's show. They didn't want responsibility. So they wanted me to behave. It was like being on an airplane and seeing that an engine is on fire. When I said, 'Hey, the engine is on fire,' they told me there was a smudge on the window I should take care of."

Richard responded to Steve after the meeting in December of 1982. "I was disinvited to all future Board meetings. That was Richard's way of dealing with it."

In 1983, Yvonne dealt with it by consulting a higher power. "I went to the Zen Center lawyer and asked, How vulnerable is the institution?" This might be considered the moment that Zen truly took root in America—when the branches of an ancient lineage were grafted onto the well-established stand of civil law and legal precedents. "The lawyer did some research and got back to me and said, 'Zen Center doesn't have a chance.' The precedents made it clear that the institution was responsible for the behavior of an employee—in this case the Chief Priest. 'Do whatever you have to in order to settle with Paul Hawken,' he told us, 'because, with a lawsuit, he could take Zen Center all the way down.' And it was plausible at that point that Paul might sue Zen Center. Paul was so frantic and upset that he talked to everybody. Inside Zen Center there was an unspoken but potent message—You don't talk about things. But Paul was enough of an outsider that the first thing he did was to talk to all of his friends, who were part of the very significant Zen Center support system."

After that first full meeting of the Board in 1983, "that stunned day of truth telling," Yvonne and the Board informed Richard, who had returned to Tassajara without Anna, that he had to come to the city immediately.

Willem spent a lot of time with Richard and watching Richard during the days before he was called back to City Center. "No one was keeping the schedule [of meditation]. It was clear that the Board had realized it could not make Paul Hawken disappear. For years, Richard had been young enough and strong enough to make a lot of other guys pack their bags, including a lot of senior priests who'd been expecting to get Transmission from Suzuki-roshi. Paul Hawken was a little different. He had written. He had a track record and money. And he was an idealist. He was the first peer on the inside. And he was a peer with Laurance Rockefeller and Governor Brown. Paul put the Board against the wall. And Baker realized he was playing a losing hand."

Willem holds his face in his hands when he says, "I was concerned about him. I thought, if I was in his place, I would commit suicide." Willem gently slaps his face, waking himself up to the facts. "Ultimately, though, Richard wasn't going to bite the dust and cry out for help. He was reeling, but not ashamed." Instead, says Willem, "he spent a lot of time on the telephone trying to contain the damage in the outside world. He was concerned about funders, and how it would ripple through the whole Buddhist network. Then they took away his phone rights. He looked ash gray, and he took almost a week to write a short, open letter, to say he felt bad, but he was still the master. People felt it was not humble enough— too little, too late. I think if he had eaten shit, it would not have been enough."

"The Board gathered to meet Dick upstairs in the Guest House, surrounded by all that name-brand furniture Dick had picked out," remembers Ed Brown. "We were sitting in a circle, and there was one empty chair. Dick comes in, walks right past the chair, sits down on the floor in *seiza* [Japanese kneeling posture for meditation], and starts talking. And there was a collective gasp—disbelief. Didn't you agree to come in to listen to us? And Dick started sort of schmoozing, and though it was hard to know what he thought he was doing, he apparently believed he could talk his way out. Finally, Yvonne interrupted him."

"I said, 'Richard, sit in a chair like the rest of us.'" When Yvonne flattens out her voice and raises the volume, no sentient being could mistake the seriousness of the moment. "And Richard did a whole shamble about being humble, and I said, 'Sit in a chair like the rest of us.' And I had to say it three times. I was not willing to have the meeting proceed until he sat in a chair."

"No one had ever done this before," says Ed. "She told him we'd invited him to listen to what each of us had to say." For a few months, the community was flush with gratitude for Yvonne, but it faded when a number of Richard's fiercest critics found a new use for the Abbot's theory about spurned women. Ed remains steadfastly grateful to Yvonne for her leadership. "We did have a quorum as a Board that day in the Guest House, after all those years, but Yvonne is the one who did it."

For at least a moment, in 1983, Yvonne believed the questions facing Zen Center were simple. "What's the truth? Is this a sham we have been living? And what is the cause of this heartbreak and suffering?"

"It was actually hopeless at this point," whispers then-Treasurer Steve Allen, looking away, looking a little dizzy. "It was all out of a sense of goodness, from Richard on down, but there were too many unresolved efforts—including the ideals the community had set up and the policies and practices that Richard had invented to fulfill his responsibility. It was impossible. Am I Japanese or American? Am I practicing or managing? Am I a priest or a CEO?"

Ed remembers that Reb was one of the last to speak. "The message from everyone had not been about the affairs. The message was [Richard's] failure to listen. And when Reb said, 'Well, it looks like we have a person here who doesn't listen very well,' Dick said, 'If I have a problem listening, it is because you haven't taught me.'" Ed nods his head—yes, yes, yes, yes, yes, that's what he said. "Even that was our fault. Here's the person who has been taking responsibility publicly for building all of Zen Center, and the problems are our fault?" Ed nods again—no, no, no, no, no. "It's an old trick of spiritual teachers. You know, It's not a problem if I screw the students, it's a problem that you want to talk about it; *you're* screwing with the sangha." Ed closes his eyes. "I'd always wondered, if only to myself, How can he be the Abbot of Zen Center? And he couldn't."

"Later, in the fall [of 1983]," says Yvonne, "the Dalai Lama offered to Dick that he go to Dharamsala," in northern India, where the exiled Tibetan spiritual leader makes his home. Dharamsala does seem a more reasonable refuge than Disneyland. "His Holiness would provide a place for him to go into retreat and would be available to him to help him sort out what had happened, and to figure out where he was. And Dick initially said he couldn't go because he had no money. So somebody gave him a plane ticket. He never went."

"At Tassajara," Willem remembers, "people were walking around wailing. Loud. Lost." Willem took to his bed. "I was disappointed in Baker, in Zen Center, and in the senior students. But I was twenty-eight," Willem adds, sadly. "I just felt very disappointed in myself. It was a crisis for me. I was half-hallucinatory, going back through everything that had led me here. How could I have made the bad decisions that kept me here? My spirit had escaped me. What did it mean to be wearing a black robe now?"

8.

"I THINK ONE MAKES THE COMPARISON with Watergate. I don't think the perpetrators of all that happened at that time really knew or saw what they were doing, at the time, in the kind of light in which ordinary people might. One would start rewriting one's code of ethics—a little bit here and a little bit there." Grahame Petchey is a very tall, very thin man in his sixties with a very pronounced English accent. He has not lived in England for forty years, but his speech is still inflected with a very British precision and, occasionally, derision. "My relationship to Zen Center is formal in the sense that I was the first President, and I incorporated the organization, which can never, ever be changed. But it is informal in the sense that I very rarely go there."

Grahame was the first Zen student ordained by Suzuki-roshi in America and, in 1963, he became the first Zen Center practitioner to wear a black robe. "But by 1983," says Grahame, "I was on the periphery of Zen Center. There were aspects [of the accusations] that I was very well aware of, but I was surprised by the extent of his—womanizing, shall I say? I thought it was one or two, which does happen, but it was more extensive than I ever would have imagined." Grahame recalls that "Richard was not seeking advice," but Grahame "felt it was appropriate, as one of his very close friends, to give him my opinion." Richard talked to Grahame about the situation "from his perspective." Finally, Grahame said, "'If it were me, I would step down graciously from the Abbot's position for at least a year, or two years—whatever it takes. I would stay at Zen Center and go to work in the gardens and continue to practice in a humble and thorough manner,'" which Grahame characterizes as "some contrition and some reconnecting with the really fundamental spirit of Zen Center, of zazen itself. Understanding of life."

Grahame's habit of suddenly going silent complicates the effect of his casually elegant diction. He makes space in time, and his words reverberate there.

Understanding of life.

"Grahame was the only other person who was committed to Zen as a life," remembers Richard. "Or as the possibility of a life. [He and I] took practice seriously, not as something you did on the side." Richard remembers a car trip; he and Grahame were in the backseat and Suzuki-roshi was in front. Richard had been practicing for a few months, and said, "'Suzuki-sensei'—everybody called him *sensei* [teacher]; it was Don Allen and I who started calling him *roshi* [master] because we found out he was a roshi—I said, 'Do you think we can learn Zen Buddhism?' We Westerners, I meant, and he knew what I meant. He turned back, and his eyes locked on to mine, and he said, 'If you want to.'"

Grahame is silent a while longer. His stillness and composure in these odd moments seem perfectly British, or perfectly Zen—or, maybe, neither and both. "Had Suzuki-roshi really been in charge, it would never have happened," says Grahame. "He was officially in charge, but he didn't have hold of all the reins. He let it happen, to see where it would go."

Grahame scoots away from his desk and opens and closes the door that separates his office from his living room, and then he opens and closes it again. He points to the piles of manila folders and photocopies on his bed and shrugs apologetically. His office is also his bedroom. He pauses to stare out through the sliding glass doors into his sunny backyard, and he tilts his head, as if something is missing out there.

If I were you.

"If I *were* Dick, I would have given my life to Zen Center; it would have been my life's work." Grahame has opened another space in time, and whatever he sees there, he stares it down and, finally, says, "And I'd know that I had done a magnificent job. [Dick] is the only person I know who could have done it."

It is Zen Center. But it was not Zen Center when Grahame first sat with Suzuki-roshi in 1961. It was just Zen.

Shunryu Suzuki, a Japanese Zen Buddhist priest, turned up in San Francisco in 1959. He installed himself in a strange old wooden building on Bush Street, near the corner of Laguna Street, in Japantown. He was fifty-five, just over five feet tall, and he was just about as unlikely a candidate for establishing Buddhism in the West as anyone could have imagined.

Throughout the nineteenth century, Buddhist émigrés and converts and bits of Buddhist culture had made their way to America from Asia, but it was many decades before Americans cultivated an indigenous Buddhism—rather like the soybean, which Americans did not cultivate in quantity until World War II and is now a leading export crop, sold principally to the Japanese. In their attempts to date Zen Buddhism's official debut in America, many historians follow the lead of Rick Fields and cite the significance of the 1893 World Parliament of Religions in Chicago; others point to the subsequent arrival of a particular teacher. The undisputed fact is that it was not here until the twentieth century, and it was not able to flourish until a monastery was established at Tassajara in 1967.

Why? Why hadn't it emerged from Walden Pond? Thoreau, like Emerson, was deeply interested in India's religious and Tantric traditions, and according to Richard Baker, the philosophy and prose of the Transcendentalists carries a sense of the dharma, the teaching of the Buddha. "The words of the Transcendentalists were very similar to Buddhism," he says. "But they didn't have the practice."

For 2,500 years, the Buddhism that filtered into the West was the provenance of scholars, philosophers, curators and collectors, and poets. Until very recently, there were more statuary Buddhas in our museums than there were Buddhists in America. The material of Buddhism had been deracinated, cut off from the practice of Buddhism. For most Americans, it was esoterica, puzzling stuff that someone else prized. If you were one of the few who'd heard about Buddhism and wanted to know more, you really couldn't do anything about it unless you traveled to Japan or China.

Of course, you could read a book or two about Zen Buddhism. *Zen in the Art of Archery* was translated from the German and published in America in 1952; Robert Pirsig's *Zen and the Art of Motorcycle Mainte-*

nance was published in 1972. In the intervening decades, Zen best-sellers became a mainstay of the publishing industry. In thousands of wildly disparate books and essays, Zen was identified as a principle of particle physics and the secret to the game of tennis; it superseded Existentialism in university philosophy departments, and anticipated the deconstructionist movement in linguistics that spread to our literary and cultural criticism. Americans did not take to Zen practice, but they took Zen into their lexicon. By the mid-sixties, uttering the word *Zen* had become a way of acknowledging the unutterably elusive essence of—well, of everything.

"It's so Zen," perfectly reasonable people said, when they meant, basically, "It's so groovy," but Zen gave it gravitas. Zen, in America, was not a rigorous, rigid, formalized religion; it was a head game, a mind fuck, a profound riddle. This was typified by the famous formulation from the Heart Sutra, the heart of the ancient *Prajnaparamita*, which is chanted daily to make students mindful of the allness and nothingness of each moment. *Form is emptiness; emptiness is form.*

How paradoxical. How very Zen.

Only it is not a paradox. It's a pair of equations, really, a simple bit of math, as Suzuki-roshi made eminently clear in his lectures to students.

If	FORM	=	EMPTINESS
And	EMPTINESS	=	FORM
Then	FORM	=	FORM
And	EMPTINESS	=	EMPTINESS

Which just makes sense. Be mindful: The nature of a thing is the nature of everything. It's that simple. Rather like the practice. Just sit. But it sounds almost psychedelic when you spell it out as, *Form is form, and form is not form (it is emptiness), and form is not not form (it is emptiness, which is form), and emptiness is, is not, and is not not emptiness or form.*

Spelling it out is the antithesis of practicing Zen. In his introduction to *Zen in the Art of Archery*, the eminent Japanese scholar D. T. Suzuki wrote that Zen practice leads to the recovery of *original mind* or *everyday mind*, which "is no more than 'sleeping when tired, eating when hungry.' As soon as we reflect, deliberate, and conceptualize, the original unconsciousness is lost and a thought interferes." Thus, reading reinforces our remove from original mind. Why, then, did D. T. Suzuki write about Zen? Perhaps because he believed Westerners would never take up the practice, and reading was as close as we would come. His lucid essays alerted Carl Jung, Aldous Huxley, and John Cage to the idea of Zen. But he did not expect his readers to meditate. In his many celebrated books and essays, he devotes not a single chapter to zazen.

When Alan Watts, an Englishman living in the Bay Area, published his widely read primer, *The Way of Zen*, in 1957, he explicitly warned readers against trying to import Zen practice to America. Like his predecessors, Watts emphasized the poetical habits of mind that had fascinated Emerson, Thoreau, and Whitman, as well as their Beat and beatnik descendants. In the first sentence of his first chapter, Watts describes Zen as an indescribable reality that eludes "the formal categories of modern Western thought," striking three resounding notes for American readers standing at the edge of the sixties—social and philosophical formalities were impediments; modernity was problematic; and the East was a repository of ancient remedies. Watts identified himself as neither "Zenist" nor Buddhist. "It is not a religion," he wrote, a claim that is frequently and emphatically made by American adherents. But it is not *not* a religion. Watts called Zen "a way of liberation," which rings true, though it doesn't fully account for the priests, monks, incense, chanting, bowing, and altars.

The message was clear. Form is emptiness. No one bothered to add, Form is form. No one expected Americans to shave their heads, don black robes, and sit cross-legged for four or five hours every day.

"It was 1960, when I was in Kyoto," recalls Gary Snyder, "that I first got a letter from friends in San Francisco that Shunryu Suzuki, a Zen priest from Japan, had arrived and was beginning to set himself up in the old temple on Bush Street. And then several poet friends of mine wrote and said that they had been over there to sit the very first morning he had hung up his shingle, which said *zazen*. And that was my first knowledge of Suzuki-roshi being in San Francisco. He was, at that time, one of the very first and maybe the only Zen priest on the West Coast who was openly and willingly engaging with non-Japanese people. Over the next couple of years, I got glowing reports about what a wonderful person he was, and more and more people were joining him at zazen, and studying with him."

Suzuki-roshi had agreed to serve as head priest at the Zen temple on Bush Street for a couple of years. Having taken a leave from his temple in Japan, he arrived in San Francisco in 1959 without his wife or any of his four children. It was not an extraordinary choice. Buddhism is a missionary religion. There was an established Soto Shu in America, a mission branch of the governing Japanese authority; the American Zen bishop resided in Los Angeles. With no indigenous training monastery, American Zen temples had to rely on Japanese priests, most of whom did not live out their careers in the States. Bishop Yamada, for instance, served a five-year term in Los Angeles and was then appointed to the presidency of Komazawa, the Soto university in Tokyo.

Sokoji had opened as a Zen temple on Bush Street in San Francisco in 1934; the building was originally a synagogue. From any distance, it looks like a mock Romanesque church carved out of inexplicably wan sandstone. You have to get near enough to touch the façade to believe that it is strips of unstained, weathered wood that were bent and carved to assemble the elaborate, inscribed central arch that frames the front doors. A blank, tan rectangular tower stands like a sad sentinel at either side. It is empty now—a hulking, haunting presence on a street of pristine white row houses, but even in the early sixties, Richard says, before the gentrification of the neighborhood, Sokoji was "Kafkaesque," and if you peek through the metal grates bolted to the doors, you can see that the walls and ceiling of the lobby are still painted ghoulish red. Sokoji was closed for several years during World War II, when the Japanese Americans were herded into distant internment camps, but it reopened upon their return to San Francisco. The routine Suzuki-roshi could anticipate at the temple on Bush Street was not unlike the routine at any small Soto temple in Japan, of which there are more than 15,000. Most of the parishioners were farmers who spoke Japanese, did not meditate, and relied on their priest for Sunday services and ceremonial Buddhism—weddings, funerals, and occasional rituals.

Betty Warren and Della Goertz were schoolteachers who'd enrolled in an evening class in Zen Buddhism at San Francisco's Academy of Asian Studies. "Our teacher was Dr. Kato, a Buddhist priest at Sokoji," Betty recalls. He typically lectured on the history of Zen and its cultural significance in Japan. Soon after Suzuki-roshi assumed the duties of head priest at the temple, Kato brought him to the class. "We were all charmed with him," Betty says, and then she closes her eyes and shrugs, as if to say, Who wouldn't be? "He was small, and his English was hesitant—he had book English but not the practice of speaking. And he was shy. Pretty soon, before he said too much, he had everyone on the floor, sitting zazen. It was our first taste of the real thing."

Betty is seated at the far end of a cozy old sofa. Her house is perched in the hills of Sausalito, shaded and scented by eucalyptus trees, and from her living room you get to look down on the fancy boats in the bay. She's dressed for a hike—slacks and a sweater and sturdy shoes. Since 1988, she's been leading people on four- and five-day vision quests in the desert. She's in her eighties. "At the end of that class, Suzuki-roshi said, 'I sit every morning at six o'clock. Please join me.' We did. Della and I went, and there were a couple of other people who had been showing up, and they sat with us."

For five years, Betty sat at Sokoji every morning. "From the very beginning, we knew we had a gem. I had been listening to Alan Watts on KPFA radio, and I was interested in his thoughts. I'd bought a couple of books. But it was the practice that made sense immediately. I was teaching in Oakland and living here, in Sausalito. I got up in time to get to the temple by six, I think—everyone remembers a different time, but it was early. We had the sitting and a little service and chanting. Then I was on my way to school. I took my breakfast—a thermos of coffee and a sandwich—and sat in the teachers' lunchroom and prepared my lessons. Not many people knew me well enough to suggest it was weirder than what I usually did. I was radical politically, and I guess people expected I might do something else a little odd. Before classes—Oakland was a tough place to teach—I would think, I have done the hardest thing already; the rest of the day I can handle. Zazen is painful at first, but we had camaraderie, knowing that everyone's knees or back hurt. And sometime during meditation you see, or have a feeling, and that's it—this is what you've been looking for all of your life."

Within a few years, Betty remembers, five or ten regulars "started doing things together. We'd meet on Saturday mornings to paint the walls, sand the floors, or carry the pews up and down the stairs when they were needed for services. And we had these capable and bright young men—Richard and Grahame—who knew how the world worked. The thing was to find a way to support our teacher. And they managed to get up the idea that we should form a nonprofit corporation. They knew how to go about it legally. This pleased Suzuki-roshi. He depended a lot on their know-how."

"The Zen Center I remember," says Grahame, "was this small, vital group of people at Sokoji. I do wish it had been kept simple in the way it was in the Sokoji days. The practice had great meaning. And there is far less opportunity for things to get out of hand if one has poverty."

"The Japanese were very surprised by Zen Center," Gary Snyder recalls. "When I first went to Japan in the fifties, the general opinion was that Zen is too hard for Americans. Many Japanese said, Well *we* can do it, but what makes you think *you* can do it? So they were seriously impressed by the dedication at Zen Center—that those people really were sitting cross-legged, and they didn't move on their cushions." Gary laughs. "All those important things."

Form.

It was empty for Betty. "I didn't go in for ceremony—all the proper things to put on an altar. That has nothing to do with my relationship to people and nature—which is doing something to try to help peace, such as it is, in this world. Sometimes Suzuki-roshi would lecture on the *Blue Cliff Record*"—one of the major collections of koans and commentaries by Chinese masters—"but it was just words. They didn't sing to me. A lot of words about something that cannot be put into words."

It's like trying to stuff a tall, skinny white man into a black Japanese robe.

"That's a problem," says Gary Snyder. "The role of the formal priest—the shaved head and the robes—has been established for centuries in

Japan and China. Priests have a role when they go into the community. They don't just teach the dharma. They do marriages and funerals. They teach flower arrangement and tea ceremony. These are cultural teachings. Calligraphy. And the priest is taken as a neutral person—a mediator and facilitator—and plays that role very well, and—" suddenly Gary waves his hand, indicating that this is not the half of it. "There was no community role in America for the person in the costume of a Zen priest," he adds summarily. "And there is a real question here. Is our Buddhism in America going to be a lay Buddhism or a monastic Buddhism?"

The question did not go unaddressed at Zen Center, though it has never been resolved. "You are neither laypeople nor monks," Suzuki-roshi often told his students during his twelve years in America. But in 1963, Grahame, a layperson, had a wife and a child. How did they fit into a monk's black robe?

"In those early days, Grahame was a very strong practitioner," says Yvonne, reflecting on the lore that was in place by the time she started sitting at Sokoji in 1965. "He sat well. He sat still. He was a good student from the Japanese perspective. He was the stalwart until he went to Japan."

"In September of 1963, I got on a plane and flew to Japan," says Grahame, as if it stills seems unlikely to him. "It took fourteen or fifteen hours to get there. It was my first experience of jet travel. I arrived at six o'clock in the evening, went straight to Tokyo station, and took a night train to arrive at Eiheiji," one of the two major teaching and training monasteries for the Soto sect. "I had no idea whatsoever of what was going to happen to me. Suzuki-roshi had ordained me just prior to my leaving. He had not taught me anything about being a priest. He had not taught me how to tie the robes, how to eat [in the silent, ritualized *oryoki* style]. Nothing."

Grahame was not the first student to be sent to Japan. Incredibly, he was the best prepared. Richard remembers very well his encounters in 1962 with two of the first students who'd been sent to Eiheiji monastery. "Two of Suzuki-roshi's disciples went crazy—[one] who went to Japan and flipped out. I knew both of them quite well. I remember sitting with [one of them] in the lobby of Sokoji, that strange old red-painted place, and he was telling me flames [were] leaping all around me. A lot of people were very disillusioned because they thought Suzuki-roshi should have helped him, but I didn't think Suzuki-roshi could've helped him. This guy had problems that Zen is not trying to address."

Grahame was aware of the precedent. "I kept a diary to keep myself together in that very, very strange culture. You could say I had come from the 1960s in California and stepped back 700 years in a single day. This was as close to a time capsule as you can get."

And Eiheiji monastery was as far away as you could get from American storybook Zen.

"The diary is pretty horrific, as to what I was going through. I have many times thought of destroying it," says Grahame. "I feel ashamed that I could be so weak." He was "persuaded not to [destroy the diary] because it is a record of an extreme case of culture shock." Grahame looks out into his empty backyard again.

When Grahame turns around, he is smiling. Almost. He aims his gaze at the blank white door to his living room, and he speaks slowly, steadily, as if he is reading aloud from a story he knows by heart. "It could never have happened in the history of the Eiheiji monastery that anyone showed up as uninformed as I about what was to happen. Plus the fact that I hadn't slept, was jet-lagged, culture-shocked, and totally dazed. Suzuki-roshi's son [who was an ordained priest] met me at the train station and took me to a shop where they ordered robes for me and shaved my head, removed every personal object from my body—my wedding ring and everything. And then they dressed me up. It was pouring rain. I was pretty down by that time, but I had to go through the interview at the entrance—sitting for long hours in an anteroom—*Why are you here?* and other questions one cannot answer. If you do answer, you just get hit. Then to *tangaryo*"—sitting in zazen posture until you are admitted to the monastery. "After a couple of days of tangaryo, I thought, What have I done? Physically, it was very tough.

"I survived several days of tangaryo and entered the *shuryo*, where the young monks first get training—hitting bells, cleaning the floor and toilets, and ten thousand other duties. I was sat down in a room, which had a schedule that covered an entire wall. It was mostly in Chinese characters.

I did not understand a single one of them—Japanese or Chinese. But I had to learn the schedule. The routine was, you learned it, and then you were questioned each evening, and every mistake you made was clearly brought to your attention—which, you understand, is a British understatement. You were subjected to torture for your errors. I couldn't pass even one. I hardly even knew what they were saying."

Grahame was a long way from Sokoji and Suzuki-roshi's way with his students. "I was hospitalized twice. The biggest problem was malnutrition. Not that the food wasn't available or wholesome. One had to absorb very large quantities of rice—coarse rice—and we had only twenty minutes to eat, start to finish, and ten minutes, at least, was taken up by chanting. When the time came to eat, the Japanese could shovel it down without chewing. It went straight to their stomachs. As Suzuki-roshi said when I told him about it, 'Oh, Japanese stomachs just come out and grab the food. They don't use the mouth.'"

Even before he had completed his first days of sitting and waiting to be admitted, Grahame remembers that "the determination to stay waned. It was so impossible that the only thought which enabled me to endure it was that if I failed, I would be failing everyone else, who might be stronger than I." Before his arrival, he says, "Eiheiji had admitted Asians from other countries, and Americans had been allowed to visit as lay students. But this was the first monastic experience for the Zen Center group, and the first time ever that a white man had been admitted to the sodo, where the monks live. I was a genuine initiate in the system."

9.

"ONE OF THE FIRST THINGS SUZUKI-ROSHI said to me was, 'At my age, coming to this country, I need a disciple who is already well prepared. I think an understanding of Western Transcendentalism would be a good preparation,'" he added, recalls Richard. "'Can't be here so long. I need a disciple.'"

This almost makes sense. However, Suzuki-roshi's eldest son, Hoitsu, was a Zen priest in Japan. According to Japanese practice, he would become his father's successor (by receiving Transmission) and inherit his father's temple. In fact, when Suzuki-roshi left for America, Hoitsu took over the priestly responsibilities at his father's temple in Japan. Why, then, did Suzuki-roshi have to go to America in search of a disciple?

"He was opposed to the whole tradition that temples are passed from father to son," says Richard. But even Richard looks a little daunted when he says, "Suzuki-roshi also said, 'I want you also to reform Buddhism in Japan.' He was actually rather proud of the fact that he was the disciple of a Zen master who was not his father." This made Suzuki-roshi something of a renegade in Japan. As Gary Snyder explains, "We are, by now, into the third or fourth generation of Buddhist families in which Japanese sons perform the outward monastic forms knowing they will inherit their fathers' temples."

"If one practices as a [Soto Zen] priest in Japan, one does what I did," says Grahame. "Go to the Eiheiji monastery and spend a year, or more." Most of the black-robed priests Grahame sat alongside at the monastery were under twenty-five. They had been ordained by their fathers before arriving for an intense period of training at Eiheiji. In America, the word *roshi* and the brown robe worn by Suzuki-roshi were symbols of enlightenment. In Japan, Grahame learned, "When you're ready, or when your father says you're ready, you will be given Transmission, and you will go back to Eiheiji again for a day or two, and you'll have a wonderful ceremony with the two of you there. These young men are called one-day roshis. Transmission is fairly routine, not the big, big thing it is here."

Richard remembers, "When I was at Eiheiji [in the late sixties], all the kids had their brown Transmission robes. They couldn't wear them—they didn't have the positions yet. But they had them." Most important, says Richard, was the idea that Suzuki-roshi "wanted to come to America to make [Transmission] real." It was clear, says Richard, that his teacher did not want to re-create Japan in America. "Suzuki-roshi thought that the fact that Buddhism would have to be reconceived in America gave it a chance to survive."

In notes from the early membership meetings, it is clear that Zen Center students frequently talked about the possibility of owning and running a genuine monastery. They imagined themselves as full-time monks performing chores on the monastery grounds. Who might pay them to mow the lawn and mop the floors was not discussed. As early as 1962, Suzuki-roshi and his American devotees were taking day trips to look at available land and buildings in Northern California. Typically, the purchase price squelched enthusiasm. Their more pressing fiscal concerns were the affordability of a commercial telephone listing, and whether a proposed bazaar and bingo event could be cosponsored by the "Caucasian and Japanese congregations," which proved unfeasible. "This is the level at which we were operating," says Grahame.

The organization was funded by member dues (typically $10 to $15 annually), donations, and minimal charges for some events (for instance, 75 cents per meal during *sesshins,* the one- and five-day meditation sessions). In 1962, assets after expenses—principally, $1,000 to the Sokoji congregation for temple maintenance and $1,200 toward Suzuki-roshi's salary—totaled $550. The financial picture did not change substantially for four years. In 1965, the year they decided to try to buy the $300,000 Tassajara property, Zen Center's total assets were $2,394.25, which included a single $1,000 bequest. The annual operating budget was $5,419.22, which funded a newsletter, sitting cushions for the zendo, maintenance of the temple they shared with a congregation of Japanese-American Buddhists, stipends to visiting Zen priests, and a contribution to the meager salary of their teacher.

No one in Japan had commissioned Suzuki-roshi to launch a reform of Buddhism. "To this day," says Gary, "I'm sure the Japanese are mind-boggled by the historical accident that American bohemians became the caretakers of Zen in the West." Neither did Suzuki-roshi's congregation of Japanese Americans at the Bush Street temple support his increasingly unorthodox approach to practice with his Zen Center group. "We were all Caucasians," explains Della, who was at the time a married schoolteacher. "We knew we were imposing on the Japanese congregation at Sokoji, taking time from their ceremonies. We were eager to know more about them, but they didn't meditate. Suzuki-roshi said farmers were too busy to meditate. He tried to get them to sit, but they never did. On Sundays, sometimes we stayed after our services to join their services, but I am not so sure they really welcomed us. I don't think so. This made it very hard for Suzuki-roshi."

One of the difficulties was that he needed a cadre of ordained priests with a deep understanding of monastic traditions if he intended to open a monastery, let alone reform Japanese Buddhism. This was not in line with the goals of the Soto Zen mission in America. In 1964, along with ninety Japanese and twenty white Americans, Suzuki-roshi traveled to Los Angeles for the first Soto Zen Conference in America. Most of the Americans met separately because the proceedings were conducted in Japanese. Among the resolutions adopted by the conferees and reported in *Wind Bell,* the Zen Center newsletter, was a request for all American temples to sponsor second-generation Japanese members of the congregation for the priesthood, which would entail time in Japan. Six months earlier, Suzuki-roshi had performed his first ordination in America and sent the tall, white, transplanted Englishman—Grahame—to study at Eiheiji. Suzuki-roshi did not seek out or cultivate a Japanese or Japanese-American disciple. He had quietly secured his status as a renegade in America and Japan.

It was 1962 when Suzuki-roshi told Richard he needed a disciple. Richard had known Suzuki-roshi for a few months. He and Virginia had become friends with Grahame and his wife Pauline. "Then Virginia and I became pregnant. We weren't married. I went to see Suzuki-roshi and said, 'I am thinking about getting married.' He basically said, 'If your wife supports your practice, it's okay. The problems of being married and the problems of being single are about the same. You have problems both ways.'"

It's true, of course. But set against the history of marriage in Japanese Buddhism, or the complicated history of his own marriages, it does not seem true enough.

Richard talked it over with Virginia. "I said, 'Practice is my highest priority.'" Richard looks suddenly sad when he says, "This was, I think, a kind of mistake. I said, 'My marriage is always going to be second to practice, and that's just the way it is. I can't survive otherwise.' And that was probably true. And she agreed. Suzuki-roshi married us."

"Married monks." Gary Snyder winces, as if he has banged two dissonant bells. "Married monks?"

Suzuki-roshi had come to America alone in 1959. In 1961, his third wife and his youngest son joined him in San Francisco. "We almost resented his wife coming," remembers Della. "When she came, we couldn't have lunch with him every Saturday after the lecture or do things with him as we had during those first two years. I'd get out of school at 2:30, and often he would call and ask me to take him shopping or to the airport. But then his wife was there, and she was able to do things for him, so we didn't have so many chances to eat with him and just be with him. It was a big change. It was hard."

"The questions of marriage, family, and sexuality have never been resolved," says Gary. "Not by the Japanese, and less so by the Americans. They just overlook them. They don't know what else to do with them."

This may explain Richard's confusion when the details of his marital and extramarital life showed up as agenda items for public meetings in 1983. Until then, Zen Center had operated under a code of public silence at the dangerous intersection of monastic practice and sexuality. When questions were asked aloud, they were typically answered with elusive, epigrammatic statements. Richard is blamed for the code of silence that stifled open discussion of the wide-ranging sexual practices of Zen Center's membership; it fits well with his reputation for empire building and the attendant atmosphere of court intrigue at Zen Center. But Richard did not invent the policy. Suzuki-roshi had taught his students not to ask. "We understood it was a sign of respect not to ask anything but polite questions about his kids," recalls one of the men ordained by Suzuki-roshi.

"We really didn't talk much among ourselves, not about that stuff," Betty remembers. "We didn't talk about our own lives that way, either." This may well seem odd; romance, marriage, family, and children are the ordinary concerns that might normally occupy *ordinary mind*, or *everyday mind*. However, like the fate of the young man who went mad in Japan, Suzuki-roshi's family life, his three marriages, and his relationship to his children "were not problems Zen was trying to address," according to his students. In fact, until 1983, they were the very problems Zen Center was trying *not* to address.

Richard, Yvonne, and other Zen Center students do recall a few conversations with Suzuki-roshi and his third wife, Mitsu, late in his life, during which she chided him for being a bad husband. She was not forthcoming with details. It was from David Chadwick's 1999 biography that students first learned of Suzuki-roshi's first marriage; his young wife contracted tuberculosis and returned to her parents' home soon after she'd married Suzuki-roshi. His relationship to his four children, all from his second marriage, was, according to a devoted disciple, "mystifyingly unclear."

"One of the problems for the married priest," according to Gary, "is that there still seems to be the feeling that you have to maintain a celibate, unmarried, priestly look. A wife and children feel like second-class citizens. They know they don't quite belong. This is a deep problem."

Suzuki-roshi's youngest daughter, Omi, hanged herself in Japan in 1964. She'd been living in a mental hospital for nine years, according to *Crooked Cucumber*, the narrative biography David Chadwick wrote about his beloved teacher. His no-judgment summary of the facts tallies with other students' recollections; David's account is singular by virtue of his willingness to make it public. Omi's mother, Suzuki-roshi's second wife, had been brutally murdered by an erratic, antisocial monk whom Suzuki-roshi had retained as a temple assistant, despite contrary advice from colleagues and neighbors, as well as complaints from his wife and children. After Omi's suicide, Hoitsu, Suzuki-roshi's eldest child, an ordained Zen priest, asked his father to return to Japan to join him and his other sister for Omi's funeral and memorial services. Suzuki-roshi did not go to Japan at that time. Instead, according to Chadwick, he waited six months to report Omi's suicide to his teenage son, who was living in an apartment across the street from his father's temple on Bush Street. This young boy soon thereafter joined the U.S. Army. He volunteered for service in Vietnam at just about the time that several young conscientious objectors were taking refuge at Zen Center, having convinced the Selective Service and themselves that Buddhists were pacifists.

"So," says Gary Snyder, several times.

So?

"It's an old realization in the Zen tradition that the roshi makes mistakes. The roshi is enlightened. And enlightenment is nothing special; it is not perfection. *Kensho,* wisely enough, literally means, *Having seen a corner of the nature of things,* or, *Getting a glimpse of it from time to time.* Every roshi is pretty good. A few roshis are really good. But we make do with pretty good roshis."

So?

"So you get the best you can from the guy, and you don't imitate his bad sides. That's basically the way monks and laypeople approach the teacher in Japan. In fact, it is a commonplace among monks in Japan. They say, 'I want to get my teacher's dharma, but I don't want to be like him.' This is so common that it is a joke."

At Zen Center in the early sixties, they didn't really get the joke. They did get the sense that their teacher was enlightened. Like their teacher, they did get married, but many of them didn't know that they were stepping into a breach in Buddhist history.

"Married monks are an unresolved question in Japanese Buddhism," explains Gary. "The difficulty is simply this: In the rest of the world, Zen priests are celibate—well, maybe they're not celibate, but they are not married. In the nineteenth century, at the end of the Tokugawa Era and the start of the Meiji Restoration, all of the Buddhist sects in Japan were taken out of government control. For centuries, they had been legally managed as if they were government agencies. Part of removing them from government control was removing the legal stipulations—including the stipulation that a priest may not be married. Now, oddly enough, in the Buddhist world, a monk's unmarried state is not brought about by legal stipulation. It is the tradition, the customary condition of a monk. But in Japan, they had been under legal controls for so long, they figured that if the law wasn't there, you could do it. And they were encouraged to get married by the government. It was an attempt to break up Buddhism. That's what I believe. It was a very clever anti-Buddhist move."

The logic was simple and sound: Without practicing monks, the monastic tradition would die out. This bit of reasoning demonstrates either the limits of logic, or the illogic of Zen. When Japanese Zen monks began to marry in the nineteenth century (and almost all of them are married today), they gave up the defining practice of monasticism—celibacy, aloneness. But they refused to turn in their costumes or close their theaters. Instead, they altered the forms. The lineage charts, through which a Zen master can trace his descent back through generations of Transmitted teachers to the Buddha, often resemble family trees. And as Richard points out, "It's not that simple, because sometimes the person you pass the temple to is not your son; you adopt him so he becomes your son. So most of these lineages involve a daughter's husband or an adopted child. It has to have the shape of a blood lineage."

Transmission had become an empty form.

Suzuki-roshi left Japan and the Japanese system. To establish his teaching, he needed a genuine disciple.

It almost makes sense. However, in 1966, five years before he gave Transmission to Richard, Suzuki-roshi traveled to Japan to relinquish his temple there. Zen Center was purchasing Tassajara. Suzuki-roshi was committed to his role as Abbot of the new monastery in America. But while he was in Japan, he installed his eldest son as the new head of his temple. Hoitsu had never studied with his father. He had done his time at Eiheiji monastery. And he had received Transmission from his father. Hoitsu is on the lineage charts as his father's dharma heir. And before he returned to America, Suzuki-roshi gave Transmission to another young priest whom he had never taught; it was, he told his students, a favor to an old friend.

At Zen Center in the early sixties, and over the ensuing decades, no sense of fraudulence attached to Suzuki-roshi or his teachings as a result. "I asked him about that, in the context of his being so critical of Japanese Buddhism," one of his earliest American disciples confides. "He told me he hadn't felt ready to give his son Transmission—Hoitsu was too young— but finally he was forced into it. The parishioners at his temple in Japan refused to accept someone else [as their teacher], so Suzuki-roshi gave his son Transmission against his own wishes."

This capitulation might have been seen as an attempt by Suzuki-roshi to keep a foot in both worlds by securing an heir in two distinct traditions. It might have caused his Zen Center students to rethink the relation-ship between Transmission and enlightenment. Instead, the significance attached to Suzuki-roshi's selection of an American dharma heir was heightened, as if he had performed the two Transmission ceremonies in Japan as warm-ups for the real thing.

"It's interesting to think how the failure of skepticism, or the rise of credulity, enters this story," says Gary.

His American students seem to have construed it as a mark of Suzuki-roshi's sincerity that he let it be known that his two dharma heirs in Japan—one of them, his son—were not his disciples. The insincerity they identified was institutional ("The *Soto Shu* is the Vatican of Zen"), cul-tural ("The Japanese observe form at the expense of everything else"), and historical ("The entire Japanese royal family lineage is a myth, a political invention. Maybe every lineage is invented").

But form is not empty. Suzuki-roshi did not live forever, but the metic-ulous lineage charts preserved and updated by the authorities of the Japanese Soto Shu just might. On those charts, it is plain to see that Hoitsu and Richard are both acknowledged Zen masters, both heirs to the Buddha-dharma as it descended through the life and teaching of Suzuki-roshi. The only difference was that Hoitsu could guarantee the survival of the lineage. In the Japanese system, which the Americans considered cor-rupt, Eiheiji monastery—which the Americans considered the model for Tassajara—is a training center. It is a school from which priests graduate.

In Japan, there are thousands of temples that need new priests. Hoitsu had a temple and parishioners to support his family, a temple that his chosen dharma heir—presumably a son—would inherit. "Here," says Gary, "there was no place for them to go. In this country, they built a monastic training school, but they did not build a temple network. And yet they all got married and had children. I talked about this early on with Yvonne. I told her I thought Zen Center was headed for a problem. The best they could hope was that they would attract a lot of entrepreneurial people who were willing to go out and start their own little temples. As it turned out, very few people wanted to leave the nest."

As Suzuki-roshi had told them—maybe it was a warning?—"You are not monks, and you are not laypeople." They were strange birds, indeed. By the mid-seventies, the three branches of Zen Center were crowded with ordained priests, their spouses, and dozens of little chicks. So when Richard began to behave like the Abbot of a wealthy, ancient, and powerful Japanese monastery, he appeared to be feathering his nest.

"So," says Gary, one last time, "in the early 1960s, when the forms of Soto Zen and its semimonastic style were brought to the States and enthusiastically taken up by many Americans who had no idea what they were getting into, it struck me as not a great idea."

10.

love story: falling in love with a stranger; falling so far that you forsake all others; falling away from yourself until you are not an American and you are not Japanese and you are not a layperson and you are not a monk and you find yourself wrapped up in a black robe and falling on your knees to bow down in gratitude to the person who occasioned this fortunate fall.

"I don't like the word *refuge*. And I don't think it helps to think of a place or a person as refuge. But that is how I came to Zen." Bill Kwong smiles. "I had a family, and I worked a forty-hour week. And in those early days, I was preoccupied with myself. But I went to Sokoji. I used it as a way of getting away." He closes his eyes—refuge?—and then he whispers, "I loved Suzuki-roshi."

As Della Goertz says, "Suzuki-roshi was my teacher and my friend. I never felt as close to anyone as I felt to him."

As Teah Strozer says, "I felt he saw me, and he accepted me to the depths." Teah was raised in a Conservative Jewish family, but she "had not found a teacher to answer the questions I wanted to speak." She met Suzuki-roshi when he gave a lecture in Los Angeles in 1968. "And I wanted to be around him. There was peace with him. I would go to him with some neurotic problem—I was very neurotic at the time—and after ten minutes, it didn't seem like a problem anymore, as if all the words had spilled out of my mouth, fallen on the floor like a pool, and then I could breathe, and just be with this beautiful man."

As Lew Richmond says, "I loved Suzuki-roshi like no other person. He was the most important influence on my life. We were his students, and he had no interest in life but us. He would have died for us. He did die for us. He was devoted to us. He would tell his wife, 'Have to be with my students.' And Suzuki-roshi loved Ed Brown particularly because Ed had a real hard time, like Suzuki-roshi did when he was a kid."

As Ed Brown says, "He taught me to trust. Suzuki-roshi gave me a wonderful ordination name—Longevity Mountain Peaceful Sea. After the ceremony, when I told him I liked my name, he said, 'You will be like a mountain surrounded by a sea of peaceful people.' And once in a while, I am."

As Katherine Thanas says, "The third time I came to sit at Zen Center, I was afraid he was going to throw me out because I couldn't sit still in the zendo, and it looked to me like everyone else could. He came by and adjusted something in my posture—he touched me—and there was so much kindness, or acceptance, in his touch that it was like I'd been in a drought." Katherine was forty and studying art in San Francisco. "Here was a loving person, at last."

As Gib Robinson says, though he joined Zen Center after Suzuki-roshi died, "He was what we were doing there." Edward Sattizahn, who later launched himself into a software career as a senior executive with the Learning Company, gave Gib "an unforgettable impression of Suzuki-roshi. In the fall of 1971, just before Suzuki-roshi died, Ed was doing menial tasks at Zen Center and agonizing over whether he should leave and finish his Ph.D. in mathematics. Yvonne brought Suzuki-roshi back from Tassajara, and he was very sick at that point. Ed had been waiting to ask his question. He was right there, waiting. And Ed looked at Suzuki-roshi, and what he saw was his own face. He never asked the question. It dropped. He stayed."

As Tim Buckley says, "What I had to hold onto in my life was my meditation experience and my helpless transference onto Suzuki-roshi." Tim had been "in and out of Harvard" starting in 1960, and he sought out many teachers—scholars, artists, and philosophers. In 1965, he went to Sokoji and met Suzuki-roshi. "I knew. This was the guy. I never even try to praise him. I don't have the words."

As Dan Welch says, "It took me seven months. The turning of my life happened after seven months of living at Tassajara [beginning in the spring of 1967]. What touched my heart so deeply was to find out who

Suzuki-roshi was, what his teaching was, what his practice of teaching was—and this unequivocally changed my life forever."

As Yvonne Rand says, "He was a sneaky teacher. He had much more influence than we realized. In some curious way, for myself, I was learning from him in ways that made sense in his culture and were not on the map in my own culture—learning by watching; imitating the way he sat, got up, and stood; the things that he did to keep the quality of ease. I remember one of the first lectures he gave after we moved from Sokoji to Page Street." This was 1969, and Yvonne had been sitting with Suzuki-roshi for more than three years. "He had a cup of water. He picked it up and took a drink. And it was apparent he was drinking nectar. He would smack his lips, and he was just there."

As Betty Warren says, "He sort of captured all of us."

11.

RICHARD BAKER REMEMBERS THAT Suzuki-roshi "stopped looking at me for a year. Suddenly, he just stopped looking at me. I'd come in after zazen and bow to him, and he would look away. I'd come into the office to talk to him about something, and he would look away. He would actually not acknowledge me. After a few weeks I thought, Well, he is still my roshi. Whether he likes it or not, I am his disciple. That is just a fact."

"Suzuki-roshi recognized Richard's administrative skills and respected his management skills," says Tim Buckley, who dropped out of Harvard for fifteen years and studied with the photographer Minor White, and then Suzuki-roshi, and Richard, and then with Harry Roberts, an Irish-American teacher who lived and practiced with the Yurok Indians. Tim is a professor of anthropology at the University of Massachusetts. "Suzuki-roshi knew that Zen Center needed a good aggressive businessman. Many people have said all of this about Suzuki-roshi choosing Richard as his heir. And all of it is true. And all of it misses the central fact. Suzuki-roshi chose Richard Baker because they understood each other."

"I have one lifetime objective," says Richard, "which is to continue Suzuki-roshi's lineage. And I think he had that objective," he adds, explaining that "it's a complex idea of carrying together, bringing a stream into focus, and intimacy—sometimes it's called elder-to-elder intimacy—two people sharing a vision and feeling for the world. What can be more intimate? You feel another person at a level where you share a way of knowing the world. It's like being in love," he says, but adds that "Buddhism says this is a capacity of human beings," not simply to fall in love but to "*be* in that state."

"He wooed Suzuki-roshi," Mel Weitsman told colleagues in a conversation recorded in 1997 about his thirty-year association with Zen Center.

"Suzuki-roshi didn't get it, that Dick was a predator," says Yvonne Rand.

Biographer David Chadwick says, "Suzuki-roshi was the least fooled person I ever met."

"I think there is much too much weight been put on Transmission *period*," says Grahame Petchey, "and on the meaning of the Transmission from Suzuki-roshi to Dick."

Before he gave Richard Transmission, Suzuki-roshi asked Mel what he thought. Mel responded with a question. "Do you think he's ready?" And Mel remembers that Suzuki-roshi said, "Sometimes we give it when a person is ready, and sometimes we give it to somebody and hope."

Dan Welch says, "Suzuki-roshi knew who Dick was; he absolutely knew that and told us to honor him for what he was. I see that because I see how Suzuki-roshi honored who I was."

In the stories he tells, Richard was a smart, socially unsophisticated ("primitive," he says) son of a mild man ("Mr. Milquetoast"), a university professor who, when Richard was seventeen, went to work for an aircraft manufacturer on Long Island. His mother was progressive ("A women's libber in the thirties; a flapper") with libertine leanings. ("She always presented to me a world where women love sex. Men are there to supply it.") He has his mother's maiden name as his middle name and her distinguished lineage. ("My eighth great-grandfather Dudley gave the land for Harvard. He was always angry and had a big nose. There was always a feeling of connection with Harvard.") Richard got the old man's nose, but the Dudleys who preceded him got rid of the family fortune.

Richard is forthcoming with the details of his youth; however, he interrupts himself in the midst of every anecdote, abandons stories in mid-sentence, and his digressions and circumlocutions muddle and overwhelm the facts until you feel you are trapped in a car with a man who is determined to show you his childhood home in a neighborhood that evidently does not conform to his memory. You back out of the same dead end often enough, and you begin to suspect that he's hoping you will claim to have seen his house a few miles back so he can head for highway and you can both get the hell out of town.

"I think the degree to which I don't know who I am—or what I am, rather; that is probably better—is actually a factor in the Zen Center mess," says Richard.

Too much has been made of the material of his life, and it seems worn out now, even in his hands. The same autobiographical details and behavioral patterns that once seemed an oddly apt preparation for his unlikely career as an American Zen master were scrutinized and pathologized in the aftermath of the Apocalypse. By 1984, the public portrait of Richard was a caricature of failed ambition—another Dudley who'd squandered another fortune and ended up with a nose of Pinocchio proportions.

Richard's self-portraits are all sketchy, but they clearly suggest a Byronic temperament. He loved literature, and poetry especially; he admired artists, none more so than poets. ("I had experiences in high school—some kind of ecstatic experience, which is, I think at the root of many writers' poetry.") He was nocturnal, with a precocious flair for staging dark nights of the soul. ("When I was five, my grandmother's house had burned partially down, mostly because my grandfather did all the wiring, but, anyway, I decided I should protect my family. I would wait till they all went to bed, and I would get up and go out and walk around the house to make sure it wasn't burning. My father finally decided I should see a psychiatrist.") He sees himself sneaking into museums at night through steam tunnels, sleeping on the gated lawn of a hospital ("it was kind of a meditative experience, with the stars; I'd sleep a great kind of intense sleep"), and perching on roofs at Harvard. ("I used to spend a lot of time running around—you know those Georgian banisters on the edge of the roofs?—I'd go out and run in the night dressed in black, and leap across the corners of the roof. I loved being on the height. I loved being on the edge. I'd be on the roofs all over Harvard Square. I'd just sit there and look at things and feel the lights and the night. Happy to be alone. Kind of mixed up.")

By his own count, he broke with his family definitively three or four times, at least, beginning early on ("I decided at seven or eight that the relationship between my parents was not good, and I couldn't depend on it, and I was on my own"), and including a confrontation when he was eleven, during which he threatened his father by picking up a chair. ("He gave up. He was bewildered. I was kind of serious.") This culminated in almost a decade of no contact with his family after he left for college.

"Dick let me know his family," says Yvonne. "He introduced me to his sister, who later killed herself. Another sister barely managed to stay sane by having no contact with the rest of the family. And one time I went with him and spent three days with his mother. I remember sitting in this little puddle-jump plane, watching her walk across the tarmac before [Dick and I] left to go to Boston to see the rest of his family, and I looked out the window, and I said to him, 'She is a textbook case of a schizophrenogenic.' He said, 'What's that?' I said, 'That means *crazy-making.*' And that was the end of the conversation." Remembering the scene, Yvonne looks genuinely surprised—a rarity. "I have a lot of heart-feeling for how he came to be the person he is."

Richard dropped out of Harvard in his senior year. ("I didn't want to have a Harvard degree. And probably also a certain amount of shame because I didn't do as well as I should have.") He did a stint in the Merchant Marine in 1957–58, where he met his lifelong friend Earl McGrath, now an art dealer, and president of Rolling Stone records in the seventies. "Earl bought my ticket from New York to San Francisco—eighty dollars—and I arrived with thirty-five dollars. I wandered into City Lights bookstore. This is 1960."

This visit led him to Don Allen ("I'd known him in New York. He'd edited the *New American Poetry* anthology"), who found him a room and introduced him to Robert Duncan and, eventually, dozens of the poets and aspiringly poetic people who, for one brief moment, had managed to make poetry come alive in America. The new poetry scene—Duncan, Snyder, Joanne Kyger, Allen Ginsberg, Michael McClure, Charles Olson—was white people's jazz, a performance art that celebrated improvisation and experimental riffs on traditional forms, blurring the boundary between high art and popular culture. In the Bay Area, clubs, coffeehouses, bars, and, eventually, major theaters and auditoriums were crowded with fans of the new hip, colloquial, free verse. For the first time, the West Coast could boast a cultural scene that was a worthy rival to New York. Bookstores—many of them operating as independent publishers—sprang into existence in San Francisco, Oakland, and Berkeley at a rate not matched again until Starbucks started replicating like mold spores along America's city streets.

"My image of myself at that time was kind of to collect pop bottles and turn them in and live off of that," says Richard. "I wanted to be outside—a bohemian thing I inherited from my parents and the kind of literature I liked." He'd heard about Suzuki-roshi from George Fields at Fields Bookstore and, again, during a sensory-awareness workshop given by Charlotte Selver. He'd been immediately impressed by Suzuki-roshi. "He was extraordinary," says Richard. "I'd studied a little bit—gone to lectures at Harvard [by Paul Tillich and other eminent theologians and philosophers], and they didn't lead me anywhere. When I heard Suzuki-roshi lecture, something ancient was here. He *was* what he was talking about." But his turning moment did not come while he was on a cushion in the zendo. Instead he remembers a dinner with a novelist friend. "He and I went to a Mexican restaurant." The novelist had been enthusiastic about Zen practice in the early days, but he was going back to the East Coast. Richard remembers his friend suddenly saying, "'If we knew what we were doing, we would just practice Zen for the rest of our lives.' And when he said that, a kind of door just went *clunk*, and my previous life disappeared."

It's a curious truth about Richard; he loses lives the way other people lose their car keys. Impermanence, of course, is one of the Four Noble Truths of Buddhism:

1. The truth of Suffering, which is the truth of existence.
2. The truth of Desire, which is the cause of suffering.
3. The truth of the End of Suffering, which requires the elimination of desire, which is caused by the illusion of permanence.
4. The truth of the Eightfold Path, which is the means by which the elimination of suffering can be accomplished.

Suzuki-roshi was very good at losing things, too. "He was always losing things," says Lew. "He was incredibly forgetful. He never knew where he'd left his overcoat." Among the stories David Chadwick collected for his biography of Suzuki-roshi, missed appointments, overlooked commitments, and lost items figure prominently. And after he died, many of his ordained disciples claimed that Suzuki-roshi had intended to give them Transmission but had forgotten to do so; he also forgot to prepare the simple documents that would have validated their claims.

"I think he had a whole bunch of people he was going to give it to, including me," says Grahame. "But it just wasn't the time, and he'd do it somewhere down the road, and—he was very vague in all sorts of ways." Grahame has the very un-American habit of not trying to explain things he cannot possibly explain. "I was, frankly, very surprised that it was just Dick, only one person. I could not understand why [Suzuki-roshi] was choosing to go that way. I was fully supportive. This was Suzuki-roshi's decision." Other disciples were not so supportive and were much more disgruntled than Grahame. Several of them left Zen Center almost immediately. Of course, Suzuki-roshi had also left behind disgruntled parishioners when he resigned from his temple in Japan (when, you might say, a kind of door just went *clunk* and his previous life disappeared) and again *(clunk)* when he resigned from Sokoji to devote himself full time to Zen Center.

See Noble Truths, 1.

Whatever Suzuki-roshi recognized as singular about Richard, he must have noticed that Richard suffered suffering well. He had been sitting at Sokoji for only a matter of months, but Richard played the drum for his teacher's *Shinsanshiki*, the ceremony during which Suzuki-roshi officially assumed duties as the Abbot of Sokoji in May of 1962. "I had been practicing to do the drum—a big drum, an Indian drum. I had been learning how to do it. [Suzuki-roshi] had been showing me how to do it." In order to play the drum properly, in fact, "I had made the drumsticks from children's bats because the sticks they'd been using weren't heavy enough."

Shortly before he was to play the drum, Richard had an accident. He was riding his bicycle from morning zazen amidst San Francisco's commuter traffic to catch a bus to Berkeley, where he worked for the university's Extension program. He felt his front wheel jam. By the time he'd extracted himself from beneath a parked car and been to a hospital, his elbows were swollen with fluid and had to be aspirated. Suzuki-roshi was about to be installed as Abbot. "I had both elbows in casts. And I just said I was still going to do it," remembers Richard. His teacher never asked how. As is traditional, Suzuki-roshi's procession began several blocks away from the temple. "As he came in [to Sokoji] down below—I was up in the balcony looking down—as he came in, I was beating the drum with my arms in casts."

What was understood between them? Suzuki-roshi said nothing about Richard's heroic drum performance. A week later, Suzuki-roshi married Richard and Virginia. A year later, he was planning a trip to Japan to begin the process of turning over his temple to his son. Richard was working on a master's degree, working as an administrator in the Berkeley Extension School programs, working on being a husband and a father, and spending a lot of time pretending San Francisco was a monastery. "I wanted one, and I didn't have one, so I pretended."

Was he manic? No.

Depressed? No.

"Beset," Richard says. "Compulsive thinking. I don't know what a psychiatrist would say about it technically. When I did see a therapist, I was told probably this would be the case for all of my life, but it hasn't been the case for all of my life." He credits his faith in practice—"that I could understand myself well enough to change that."

He does remember some hard times. "I remember getting up in the middle of the night from being with Virginia and our little baby." He was not in a good frame of mind. "I decided I would probably have to turn myself in to a mental hospital." This was 1963, and Richard says at that time not only did he pretend San Francisco was a monastery, but "I also pretended [San Francisco] was a madhouse. And I said, Okay, I'm in a madhouse already, so I will just try to function." Richard walked to Bush Street, and stood outside of Sokoji. It was midnight. "I stood looking up at the tower," he remembers. "The light was not on. I was going to tell Suzuki-roshi, but I thought, What can I tell him? When you go crazy, where do you go to? I decided to go home."

What was understood between them this time? This was almost one year after Richard's plaster-armed drum solo. Again, not a word was spoken. Richard went to zazen the next morning. After sitting, "we all go out of the zendo and bow to [Suzuki-roshi]." Suzuki-roshi had set out the drumsticks Richard had made to play the drum. "Suddenly—they hadn't been seen in a year—they were sitting unmistakably right where I could see them." It is a long time before Richard says anything else.

Wordless transmission? Heart-mind to heart-mind?

Richard blows all the air out of himself, and then he says, "That gave me confidence. There was some . . . I didn't feel like he didn't know."

It is clear that Suzuki-roshi was a subtle, intuitive teacher. Subtlety was not Richard's forte; in fact, he was becoming a master of the grand gesture, and Suzuki-roshi seems to have appreciated the scale of Richard's performance. It is not clear, however, that Suzuki-roshi intuitively understood that Richard was swinging those baseball-bat drumsticks for more than strictly ceremonial purposes, scaring away a lot of people.

"I was the first *doan,* the one who hits the percussion instruments," says Bill Kwong. "I started because one day Suzuki-roshi was sick. It was 1960 when I first did it, and after that I was the doan. Richard was not even there yet." He smiles. "Richard and I have definite karma together." He smiles again. "Everything that happened was perfect."

Bill Kwong's role at Zen Center was clear to everyone. Betty says it was evident that "Suzuki-roshi's methods just brushed off on him. From the start, he was showing the signs that he would be a great teacher. I don't think we've had a teacher of the caliber of Kwong—he's the teacher I see who came out of this. And early on, everyone could see that Bill was the biggest help to Suzuki-roshi."

Bill is sitting in his own Zen center in Santa Rosa, fifty miles north of San Francisco. His Chinese ancestors are present in his features and his voice, and maybe in his sense of time, too. He says that the first ten years of sitting zazen is just learning "to have a good seat—sitting on the zafu [cushion] and getting a glimpse of your original nature, your Buddha nature. It's a bridge, those ten years, from the zendo [meditation hall] to your practical life." Bill is robed, seated cross-legged, and his composure is pacific. At the end of many sentences, he smiles—a big, delighted smile that somehow illuminates the goofiness of human behavior. "The most difficult thing is transformation," says Bill. "It comes in spite of us. Suzuki-roshi said, 'People expect something. That's when they become discouraged.'" He nods. "And, of course, that is the turning point." He smiles.

"We were competitive, Richard and I," says Bill. "It goes back a long time." Smile. "When Suzuki-roshi left for Japan in 1963, he didn't leave any instructions. So I hit the bells every morning. Richard came up to me one morning and confronted me. 'Why do you do the bells? Why can't I do the bells?'" Smile. "Well, I knew this was not a good situation. I was very introverted at the time—I hardly talked to anyone for the first ten years. Richard was very bold, an extrovert. We were opposites. I realized that if I didn't step down—well, I knew there would be trouble. So, I stepped down. There were a few of us regulars then. And a few people left because I didn't stand up to him. But I wanted to keep the harmony."

Richard recalls that Suzuki-roshi "very specifically told me to be the doan while he was in Japan." He remembered asking the group to settle the issue, "and they asked us to take turns, which was good."

When Suzuki-roshi returned from Japan, Bill was no longer sitting daily at Sokoji. He had started to sit zazen with a few friends nearer his home and family, in Mill Valley, fifteen miles north of San Francisco. Bill remained Suzuki's devoted student, a regular at weekly organizational meetings, and a frequent visitor, but he was not quite at Zen Center. Over the years, most students at Zen Center assumed that Bill would receive Transmission and, thus, would be named Suzuki-roshi's dharma heir. It didn't happen. "Before he died, Suzuki-roshi asked people to take care of me. They didn't. And I was angry. I kept boiling for four or five years." Smile. "Suzuki-roshi once said, 'Three things cause problems. One thing—you're always trying to do something. Another thing—you're afraid to do anything because you know it won't work. Third thing—you rely on something.'"

Richard's understanding of his own behavior is illuminated by a story he was told by Robert Duncan. "'Two young men come to me with their poetry'—as was often the case. 'One young man shows me he is clearly talented. Another young man shows me a rather clumsy poem, but when I look at him I know he is going to write poetry all his life. [One] has a lot of talent; I don't pay attention to him. I pay attention to the one who has the commitment to stay with poetry, to work his life out through poetry.'" Richard shrugs. "In Zen, you can see some people who are just going to do this—they'll do it like they wash their face in the morning or go to sleep at night." These people, not necessarily the brilliant students, "I am going to pay attention to." This, he says, "is built into the conception of Transmission. There is a predictive element."

Richard certainly bathed in the waters of practice, morning and night. The only thing he seems not to have done is go to sleep for several years.

In 1964, Gary Snyder "took a break from Japan" and was hired to teach for a year at Berkeley. "I contacted my old friends, many of them active with Zen Center. I met Dick Baker. We had lunch with each other in Berkeley frequently," remembers Gary. "He was very active with Suzuki-roshi; he was by no means the only one. There was a growing group of people, and they were all extremely active. Dick actually was intent on the summer of 1965 Poetry Festival that he sponsored—it was his idea, and he organized it."

Richard says, "Zen Center was my only life. Everything else was secondary. Or tertiary." He sat every morning and evening at Sokoji, traveled with his teacher to look for a monastery on weekends, and, occasionally, accompanied him on fund-raising trips, and as a secondary occupation he completed his master's degree and conceived and organized a series of influential and memorable academic conferences.

"And he did it with a graceful style," adds Gary. "The 1965 event was modeled on the Vancouver British Columbia Poetry Festival just a few years earlier that had had such an impact, nationally, on the poetry world. He got things done. He is a great administrator."

But he is not a poet, as Robert Duncan pointed out to Richard rather directly. "I was very close to Robert, and I hung out with him and Jess [Collins, the painter who was Duncan's partner for more than thirty years]," says Richard. "They were having a little gathering—during this conference that I had put together. And I assumed I would come, but [Robert] said, 'No. You're not a poet.'" Richard nods, as if to say, fair enough. "I was clearly excluded. I wasn't part of the inner circle."

It might have been devastating. But by 1965, Richard could afford to be philosophical about it. He had finally figured out who—or, rather, what—he was.

By his own count, he waited five years to ask Suzuki-roshi about his status. "We were coming back from [Los Angeles] in an airplane. All these people in L.A. had asked if I was his disciple, and why I traveled with him, so I said on the plane, 'Can I say I am your disciple?' He said, 'Yes.' To me, that was the fact of it."

"Dick said to me, 'The fastest road to upward social mobility is as an artist or as a priest,'" remembers Lew. "He said, 'Those are the two roles in the society that can take you all the way up and all the way down.' He knew that."

"Life is a series of exclusions," Richard says. "And it is also inclusions." In 1965, he knew he was in, and he was on the way up.

Paul Lee remembers meeting Richard during the 1964–65 academic year at a conference on identity that Richard had organized at UC Berkeley. "The first evening, we were having a drink at the bar," says Paul. "Virginia and Richard told me they were both practicing Zen with Suzuki-roshi. I'd heard of the philosopher D. T. Suzuki, but not this guy. I sat there surprised and intrigued that this American was going to receive the Transmission!" Paul pauses. He is one of Richard's oldest and closest friends. "I mean, I did not intuit that."

Inside and outside of Zen Center, people understood that Richard had a singular relationship to his teacher. To Paul Lee, for instance, it must have looked simple; Richard was The One. However, unlike the poets and professors whose access to Suzuki-roshi was through Richard, everyone practicing at Zen Center also felt a personal, singular, unmediated connection to Suzuki-roshi. What looked like an exclusive status from the outside was seen as an inclusive status on the inside. At Zen Center, there was no *one* one; among practitioners, everyone was the one.

In retrospect, Richard reads his own behavior as passion. It might have unnerved or put off some people, but "If you're going to live your life, you should live a life where you can be as close to other people as possible," he says. "Suzuki-roshi was the most complete aspect of that feeling for me. Then Virginia and [our daughters]. And then this feeling extended to my friends." He says he didn't proselytize among friends "because I don't *believe* in Zen, and I don't believe it's the way to help everybody," though he later adds, "to some extent, I still think it is the way to help our society." More to the point, he says, "I had such a strong feeling that nothing was offered to me from our culture or schools . . . that answered any of the longings or desires or visions or feelings or insights I'd had—the whole society was somewhere else. When I met Buddhism, I finally thought, This is it."

Paul Lee first met Richard over the telephone. "He was calling and fishing for Paul Tillich and Erik Erikson. I was in Cambridge, teaching at MIT. I'd been Tillich's teaching assistant at Harvard, and Erikson had been my thesis advisor. Tillich was unavailable, and Erikson was in India working on his Gandhi book. But Richard gives really good phone—I mean, I've heard him chum up more people. And I said, 'What am I? Chopped liver?'" Paul asked Richard to invite him to the conference. "He said I could moderate a panel."

Richard had learned to be inclusive. When Suzuki-roshi said Yes, Richard learned to say Yes. It was a transformation. The urgency and restlessness that had earned him the nickname El Darko in college did not evaporate. And on Bush Street he continued to ruffle feathers; outside of Sokoji, however, his energy was "magnetic," "unbelievably charismatic," and "he was a human vortex, drawing everyone in toward Zen Center."

Gary Snyder visited from Japan again in the spring of 1966. "I saw more and more of Dick, and on that occasion, he said to me, 'Do you want to go and look at this piece of land up in the Sierra Nevada? Suzuki-roshi asked me to look for some land for a monastery, and I've narrowed it down to two places—this land and Tassajara. Roshi liked both places, but he decided he liked Tassajara better because it had hot springs. But this other one is good. Maybe you and I and Allen Ginsberg should buy it.' We took a day and drove up here and looked it over. I said I would be interested, and Allen said, Me, too, and so we put down our down payment. I had a little money saved up from teaching at Berkeley, and that paid my share. It was two hundred dollars an acre. And then I headed back to Japan."

By 1966, Paul Lee had accepted an offer to become "the psychedelic professor" at the University of California at Santa Cruz. "I'd gotten involved with the Timothy Leary group at Harvard. I was the founding editor of the *Psychedelic Review,*" he says, and Santa Cruz "was a university organized around acid. If you wanted to smoke dope and drop acid, you came to Santa Cruz. It was like a country club for psychedelics in the redwoods."

Paul is a red-faced, silver-maned giant who laughs a lot, and sometimes he laughs so hard that he has to stomp his big foot or bang his heavy hand on the table to stop himself, and then the pots and pans hanging in his kitchen rattle for a while. He is retired, but he lives only a few blocks from the Santa Cruz campus, and he gnaws on a chunk of ginseng root as he speaks. He had been hired to teach philosophy, "but I founded a religious studies program, and they even had a Ph.D. program in the history of consciousness! That was perfect for me."

Just before he moved to Santa Cruz, Paul urged Richard to organize a conference around the growing academic interest in LSD. "Everybody came. And because he had invited Allen Ginsberg, the University [administrators] thought it was too controversial and told him he had to uninvite Ginsberg. It was an ethical issue for Richard. But it was that or shut it down."

Life, as Richard says, is a series of exclusions; some of them are especially poetic.

"It was the summer of '66. All the heavyweights were there speaking and partying." Paul takes a big breath before he dives into the past, and then he's good for several uninterrupted minutes in the deep end. "It was a phenomenology of freaks. We were from Harvard with button-down shirts and three-piece Brooks Brothers suits—even Leary wore the [academic] uniform. And there were these California freaks, and it was like, *Who gave them permission to look like that?* We thought of ourselves as the guys running the show, and here was this whole West Coast development that we hadn't a clue about until we got here. The Psychedelic Bookstore had just opened in Haight-Ashbury, and Owsley [who manufactured and supplied LSD for Ken Kesey's early Acid Tests] was in the house handing out acid to everybody. The law had not yet gone into effect banning it, though it was about to—it was banned a month later.

"So on Sunday afternoon, sort of to launch the event, we go to a rented mansion in San Francisco with a huge swimming pool with about two or three hundred people—two thirds of them nude—and every size and shape and age. And people were smoking gigantic joints rolled in newspaper. I thought, That's really spectacular . . . joints like stovepipes. And then The Grateful Dead came out to play, and before they got going some-body announced that we were all going to have to move our cars because there had been a complaint. And I thought, This is it. This is the test. And the cars were all politely moved. And I was reassured. I figured, whatever is coming our way, we'll probably get through it all. And then The Dead played. One guy had his head in the speakers the entire time they played. I asked everybody who he was. It was Neal Cassady [Jack Kerouac's *On the Road* companion, the model for that book's Dean Moriarty, and, later, Allen Ginsberg's lover], of course. Man, was he *gone.*"

Paul comes up for air. He stares at the ginseng root in his hand—which is clearly not what it used to be. "That was my introduction to the move-ment out here. And the week was not problematic at all. Richard handled it all beautifully."

Form. Richard had mastered it. El Darko was now a colorful character, wrapped up in a seamless garment he'd sewn of poets, priests, professors, psychedelics, sensory awareness, and sitting. "I asked the university if I could have two or three phones instead of one," says Richard. "Already at that time I was—I'd begun to realize I'm sort of multitrack." Richard was everybody's cultural attaché.

And as if his life wasn't complicated enough, Richard was about to turn it into a sleepover with another grand gesture—the promise he would make to Suzuki-roshi that he could raise $300,000 and turn their dream of a monastery into reality. Ten thousand people across America were about to be issued invitations to Tassajara. It transformed everyone. Richard never quite turned into a monk, but as Suzuki-roshi's disciple, he could not be a layperson. Richard remembers that he and Suzuki-roshi did not discuss his decision to be ordained. Seeing the need for Caucasian priests, and knowing that his teacher wanted him to be a priest, Richard remembers, he asked to be ordained at Tassajara. He was about to find out what did and did not fit into a black robe. "Dick argued with Suzuki-roshi until 1967; he did not want to be ordained as a priest," remembers Yvonne. "But Suzuki-roshi wanted it to happen. It was traditional. Out of his love for Suzuki-roshi, Dick went along with a form of practice that, perhaps, never was a fit for him. I think that was a mistake."

It was in 1965 that Yvonne and Virginia Baker became friends. "I was taking a weaving class with Virginia. We had daughters who were within two weeks of each other in age, and after we'd known each other for about a year, Dick and I had a conversation. He discovered that I had studied Buddhism as an undergraduate at Stanford, and he suggested that I go hear Suzuki-roshi in one of his Wednesday night lectures, and I started sitting immediately, although I found myself fairly unnerved in the face of zazen. My life was in transition and my marriage was in stress and strain."

Zen Center was not a residential community yet, but a handful of practitioners had formed a cooperative in a couple of subdivided townhouses directly across from the temple on Bush Street. "It was a time when people were more bohemian, and many were interested in living in Japantown—you could live modestly but quite well. Later they were identified as hippies. I was as interested in what was going on with the people around this teacher as I was with Suzuki-roshi himself," remembers Yvonne. "This was the late summer of 1966. The dream of Tassajara was very compelling. In hindsight, it was a way to not be so lonely, and to distract myself from the suffering in my personal life."

Refuge.

By the spring, though, Yvonne was the Secretary of Zen Center. "I was right in the middle of fund-raising for Tassajara."

"People say all of this made Zen American," says Bill Kwong. "Even the scandal." He smiles. "You see, in 1983, I felt that the other people should have left Zen Center, not Richard, because Suzuki-roshi had entrusted Richard as his first successor. I'm sure that's how traditional people feel. Traditional people in Japan and here, too." Smile. "Maybe it all makes it American, though. Right?" He narrows his gaze and shakes his head. Dubious. "I don't know. American Zen? I don't think so. Zen is Zen. The change is really just the food in the bowl."

**12**

Clunk. YOU CLOSE A DOOR.

The door opens. You close it.

It opens again. You close it.

Open. You close it. You wait. You wait.

It opens. You close it.

You wait. You wait. You open it.

Why wait?

"In the early years at Zen Center, I think it probably was I who seized on the concept of finding land and opening a monastery more strongly than anyone else," says Grahame. But on the very day that Richard informed Grahame that Zen Center was committing itself to the project of acquiring Tassajara to make a monastery in America, "I parted company with Zen Center—well, I don't want to say *parted*, but events took over, and I was not there, and, thus, I was not participating."

Karma?

Grahame never thought that he would not eventually rejoin Zen Center. He visited occasionally throughout the sixties and seventies, and hints of his imminent return appeared periodically in *Wind Bell*. His administrative skills and his deep monastic experience would have profoundly shaped the work being done by his teacher and the new young students who streamed into Zen Center as Tassajara was established. But he never rejoined Zen Center; in fact, within months of Suzuki-roshi's death in 1971, few of the earliest, most senior students had roles in the daily life of Zen Center, save Richard Baker.

"Intentionality is the formal definition of karma," says Lew Richmond. He was ordained by Suzuki-roshi in 1971 as a Zen priest (or monk; the terms are used interchangeably, though ordained people who assume teaching or administrative roles at Zen Center typically are referred to as priests). After Suzuki-roshi died and Richard became Abbot, Lew became Treasurer of Zen Center, and only Richard and Reb were perceived to rank above him in the hierarchy of spiritual leaders in the 1970s and early 1980s. However, when Lew left Zen Center in 1984, he was not an acknowledged Zen master; neither Suzuki-roshi nor Richard had chosen to given Lew Transmission and recognize him as a dharma heir.

Lew says, "Karma occurs because of the thought that grows into action."

It was not until the 1980s, after several entrepreneurial successes in Japan, that Grahame returned to live in the Bay Area—just in time for the Apocalypse. "I came back to Green Gulch Farm and lived very close by in a house owned by Zen Center. I was right there," he says "when everything happened" in the spring of 1983. "I had taken a position with the Smith and Hawken garden tool catalog, in the early, entrepreneurial days. The company was still in Palo Alto; it was supposed to [have moved north] to Mill Valley [a few minutes away from Green Gulch], but that didn't happen, so I was commuting each day, which precluded my really taking part in Zen Center. I had to get up at five-thirty every day, and I got back from work at seven." Grahame was trying to establish his life in America "with my second wife and our son Mark, too." Grahame grins and leans back from his desk, apparently to achieve a sardonic distance. "It was complicated," he says, with a wince. "You see, Richard had introduced me to Paul Hawken," he says flatly, and then he adds, "Complicated, indeed."

"We have a lifetime of karma," says Pat Leonetti, a big, black-haired woman with a generous sense of humor who was ordained by Reb Anderson. She is reluctant to say anything else for a few minutes. Karma is complicated. "Of course, karma is not contained in a single lifetime," she says. Pat is more than a little skeptical about the likelihood of anyone explaining something so profound. Karma is created by intentions and actions. The effects of karma shape our circumstances but do not determine our behavior. And karma is manifest over the course of existence, which, according to traditional Buddhist teachings, unfolds throughout the cycle of rebirth.

To escape, by achieving liberation from the cycle of rebirth, the individual must transcend desire, hatred, and delusion. At that point, the will of the individual is still; the individual intends nothing; the individual creates no karma. This liberated state is *nirvana*, popularly known as *perfection*, though it translates literally from the Sanskrit as *extinction*.

"I don't know anything about rebirth," says Pat. She stares at her folded hands on the table and shakes her head, and it's not clear whether she wants to change the subject or meditate on the truth of not knowing anything about it. Her eyes are still downcast when she says, "And if you have a definitive idea about rebirth . . ." Her voice trails off and she lowers her head a bit more, until her face is almost flat against the table. After a minute, she raises her hand, signaling her readiness to say something, then she slowly lifts her head, and when she tries to finish her sentence, she laughs out loud. "Rebirth is a just a big *I don't know* area," she says. "I don't try to have a concept." This just seems right. It *is* funny to talk about human perfection as if we might recognize it. Any concept of rebirth, as Pat says, is a matter of faith.

"But this was not the consciousness in the community when we were trying to establish a monastery," says Lew. "There was a kind of complacency. We were doing zazen. And the main point was, zazen leads to enlightenment, enlightenment leads to perfection, and the rest will work itself out. We were Buddhist heroes. That was part of the shock. We were blind. We're not so special."

Pat is still smiling when she says, "In this lifetime, what we do at Zen Center is we try to sit with our karma. That's all."

Grahame opens the door that separates his office-bedroom from his living room. Although he was the first Westerner ordained as a monk by Suzuki-roshi, Grahame has lived most of his life as a layperson. Opening that door is one of the routines of his ordinary life. He is monitoring his seventeen-year-old son Mark, who is lying in a bed in the living room. A car accident in the summer of 1999 left Mark paralyzed and unable to speak or feed himself. Grahame sits with his son all day, every day. The prognosis for Mark is not clear. Theirs is a moment-by-moment, day-by-day life. It's a life of stillness and, paradoxically, a life fraught with unforeseeable, unpredictable possibilities for change. Maybe it's the life we're all living, try as we might to keep that door closed.

The first person to open the door for Grahame was a minister at a Church of England boarding school. Grahame was twelve when the minister told the students in his religion class that they couldn't just accept spiritual teachings as they were presented but should find God themselves. "I don't think many of my classmates were aroused, but I latched on like, Wow!" When Grahame discovered that the minister could not answer all the questions he asked, he "looked elsewhere," including a Carmelite monastery where he spent a rewarding summer when he was nineteen. "It was almost like paradise," he remembers. "At the end of the summer I wanted to stay, and they wanted me to stay, and I didn't share their beliefs."

Grahame eventually found Buddhism in books in his mother-in-law's library, and within weeks after he and his wife moved to San Francisco in 1961, he found Suzuki-roshi. "I called Sokoji, and Suzuki-roshi gave me the wrong time to arrive, and when I turned up, they were all in the midst of zazen. I waited in the entry room." When the door opened, "a big troupe of people came out, and it was shock to me," says Grahame. "I had expected to see robed monks and bald heads—out comes one in blue jeans, looking like he'd come from a construction site, and people in sweaters, just normal, everyday people."

Suzuki-roshi "kindly offered" to sit with Grahame, "and we sat together for about thirty minutes. Then he said, 'You take the posture very well. Please join us. Please come back tomorrow at 5:45.' I said, 'I am married. I have a job.' I couldn't believe it. Sunday at ten o'clock—something like that, yes. But I went. I don't think I missed a morning thereafter for two years. The first time I missed was the day my son was born." It was after two months of the 5:45 sessions that Grahame went to Suzuki-roshi and said, "'I'm not getting it. I'm not really understanding what I'm doing.' He said, 'Oh, in that case, then please come in the evening, as well.' I thought, Well, okay."

Grahame organized his life around Suzuki-roshi and Sokoji—sitting twice a day, including weekends and, occasionally, daylong and weeklong sesshins. His wife was sitting at Sokoji regularly, he says, "until the children came along." But after two years, he still wasn't getting it. "So I went to Suzuki-roshi and said, 'Look, we've done this, and you really have not helped me solve what I am trying to solve.' This is when Suzuki-roshi said, 'I think you should go and study in Japan.'"

In the autumn of 1963, Grahame left his wife and children and endured three months as the first Zen Center initiate in the Eiheiji training monastery. After that humbling experience, Grahame returned to San Francisco and sat with Suzuki-roshi every day for another year and a half and became an organizational leader, as well. "Then, the same questions. I told him after three and a half years, 'I just don't understand it.' On this occasion, Suzuki-roshi sighed and said, 'Nor do I. I think you'd better study with someone who really understands the meaning of Zen. And I only know about six people who do.' And I said, 'They're in Japan, aren't they?' He said, 'Of course. Maybe there are twelve. If I know six in Soto Zen, maybe there are six in Rinzai.'"

Grahame took the six names, his wife and children, and his mother-in-law; his family lived in Kyoto and Grahame went back to Eiheiji, where he was eventually carried out of the zendo in front of 140 monks and a crowd of guests and visitors in the midst of a public ceremony. He had developed water on the knee. He'd been hospitalized several times already. "Dogen [the great master who founded the temple in 1243] was always going back to Kyoto to recover from the unhealthy atmosphere of Eiheiji," which is in a deep valley, says Grahame, with high humidity that "rolls down the hills and just sits in the temple, which is very cold."

Grahame looked at Suzuki-roshi's list of six names, and he found Sawaki Kodo, one of most eminent masters of the twentieth century. Sawaki Kodo had a small temple with a few monks, which appealed to Grahame, especially in contrast to the high dudgeon of Eiheiji. "There were no big donors at this temple. There were no telephones. The monks went begging for their livelihood—not ceremonially, but really begging." The spirit of this temple was coherent with the spirit of the Carmelite monastery he had visited as a boy. While Grahame was at his temple, Sawaki Kodo died. Grahame and the other monks sat a forty-nine-day sesshin. "Sitting day after day in midwinter, one's mind becomes incredibly calm. I could literally hear the insects walking on the tatami [mats]. It was during that period that I recognized that I had not exactly answered my nagging question, but the questions had quietly gone away."

When the sesshin dedicated to Sawaki Kodo was complete, Grahame recognized that "it was time to go on." He headed back toward Zen Center. But he stopped with his family to see his parents in England, received an offer to start a language school in Japan, and signed a contract. "The day after I signed the contract, I received word from Dick about the prospect of Tassajara. I was devastated." It was not only his monastic experience and his devotion to the practice that informed Grahame's reaction. "I wanted to pursue the formation of a community where we could spend our lives in this pursuit. I felt equally obliged to honor my contract and to do what we had always hoped to do at Zen Center."

Grahame asked for help. What is striking is that he received a direct reply. "I wrote it all out in a telegram to Suzuki-roshi, and he wrote back telling me I should go back to Japan."

Grahame says, "I think Suzuki-roshi had two motivations. He agreed with me that one should fulfill a contract. More important, I think, he wanted me to have more exposure to Japan, to become more fluent in the language, to become totally saturated with the culture." Suzuki-roshi was trying to cultivate priests who could train the blind young heroes who were volunteering for duty at the Tassajara monastery, and as far as his students understood, he clearly intended to open a practice center in Japan, too, as part of his desire—you might call it a blind ambition—to reform Buddhism there. So, in a single lifetime, at any single moment, a single action might be conditioned by more than a single intention. Grahame did go back to Japan. "And these days," he says, "I very rarely go to Zen Center. Not because I don't want to, but with Mark, it simply is not possible to go anywhere."

"When I was a very new student," says a former Zen Center resident, "I heard Ed Brown say, 'Karma is merciless.'"

Pat Leonetti says, "I've actually experienced in myself patterns of behavior that are so deep they are like troughs. You can use the word *karma* for those conditioned ways of doing and thinking," she says, and then adds, "Those troughs seem to soften with examination. With under-standing, they fill up from the bottom and seem not so deep. I think there is karma, deep conditioning, and there is a way to soften and change it. The idea is to try not to be driven from behind or beneath by your karma."

Suzuki-roshi said many times, "It may be quite difficult to know how to help another person." But people asked him for help. What could he do? Once, he sent a telegram. Once, he placed a pair of drumsticks on the floor where a student would see them. Once, he opened his home and family to an antisocial monk whom no one else wanted around. "Trying to help often creates more problems than it solves," Suzuki-roshi warned his students. "Sitting in zazen is the easiest, safest way to help yourself and others."

"See, you commit harm whenever you do anything," says Lew. "You cause harm when you breathe. This is one of the realizations of Buddhism. The first precept is to do no harm, but everything you do causes harm." You cannot avoid trouble in the world. You cannot control the circumstances of your life. "You *can* work on the intention behind what you do and don't do," says Lew. "It has to do with what happens in the psyche."

13.

"GOING OVER SUZUKI-ROSHI'S teachings, again and again I come across that the work is to accept suffering. It is not to put an end to suffering." Dan Welch was among the initial, small cohort of novices who took up residence at Tassajara soon after it was purchased. They worked on the physical transformation of the land and buildings, often alongside Suzuki-roshi.

Something of Suzuki-roshi rubbed off on a lot of people. But something of Suzuki-roshi rubbed Dan another way. He is a tall, slim, strong, sweet man with blue eyes and shiny white bits of hair by the end of every week, until he shaves his face and pate again. He is a practicing Zen priest. This surprises many of his former colleagues. Dan was known for being who-knew-where and for having taken off his ordination robes in 1984 and then—depending on who is telling the story—giving away those robes, or selling or burning them.

He says he had no idea that people had been thinking about the fate of his robes. "You're stirring up a lot of dust," says Dan. His grin as he says this is about as convincing as a mustache painted on the *Mona Lisa*. Then he goes silent, and the temperature in the cab of his white truck seems to rise. "You're in the story now," he says, turning his gaze from the road to me and reaching toward me with his right hand. He is leaning in way too close. In the moments that have passed since I mentioned my conversations with other people about his robes, he seems to have grown taller. And the heat I feel is not coming from the vents, and it's not all coming from me. Dan is actually hot. I can feel him. Also, his face and neck are red, and that's a signal, which I interpret as *Not good*. Or am I misreading the signals? He pinches the sleeve of my blue sweater and I am thinking,

Again, not good. And I don't know who this man is or what he is apt to do next. And I do not want to believe I am in this story any more than I want to believe I am stuck in a truck on a highway in the New Mexico desert with a man who is either much more intense or much more annoyed than he seemed just one hour ago, when we first met.

I know way too much about Dan Welch. Before he offered me a ride from Santa Fe to Crestone, Colorado, two dozen people had told me about the fate of Dan's robes. More than a dozen people had recounted escalating versions of the morning at Zen Center in the mid-seventies when Richard Baker had taken the stick (more typically used to prod sleepy sitters during meditation) and "beat on Dan," in the words of a young student who arrived at Zen Center years after the incident. It was one of the stories that was passed among students below the surface of official teachings for several years, and it broke to the surface in 1983. "It was after a Zen Center party," a senior priest and colleague of Dan's recalled, in the version most often repeated at Zen Center. Richard had heard of some flirtatious activity between Dan and a younger student. Dan was married. The next morning, Dan was called in for a private interview, or dokusan, and Richard used the stick. In fact, as the story was told, Dan and the woman had gone their separate ways without acting on the attraction.

Physical reprimands and apparent emotional cruelty were, to some degree, understood as traditional elements of the practice. "You have to pass through the master to be a master," says John Bailes. But, he adds, "I think people were putting their best efforts forward to try to practice Buddhism, and when it was slammed in their faces in some way, they were afraid to put their best efforts forward. It could have been anyone, not just Dick," says John, who remembers that Reb was just as tough on students. "I couldn't figure out what their fraternity was," he adds, "it was beyond me."

"Dick was physically punishing students for behavior that was his for his entire life as a Zen practitioner," says Yvonne. "Essentially, *I am above the rules. The rules for you do not apply to me.*"

John remembers several people, including senior priests, who fell apart under the strain of psychological treatment that registered in his own life as "having the shit kicked out of me." All that was clear, he says, is that "Dick and Reb had all the cards."

Richard says he was always ambivalent about the stick but did use it; however, he remembers using it to "hit [students] on the shoulder, not hurting them," to signal that an answer to a question during a private interview with him didn't make sense. "Boy, when '83 came, they got me back for that."

Many elements of Dan's story became public in 1983, and they figure in other people's understanding of their own stories. Often, I was asked if I had heard about Dan's sister, though it turned out I was being told about Dan's sister, Jeannie Campbell, who had started the sitting group that later became the Berkeley Zen Center, had an affair with Richard in the early sixties, managed one of the first Zen Center businesses, and killed herself in 1973.

The first thing Dan told me about himself after I'd climbed into his white truck in Santa Fe was that he had landed at Tassajara in 1967, and that Jeannie had led him to Zen Center. But before he said that, he wanted to know about my first impression of Zen Center.

On an autumn day in 1997, Wendell Berry was invited to speak at Green Gulch Farm, and his editor, Jack Shoemaker, was going with him, and Jack is my editor, and I was in San Francisco at the time, and Jack invited me to join them for the day. It was one of those is-it-raining-or-not days in the Bay Area and, in truth, my memory of the day is drizzly, too. I remember that the land impressed me because you couldn't see it until you were there. I was riding in the backseat of a big white rental car with pleasingly springy shocks. We bounded up the twisty hills of the Pacific Coast Highway on the edge of the Muir Woods, and suddenly the snug bunker of land on our left gave way to cliffs, and the vast Pacific flashed and splattered a few hundred feet below, and as the road rolled to the right, our sedan lurched to the left, and I thought, *Here we go.* Instead of plummeting over the cliff, though, we slipped down a bumpy road into a hammock of land—115 acres slung beneath the highway. The road ran down through dense patches of old growth pines and stands of sweet and stinky eucalyptus toward a flat patch of cultivated valley, and beyond that the land sloped up toward promontory pastures high above the ocean. There were a few large, low white buildings with shingled roofs half-hidden by bends in the road, the web of weepy eucalyptus limbs, and thickets of vigorous shrubs and vines. It reminded me of Burma, where I have never been. The air was green.

The road dwindled to a path that drew us down and out from underneath the canopy into a clearing where the grass is green, the soil deep, and we toured the twelve-acre organic farm and garden. The mud sucked off my loafers several times, which later complicated the custom of taking off your shoes before entering a building, since my socks had become slick and slimy. Our guide wore waders. She said it was a good day to try to answer questions about Zen because practicing Zen is like walking in a light rain. You just walk in the mist with your teacher. You do what you're supposed to do. Before you notice, you'll find that your robes are soaking wet. You don't have to think about what's happening to you.

We were ushered into a few beautiful wooden guest facilities; we were not shown the insides of the trailers and saggy barnboard shacks where the younger priests and students live. When I finally figured out that Green Gulch Farm was one part of the three-part San Francisco Zen Center, I asked a couple of people how a few hundred otherwise unemployed Zen students had financed three spectacular locations, and I was told about the farm's plant and bake sales, a couple of the businesses that Zen Center no longer runs, Ed Brown's bread book, overnight guests—and someone said they used to keep chickens and sell the eggs from a farmhouse they owned in Jamestown, at the bottom of the road to Tassajara. Eggs, muffins, and fresh vegetables didn't really add up to an empire, but by then Wendell Berry was seated in a chair—an elder statesman—and the rest of us were sitting on the floor around him, all of us muddy, which might have engendered more camaraderie had we been allowed to look at each other or speak. The students and priests seemed to be teaching you not to look at them, though; they kept their eyes averted. Most everyone was dressed in a homey, folksy way, and a lot of the cultural material in the room seemed secondhand and rag-taggy, as if we were gathered to sing Pete

Seeger songs in Japanese and share a ceremonial bong, which, I remember thinking, might take the edge off all this earnestness. Instead, Wendell spoke about sustainable land-use habits and a prison-farm in the city that was being established with the help of Green Gulch residents, and then the students served tea out of pasta pots and weren't unfriendly. Whenever someone asked for either a refill or an explanation of rebirth, they smiled, but those smiles were brief as winks.

That's how I ended up in a blue sweater in a white truck on Highway 91 in New Mexico in the summer of 1999, pretending not to know what Dan meant when he said I was stirring up a lot of dust, until I realize that I *don't* know what he means, exactly.

Karma is merciless.

I don't say anything, and Dan doesn't say anything, and he has one hand on the wheel and one hand on the sleeve of my sweater, and I have a tape recorder in one hand, recording every word neither of us is saying, and on the other hand, I am wondering if now is the time to ask him about Richard, and that's when I feel my sweater pook back into place, and Dan is rolling down his window, and then he sticks his fingers out as if he has picked something off my sweater, and he lets it go into the stream of air screaming by—maybe it was a speck of dust, maybe a spider, or maybe it was a teaching—and I stupidly roll down my window, which creates a deafening wind with force enough to blow my brains out of one of my ears and into one of Dan's.

We rectify the window situation, and I say, "That was confusing." It is July in New Mexico, but it is morning, and the air is still cool.

Dan says, "I'm sure some people have told you I wanted to kill Richard. Right?"

And I don't say, You read my mind, but I guess he has.

"Long body," says Richard. It is a snowy February day in 2000, nine months after my first conversation with Dan. I am back in Crestone, Colorado. Richard is not talking about Dan, but somehow everyone in this story is always talking about Dan to me. "We have a cultural view that space separates us. You are there and I am here." But something is going on between us, he says. "That is the experience of long body. You pick up the phone and somebody says, I was just going to call you. Buddhism assumes there is a connectedness, a nonlocal consciousness."

It's not mind reading, and it's not some Buddhist trick. The trick of Buddhism is to get you to sit still long enough to become aware of the causes and effects. If you have a view that assumes that space separates us, "that view is lodged in the way the mind functions prior to perception and conception. All of your perceptions will reinforce separation," explains Richard, who has a gift for serving up Buddhism's most exotic fare without any pomposity or mysticism, as if it's just a few chunks of fresh mango and kiwi he's thrown into the canned fruit cocktail Americans customarily eat. "If at some point—and there are practice techniques to help us do this—you can get the view that we are connected prior to perception, perception starts showing you that we *are* connected." Later, he points out, "There are a thousand handy phone calls and television stations in this room right now; we just don't have the sensory apparatus to tap into them. Zen assumes that there is a lot going on here that we don't have the apparatus for."

Long body. Dan might have the longest body in America. He's certainly been on the mind of everyone I've met since I started asking questions about Zen Center. Despite the Buddhist ban on gossip, which falls under the rubric of Right Speech, Dan was famous all over American Zendom, and not least of all for what he intended to do to Richard Baker a few years after both of them had left San Francisco.

"He came to Santa Fe to kill Baker-roshi," Willem told me.

Dan is more modest about his ambition. "My feelings about Richard have been misconstrued. What I wanted was to get his undivided attention. It was 1987 when I found him in Santa Fe. I was studying with Clint Eastwood at the time. I mean that facetiously, and I mean that dead seriously. I had tried to get Richard's attention for years. He could never give it to me, bless his heart."

Bless his heart. It's not edged with sarcasm. It's not edged with sancti-

mony. It's not edged with anything. It's funny and affectionate and somehow soft, as if the edge has been rubbed away, rounded off. And that's
what Suzuki-roshi did to Dan Welch.

Dan's story is singular, and his path has been singularly circular. To
many of his former colleagues, it just looks loopy, as loopy as Suzuki-
roshi's unfulfilled desire to circle back and reform Buddhism in Japan.

We are speeding north toward Crestone Mountain in southern Colorado, 14,000 feet above sea level, where Richard is the Abbot of a small
residential training temple he established in 1987. What does Dan want
with Richard now? "To see me, or to see Richard—to see what happened
to any one of us at Zen Center, and to see what happened to all of us—you
have to see Suzuki-roshi," says Dan. "His own life as a teacher was difficult. He didn't come to America as a Zen teacher. He was a modest guy, not
a miraculous guy, who got here almost by default. He had qualifications
for putting the teaching into place, but he'd had no opportunity. The
strange circumstances of our time provided, instigated, and nurtured it."

Dan doesn't say, Karma.

I don't say, An accident waiting to happen.

Dan says, "There is something true about saying *I cannot help humanity*. Humanity does not want my help. And there is really nothing I can
do for it. But I do feel I want to do something," he tells me. "This is what
Suzuki-roshi taught me. If you feel you want to do something, if you
want to do something as small as picking up a speck of dust, you should
know unequivocally, it is going to cause myriad problems. Don't fool
yourself. Be fully prepared to pick up all of the suffering of the world with
that speck of dust." He is grinning again, and reading a map spread out
on his lap. I'm watching the road. He says he is looking for a lake. I figure
he has a better chance of finding it on that map than in this desert, and
the truck seems to be about thirty seconds away from a header with a
medium-size mountain. Dan looks up, takes a sharp left, and we bounce
down a dirt road. "These are the foothills of the Sangre de Cristo," he says.
Red sandstone hills and cliffs erupt out of the desert dust. This is the
Blood of Christ.

Really.

"When you look at the Zen Center experience," says Dan, "it looks like it increased suffering, but let's look at it again. It is 1965, 1966, 1967. In this wide, wide world, I am drawn into one beautiful moment in a beautiful valley. Tassajara. I can abandon it. I can embrace it. I can do anything. What do I want to do?"

During the last three years, I've met a lot of people who have practiced at the San Francisco Zen Center. I asked each of them the same question: What led you there? No one said, I was so happy and fulfilled that I wanted to find a new way to express my joy and gratitude. Discontent, depression, sickness, bad luck, and loneliness had paved the way. Suffering shapes the place more than the sixties, or any particular cultural moment, or any one woman or man. Suffering is the recurring moment, reborn every time someone new turns up.

"I wanted to do something. I wanted to help start a monastery. I wanted to pick up a speck of dust," says Dan. "And now I hear Suzuki-roshi's voice. *Be aware. You will pick up all of the world's troubles.*
    "And we did."

14.

THE DUSTY ROAD TO TASSAJARA
has never been paved. "It's a whole lot safer and smoother today than it was when Zen Center got hold of the place in the sixties," says a retired teacher who first visited in the early 1950s, "but it's still a rough ride."

In the spring of 1966, Richard drove Suzuki-roshi up the rutted road. For five years, everyone at Zen Center had known they were looking for a place to start a monastery, but no one had any clear idea of what it might look like. "[Suzuki-roshi] told me once that most people are not making practicing in the city work the way you're able to—words to that effect. That started my desire to get Tassajara," says Richard. Suzuki-roshi thought it "would help him continue with most people who were too caught up in their daily lives—they weren't as fanatic as I was or as worried about going crazy, so he thought a monastic type life would be good. So we went on a hunt. We looked for places. All of them he nixed. And he had a great sense of land. He'd look down and say, 'There's gonna be a water problem down there.'"

Grahame and his wife had camped at Tassajara in 1961, and Richard and his wife had followed their lead, but it was years later that Richard heard that the land was owned by Fred Roscoe, who owned the Discovery Bookstore. "I knew Ferlinghetti and those people [who owned City Lights bookstore next door] much better, but I used to shop in Fred's store," too, says Richard, who telephoned Fred, "and he said 'I was the partner but I got out of it, and now Bob Beck is the sole owner, and here's [his] phone number.' I called Bob Beck. And he wanted to sell a portion of the land."

The $150,000 asking price was inconceivable to almost everyone but Richard. "I just think things are possible," he says. He was mindful of having "developed a large range of contacts," and he had "a kind of confidence" that America was ready. Almost every wealthy family in America had someone involved with meditation or yoga, "and here was an opportunity to practice. This might capture their imagination." A little later he mentions one other factor. "I've never been afraid of failing," says Richard, and it takes a minute for the memory of his own history to catch up with those words.

"I didn't know I was going to fail on such a big scale," he adds.

A little later, he adds, "I always feel I have nothing to lose."

With a $2,500 down payment and Suzuki-roshi's blessing, Richard organized the fund-raising effort at Zen Center. Yvonne remembers that "ten or fifteen of us met every Thursday night in my living room for the next two or three years, wondering, How are we going to do it? We felt our way along. Somebody would get an idea—one person could write to her grandparents, somebody else would think of a college professor—and from one week to the next, someone's idea would energize someone else. It was very grass roots and small scale, and that was significant. What made the project happen on a bigger scale were the two foldout brochures. Richard had the vision to do those—designing them and getting well-known people to give quotations."

In addition to supportive words from Gary Snyder, Paul Lee, Alan Watts, and eminent academics, "I wanted a brochure that you got physically involved with," says Richard. "My conception was [of a man opening his mail and yelling,] 'Emmy! I got this brochure in the mail. Would you come over here and grab this other end?'" The 9" x 9" square unfolded into an unwieldy 18" x 27" rectangle. "When you opened it up, your body was involved."

Zen Center was finally on the road to Tassajara; however, there was a little bump. Bob Beck had not agreed to sell Zen Center the hot springs resort, which is what Richard and Suzuki-roshi wanted to buy. Instead, he had sold them a 160-acre parcel of mountainous land near the hot springs resort, known as the Horse Pasture. It included forty acres of relatively flat land at the valley floor with a reliable, spring-fed water supply, and not a single habitable structure.

Richard was confident Beck would eventually sell them the resort, which was clearly not being run at a profit. Suzuki-roshi was confident about Richard's confidence; in the summer of 1966, he traveled to Japan to resign from his temple and turn it over to his son.

The first brochure was mailed out in the fall. Within six months, more than $90,000 in donations had been collected. In addition to black-and-white photographs and an introduction to Suzuki-roshi's teaching, the brochure included the following details about the construction and development plans: _____.

That's right; not a word.

"Richard had the capacity to make us feel we could see way up the road into the future," says Lucy Calhoun, who lived at Zen Center in the seventies. "Suzuki-roshi made us feel we didn't need to look ahead."

"It was a dream, really," says a former Board member. "The cost and dangers and logistics of a major construction project in the Horse Pasture would have proved prohibitive. If anything had actually materialized, it would have happened on a much smaller scale, and it would not have happened for at least ten years. Suzuki-roshi wanted one thing—a place to cultivate the practice. But he had no practical plan for making it happen. Richard said, essentially, Trust me. I can make it happen."

As Dan Welch says, "Richard likes to say, 'If you can think it, you can do it.'"

"Suzuki-roshi was not a naive or an innocent," says Tim Buckley. "He understood what he couldn't do and what Richard could do. One-mindedness between teacher and disciple is a cliché, but it has meaning. And it does not mean *my mind alone*." These were two minds, they felt, that were working as one.

And it did work. Before the end of the year, Bob Beck told Richard that he wanted to retract the sale of the Horse Pasture, and instead offered to sell Zen Center the resort property. This time, the purchase price looked like more than a bump in the road. "I called Suzuki-roshi at twelve-thirty at night. I'd been talking to Bob Beck all evening, and he wanted $450,000. I told Suzuki-roshi, 'This is a businessman's price, and we're not a business. I ask your permission to step out.' Suzuki-roshi said, 'Fine. We should only do it'—and this is a rule I have always followed—'if the person really wants to sell it to us. If the feeling is it is partly a gift, we do it;

if it's not partly a gift, we're out.' So I hung up and said [to Bob and his wife], 'We're out. It's over.' And then, an hour or so later, Bob changed the price to $300,000." Richard suddenly looks exhausted. And chastened. He looks happy when he says that Bob Beck "changed Buddhism in America by selling that place to us."

By early 1967, several students had begun to renovate the buildings, construct a zendo, and refashion the Tassajara grounds to accommodate Zen Center. The market value of their first few months of donated labor was estimated at $50,000. Still, Zen Center was in debt for the first time—to the Becks and to Richard. But Zen Center—and Richard—also enjoyed a windfall of prestige. Gary Snyder, Alan Watts, poet Gerd Stein, and their friends organized readings and participatory Zen-events to raise money and consciousness for Tassajara; The Grateful Dead, Big Brother and the Holding Company, and Quicksilver appeared at a "Zenefit" at the Avalon Ballroom, courtesy of Bill Graham; Ali Akbar Khan and other Eastern Arts musicians also played a benefit concert; Edward Avedisian, Sister Mary Corita, and Mike Dixon donated paintings to be auctioned or sold.

"Richard had put an ancient and rich tradition right into the center of the Bay Area scene," says Esalen's Michael Murphy, who met Richard that year.

"Plus, we had the best hot tubs in California," says a former student.

Zen Center stayed well ahead of its payment schedule for the Tassajara mortgage, which was actually an interest-free loan to be repaid to the Becks over five years. The second brochure, as big as the first, appeared that spring. Anyone who had seen the first brochure could plainly see that the dream of a monastery had become real in a matter of months. Celebrity endorsements arrived from Joseph Campbell (who called the founding of a Buddhist monastery "a disclosure of America as home"), a Catholic missionary ("As a human being, the seven years spent in Bolivia were the best years of my life. As a spiritual being, the month at Zen Mountain Center was the best month of my life"), and Michael Murphy. In addition, three key benefactors became publicly associated with the Zen Center project: Nancy Wilson Ross, a powerful New York socialite and author of The World of Zen, joined Xerox Corporation founder Chester Carlson (the first six-figure donor) and Edward C. Johnson II, chairman of

Boston's Fidelity Mutual, in a public statement of support for Zen Center, for Suzuki-roshi, and for Richard Baker, the young American man who had accompanied the Zen master on his trips into their homes and into their hearts.

Almost a thousand contributors had responded to the first brochure. "Over half the money we needed came from people who made donations of twenty-five dollars or less," recalls Yvonne. "That sense—many people doing a small bit—is one of the most inspiring facets of the actualization of this dream."

The major gifts, then and later, came from "high families," says Tim Buckley. "Naturally, the link into America was through the aristocracy and the nouveau riche. It was not a populist movement, no matter how comfortable Woody Guthrie might have been at Tassajara. This is the East Coast tradition right back to Thoreau and Emerson. And remember, all of the Sutras from India begin, *O sons and daughters of good family. You people who can afford to be listening to me, who aren't starving to death in the gutters, who aren't working dawn to dusk in the fields and have a life of comparative leisure, who can afford to be Buddhists.* Richard didn't invent this. And I'm sure he would not have been so successful had he not seen the way Suzuki-roshi held a fork in public."

Most Americans didn't have a professor of anthropology on hand to decode the list of contributors when they received the second brochure in the mail, just a few months before the Summer of Love. It was hard enough to puzzle out the meaning of the brochure's appealingly cryptic title, "An Unconditioned Response to a Conditioned World." In 1967, you probably didn't have to be a Buddhist to respond to the idea that you had been conditioned—by the Establishment, the Military Industrial Complex, Multinational Corporations, or your hopelessly reactionary parents. You probably did have to be a Buddhist to understand that "unconditioned" was a way of declaring Tassajara a karma-free zone—an egoless response to America's social circumstances. The road to Tassajara, apparently, was *not* paved with good or bad intentions.

Of course, it was not a literal claim. Zen is not literal. But no one was saying you could *not* find perfection at Zen Center. "Japanese Buddhism has this incredible flaw," according to Lew. Buddhists long ago articulated a set of precepts for everyday life, he says, and Japanese Zen "separated itself from those precepts to accommodate the samurai class—the samurai were professional killers—and it went downhill from there." Lew remembers that Suzuki-roshi's attitude in his lectures was that the precepts are "flexible and situational to a certain extent. And that sort of fuzziness has been part of Buddhism's genius and downfall. You can ultimately rationalize anything. And some Zen masters do."

"The second brochure articulated—visually and in text—a dream, at a time when many people in this country responded to the dream of an authentic spiritual practice," explains Yvonne. "We were mailing out thousands of them. Many people who never imagined they would see Tassajara supported it. They wanted it to happen."

Charlotte Selver, one of Richard's mentors and a faculty member at the New School for Social Research in New York City's Greenwich Village, extolled Tassajara in Edenic terms, as a place "where no doctrines or authorities are superimposed and where the reality of living and working for its own sake already appeals deeply to the young."

And hers was one of the more sober endorsements.

"It would have been much better," says Lew, "to have an institution that thought of itself as part of the world. The early Zen Center was the healthiest Zen Center. Everybody had a job and an ordinary life and came together to meditate."

"When the opportunity to go to Tassajara came up, I got on the bus," says Tim. He'd dropped out of Harvard in the early sixties and moved to a cabin in Maine with a friend. "We were still acting out these Beatnik scripts—this was the *Dharma Bums* moment. But I had begun sitting, sort of with a book in one hand, doing it wrong, probably, but doing it." After Tim left Maine to study photography, his cabin-mate moved to San Francisco and urged Tim to join him. "He told me to get out to the West Coast, that everything we ever wanted was out there—women, booze, and Buddhism in a beautiful city, very far away from the Episcopal church and my parents."

On his way to say good-bye to his parents, who lived in western New York, Tim met Philip Kapleau, an American who'd spent several years studying Zen in Japan and would soon establish one of the most influential East Coast practice centers. "Kapleau had just published *The Three Pillars of Zen*. He was making his entrée to Rochester and visiting a family friend. He invited me to stay and study with them, but it was 1965 and the whole continent was tilting west. Kapleau told me to find Shunryu Suzuki," recalls Tim. "And when I got to San Francisco, all the photographers I met knew about Suzuki-roshi, which made sense," because the photographer Minor White was Tim's connection to them, "and he was a genuine visionary and a genuine disciplinarian." Tim also had "all these hippie friends, and I messed around for a while, until even I could see I wasn't getting anywhere, so I finally went over to Sokoji on Bush Street, and Boom! Suzuki-roshi. Recognition." Tim shrugs. "Is that another cliché? Like everyone, I'd looked around a lot. The Tibetans were just arriving on the West Coast, and there were a lot of gurus available, but I'd never seen another human being who could present himself flawlessly in the world." Flawlessly? Tim nods. "Suzuki-roshi was like Ulysses; he was up for every moment, and he was never inadequate to the moment."

"Once those brochures went out," remembers Yvonne, "people started showing up at Sokoji with backpacks, saying, Here I am. Take me. I'm yours."

"In the first summer that we took ownership of Tassajara," recalls Tim, "everyone was desperate. The quality of practice then—it was like being in the catacombs. We were fugitive heretics—junkies, prostitutes, screwed-up adolescents, and runaways—and most of us were too young to know what to do with the serious life experiences we'd had in the world."

"This dream of a residential community was courageous and visionary," says Lew, "and it made us feel that we were leading the way, leading the world. But the whole notion that we created something called *the world* was problematical, and not a very good idea."

15.

THERE ARE MANY PATHS TO Tassajara but only one road. And in the spring of 1967, that one road was closed down for almost three weeks by late snow and mudslides. It was more than a metaphor. Thirty novice students had taken up full-time residence at Tassajara, and even in good weather, they were basically on their own. They meditated and worked at a provisional monastery with no ordained Zen priest in residence. Until the summer, Suzuki-roshi typically visited only on weekends with Richard, Yvonne, and the other senior students who were devoting themselves to the practical business of paying for the project and overseeing the daily business of Zen Center—which included an increasing number of Americans practicing daily in the city, and the increasingly discontented Japanese-American parishioners at Sokoji. And until just shortly before Suzuki-roshi's death in December of 1971, the monastic routine at Tassajara remained a matter of improvisation.

Ed Brown was the cook. He had dropped out of college in 1964. "In the second semester, I was taking a course in social psychology. It seemed pretty obvious that sociology and psychology weren't about anyone we knew. It was purposefully objective. I wrote a paper about alienation and anxiety—causes and conditions. I got an *A*. And I was as anxious and alienated as ever," he explains. His brother had met Suzuki-roshi and sent Ed excerpts from Paul Rep's 1957 collection of enlightenment stories, *Zen Flesh, Zen Bones*, in which a young man is advised to go to the mountains and attain true realization. "At the end of the year, I withdrew, and they sent me an exit survey asking me to explain why, and I put down, To go to the mountains and attain true realization. And two years later I was at Tassajara."

It was 1964 when Ed left Antioch College, and the Vietnam War was on. He sat at Sokoji. "The practice had an effect on me. Unlike scholastic work, it did not objectify people; it was something a person could do." He was granted a military-service deferment on the basis of Suzuki-roshi's word about his sincerity as a priest-in-training, and an intensive FBI investigation. ("They talked to people whose lawns I'd watered when I was a kid. By the end, the FBI knew more of the people I knew than I knew.") Eventually, Ed was given conscientious objector status. He first went to Tassajara in the summer of 1966 as cook for the last season under the ownership of Bob Beck. "And then I just stayed on when Zen Center took over, and I did two years of alternative service. I served my country by helping to cut trails, fight forest fires, and cook at a monastery."

If you didn't want to travel to Tassajara, or even to Sokoji, in 1967, you could take refuge in tofu, wheat berries, and miso. Variations on the so-called Zen macrobiotic diet sustained a lot of Buddhist sympathizers, but not the students at Tassajara, who rose at four in the morning for a day of meditating (morning, noon, and night) that ended at 9:30 in the evening, and included heavy labor—refashioning the resort's bar and lounge into a zendo and restoring crumbly stone walls and antique plumbing, as well as digging, plastering, dredging, and painting. After a few weeks on the macrobiotic starvation diet, eggs, cheese, and other fat- and protein-rich foods began to appear in their bowls. As did gruel, almost every day—sometimes as breakfast (yesterday's rice boiled with water to a slippery, slimy consistency), and sometimes as lunch (a soupy stew of yesterday's rice, soup, and uneaten vegetables). And Ed made bread.

All meals were eaten in silence with *oryoki,* ceremonial bowls whose noble, practical function was restored at Tassajara. At Zen Center today, oryoki are used only occasionally; you are most apt to see them during a sesshin, an extended period of meditation (typically, a week), during which practitioners sit a twelve- or fourteen-hour schedule of zazen daily and take their meals on their cushions in the zendo.

For the uninitiated, oryoki is a baffling combo of a meal and a shell game. It goes something like this: You start the game with three nested bowls, a pair of chopsticks, a little wooden paddle with a cotton tip, and a cloth or straw place mat—all of which are wrapped like a gift in a generous napkin, whose ends are knotted so the tails stick up and the whole package can be quickly undone. If you are not expert, it is not so easy to undo the knot, spread the cloth, and organize your bowls before the servers start zipping around with the first of three vats—say, vegetable gruel, some sweet potatoes or scrambled eggs, and maybe a salad. The servers arrive at your place long before your bowls are properly aligned. (Also, your chopsticks were supposed to be laid out like compass needles; they point in one direction before you eat and end up in the opposite direction and balanced on one of the bowls when the wooden clapper signals the end of this ordeal.) You can waste a lot of time surveying your neighbors' arrangements, and, thus, barely get a bite to eat. There are also some secret hand signals you have to master to indicate to the servers whether you want the soup, and how much, and if you don't give the proper Stop! sign, you are supplied with way too much gruel or sweet potatoes, and then the lickety-split meal is ending and someone is standing before you with a giant kettle of boiling water, which is aimed at your biggest bowl (which should be empty by now, but you took way too much gruel; learn the hand signals). Here's where the little paddle comes into play; you use it like a big Q-tip to swish and swab the hot water in each bowl in succession—your oryoki will not be otherwise cleaned for a week—and then you drink the dregs, and stack and wrap the bowls up as fast as you can.

Properly performed, it is an elegant ceremony. Nothing is wasted—not a grain of rice or a drop of water, not even a word. At ordination, a Zen monk receives the large oryoki bowl, which was the sole possession of the first disciples of Buddha, who were homeless and begged for every meal.

"Our way is pretty complicated," Suzuki-roshi told his students at Tassajara. "Someone pointed [this] out about oryoki. But the city is more complicated and busy, and in some sense, more formal. It looks like there is more freedom [out] there, but not actually," said Suzuki-roshi. "But try not to understand it completely. It is impossible! Just enjoy it."

"The first time I met Suzuki-roshi was when he was trying to raise some real money for Tassajara," remembers David Padwa. "Richard Baker brought him to New York, and we all went out for a lobster dinner."

Padwa was living on the Upper East Side. In 1960, he founded Basic Systems, a company whose technology made possible the first practical applications of programmed computer instructions; five years later he sold the
company to the Xerox Corporation. "I was surprised when Suzuki-roshi
ordered the lobster, and he was astonished when a bib and tools arrived,
and especially when the lobster showed up whole and still in a shell. He'd
been expecting lobster sashimi. Suzuki-roshi was tremendously good-
humored about the lobster and all the tools," says Padwa. "I remember he
was good-humored about everything."

Padwa had known Richard for years, "basically from the party scene in
New York," he explains. "And I'd been a contributor to Zen Center. That
wasn't why I was visited in New York, though." Padwa's contribution was
to get them an appointment with Chester Carlson at Xerox, which he did.
"I was impressed by Suzuki-roshi. I mean, I didn't think he was divine,
but he was serene."

"Suzuki-roshi would very quietly go off to meet powerful people,"
remembers Tim, "and do Buddhist things for the aristocracy of America.
He never made a fuss about this sort of—" Tim hesitates, searching for a
genuine way of saying what he means to say—"well, *fund-raising* is too
extreme a term, but that was certainly part of it. Very, very few people
were aware of Suzuki-roshi's work with these High Families." While he
was at Tassajara, Tim married into the Saltonstall family, whose political
and social prominence in America dates to 1630, when Sir Richard Saltonstall, a member of the Massachusetts Bay Company, left England with
colonial governor John Winthrop. Thus, Tim saw more than most of his
colleagues. "Richard was learning how to [work with High Families], but
he did not yet have Suzuki-roshi's seamless way," says Tim, who recalls
"hearing famous names dropped by Richard" after his trips East. "Richard
was very young, [and] he tended to talk about where he'd been and in
whose home he had eaten. And, it started to look like a raggedy contin-
uum from the zendo to [Chester] Carlson's dining room. But Tassajara
was enormously expensive, and unlike the rest of us, Richard understood,
as Suzuki-roshi understood, that someone had to pick up the tab."

———

"Suzuki-roshi brought me back into the world," Richard says. This path led him in the opposite direction of almost everyone who was headed to Tassajara.

Richard had invented the monastery out of the thin air of his teacher's dreams ("No one has worked harder, or is singly more responsible for this project's success," reported the *Wind Bell* in February 1967, summarizing Richard's contributions), but he did not want to move to Tassajara. "I had decided I should have an ordinary life," he says. He did not want to leave the world. He'd tried that already by dropping out of Harvard, cutting all ties with his family, and intentionally flunking the physical and psychological tests when he was called in by the Selective Service ("I put dirt on myself and carried *The Good Soldier* to add a little irony"). Suzuki-roshi turned him around. "Really," he says. He voted for the first time; he also married, completed two degrees, and made a career for himself. "Had Suzuki-roshi been in my life earlier, I probably would have gone into the military. Somehow being with Suzuki-roshi made me think you just have to accept society as it is and work with it, and work within it."

Of course, like Eiheiji in Japan, Tassajara was not supposed to be a permanent refuge from the world for anyone. It was a training monastery; however, a few facts mitigated this concept. First, almost no one who arrived at Tassajara had any previous training, so it was clear that a year or two would not make them masters, capable of starting and sustaining their own Zen temples. Second, there was nowhere else in America for students to be trained, and very few had had the wit or the wherewithal to get themselves to Japan. Third, Tassajara needed a reliable labor pool for year-round restoration and building projects, as well as competent staff for the summer guest season, which was essential to the monastery's viability.

"I didn't notice it at the time, but from May of 1967 through May of 1972, I was mostly at Tassajara," says Dan Welch. "Five years. For virtually the entirety of that time, Richard didn't live there. He was back and forth from the city for the first two years, and then mostly in Japan. I had that unique time, while he—who had done so much to get Tassajara together—was gone."

Dan already had a long history with Zen by the time he "landed at Tas-

sajara," though he did not have a long history with Zen Center. His interest in Zen "was piqued by my curiosity about Gary Snyder. I'd read
Kerouac's *Dharma Bums* in 1960, when I was a senior in high school."
Snyder was the model for Japhy Ryder, the mystical, mountain-trekking
fire-lookout in the novel. "Gary was not an integral part of Zen Center,
but he is indelibly a part of my life." Following Snyder's tracks, Dan went
to a Rinzai Zen monastery in Japan a couple of years after high school.
"They'd given me a tiny little room with a little window and two tatami
mats. It was six by six feet," says Dan, who is six feet plus.

"It was breaking my heart that I wanted to leave. And one early winter
afternoon I tried to articulate why. I loved the wholeheartedness—working, begging, sitting—and their sense of fun, teasing each other with delight. I was uneasy with it—I was often the object of [the teasing]—but I
liked it. I liked the playful intensity." Dan says he didn't approach Buddhism intellectually. "It's always been a feeling, and I was drawn to the
Zen emphasis on the individual directly realizing the role—not vicariously through books or gurus." Dan asked himself what was missing.
"There was increasing pressure for me to have an enlightenment experience. Enlightenment eluded me. And everything seemed to follow from
enlightenment, so I felt trapped."

During the next two years, his sister, Jeannie Campbell, got to know
Suzuki-roshi and Richard Baker. Dan eventually moved in with Jeannie
and her husband Howard Campbell in Berkeley, where they'd started a
sitting group for people who could not travel daily to Sokoji. Dan didn't
join the sitters. "My experience in Japan left me sad, as if Zen were beyond
me." He was deeply aware of Jeannie's devotion to the practice, and he visited Sokoji a few times, "tenderly approaching thinking about practicing."
He was also working for Goodwill Industries, his alternative service. Dan
had an easier time than many who sought conscientious-objector status
because he had been raised as a Quaker.

These were people who had pursued alternatives to the mainstream
American culture for many years. "My sister was an activist. She worked
against the House Committee on Un-American Affairs and in the early
civil rights movement." Jeannie and her husband, Howard, "were becoming estranged, and in February of 1967, Howard moved to Tassajara."

Jeannie stayed in the city. "She was a devoted Zen student. She loved the practice." And she began an intimate relationship with Richard. Jeannie's marriage ended; Richard's marriage endured; for a time, Jeannie's and Richard's paths put them on the same road, but they were moving in opposite directions.

Dan had joined a commune, "and I soon began to think I could do something more useful with my skills. I talked to Jeannie a lot, and we worked it out so that I was accepted by Zen Center and the draft board as Tassajara's volunteer fire marshal." Dan became the Japhy Ryder of Zen Center. "I was living with a woman, and we rode together up that long road [to Tassajara] on our Harley-Davidson three-wheeler with most of our worldly belongings in May of 1967. I had long hair, and I was seeing the land through Gary Snyder's eyes and poems, and I was ready to drop all of my alternative agendas. I'd said No to a lot of what the world was offering me. In this remote place in the wilderness, I was seeing the remote possibility of Yes."

16.

David Padwa credits Suzuki-roshi and Richard Baker and the collaborative effort known as the San Francisco Zen Center with the genuine establishment of Buddhism in the United States. "But I am skeptical about the overall or enduring effect of Buddhism on American life," he says. "America does not seem to me a more compassionate, kinder, safer place because of it."

Nor did Zen Center.

"Suzuki-roshi said to me once, 'Why are you making it so big?'" Even now, Richard looks more than a little sad when he hears himself speak the question. Well he might. It is at the heart of the heart attack that seized Zen Center in 1983—the too-bigness of Richard's vision and behavior. "I said, 'Because when I come back from Japan, we will need enough people and resources so it will last in America,'" Richard remembers. "And he kind of accepted it, but he was worried."

It is a remarkable and strange exchange, even when judged by Suzuki-roshi's remarkably high and strange personal standard. Suzuki-roshi often engaged his students' questions with puzzling proclamations. A remarkable example appeared in the Fall 1967 issue of *Wind Bell.* During the first practice period at Tassajara in the summer of 1967, when asked to explain the difference between the Buddhist idea of ego and the psychiatric idea of ego strength, Suzuki-roshi answered, "Ego."

(My advice? If you are prone to vertigo, get out of this parenthesis right now, as the rest of his response is genuinely dizzying. Suzuki-roshi went on to say, "Strictly speaking, ego does not exist. By stressing it, you put emphasis on some point, on a stream of successive activity in your*self.* But it is not just a continuous ego; it is changing moment after moment.

Here, here, here. That is why we say the ego does not exist. No such thing as ego, you see? Firewood does not become ash. Here is firewood this moment; here is ash, the next. So there is no firewood and no ash. No ego. But still something exists moment after moment. You can understand the same thing in two ways. One is successive ego; the other is discontinuous ego, which changes.

"Even the smallest particle of time imaginable exists because it appears. So something which does not disappear actually does not exist. Whatever it is, what appears should disappear. This is true. So ego is something which should disappear and which should appear. Ego has two meanings. Sometimes we say ego exists and to strengthen your ego is to have your own world, to have your own practice. That is to stress your ego. But if you attach to some particular state of mind, that is delusion because it does not actually exist. So the ego exists because it disappears, isn't that true?

"When we talk about ego, the concept of time is involved and time is continuous and discontinuous. We say time is continuous; but when I say nine o'clock, that is the idea of discontinuity. So even time is continuous and discontinuous. So is the self; it is continuous and discontinuous; it appears and disappears. And yet it continues in some way. But it changes. And as long as it changes, the same ego does not exist. Did you understand? So to strengthen your ego means to have your own practice, to live in your own world and let everything live in its own world, and let everything have its own position. That is true mercy. To keep a dog in your home is not always to love the dog. Do you see?")

Not even this discourse on ego is as strange or suggestive as the simple question Suzuki-roshi asked Richard in 1969.

"Why are you making it so big?"

Richard's reputation for grandiosity makes the question seem reasonable. Even he thought it reasonable. Richard answered his teacher, taking the credit with the blame. Was it ego that made Richard unable to see that the bigness of Zen Center was not entirely his doing?

In November of 1971, just before he died, Suzuki-roshi said to Richard, "I am very sorry for what I am about to do to you." And he started to cry. Perhaps because he knew he had already done it to Richard, and in a big way.

The formal opening of Tassajara was in July of 1967. "From the time I arrived in May until then, I saw a lot come together. People threw their life energies into this," says Dan Welch. "The traditional monastic roles and responsibilities—we didn't even know what to call most of them at that point. We had no precedent—men and women living together, not exactly monks, and no initiation period of prior practice in the city, as there is today. We were totally creative, and mostly we worked hard and sat zazen. I didn't have seniority, obviously, but I was the only one in residence who had lived in Japan. It was a kind of borrowed seniority, and the teachers honored that. Within a year, I was participating as a Board member, and I had leadership roles."

Suzuki-roshi could not be there to give his students daily guidance. He had responsibilities at Sokoji. He was also trying to cultivate the practice with weekly visits to three small sitting groups maintained by people in Berkeley, Mill Valley, and Los Altos who could not travel daily to San Francisco to sit with him at Sokoji. It was too much for one man. The Soto Shu, the spiritual and administrative leadership of the Soto Zen sect in Japan, and its American authorities may have been ambivalent about Suzuki-roshi's renegade mission in America, but in 1964, an ordained priest who'd been sent from Japan to the Los Angeles Zen temple was reassigned to work as Suzuki-roshi's assistant at Sokoji. Dainin Katagiri was in his thirties when he arrived, and his wife and young child were brought over from Japan at the end of the year—another missionary who seemed inclined to stay. Whatever the Soto Bishop in Los Angeles had intended, Katagiri soon was devoting most of his time to American students. Katagiri had Transmission in a lineage distinct from Suzuki-roshi's teachers, but he filled in for Suzuki-roshi at Sokoji and at the satellite zendos, and often at Tassajara.

"Katagiri was a great ritualist," remembers Gary Snyder.

"Katagiri was a wonderful, stern man—Mutt to Suzuki-roshi's Jeff," says Tim Buckley. "They were a perfect teaching pair. Suzuki-roshi was laissez-faire and graceful and up-to-the-moment. And Katagiri would say, 'Sit like your hair is on fire.' And we did."

Mel Weitsman, who had brought the Berkeley Zen Center to life after the informal group begun by Dan's sister Jeannie had dissipated, always saw Katagiri as a model for the students at Zen Center; Katagiri was at Zen Center to show the Americans how to relate to a teacher.

"He was always clearly there to help Suzuki-roshi," says Yvonne, who eventually received Transmission from Katagiri. "It was not until much later that he became a teacher in his own right. As long as Suzuki-roshi was alive, he was the [one] teacher. That's traditional form. There was no question in Katagiri's mind about that."

Zen priests visited Sokoji and Tassajara regularly from New York, Los Angeles, and Japan, but Suzuki-roshi needed more full-time help. A second young Japanese priest, twenty-nine-year-old Kobun Chino, arrived in 1967 and spent much of the next two years at Tassajara, helping the students establish a monastic schedule.

When it came time to open the first intensive monastic practice period at Tassajara in July, Suzuki-roshi had two full-time Japanese priests assisting him. Six of his own students had been ordained as priests. In addition, Bill Kwong continued as Suzuki-roshi's student while he led his sitting group in Mill Valley. Mel, in the leadership role at the Berkeley Zen Center, also was available. Several other longtime students, who along with Richard and Yvonne had traded places as officers of Zen Center over the years, were also at Tassajara. Suzuki-roshi decided to open the practice period by shaving Richard's head and ordaining him. Tradition required Suzuki-roshi to name the most senior priest to the position of *shuso*, or head monk, for the practice period. As was often his way, Suzuki-roshi ignored tradition; he overlooked the other, more senior priests and students and appointed Richard Baker as Tassajara's first head monk.

At the end of the practice period, according to tradition, the shuso answered questions. Richard, robed, sat on a raised platform. Bill Kwong, in slacks and a T-shirt, approached. He shouted, "Kwatz!" It is a traditional nonsensical syllable, often used by Zen teachers like the stick, to prod or provoke students. Richard then asked Bill if he had anything else to say. Bill stomped his foot, bowed, and walked away.

"People remember I did that," says Bill, years later, smiling. "Maybe teachers don't have to talk so much."

Suzuki-roshi did not want his lectures to be recorded. Zen, of course, has a long history of eschewing texts. Until 1965, *Wind Bell* reprinted his talks and comments as they were recalled by Trudy Dixon, a devoted student, which proved to be an appealingly idiosyncratic and imprecise compromise.

Trudy was married to Mike Dixon, a painter, and they were close friends of Richard and his wife Ginny. In her recollected versions of her teacher's lectures, Trudy managed to preserve both Suzuki-roshi's inventive English grammar and his indirect habits of mind. Still, the text is blatantly ersatz. Long passages are summarized, so you get a sense of what he was saying, but you also have a clear sense that you missed something. ("When you take a cup of tea, you help others and you help yourself," Trudy recalled her teacher saying during a 1964 lecture. "Even if you sit alone in the zendo, you are helping others. And if you do something quite different, you are sitting in the meditation hall. Practice is one.") By the end, you get the sense that every memorable assertion or example was precisely what he was saying Zen practice was not. This is not unlike the confusion his students felt when he spoke to them, but it is not exactly the same. "Often," says Dan, "I didn't know what he was talking about in lecture, but his words took root."

Long Body. Suzuki-roshi wasn't lecturing for posterity but for people whom he could see, whose collective heat he could feel. If you weren't there when he spoke, you missed the moment of Suzuki-roshi. His teaching is embodied in his students, not in the words he might have said or the words one of them recalled.

By 1966, some of Suzuki-roshi's lectures were being tape-recorded and transcribed. Whenever he visited the Los Altos sitting group that met in her garage, Marion Derby pressed him to allow her to record his words, because some members inevitably could not be present when he put in one of his infrequent appearances and a tape recording of his lecture would be better than nothing, she reasoned. Suzuki-roshi relented. As a result, a relatively novice student had soon assembled a book-length series of introductory lectures by the most sought-after Zen teacher in America.

It really wasn't better than nothing, but it certainly was bigger. The book—*Zen Mind, Beginner's Mind,* released in 1970—became the bestseller for Weatherhill, the company that published it, says Richard. It also became one of the best-selling books on Zen in English. For Suzuki-roshi, who didn't want his words plucked out of time and repeated at moments when they might not apply, this was either a case of really good *bad* luck or really bad *good* luck. He had become an authorized text, unembodied words set into type. An edited transcription of the words he happened to say in a Los Altos garage would survive him. ("If you attach to some particular state of mind," Suzuki-roshi told his students in his lecture on ego, "that is delusion.") His grammar was ironed out, and gaps were filled in. The book altered the tone and scale of his teaching. After the book's publication, students of Zen who had never met Suzuki-roshi could memorize what he hadn't exactly said and quote him out of context.

Trudy, who edited the transcriptions of her beloved teacher's tape-recorded lectures for publication, died in 1969 of cancer at the age of thirty. Her dying was long and unashamed. She traveled to Tassajara one week before her death and drank a handful of creek water. She sobered and inspired her colleagues. At her funeral, Suzuki-roshi asked, "How can I express my true heart?" As if he might otherwise be misunderstood, he did not utter a word. He roared in an immense, ascending voice.

Emptiness equals emptiness. Words are emptiness. And emptiness is all there is to say.

"Trudy was my main compatriot in understanding Zen practice," says Richard, who was also involved with Trudy in what he now calls an "impassioned relationship." In a more forthcoming moment, he says simply, "I loved her." Richard wrote the introduction to *Zen Mind, Beginner's Mind*. "The book was our way of working together."

Trudy's husband, Mike, provided the one illustration in the book—a simple ink drawing of a fly in the corner of a blank page. It seems artless at first glance. And the fly somehow makes you more aware of the empty page than of itself, which makes you mindful of Suzuki-roshi, who is not there on every single page, but who was somewhere once, and did his business, and then took off, and that's as good an introduction to Suzuki-roshi's teaching as could be written. Why did Mike make the fly so big? No one asks. In the case of the fly, *big* and *little* are immaterial; such distinctions don't matter—they don't even occur to you. That's the art of it.

———

Richard remembers a seven-day sesshin that was led by Suzuki-roshi. During the breaks between the many forty-minute meditation periods, Richard noticed that a brush-stroke painting on a far wall was crooked. Finally, during one of the breaks, while others stretched their backs and legs or left the zendo to use the bathroom, Richard walked across the meditation hall and straightened the painting. He sat down. Later, Suzuki-roshi stood up, walked to the painting, and made it crooked again.

"It's a lesson I still haven't learned," says Richard.

In 1970, Zen Center was not any bigger than Suzuki-roshi had made it with the help of his students and supporters. That's the truth of it.

"Why are you making it so big?"

Richard might have said, I didn't do any more than anyone else.

But thirty years later, he is still trying to straighten out the impression people have of him. "It's true [Trudy] helped me edit the book," he says, sort of diminishing Trudy's role and not looking any bigger for it. "I put her name on it, and in some ways I now wish I'd said edited by Trudy and myself, because Zen Center has fought me for control [of the copyright], which is kind of irritating."

The debates that have ensued about the relative size and merit of each person's contribution don't make anyone at Zen Center look big. After 1983, "they truly tried to diminish my existence in the world," says Richard. "One of the first things they did was to write to the publisher and say, The book is really Zen Center's; send the royalties here now, and we will decide what happens to the book now, not Baker." In retrospect, no one can get the proportions right. "But there's a contract," says Richard.

Contract. Words on a page. You can apply them to the problem, but they make an ineffective salve. There's no fly in this ointment. The contract is a record of an agreement, but the spirit of agreement has been lost. "I'm his literary executor for this book," says Richard, and he adds, "Suzuki-roshi let me distribute the royalties. Suzuki-roshi got sixty percent, Zen Center ten, Marion got ten, Trudy got ten, and I got ten."

And Zen Center got bigger.

———

"The overriding thing for me," says Richard, "was that in 1967 Suzuki-roshi told me he wanted me to be his successor. From that point on, he was preparing me and [he] related to me as his successor."

Suzuki-roshi did not talk about this with other students at Zen Center for two years.

Richard left his job at Berkeley. He was President of Zen Center, the editor of *Wind Bell*, and Director of Tassajara. Yvonne was Secretary of Zen Center, manager of the San Francisco office, and Suzuki-roshi's principal assistant. They and the Japanese priests were the only salaried employees of Zen Center. Several other students with independent incomes also worked full-time for Zen Center, and the other positions were staffed by part-time volunteers.

In May of 1968, Richard resigned all of his many Zen Center jobs. "I got a call from Dick," recalls Michael Murphy. "He told me I was one of three people he was going to confer with about whether or not to accept Suzuki-roshi's choosing him as Dharma heir. 'First off,' he said, 'I'll have to go to Japan. I'll have to give up everything. I will just be a priest. It's huge.' We met in Chinatown. It wasn't like, *Gee whiz, this is great*. It was fateful."

"And that's why we were in a cabin at Tassajara in 1968," says Tim, "wondering if we could really give Richard $10,000 to go to Japan." Richard was to spend time training at Eiheiji, as well as other Soto and Rinzai monasteries.

Richard remembers people at Zen Center who wanted to go to Japan, to Eiheiji, but "I didn't want to leave," says Richard. Two years earlier, after receiving a grant to study in Japan, he turned down the opportunity so that he could devote himself to the Tassajara project. "I wanted to stay with Suzuki-roshi because of this feeling of friendship and communication there—it was more than temples or titles." But Richard could not reasonably expect to complete his training in America.

Nor could he reasonably be expected to pay his way to Japan. "His personal income from Zen Center was minuscule," says Tim. "I remember the meeting with Silas [Hoadley], Yvonne, Peter [Schneider], and Suzuki-roshi. Richard was out of the cabin. And there was a concern that he would squander the money—like the Tom Waits song 'What's He Doing in

There, Anyway?' But it turns out that Richard was kind of heroic. He had already raised hundreds of thousands for Zen Center, while other communes and Buddhist groups were trying to figure out if they could afford to patch their roofs. That said, he was not as mature in the practice as Suzuki-roshi, and he didn't make it easier for us. He was a very independent man, and a man of some hauteur in those days."

Suzuki-roshi, says Richard, "wanted me to *not* be [at Zen Center] as one of the guys who suddenly became his successor. He wanted to say, He is in Japan." Then, Richard could be brought back in a new role.

"I came back to the States from Japan for good in 1968," says Gary Snyder. "I saw a lot of Dick and Ginny [before they left for Japan]. We were family friends. I didn't go to Zen Center much. I certainly had not lost interest in Zen. But it was not Rinzai Zen [Zen Center is in the Soto Zen tradition], which means a little bit to me." Gary is an ordained Rinzai Zen priest and completed the systematic study of koans with an acknowledged master prescribed by the Rinzai sect. "And largely," says Gary, "my time was really involved in making the move up to the land in the Sierra I had bought with Dick and Allen Ginsberg, and reacquainting myself with America. It was all new to me. I did drop in to see Suzuki-roshi from time to time. We always talked in Japanese. He said, 'Oh, Americans. They don't have enough sense of humor. They're much too serious.'"

"Suzuki-roshi used to beat up on me," says Richard with a half-smile. He recalls that it happened a couple of times under similar circumstances. And he says he vividly remembers an occasion on which he had come out of his office to bow to Suzuki-roshi, went back in to talk to somebody, "and suddenly he grabbed me, took me by the shoulders—and he was a little man, but I never thought of him as little until I saw a photograph of us beside each other. He just pushed me down *Poom!* to the floor, and he began hitting me with the stick everywhere, [yelling,] 'You should understand under my anger! You should understand under my anger! You should understand under my anger!' *Poom!* What the heck was he doing? I actually knew that ninety percent he was criticizing that person over there, but he couldn't say this to him, and he *could* do it to me. I also knew he was saying something to me."

Was Richard shifting blame, or was Suzuki-roshi? Richard's understanding tallies with the experience of Jean Ross, one of the first of Suzuki-roshi's American students to spend time in the Japanese monasteries. In letters to her colleagues in San Francisco, Jean explained that she would be made aware of her own mistakes and ineptitude indirectly. A Japanese priest seated beside her would be reprimanded or hit, and she understood that she was being criticized.

In recent years, the archivist and priests at Zen Center have transcribed and published many of Suzuki-roshi's lectures and informal dharma talks; brief as it is, the *Poom! Poom! Poom!* lecture has not been included.

Richard moved to Gary's house in Kyoto with his wife and daughter in the fall of 1968.

He returned to the States for three months in the fall of 1970. During his two-year absence, someone—Suzuki-roshi apparently could not figure out who—had made Zen Center much bigger, much more formal, and much more expensive.

In July of 1969, Suzuki-roshi had resigned his position at Sokoji. After that, he and the other Japanese priests were entirely devoted to, and dependent on, Zen Center. They also needed new digs. In a move so grand in scale, so precipitous, so inventively financed, and so nicely flecked with irony that it was almost Richardesque, Suzuki-roshi traded his little apartment in the Zen temple (which was formerly a synagogue) at the corner of Bush and Laguna Streets for a three-story brick building that had been designed as a residence for Jewish women in 1922 by Julia Morgan; the building was less than a mile from Sokoji, on the corner of Laguna and Page Streets. The purchase price was $325,000, just a bit more than the price tag for Tassajara, on which $62,500 was still owed. Most of the students who had migrated to Japantown over the years could also move in with their teacher. And they did. The former Emanu-el Residence Club would accommodate seventy residents. The bedrooms of single Jewish women became monks' cells, and the basement gymnasium was remade into a zendo.

The three-story building at 300 Page Street has at least three common names: Beginner's Mind Temple; City Center; and, sometimes, just Page

Street. For years, taxi drivers have called it the Woodpecker House, because when they are in the neighborhood they hear a mallet against a wooden board, the *han*, calling students to meditation. It is an assertive American building, and its brick and concrete façade looks like a bulwark, a promise of permanence. The neighborhood, in 1969, was mostly peeling Painted Ladies rented out by absentee landlords, empty lots, and some of San Francisco's most shameful public housing. But inside, what's outside feels faraway. A long, broad, calm hallway with dimly glowing stone floors connects administrative offices and a large hall for ceremonies and lectures to the dining room and kitchen. The building reads as a rectangle, with a central, open-air courtyard on the first floor. On the roof, above the two floors of bedrooms, is a deck overlooking San Francisco and its beautiful and baleful bridges, and you can see what Buddhists mean when they talk about the phenomenal world—you only really see it when you're not in it.

The payment plan involved a $175,000 mortgage, $86,000 in private loans, a $20,000 bank loan secured with a patron's stocks, and $33,000 in cash gifts. The living scheme was a matter of invention. Someone had to devise a routine suited to a training temple that was not a monastery, and the residents had to invent rules and routines for long-term cooperative living. Just as the sixties were ending, Suzuki-roshi had inadvertently turned Zen Center into a commune.

"Zen Center was populated by hippies," remembers Lew. "It was musical beds in the early days at Page Street. Heterosexual and homosexual and every combination in between. It was a very sexually active community. But it was also open. No secrets about it. People knew. Doors weren't locked there, and you could walk around at three in the morning and see who was coming out of whose room, and whose shoes were outside the door."

Lay practice.

By 1970, Zen Center estimated its community had grown to include 100 to 120 full-time students in residence at Page Street and Tassajara; 200 nonresident students, including its affiliated sitting groups; and one teacher. Private, one-on-one time with Suzuki-roshi was no longer a reasonable expectation, especially for new students. The organization's annual operating costs had risen to $200,000.

The public face of Zen Center had changed dramatically, so when it went begging, it no longer looked so needy. Yet there was still a lot of work to be done at Page Street and at Tassajara. And for all its newly acquired space, Zen Center could not accommodate families with children except during the summer guest season at Tassajara; this stymied the growth of a rigorous lay practice, which Suzuki-roshi saw as the source of a genuine reform and renewal of Zen.

For the first time in the long history of Buddhism, however, the door was open to women. "I take credit for really being one of the people who really made absolutely certain that women were absolutely equal in the West [in Zen practice]," says Richard. "Katagiri wanted Tassajara [to be] just for men." Richard said he insisted otherwise, as did Suzuki-roshi. He would not "do a center that is not equally for men and women, and for old people and young people. We can't conceive of Zen in the militaristic Japanese way that excludes anyone who is a little older."

Of course, this led to the problems, too, says Richard, but "Tassajara really set the standard that men and women practice together. And families," he adds. "And that meant there were going to be babies. You can't prevent people having relationships."

Yvonne now sees that "it was out of Suzuki-roshi's cultural context to train women," which she better understood after a 1998 conference on his life, which "has been enormously useful to me in understanding his reluctance to ordain women as having a lot to do with his cultural conditioning." And Yvonne remembers other problems with the coresidential model. "It was not at all unusual at the end of a sesshin for someone to have a big party," she says. "There would be lots of sex, lots of drinking, and it would be like blowing all the energy from the retreat in one night. And all kinds of consequences arose from that, like getting pregnant. That's not so true in the early sixties. I was more aware of this after Zen Center moved to Page Street. But," Yvonne adds, "Richard was involved with lots of lovers early on."

You can't prevent people having relationships. And this led to problems. It led one woman to follow Richard to Japan, where she apparently mistook love letters for a contract. She was soon exported back to America. "Even then," says Yvonne, "he consistently picked fragile women."

He had also picked a fragile teacher. In 1969, Suzuki-roshi was laid up with a bad flu, and though it was almost two years before his jaundice was correctly diagnosed as a symptom of a deadly cancer, he seemed to know he was not going to finish what he had started.

He needed help. In 1969, along with several Tibetan and Japanese teachers who stayed for short periods at Zen Center, on Richard's recommendation Suzuki-roshi invited Tatsugami-roshi to lead the practice periods at Tassajara.

"He changed everything," says Ed Brown. For twelve years, Tatsugami-roshi had been *Ino,* or head of training, at Eiheiji. "It took Suzuki-roshi almost a year to figure out he'd let a snake into the hen house. Then, just when Tatsugami was planning to leave Japan and move in with us for good, Suzuki-roshi managed to uninvite him very graciously."

Many students resented Tatsugami-roshi, who imposed on them the formal rigors of Japanese ceremony, ritual, and roles. Mel Weitsman is more sanguine than most. "He did what he knew how to do. Before he came," says Mel, "we sat zazen and we worked. And during practice period, we sat a little more zazen and worked a little less. We knew what we were doing, but we didn't really know what we were doing."

Tatsugami-roshi taught the students temple ritual and traditional Japanese chants and prayers (which they memorized from phonetic transliterations, so they sounded like Japanese, although most of the students could not read or speak a word of the Japanese language). He also taught them the many discrete roles involved in traditional monastic life. Flow charts drawn under his direction were used by students to learn the Japanese terms for their jobs in the kitchen, the zendo, and on work crews; and these charts also established a hierarchy. "After this," says Grahame, "Zen Center learned to observe status distinctions modeled on Eiheiji, literally. Tatsugami-roshi, of course, had been the—well, master of ceremonies, if you like, while I was at Eiheiji. I felt the hierarchy was inappropriate there, as I felt it was inappropriate in Rome, and it was no different at Zen Center."

Contrary to the reputation Richard has acquired retrospectively, Tatsugami's style was not a style that appealed to Richard at the time. Within a year of recommending Tatsugami-roshi, Richard realized "what a mistake I had made." In his correspondence from Japan, he questioned Suzuki-roshi about Tatsugami's strict, orthodox, sectarian approach to Soto Zen. Richard was himself studying with teachers from both the Rinzai and Soto Zen sects, and he was mostly intrigued by the nonsectarian style Suzuki-roshi sometimes referred to as Dogen Zen, in honor of the great Japanese master whose practice was not limited by the sectarian divide.

"I never say anything to someone I disagree with," wrote Suzuki-roshi to Richard in Japan, "because there is always something to learn from others—like Tatsugami-roshi." Suzuki-roshi clearly believed that his students could not fully embrace nonsectarian Zen—"whole-minded practice"—without first embracing a sectarian tradition. "Nonsectarianism for us is nonduality, but we know nonduality includes duality. That's why Tatsugami-roshi is here," he wrote.

The students at Tassajara never became traditional Zen priests in the eyes of the Japanese Soto Shu, but they did learn to behave more like priests than pioneers. This was not a subtle transformation. Paul Discoe had started practicing at Tassajara in 1967. He worked for a couple of years as a carpenter. His way with wood was remarkable, and Suzuki-roshi encouraged him to go to Japan to study traditional temple architecture. "When I came back to Zen Center in 1972, Richard had just become head of the place. Eighty percent of my friends were gone," Paul remembers. "And there was definitely a new feeling at Tassajara. It was more than a feeling, really. You might categorize it by saying that the people who were now at Zen Center, if they were outside, they would go inside to pee. Men and women alike."

Moreover, while Tatsugami-roshi was in charge, renovations and improvements to Tassajara and Page Street—many of them mandated by government health and safety codes; others required to make the summer guest season profitable—were delayed so the students could practice their bowing and chanting. And revenues were consistently lagging behind costs. By 1970, nearly one-fourth of the residential student population was being subsidized with full scholarships, and other students paid only $90 a month for room, board, and instruction. With Richard in Japan, Zen Center had achieved institutional proportions without institutional means. A fund-raising letter from Peter Schneider, then President of Zen

Center, expressly stated the need for an endowment; however, even six-figure gifts were being absorbed by operating expenses, he explained, and students were spending more and more time not earning money and not making capital improvements to the Zen Center property. In effect, the letter inadvertently laid bare the illogic of endowing the organization.

As Lucy Calhoun said, "Suzuki-roshi made us feel we didn't need to look ahead."

From the outside, looking at Zen Center as an institution, Suzuki-roshi's ability to *not* look down the road looks like a liability. "Our practice should be more personal," he wrote to Richard just months before he invited Tatsugami-roshi not to return to Tassajara. But Suzuki-roshi seems to have known that the possibility of personal, intimate, one-on-one practice was behind him by then. A new formality had been charted and grafted onto Tassajara. And Zen Center had only one recognized teacher for hundreds of students.

"He expected to have more time," says Richard. "At one point, he talked with me about leaving Zen Center and just practicing with me. To train me. He didn't think he'd have time enough to train me. Then he talked about leaving with three or four people—he talked about Santa Fe and Japan. He thought he had an obligation—and I can understand this feeling; I have this feeling now—that building the organization of Zen Center was great, but it was only great if it helped you establish the lineage in a disciple." Richard says Suzuki-roshi "was afraid it was interfering."

Leaving was a dream; it never matured into an intention. It would have required a kind of foresight that Suzuki-roshi did not practice. There was no recognized Zen teacher to assume his role in his absence. Tatsugami-roshi was gone. Katagiri had made it clear he would not stay at Zen Center much longer. As early as 1969, having been told of Suzuki-roshi's choice of Richard as his successor, Katagiri had to be prevailed upon to stay and help Suzuki-roshi through his illnesses. He could see that there was no future for him at Zen Center. In the meantime, Kobun Chino had become the full-time teacher at the affiliated Zen center in Los Altos. Bill Kwong had never reconciled with Richard, and though Suzuki-roshi told many people that he intended for Bill to have Transmission in his lineage, he never made it a priority to seal the deal himself. So, after more than ten years in America, Suzuki-roshi had cultivated not a single American or Japanese priest whom his students regarded as a teacher worthy of their singular devotion. This tallied with his history in Japan. Maybe it was just his way.

"Suzuki-roshi embodied Zen for us," says Lucy.

Where, then, would they be without him?

Richard had come back from Japan once before 1970, when Edward Johnson at Fidelity Investments in Boston "asked me to be part of their investment move into Japan."

For a man whose path had led him through Zen and into the world, this seems oddly appropriate. He was a married monk. He had a family to feed. Someone had to invent a form of alternative service.

This plot twist continues to surprise many of his former students. Richard tells it as an adventure story. He recalls that Edward C. Johnson "was just great—I love to meet people who overwhelm me," says Richard, who remembers the man credited with inventing the mutual fund as "very intense . . . he would stand right in front of me, asking me questions . . . I'd think, Couldn't we sit down?" Richard was face-to-face with a man who would never worry about bigness. "And he would take me to the Museum of Fine Arts in Boston and watch what I looked at." Richard eventually "did three months of training at Fidelity—they put me up at the Union Club—and then I went back to Japan." He told Suzuki-roshi that "I thought I could earn enough money to help support Zen Center." And given Fidelity's record over the last thirty years, that was probably a profound underestimation. But Suzuki-roshi "did not like it, and he did not want me to do that. So I did the minimum, and returned their salary, and they sent me back a month of it."

Kwatz!

Richard's former colleagues point to this episode as evidence of his insincerity or his greed. Meanwhile, they had installed themselves in a monastery, declared themselves conscientious objectors to celibacy, and many of them figured it was up to somebody else to foot the bill for their independence, not to mention any dependents who might be born into the situation. And from their remote perches, they could evidently see that it was noble for Richard to beg money from Fidelity and Xerox on their behalf, but it was ignoble of Richard to want to earn it.

Richard's flirtation with Fidelity was brief, but it was not an isolated example of the distance between him and his colleagues. By 1971, Richard's opinions about organizational politics at Zen Center were increasingly contrary, and sometimes anarchic. From Japan, he wrote copious responses to Board notes he received via Yvonne. "I think Ed should have been given the largest portion, perhaps 60% of the royalties from the cookbook," wrote Richard when the *Tassajara Bread Book* was published. "Suzuki-roshi is getting 60% from his book," he argued. "If we don't work out such things along lines that include our own social morality in its best sense, so that the individual is given as much identity recognition as the group . . . [or] if you introduce a value scale of what identities are more important (that is, Roshi more important and more de- serving than Ed), you are really laying a moral good-bad discrimination trip on the world."

His suggestion was ignored by the Board; after 1983 it was forgotten, and Richard was accused of hogging all the profits from Ed's book. In fact, in 1971 Richard had argued that Ed alone could best decide what to do with the profits he received—keep them, give them to Zen Center, or if Ed didn't want to deal with them, the royalties could be "scattered in the streets, or from an airplane."

Richard also responded to news that an ordination of a young woman at Zen Center had been delayed by the sewing of robes. "Weird to me," he wrote. "When mind and body are ready, she should be ordained. Robes can be put on if she wants them later."

And Richard wrote vast treatises filled with questions to Suzuki-roshi, which Yvonne typed, read to Suzuki-roshi, and returned with Suzuki-roshi's responses. It is clear in these pages that Richard had not had a lot of fun at any of the monasteries he visited, and though he was still supposed to be looking for a practice place in Japan for American students, he was skeptical. Even at the temple where Suzuki-roshi's son and dharma heir presided, Richard advised his American colleagues against enthusiasm. If we try to set up a practice place here, he wrote, "we should make clear to him [Hoitsu] that he is not expected at all to participate in the practice, least of all as head. . . . He does not sit zazen and only chants when he has a service to do for someone."

Suzuki-roshi reminded Richard that Hoitsu had a family and two children. Did it not occur to him that Richard had a family, too, as did many of the priests at Zen Center? "I feel a kind of pain, you know," wrote Suzuki-roshi, "to see our students come back [from Japan] without anything but disappointment. . . . It will create a kind of distrust with the Buddhist way."

Why was Japan a source of disappointment to almost every Zen Center student who was sent there? Maybe it was only in Japan that they could see what they were doing.

Suzuki-roshi's students in America were laypeople who practiced like monks. This seemed so innovative, so unprecedented, that scholars and theologians told the students at Zen Center that they were the vanguard of a Buddhist reformation. And Suzuki-roshi apparently believed this was true. He had asked Richard to reform Buddhism in Japan. But seen from Japan, the Zen Center model might have looked like backwards Buddhism. For almost two hundred years, the monks in Japan had been practicing as laypeople. When Suzuki-roshi arrived in America, he inverted the model by necessity; he had to begin with laypeople because there were no American monks. It was a long road from Sokoji to Tassajara. But they got there. They escaped from the world and holed up in a monastery. And then they transformed Tassajara. And it began to look a lot like Eiheiji. During services, the Americans even managed to chant in Japanese.

What was the big difference? The distinction was really a matter of degree. What distinguished the Americans from the Japanese was their determination to sustain the intensity of monastic practice after they left the monastery.

As Tim says, "It was the seriousness of purpose of the early Zen Center group that convinced Suzuki-roshi that we were in it for the long haul. He wanted to devote his life to the practice with us. He wanted to sit. He couldn't do that as a parish priest—not in Japan, and not even after he left Japan and set himself up in America. He left Sokoji, I think, because he was tired of marrying people and burying them and having a whiskey bottle on every table at the banquets."

Unlike his teacher, Richard was looking down the road. Even if large numbers of Americans could be supported while they practiced at Tassajara, which was by no means guaranteed in 1971, what would become of them when they left the monastery? Who would put the gruel in their bowls?

In perhaps his most pointed series of questions, given his teacher's refusal to let him support himself and Zen Center as a mutual-fund manager, Richard asked about *takuhatsu*, the tradition of monks begging for their livelihood. Takuhatsu originated with the Buddha and his disciples, whose only possessions were the bowls with which they begged and from which they ate. A few smaller temples in Japan had preserved this tradition, and even at the largest temples, monks were still sent out on ceremonial begging trips for a few days every month. Of course, Tassajara was so far out of the world that the walk to the nearest town made even ceremonial takuhatsu unimaginable.

Richard knew that Zen Center had to invent a new tradition to support itself and the future of the practice. But his implicit argument with orthodoxy and the formal legacy of Tatsugami-roshi went further. Richard had done his homework. From the beginning, he pointed out, the Buddhist practice of begging was based on an ancient notion of accumulating merit—not unlike the Roman Catholic indulgence scams. By giving food and money to the monks, wealthy patrons essentially accumulated merit badges, which were redeemable in the next life. Richard wondered if the tradition of begging—on the streets or in board rooms—wasn't corrupt. "Don't we want to avoid the idea of merit?"

This question occurs at the end of eleven single-spaced pages that Richard had written out, and which Yvonne had read to Suzuki-roshi. In her only marginal notation, Yvonne wrote, "Before reading this next section, I told [Suzuki-]Roshi that it was about Takuhatsu. Roshi said, 'I give up.'"

Richard might have been ready to give up, too. "Should we set up a place in Japan just because Roshi wants to, without an understanding of what we are doing?" wrote Richard to his colleagues on the Board. "If the idea is to give Roshi a better chance to work more closely with a few students—can't that be done in America? If it means that Zen Center has grown too big, have we considered alternatives—like selling 300 Page Street or passing it on to another group and finding another place in a warm climate [for] Roshi?"

Suzuki-roshi never wanted to be called roshi, a title traditionally accorded only to the most esteemed Zen masters in Japan; it denoted not only advanced age but experience—as a teacher and of enlightenment. He felt the term was too grand for him. He preferred to be called Suzuki-sensei (sensei means teacher). Some of his students who'd been to Japan early on did call him roshi. Several students believe they were the first to do so. However, the term was used in 1961 in the very first Zen Center newsletter, and then it dropped out of general use. Richard remembers that he and another practitioner used the term early on. Most students credit Alan Watts with the widespread adoption of the title. Watts was bothered by the oddity of such references as Reverend Suzuki, and he wrote a note in 1966 urging everyone at Zen Center to urge their teacher to do just what he had said he didn't want to do and accept the roshi title, as would be traditional in Japan. And he did. Thus, Suzuki-roshi.

In mid-1970, the Board wrote to Richard in Japan to ask if Suzuki-roshi should travel to New York to try to solicit a major gift from the widow of one of Zen Center's most generous benefactors. The widow was not inclined to maintain her husband's level of support. Richard responded that Suzuki-roshi should not devote any of his time to raising money. "That is not Roshi's job," Richard wrote. "Roshi has more important things to do for us."

On December 4, 1970, Suzuki-roshi joined Richard in Japan, and he began the formal ceremonies that marked the completion of the Transmission of the dharma. On December 8, Richard became the first Western man to be recognized by Suzuki-roshi as a Zen Master. According to an ancient tradition, Suzuki-roshi gave his student an oryoki begging and eating bowl to commemorate the occasion.

In a grand gesture worthy of his untraditional teacher, Richard inverted this tradition. At the time of his Transmission, Richard gave his teacher a Raku tea bowl. And tiny as it is, that bowl somehow contains all of the confusion that accumulated at Zen Center over the ensuing decades.

"I'm the first Westerner who's ever been able to buy a Raku tea bowl," says Richard. "You can't buy one; they have to want to make one for you," he explains, unless you buy an old one for maybe $10,000, he guesses. "There are Raku-*style* tea bowls," he says, and then there are Raku tea bowls, "made by the Raku family," which has been making them for fifteen generations. Richard got a bowl, "made by Mr. Raku himself," he explains.

It was a little bowl, but it was a big gesture for a man who was receiving a $10,000 annual stipend as a representative of Zen Center. Of course, Richard didn't actually pay $10,000 for the Raku tea bowl. But you might say that as Suzuki-roshi's dharma heir, Richard represented everyone involved in the practice and, therefore, his gift was everyone's gift to Suzuki-roshi. Or you might say it was more personal, that it was between Suzuki-roshi and Richard. And you might say all the same things about the Transmission of the dharma.

What difference do such distinctions make? They are immaterial, aren't they? Surely, no one begrudged Suzuki-roshi a little piece of pottery.

As a young man, at a big port near Tokyo, says Richard, Suzuki-roshi "saw this schlocky stuff being exported to the West. *Made in Japan* used to mean *cheap*. He saw all this *Made in Japan* stuff going to America, the worst side of Japan. And he thought, they should get our real tea cups. That's one reason I gave him the Raku tea bowl. That's the best."

On November 21, 1971, Richard inherited Suzuki-roshi's American temples. On Page Street, at the Beginner's Mind Temple, Suzuki-roshi, weakened and yellowed and shrunken, stepped down from his teaching role and installed Richard as the Abbot of Zen Center in the Mountain Seat Ceremony.

Katagiri stood in for Suzuki-roshi during the more strenuous rituals.

Richard was required to deliver a sermon on this big occasion. The text is here reproduced in full. He said, "There is nothing to be said."

Bill Kwong added a couple of ritual shouts, and when the newly installed Abbot asked Bill to show his true nature without shouting, Bill bowed and took to his seat.

On December 4, 1971, Suzuki-roshi died.

And when Suzuki-roshi's widow returned to Japan to live, Richard inherited the Raku bowl.

Has Buddhism made America more compassionate?

"What I say will not settle that question," says Dan, sitting by a silver lake in the dusty red New Mexico desert. He pulls out two sandwiches, which he kindly packed for us before our trip began, before we'd met— one tuna and one ham. We've found side-by-side rocks near the water and we sit with our feet in the sandy bank. We balance the sandwiches on our laps, unwrap the wax paper, and smooth the creases against our thighs to make place mats. American oryoki. "We are practicing," says Dan. He leans toward me. He is holding one half of his sandwich in his hand, and he is smiling. We trade halves. "This is the form it has taken," he says, and we both begin to eat. I want to thank him for the polished silver lake, the lunch, the hot sun overhead—the whole grand gesture—but for reasons that seem as mixed up as the tuna fish, I realize that I might just cry if I try to speak. Dan says, "We will remember time with each other longer than we will remember each other's words."

17.

ZEN BUDDHISM OCCUPIES A SPACE in the world that does not exist. This might explain its persistence. Its detractors logically argue that there is no *there* there, and its adherents agree.

It's nothing. That's the Buddha's teaching, which is the dharma. Nothing. But as soon as you say it, it's not nothing. It is something shaped by intention, conditioned by karma, and clotted with all kinds of dust. This is why Transmission of the dharma is not a matter of words or rites, really; it's immaterial, heart-to-heart, mind-to-mind enlightenment that doesn't happen until it is possible for the student and the teacher to understand what each other means to say when either one says, "It's nothing."

Fleeting and fragile as such understandings are, this sort of thing often works out very well when the Transmission is a one-on-one affair. We know this much from our daily lives. If someone bakes a cake for a loved one, and the loved one expresses gratitude, the baker might say, "It's nothing." Of course, the cake and the baking of it are not nothing, but the loved one and the baker know it is nothing between them. This is enlightenment. This is kensho. This is satori. This is nothing.

This is the Buddha, and this is the dharma—two of the Three Treasures in which Buddhists take refuge. All that is missing is the sangha, the community, or the wholeness of intention among many people. The Buddha's original recipe for sangha is nothing but an endless repetition of the one-on-one dharma-Transmission method. It is time-consuming at first, when there is only one master chef, but as more and more sous chefs get their credentials and start working their own ovens, the business grows exponentially. Eventually, everyone gets a cake, and everyone knows it's nothing, which eradicates the delusional desire to eat the cake, which means there is no longer any cause to bake a cake, and then everyone does nothing but rest on a worldwide cushion of cakes, and that is nirvana.

"We will be very happy when people no longer need us," said Suzuki-roshi in a lecture (number 218 in his collected lectures; the text cited here was edited by Dan on Crestone Mountain in 1999). The practice of Buddhism was to make the practice of Buddhism unnecessary, he said. "The reason we wear robes may be in order to take them off," he explained, and then he added, "But Buddha's robe is a problem robe." He was talking to his students about the Genjo Koan, which is, as Dan says, "the most real koan for us," the koan that stands for all the other koans. It is the source of the Zen wisdom about the unforeseeable consequences of any action, even an action as apparently inconsequential as picking up a speck of dust. As Suzuki-roshi explained it, "In the great universe or in the great buddha land, to start a zendo is just to pick up a speck of dust. It's not a big thing."

When Suzuki-roshi started the San Francisco Zen Center, dust flew, and some of it got in people's eyes. This apparently made it hard for anyone who practiced at Zen Center to recognize a teacher other than the man sitting at Sokoji. There were thousands of acknowledged Zen masters in Asia and more than a few in America, and yet as long as Suzuki-roshi was alive, heart-to-heart Transmission for a Zen Center student always meant *Suzuki-roshi and I*. No other teacher was acknowledged. And when Suzuki-roshi died in 1971, Zen Center had one acknowledged teacher. And after Richard lost his way while walking to Tassajara in 1983, Zen Center had one acknowledged teacher. And though no one knew in 1983 that Reb had hidden a gun in his trunk so he could shoot himself in the foot after he became Abbot, a lot of senior students knew that Zen Center was not exactly producing dharma teachers at an exponential rate. In fact, Zen Center was no better at acknowledging teachers than it was at losing them.

It had become a zero-sum game.

"There was tremendous frustration just at the level of Transmission," says Richard. "What could I do?" It was a problem of scale and perception, he says. "I had no idea that these people were actually counting the years — if it took this long for Reb, and after Reb is Lew, and then there is Dan, and that's another ten years, and I'm gonna be thirty-five before he gets to me." In fact, many of the senior students were well over thirty-five before Richard left Zen Center. He shakes his head. "It was my mistake to let Zen Center get so big, and to base Zen Center in this conception of serious practice when I could not follow through on what they wanted from serious practice."

But maybe his mistake was smaller. It now seems clear that what senior students wanted was acknowledgment from their teacher. After fifteen or twenty years of sincere practice, and day-by-day, one-to-one contact with Suzuki-roshi and then with Richard, they figured something of the dharma had rubbed off on them. A Transmission ceremony with Richard would have acknowledged their readiness to pass on the legacy of Suzuki-roshi. This had been the ideal from the outset. This was how genuine Transmission of the dharma was supposed to be accomplished in America. Ceremonial Transmission, as it was given to young men in Japan after a prescribed number of years of monastic practice, was an empty formality; in America, the ceremony would not mean nothing.

But after twenty years, nothing was happening on the ceremonial front. Why didn't Richard acknowledge anyone but Reb? After he left Zen Center, Richard began to find time to perform several Transmission ceremonies. And Richard now acknowledges that Suzuki-roshi told him that he had been working on Transmission with Bill Kwong and wanted Richard to complete it; however, just like his teacher, Richard never found the time to perform the ceremonial Transmission, which would have acknowledged Bill's place in Suzuki-roshi's lineage.

To the senior priests at Zen Center, it looked like Richard was standing on ceremony to keep everyone underfoot. This was widely perceived as more than just a person-to-person, your-foot-is-on-my-neck problem. "I recall [at least] twice when someone asked Dick why he didn't give Bill Kwong Transmission," says Ed Brown, "and Dick said, 'Suzuki-roshi only started giving Bill Transmission because he was dying and he knew he wouldn't have to finish it. It was to support Bill.'" Thus, by the mid-seventies, the "bottleneck" in the Transmission process (which many people identified only years later) was in place, stunting the growth and maturation of the community.

There was a community but no singular and sustaining spirit of communion. Why?

Is it the nature of the practice? To sit zazen is to study the self, as the Japanese master Dogen said centuries ago. This aphorism is often quoted, and it is frequently included in introductory zazen sessions for visitors to Green Gulch Farm and Tassajara. It raises a question. If everyone at Zen Center was studying the self, what would occasion the birth of a genuinely shared spirit or sangha? Maybe individual practice never adds up to a sangha.

Or maybe it's dangerous to quote Zen masters out of context.

"I've always had difficulty with the technical side of Dogen's writings," says a wry and modest woman who practices in Colorado. "But Dan makes Dogen come alive. This is a good thing since, of course, Dogen is the founder of this lineage. Here's what Dogen said: To study the way is to study the self; to study the self is to forget the self; to forget the self is to be enlightened by ten thousand things."

Thus, sincere practice nurtures sangha. So what was wrong at Zen Center? "In the 1960s," says Gib Robinson, a professor of literature at San Francisco State University, "the truth is that the community was too young, and the idea of emptying out individual egos was too new. It didn't happen." This is a good description of what couldn't happen in the early years, and it is widely endorsed by priests and students who studied with Suzuki-roshi, but it is not an explanation.

"The intense practice period model, which has been the main model for teaching the monastic experience at Tassajara and Green Gulch, is not functioning very well," says Steve Allen, who was Treasurer of Zen Center during the Apocalypse and now lives and practices with his wife and occasional visitors in relative isolation, in what he calls a hermitage setting. "At Zen Center, people spend ninety percent of their time dealing with community issues and not Zen practice. I think it is not a healthy environment. Maybe a few generations down the line, if we have worked out how to live together in a communal way, the teaching will be able to come through that." Steve is basically describing a cart-before-the-horse problem. By 1972, there were three crowded residential carts that composed the Zen Center community—but there was no sangha, no horsepower. "And today? Even at this point," says Steve, "I really do believe most of the energy is going into issues of how to live together and not issues of how to transcend the dualistic framework in which we find ourselves in ordinary society. And that is what I understand practice is about—nondualistic experience and liberation from the normal limitations of social programming."

"I wanted to see if we could develop a sangha," says Gib. He joined Zen Center in the seventies. He never gave up his tenured position at San Francisco State University, but he served on the Board, and for a couple of years he did join the residential community. "But Richard kept us all apart because it was easier for him to deal with us individually." He had come by it honestly; this was Suzuki-roshi's way. But Gib says Richard's isolation of individuals within the community went beyond teaching. "He didn't like it when we formed a Men's Group. He didn't like people communicating about anything substantial without his being present. There were restrictions, god knows, not only about saying anything if you had an affair with him, but even discussing what he had said to you."

Conversely, it was often difficult to get his attention. "One of the things we discovered after the blowup in 1983 was that the only effective way to get Richard's attention was to have three of us talk to him at once," explains Yvonne. "And the three of us—Reb, Lew, and I—would get through. How did we not discover that for so many years? Why weren't we able to collaborate before this?"

"Richard wanted to keep everyone relating to him directly," says Gib. "As a result, the community itself did not develop the kind of substance that would have served him. When the break came, we were not ready to meet him as a sangha. There was no equivalent power to his. It's ironic. Had we been able to meet him as his equal, it might have been easier for him to stay."

Steve Allen thinks Richard was behaving like a traditional Japanese abbot. Or a drill instructor. "At one point, Richard said, 'You know, monastic life is quite like the army.' And that's right," says Steve. "The strong hierarchical element in Japanese Buddhism is very clear. I was born into a military family, and it was, indeed, very similar to monastic life." Of course, many of the young men who joined Zen Center had signed up for an alternative to the military system. And a lot of other people had come in search of refuge from the hierarchies of families, universities, and corporations. As a result, Steve believes, more energy was expended in the struggle to transform the Tassajara monastery into a utopian community than was expended in the struggle with the practice.

"There are two sides, and they are often at odds," says Norman Fischer, the sixth Abbot of Zen Center from 1995 to 2000. "On the one hand, Zen Center's mission is as a long-term training center for Zen Buddhist priests; on the other hand, we are this very wide and expansive community, where all sorts of people come and go with all points of view, and the community's agenda is just to benefit the world widely—forget about Zen Buddhism. This makes it complicated, and it creates conflicts, and this makes it wonderful."

The wonder of it all was lost on a lot of people in the early eighties; for people who stayed through the nineties, the project became an experiment in creating a new kind of community that could acknowledge and support many teachers and, thus, nurture the development of a sangha. It required Zen Center to release itself from its own history, and the divorce took its toll on the place. These were years—more than a decade—"of total reaction," says Darlene Cohen, who arrived on Page Street soon after Richard became Abbot, laid low for several years after he left, and yet maintained a lay practice at Zen Center through the years. In 1999, she and her husband Tony Patchell were ordained as Zen priests.

"Everybody was meeting with everyone else," remembers Mel, the longtime teacher at the Berkeley center who became Zen Center's fifth Abbot in 1988; he agrees with Darlene, although his math is more modest. "For months it just kept going on—for years it went on. Zen Center was in decline for at least five years. We had meetings where people were saying, 'Why should we have to obey the rules?' It became anarchic. City Center became a kind of hotel on Page Street—people were living there and bad-mouthing Zen Center. They had lost their faith in the practice."

There was a spiritual problem and there was a practical problem. "In terms of practical rules, nobody even knew who got to stay here," says Barbara Kohn. "And who got to make that decision? Zen Center didn't have a dictator anymore."

For a few years, Zen Center didn't really have a Board, either, or any unsullied organizational structures. According to most of the senior priests, until 1983, Zen Center was a virtual organization that was actually run by one man with a BMW. "So, when Richard left," says Barbara, "there was a lot of movement toward secularizing the administration of Zen Center, moving it away from the monastic model. In some ways, that made it an easy time to enter the community." Barbara was in her fifties when she and her husband started to sit at Green Gulch Farm. "When I came in 1984, people made it clear there was work to do." Fifteen years later, Barbara is the outgoing President of Zen Center. "Wonderful people had stayed around after Baker left, but a number of people who stayed were troubled and not productive. Most of them have since left, but Zen Center was kind of weird right then."

"Actually, in the middle and late eighties, we lost the best people and the worst people," says Michael Wenger, who arrived as Richard became Abbot and has since taken almost every position of responsibility in the community, from editing *Wind Bell* to a term as President. He is now Dean of Buddhist Studies. "The most promising people and the hangers-on did not stay during the reactionary times. The middle level of people stayed. And for those of us who did stay, mostly those years just registered as a numbing pain. Everyone was bleeding."

"Richard Baker was clearly very sophisticated," says Barbara Kohn, "and he brought in sophisticated people, but the sophistication was not integrated into what went on inside Zen Center. So the membership was naive about communication theory and Gestalt; many of them were meeting their first psychotherapists in 1984 and 1985. During the last few years, we've brought in consultants for group training, encouraged therapy when appropriate, and sent people to drug and alcohol counseling." It's not exactly traditional, but it is the American way of taking refuge. "When I first came, every New Year's Eve there would be a *sake* toast— it's traditional," says Barbara. "They didn't have the kind of awareness that you would also serve apple juice, and when I mentioned it, people thought I was weird."

Or maybe they figured that if you eliminate too many ingredients from the original recipe, you cannot expect to bake a cake.

The Eightfold Path was laid down a couple of millennia ago to lead Buddhists to the end of suffering; is it weird that Americans are certain they've improved it with the addition of several twelve-step recovery ramps? Is it weird that so many people who made the extraordinary choice to live in community sought refuge in psychotherapy—talking to a stranger instead of their spiritual teacher? You could say it is weird that faith in democracy replaced faith in singular spiritual authority. "It is really striking," says Gary Snyder, "that so very many people at Zen Center reject the term *religion* when it is applied to what they are doing. What is any religion? A little ritual, a little superstition, and some magic. That's Buddhism. At Zen Center, [some people] seem to want Zen Buddhism to be a philosophy with a practice, or purely a spiritual teaching. Well, it's not strictly a spiritual affair; it has psychological roles to fulfill. You might not want it to be a religion based on your own experience or your own understanding of religion, but that's like wanting to clean up your dreams."

And isn't it weird, wonders one of Richard's former students, that the very people who condemned Richard for his acquisitiveness and attachment to material things are still living in the kingdom he created? Yes, says Lew, but what's even weirder is that "Zen Center replicated in one generation the problem that has corrupted every Buddhist institution on the planet. When the Communists took over in China in the 1940s, who were the biggest landowners? The Buddhist monks. The monasteries had become fiefdoms over the centuries. The same is true largely in Tibet, though no one wants to say so. The Chinese cannot justify one killing in Tibet, but their sociopolitical analysis isn't all wrong. Buddhism has always suffered with the fact that the Buddha was a world-renouncing monk." The Buddha knew his palace was nothing, so he moved out. Zen Center amassed palaces, and everybody moved in. Is that not a little weird?

Barbara is *not* weird. She's direct. And she makes even the most arcane of Zen Center's policies and procedures sound almost humane and almost plausible. She was part of a work crew whose job it was to clean up the dream. And that is a strange assignment. The idea that governed Zen Center's long restructuring and policy-making period was that religious authority in the form of a single ego—Richard's—had to be replaced, or at least balanced by an administrative structure, one that *"develops by the incorporation of the perceived moral standards of the community, is mainly unconscious, and includes the conscience."* The italicized quotation is useful because it captures both the fact and spirit of the work done at Zen Center.

Oddly, the source of that italicized quotation is not a Zen Center policy manual, of which there are many. The source is the *American Heritage Dictionary*; it is the definition of *superego*. And that's what Zen Center built to replace Richard. And on paper, a superego of administration seems more benign than any dictator or guru or abbot precisely because it is spelled out. Unlike an abbot's ego, it is reliable and even predictable.

(Not quite. "Let's do it right," says Barbara when asked once too often to clarify the distinct roles of President of Zen Center, Abbot, and President of the Board. And thus begins a parenthetical sermon on the superego every bit as head-spinning as Suzuki-roshi's lecture on the ego. "There's an organization called San Francisco Zen Center. There's a director of each of the three places [Tassajara, Page Street, and Green Gulch Farm]. And under those directors are senior staff. And the directors are appointed by the President and the Abbots. The other roles are filled by the practice committee of that place. The Abbot is involved in the choosing of the director and the head of practice at each place. The officers of Zen Center are the President, Vice President, Treasurer, and Secretary, though we may end up changing what we call them after our year-long governance study—maybe a VP for Financial Affairs and a VP for Development, or a CFO. The Board is an elected body, with a certain number of appointed spots. Appointees are not supposed to be connected to Zen Center. A little confusion here: Sometimes, people with special skills are appointed even though they are nonresident practitioners. Twelve are elected and up to four are appointed. And there are Board committees, and often non-Board members sit on these. Committees need to do a lot of the work. We have not been able to be a fund-raising Board at the level we should be because we elect monks, so now we're looking at how the Board is chosen. We have an Outside Financial Advisory Board made up mostly but not entirely of nonpractitioners who love Zen Center for some reason." Not for its simplicity. "These people are very helpful in crises about rents and in business deals. Nice is nice, and business is business. We also have a not-for-profit arm," (nice or business? not clear) "Everyday Corporation, which runs Greens Restaurant for us. The President and Treasurer of Zen Center are on that Board. The Abbot's Council is another event—it is not a decision-making body, so maybe it's a misnomer. Now that we have a group of ex-Abbots, they form their own counseling group." These are the Elders, though they're not the oldest members of the community. "Norman recently changed the Abbot's Council to include the three heads of practice and the three directors, the President, and the Abbots. Primarily, we look at demographics and positions that need to be filled. This is not a decision-making body for moving people around in staff positions—that's the business of the practice committee at each of the three places. Abbots also have a vote on the Board. The Elders Council is a council of the Board formed so that the Board would not be making religious decisions of a major sort. It's unlikely that the Elders would bring forth an Abbot choice and have the Board reject it. But what conditions and finances the Abbot might want would be up to the Board. And there's the EAR Council—Ethics and Reconciliation—available for people to say, This happened, so what should I do? This is not a grievance committee—the EAR can appoint a grievance committee." Barbara exhales. "It's a complex structure, and making a decision is not easy.")

This was the real work of making Zen American. It was a tireless, often tiresome effort that involved almost every member of the community in monthly, weekly, and sometimes daily meetings, group-processing sessions, policy reviews, policy debates, policy invention, policy revision, and then another meeting. It was a ten-to-fifteen-year effort, and it exposed the inefficiencies of the democratic process. "It took forever to make a decision," says Mel. "But everyone was involved. And that involvement with each other was our practice. Still, I have to say that having sat through millions and millions of meetings, I really can't sit through meetings anymore."

If there are fewer meetings at Zen Center these days, there are not fewer policies in place. Every possibility occasions a policy; this is the American way. "I can be blamed for spearheading a document that deals with the idea that at various points in time [in your residency and training], you would make decisions," says Barbara, holding her hands above her head in surrender. "*Paths and Gates*. We were trying to put together an old-age policy. Who gets to be here at the end of their lives? Now, it is spelled out. If someone stays at Zen Center for twenty years, that teacher could go out from here and, after turning seventy, come back and live here. Room and board only—no stipend. And there *is* a bonus to help people go out after fifteen years, to encourage them to take the practice out of Zen Center." *Paths and Gates* also sets forth a model for novice students, who are expected to meet with senior teachers at regular intervals to discuss their developing ideas about the practice and their commitment to it. "If you stay beyond three years," explains Barbara, "you're on staff for sure; if you stay beyond five, we're beginning to look at someone who can take responsibility for someone else's practice; beyond ten years, it would be expected that you will go on and receive Transmission and you will teach."

It's not as fast as the Eiheiji system, but it is a system for producing ordained priests and promoting Transmission. It's not designed to be unresponsive to individuals. But systems are designed to reduce idiosyncrasies. "We never want it too cut and dry," says Barbara. "We *are* a refuge. But we don't want great numbers of people thinking they can spend their lives here, supported, when they are fighting formal practice."

Where else will people go to spend their lives struggling with the practice?

"I say to people, 'You kicked me out.' And they can't stand that I say that," says Peter Rudnick, who had a central role in developing and running the farm at Green Gulch for almost twenty years. In 1999, he was told he had to leave. He is married to Wendy Johnson, who helped to design the growing gardens and worked in the kitchen. Both of them were stalwarts of Green Gulch Farm. Neither of them ever sought to be ordained as priests.

"It seemed clearly not my path," says Wendy. "I was connected to lay practice, Buddhism in the world, growing food for hungry people. It's been my life. But ordination has become an expression of commitment and intention. The strongest students have been ordained. It's an anomaly to have someone practice as long as I have and not take ordination. In the ten years I worked with Richard, I saw the community go from being much looser, with some feeling of anarchy—a kind of fierce simplicity— to a more established, comfortable, positioned place. Richard put a real emphasis on ordination. I remember once he asked me to come to talk to him about why I had chosen not to be ordained, and I said, 'Ask me to come and talk about why I've chosen to be layperson, and I will come.' I haven't chosen not to ordain."

Wendy and (to a lesser degree) Peter were devoted students of Richard Baker, and they were also outspoken critics of Richard Baker before, during, and after the Apocalypse. Moreover, Wendy and (to a greater degree) Peter don't mind mixing it up with authority figures and hierarchies. The more democratic, horizontal organization that Zen Center invented in the later eighties made sense to both of them. They were committed to lay practice on the farm, which had been purchased and developed by Zen Center to make room in the world for the long-term lay practice that so impressed Suzuki-roshi when he first turned up in San Francisco. They survived their disagreements with Richard, and their critical admiration of him survived, too. It was not Richard's ego, which they never underestimated, that forced them out; finally, the sprawling administrative superego that replaced Richard left no room for them on the land they loved. "People said they wanted to support me," says Peter, "but, then they'd say, 'There's a policy.' There are a lot of policies. But what seems clear is that if people want to stay on the farm, they have to become priests. I think Green Gulch Farm has lost its heart."

Peter has thick, dark hair that seems to have been combed and styled by a gusty wind. Wendy's long blond hair has turned to silver. They are in their fifties, and they both have the calm, unmannered, and friendly way of people who have spent a lot of time on their knees in the sun and rain, people who have carried more than their share of heavy sacks and buckets down dirt roads. A lot of what is strong and soft about them is apparent in the way they shake their heads and smile when they talk about each other.

"Peter is a son of a gun," says Wendy. "He is an in-your-face kind of opinionated, impossible, tyrannical, hardworking Boddhisatva [one who seeks enlightenment, but puts off his own entry into nirvana until all other beings are saved]. Peter doesn't fit here anymore. He's rough, a renegade who doesn't behave, and he is linked with what happened to Richard Baker." Suddenly, Wendy laughs. "Not in any stupid way am I thinking that Peter is a teacher for this community. I only mean that when a community learns how not to deal with difficult situations, you pass that on and propagate it."

Lineage.

Peter's offense was threefold. The first was smoking dope. "I had been smoking marijuana all along. There is a prohibition against it, as there is a prohibition against drinking, but the alcohol policy is softer. I smoked here. People knew. But around the time of the trouble with our Treasurer, some of my friends saw a chance to get rid of me, too."

In 1996, practitioners learned that the longtime Treasurer of Zen Center confessed to having embezzled $60,000. The administrative response seems to have been shaped more by Richard than by the action of the Treasurer. "I don't think Bill [Lane] was doing something out of his own greed," says Mel. "He was disenchanted with what had happened with Richard." Richard's Long Body was still available for flogging thirteen years after his departure. It's impressive. "No one was watching Bill in the Treasury, and he had all this money at his disposal. I think it was just con-solation." Except for the tone of voice, that part could pass an analysis of Richard. "Bill had a drinking problem. So we finally got Bill to agree to go to detox, and a woman agreed to drive him there. On the way, they fell in love; they became lovers. The love affair didn't last too long, but it cured Bill of his drinking problem. This was before his confession. He had told her about the money, and she hinted it to Reb and me [who were then co-Abbots of Zen Center]. She said, 'I can't keep this a secret.' And then Bill came to us and said, 'I took this money over a period of time, but my aunt left me an inheritance, and I took the inheritance, and I put the money back.' And we thought, That's a great thing to do, but people should know about this. And we thought Bill should tell them. But it just took him forever to get around to telling people. In the meantime, he was still Treasurer, and when people finally did hear about it, they were pretty sore at Reb and me for not disclosing it, and we had to stand behind our actions. I still do. I didn't want to prosecute him. He made this gesture of reconciliation—in a sense, and he had been open with us. And it had not been known until he identified what he had done."

Almost. But, in a simpler sense, he hadn't been open with anyone for more than a decade, which is why no one knew what he had done. It's another version of the sex-money-power story, but this version mixes it up with drinking. Drunkenness is one problem Richard seems never to have cultivated in himself. This might have been his biggest mistake. Had Richard been a drunk, he might well be the Abbot of Zen Center today, toasting his longevity with a Raku bowl full of apple juice every New Year's Eve.

Barbara had been President of Zen Center for two weeks when Bill confessed. "It was as if he had become so identified with the job of Treasurer and his role as daddy of Zen Center, that it was all his—including the money. I think that's what happened." This sort of offhand association of daddies with isolation, abuse of power, larceny, and drunkenness is not unique to the Zen Center lexicon. It's a commonplace among many American sociologists and family therapists. It is simply more poignant at Zen Center, because Abbot is a form of the ancient Aramaic word *abba* and means *father.*

"Today," says Steve Allen, "there is new layer of social programming at Zen Center going on at the community level. It is probably necessary if you want to maintain big training centers, but I don't want to be adept at it."

Barbara says, "The point is, Bill had some problems, and he got help."

There was no help for Peter. As he sees it, his problem was not that he wouldn't give up marijuana, but that he wouldn't give up on the farm. "Most of the people who live here do not want to do farm work. They want to turn Green Gulch into a monastery. They like the image of themselves living on a farm, and they want a farm that works, but they don't want a working farm."

Unlike Wendy, who loves to sit, Peter has struggled with formal zazen practice. It was an explicit struggle that was an explicit part of his conversation with his teachers, beginning with Richard. "Richard told me flat out that I would never get ahead at Zen Center, that I would never hold a position of responsibility if I didn't show up in the zendo every day. I've always believed the farm work is the practice." Peter's formal practice was renewed after he and Wendy spent time with the Vietnamese Zen monk Thich Nhat Hanh, but throughout the 1990s, he constantly reconsidered and rejected and revised his commitments to sitting and farming.

Suzuki-roshi said Buddha's robe is a problem robe.

"The problems of my smoking and my sitting turned out to be bogus concerns. My leaving basically became a debate about what will become of the farm. We had a series of the coldest, ugliest meetings I have ever been in," says Peter. He smiles and picks up a pillow from the sofa on which we're seated, tosses it in the air a couple of times, and then he sighs, or maybe it's a soft sort of laughter. "Sometimes, I think there must be something funny about it all," he says, turning the pillow over and over. "I was ready to make one more commitment, and I wrote out a proposal, but the perception clearly was that the farm is secondary and outside of practice. My commitment to the farm didn't matter. This treatment was no surprise, really. Unless people become priests, Zen Center does not support their practice."

"If you are not walking around wearing a black or brown tablecloth with no hair, you are not serious," says Wendy. "Really. It's laughable. You think to yourself, *Come on*."

"The priest thing!" says Lew Richmond. "The priest thing! Zen Center's problem is Buddhism's problem. There is no original place for family in the psychic construction of Buddhism or its legends. We had a family — one of the first, and my wife Amy was treated as a second-class citizen because she had a job and, therefore, wasn't sincere."

What is a Buddhist layperson to do? "For me," says Peter, "the question has always been, Why are we all here and what are we going to do? I don't know that Richard had all the right answers, but Richard had a genius for making people who didn't like each other and could not get along able to work together. Something happened. As soon as he left, we couldn't get any work done. What were we doing? Despite all of the meetings and rules and regulations and elected officers, the real sense of corporation—one body—is a sense that Zen Center just has not developed. *Your* practice doesn't look like *my* practice, so *you* must not be practicing. That's how it goes here. I don't look like a priest, and my practice doesn't look like a priest's practice." He doesn't look at all like a priest. He has hair and pants. "We live on a farm. You know, *Chop wood, carry water.* Isn't that it? Farming is what we can teach people who choose to live here, and how we can help people who don't. We live in an imperfect world, and here we had a chance to create a sustainable way to feed people who don't have enough to eat." He looks over his shoulder, out the window. "We're moving out."

"So," says Wendy, sitting on a bench in the garden, "that's how I lost my place and position in the world. And for a time, I became obsessed with what was happening to Peter, and I sort of lost myself, too. We went through it forever with the EAR Council, where my colleagues said, 'We don't want to hurt you,' and I thought, 'I don't believe you.' And over and over people who were my friends said to me, 'Don't confuse yourself with Peter. Peter has been removed from the community, not you.'"

Wendy's face flushes red. "I wasn't confused. Peter is my husband."

Lay practice.

"What's the opposite of cynicism? Awareness," says Wendy. "You become alert. I woke up and thought, Enough already. Peter has been removed. We're out of here." Wendy's face is pale again, and her brown eyes dart around, and this is somehow stimulus enough to stir up the dark green aromas of the cultivated earth and the slight sweetness of second-bloom roses. "I am always searching for sangha. That puts me in the world. Mostly, my copractitioners here at Green Gulch are uninterested; they are disinclined to be politically active. Tonight at dinner, I've organized a letter-writing campaign to oppose the bottling of water on Mount Tamalpais. I sit [zazen] on the steps of San Quentin. I just find a way to keep practicing meditation and connecting it with the world. [Richard] Baker-roshi had a big vision of Zen in the world. It made sense to me. If it matters to you, then you're there," says Wendy. "You go to the soup kitchen with your kids. You stand in the line and cut the chard and make the soup. And sometimes I just make bologna sandwiches. And my kids say, 'Oh, poor mom. They make you make *bologna* sandwiches? How terrible.' And that bologna feels like rubber and it is plutonium heavy, but people need to eat."

Wendy stands and points to a path that leads under the bower of some particularly skinny, weepy trees. "It's gotten all tangled up with role, position, and hierarchy here. Who does that serve?" Wendy turns a slow circle and sits on the bench again. "Baker-roshi was always ferocious about distinguishing between community and sangha. I can hear him. He said—constantly—'Zen Center is not a community. Sangha practice is not a community. We're not building a commune or a home.' That was hard to hear, especially once we all began to breed in the seventies. It became hard not to settle in. It was hard to say, This is *not* my home, that I practice here for the well-being of all beings, without trying to own the place. But just having that vision mattered to me. Trying to see that it was not *our* kitchen for *our* food but a kitchen to feed peace and social justice—that vision of *not ours* made me want to stay here. That was something worth practicing."

Wendy stands up again. "We are at the end of something now," she says. "Not just Peter and I. Most of us here are old coots. I mean, look around. Is Buddhism really here to stay?" She suddenly points in the direction of a small stand of dark, delicate bamboo bowing to a sudden breeze. "It's supposed to be noninvasive. We imported it from Japan." She nods; it's a friendly recrimination. "That bamboo is constantly trying to take over the whole garden." Wendy smiles. She starts down the little path that leads to the dirt road that leads to a gravel walk that leads to the house she is leaving. "I love this organization, and I love the people." She stops and touches the striated bark of a small, sturdy tree. Just checking in. "I thought I would stay put. I always wanted to take care of the practice place. But what do I know? I also thought for many years that we would work on a face-to-face reconciliation with our past. It horrifies me that we're not doing it." She looks around. She looks almost amused, but she isn't smiling. She almost looks sad, too, but not. Sometimes, Wendy just looks somewhere else. Her gaze goes way beyond the garden to a time when it wasn't there. "People are afraid to have Richard Baker give a talk here. I have to wonder, Have they heard that we're dropping depleted uranium bombs on Yugoslavia? Who does all this serve? Sixteen years later, we are still trying to figure out Transmission and the lineage hocus-pocus. And the eldest students of Shunryu Suzuki himself cannot even practice together?"

18.

THE ROAD TO RICHARD IS A long one. Somewhere in southern Colorado, near the New Mexico border, you turn off the highway and head west. If you're lucky, it is not February, as it was the second time I made the trip north from Santa Fe. My first visit to the Crestone Mountain Zen Center was Dan's doing; it was summer, and Richard was in the Black Forest, where he spends about half of every year with his European students. The second time I made the trip, Richard and Dan were both on the mountain, settled into a seventy-five-day practice period with fifteen or twenty students, and I was on my own in a little rental car that looked and handled like a canned ham, and right before I hit the Colorado State line, the highway disappeared in a snowstorm that was exactly seven miles long. It didn't start suddenly; I entered it suddenly. One minute I was thinking about passing a tractor-trailer on a particularly flat patch of two-lane blacktop, and then I was sledding through a couple of inches of slush, white-blinded but for a set of red rear lights. I stuck with the truck, because I figured it provided a barrier between me and any cars coming the other way with drivers stupid enough to be doing sixty in a snowstorm, as I was. Seven scary minutes later, the road was clear and dry and the sun was shining. In my rear-view mirror I could see the storm, hanging like a curtain at the border. I never did pass the truck; it had given me safe passage through the snow, and I didn't want to appear ungrateful. Soon though, it became evident that the truck was headed to Denver, or Manitoba, maybe, so I sounded my horn as I headed west, and my horn, which I'd never heard before, sounded just like a squealing piglet.

It was months before I realized that the strange, stagnant storm hang-

ing around in the middle of nowhere was just like 1983, the year of rough
going at Zen Center. There's no getting around it.

The road that heads north to Crestone is so flat and straight and black
that your brain gets nervous on your behalf and starts decorating the distance with hills and silver puddles and other distractions that aren't really
there, just to keep you on track. This is the second largest valley on the
planet, more than fifty miles wide, and just when you start to suspect that
even the snowcapped blue and gray mountains in the distance might be
something you are making up, you pass a stand of sand dunes that rises
up hundreds of feet against the Rockies like the edge of a barrier beach.
That's where you are; where the ocean used to be.

Richard sits a few thousand feet above all of this, and right behind him
Crestone Mountain rises to a craggy summit of 14,000-feet, looking like
the oldest chipped tooth in the face of the earth. The sloping land and the
big, handsome central stone building were gifts from William Thompson
and his Lindisfarne Association. A beautiful wooden zendo, a number of
sweet small cabins, and a guesthouse chalet up the hill were added more
recently, and they are all connected by a tangle of dirt paths bordered by
juniper and scrub pine and a lot of rocks and stones of all sizes, which all
seem to be making their slow way down the mountain.

Two other buildings merit mention. The Lindisfarne Association built
a chapel on the land not so long ago. It was an instant relic, a fitting memorial to the nonsectarian, nondenominational New Age impulse of the late
twentieth century. It's a concrete lozenge bunkered into a hill, or maybe
it's an abandoned flying saucer. Inside, the atmosphere is Sophoclean
sci-fi—a big, low, windowless rotunda with sunken stadium seating,
apparently designed for the first Interplanetary Parliament.

Richard sees students for private interviews, or *dokusan,* in the splendid, unassuming Hoto-an. It's modeled on the many small country temples in Japan, which are scaled like modest open-floor-plan ranch homes.
Hoto-an is outfitted with sliding glass and paper screens and paneled cab-
inetry; one step up or down divides the little room and decks; above are
seamless fitted-board ceilings, and underfoot are wood floors planed and
polished smooth as ice. The outside walls are plastered with fine-grain
mud that registers against your skin as skin.

It's a plain and unforgettable building, and I remembered seeing one just like it on the land that Richard bought with Gary Snyder and Allen Ginsberg in Northern California. "Dick found this one when he and Ginny were living in Japan," Gary had told me. Shobo-an was slated to be torn down and replaced by a larger temple in a village outside Kyoto when Richard saw it. In 1974, *Wind Bell* reported it as a gift to Richard. He told me that his wife Ginny paid for it to be taken apart and shipped to San Francisco in a giant container and then trucked up to the Sierra. (Some people just buy paper-lantern souvenirs or postcards.) Like so many of Richard's grand gestures, this one occasioned anecdotes that people like to repeat. To wit: When the customs officials in the port of San Francisco opened the container to inspect the deconstructed temple walls and roof, they found several pairs of white gloves on top, which the Japanese crew had packed for whomever had to handle it next.

This story tells you something about the Japanese, and something more about Richard, and something else again about the literalness of the project to import Zen to America. Five craftsmen specializing in temple and teahouse architecture rebuilt the temple; the crew moved up to the Sierra to assemble Shobo-an on the land Richard owned, to finish the interior, and to make more of that miraculous mud plaster. Students from Zen Center assisted them. This was reported in *Wind Bell* as a priceless teaching opportunity. "We hope that building Shobo-an will help Zen Center develop its own skill and building craft." Okay; but it was also an opportunity for the Abbot. Richard used Shobo-an as a retreat and summerhouse for his family and guests, to supplement his residences at Tassajara, Page Street, and Green Gulch Farm, which Zen Center had purchased at his insistence a year earlier.

It was evidently very difficult, and maybe impossible, and possibly even bad practice to draw a distinction or a boundary between the communal identity of Zen Center and the identity of the Abbot—especially if you were the Abbot and sole teacher. The students and senior priests toed that line.

Richard receives questions about his appropriation of Zen Center funds and student labor for projects like Shobo-an as accusations and hair-splitting recriminations. In his analysis, everyone at Zen Center was there by dint of free will and, besides, everybody benefited. It does not strike him as suggestive that more of the material benefits always seemed to accrue to the Abbot. As Richard has said, Who cares about stuff and status? It's all just nothing. But, as former students ask, when Richard decided he no longer wanted to own Shobo-an, how did it profit Zen Center?

Richard did, finally, shrug off his California palaces. And from almost anywhere you sit or stand at Crestone Mountain Zen Center, you overlook the vast, flat emptiness of the valley floor. It's a teaching, and it's really not so easy to live with the constant reminder that you're not there. The air is thin, and the sky is just about as big as the sky, and the first night I saw the stars, they were so many that I thought it was snowing.

Two years had passed before Richard replied to one of my many letters requesting an interview. In the lineup of Abbots and other Zen Center long-timers, this placed him somewhere after Norman ("Just don't try to shape it like a normal history," Norman told me days after he received my first letter. "It won't fit") and Mel ("There is nothing I won't talk about," he said when I called him cold one day), and in front of Reb, who has yet to reply. Richard spoke to me the night I arrived in Crestone, and he told me he was still uncertain about being tape-recorded, but he would talk to me as long as we didn't talk about 1983.

I didn't particularly want to talk about 1983, either, as I had told everyone I'd interviewed. I was most interested in the inventive, intrepid community work-practice projects that were launched in the seventies. But even when individuals had explicitly ruled out questions related to 1983 prior to our meeting, they often resisted opportunities to talk about other periods or events, returning again and again to 1983, or to the causes and effects of that storm. This made perfect sense to Darlene. "We spent fifteen years and thousands of dollars on psychologists and consultants trying to learn how to talk about it. We should talk about it."

I spent four days with Richard. His wife of six months was with us each time we met, which was often. I had a tape recorder; Marie-Louise had a tape recorder; Richard had this to say the first time we were all plugged in and provided with some superb green tea.

"In some sense my life has not changed much. What's interesting to me—and I don't want to talk about 1983 particularly, but just for now I'm talking about it, and maybe it is unavoidable—I deeply would like to deal with what happened, and in what way I caused so much pain for so many people. But it's also somewhat mysterious because I'm really not much different now than I was then. So. What's different? I mean there are some things you can say are different—differences in gradation. What's different? Well, there are some obvious things. If it's the obvious things, then it is pretty easy to understand. I just should have been more careful with the way people saw me. But I can't believe it is that simple.

"But as a symbol of it not being that different, this is the same Thermos I used at Tassajara in 1972. It's still with me." It is pink and white, and it is filled with hot water that is not getting cold as he speaks. "Still do the same things. Still pretty much the same.

"I want to concentrate on trying to limit myself to see if I can, for the most part, be in a state of mind as if it were 1982 and someone were asking me about Zen Center. I say this happened, and this happened.

"One of the problems people have with me talking about it, and [my wife] reminds me, is that I too often say *I* did this, and *I* did that, and it's hard for me to avoid that, because at a certain scale, as far as I can tell, I *was* the person who did these things. At another scale, I wasn't the person who did many of them; obviously, Zen Center is the creation of a lot of people.

"But it's also a little like—they did a study during the Second World War—one of the things I studied in graduate school is the history of science and technology, a parallel interest to my interest in poetry and Buddhism—they did a study of the development of radar. And all the way up the line—it was secret; nobody was even supposed to say the word during the Second World War—they interviewed [people about] how it developed. There were many people who said they made the decision. But they were all people who could have stopped the decision. It came to their desks, and they said, Okay, go ahead, and it got passed up. And the next guy said, Okay. And they all think they made the decision.

"There may be that factor.

"I say that because I am completely aware that this whole thing was a creation of an energy coming out of a lot of people. But to initiate getting Green Gulch Farm, or to initiate getting a Buddha, or to initiate how many sesshins a year, it's just like here [at Crestone]. At this scale, no one argues that this is my temple. No one argues about it. But when there are suddenly two hundred people on the payroll, and you have this thing that has *happened* . . ."

And I am thinking about radar. It's another Transmission story. Pulses of electromagnetic waves (the dharma) are transmitted by an antenna attached to the radar unit (the teacher). A distant object in the path of those pulses (the student) reflects them back to the antenna. The radar unit (the teacher) absorbs and interprets the reflected signals to create an image of the distant object (the student).

The dharma does not alter the relationship between people; the dharma does not transform teachers or students; the dharma is the immaterial means by which we locate and identify each other.

When I was in college, almost twenty years after Richard studied the development of radar, I took a course in the history of technology, principally because the other options for fulfilling the undergraduate science requirement involved real science. The teacher of that course was a somber man with silver hair who stood behind a podium in a three-piece suit and delivered long, fact-filled lectures in a soporific monotone. And almost every word he said was fascinating. He had news for us, and it was news of our world. I don't know what that teacher made of his students that semester; I don't know how our typewritten essays and handwritten exams registered on his screen. I know he never said the word *sangha*, but I know that he successfully transmitted to us something about the collective human spirit that fuels the scientific enterprise.

No one man developed radar. Between 1935 and 1940, radar technology was widely understood as a possibility. Several teams of several scientists in several different countries realized that possibility at the same time.

In time, stories change. Like everything else, even our history is impermanent. Radar remains a singular achievement, but we now know that it was achieved by sangha.

19.

WHEN THEY ARE SEARCHING FOR the right word to describe Suzuki-roshi, his students often settle on the word *seamless*. The difference between Suzuki-roshi in the zendo and Suzuki-roshi in a hot tub at Tassajara was no difference. Seamless. It applies to his teaching, his practice, and his presence.

"Suzuki-roshi's quiet, gentle teaching was the opposite of putting pressure on you to have an experience," says Dan Welch, sitting on a rock on the side of Crestone Mountain. "He acknowledged that you were here. Stay here; that's all. Studying Suzuki-roshi closely, I saw that it was seamless. There were no gaps. What he didn't do was as important as what he did do. When I took my questions to him, he didn't answer. He would dismiss me—with a glance, a bell, or he'd look away. It finally occurred to me, in the middle of a sesshin, Oh, yes, this is what I want to do. I went to see him in dokusan and said, 'I don't know what it means but I want to practice this way for the rest of my life and I want to take you as my teacher.' He didn't make a big deal. Okay. Six months later, I thought maybe I hadn't been clear and I ought to do something. I talked to him again. His reaction was the same, a slight nod, a whispered 'Okay.' This went on for two years, and then he said he was going to do an ordination with me and Peter [Schneider]," then Zen Center's President. That's why Dan became a Zen priest in 1970. "Suzuki-roshi was watching me."

Suzuki-roshi also seems to have been watching the fabric of Zen Center itself, which was being stretched beyond its limits. By 1969, it was evident that Zen Center needed priests to spread the practice to new members. In 1967, Richard had become the seventh of Suzuki-roshi's students to be ordained. No one was ordained again until Mel, in 1969, the year

Suzuki-roshi began to announce Richard as his dharma heir, Zen Center acquired its residence on Page Street, and Suzuki-roshi began to disappear. It was a gradual, quiet, but determined abdication. In the last two years of his life, eleven of Suzuki-roshi's disciples were ordained. His health declined precipitously, he deferred to Richard's judgment about fund-raising and organizational planning, and he withdrew from commitments involving longtime donors and new practitioners alike, in order to minister to his most senior students.

From the end of 1969 until the end of 1971, Suzuki-roshi hastily stitched together a lot of disparate material. Zen Center survived this interregnum, and from any distance, the history now looks like whole cloth. Until 1983, it was treated as whole cloth, as if the miraculous Transmission of the dharma had made of many scraps and bits of cloth a single, continuous garment. It was a story that served everyone and, many believe, benefited Richard most. But Richard cannot be blamed for this; even he does not take credit for inventing Transmission or the meaning with which it was invested.

On close inspection, the seams in the legacy of Suzuki-roshi do show. Various attempts have been made to cover up and smooth over the scar of these hastily made stitches. Today, some people at Zen Center will tell you that the scrappy and patchy parts are not his handiwork. But even the nastiest bits of stitchery bear the mark of the master—they cannot be undone. The imperfections are permanent.

"Suzuki-roshi had an opportunity to manage the transition a heck of a lot better than he did," says Lew Richmond, "but by the end, the man was dying faster than anyone understood. He thought he had months when he had only weeks. His vision was to give Transmission—that is, to empower—a whole group of people. He explicitly told people that's what he wanted. But he did what he did."

After 1962, no lay ordinations were performed at Zen Center for eight years. Zen students typically take lay ordination after one or two years of sincere practice. They sew *rakusus,* stitching together patches of cloth to make a rectangle that is attached to a neck cord and worn in memory of the Buddha's patchwork robe, and they also receive the Precepts, the Ten

Commandments of Buddhism. In 1970, Suzuki-roshi suddenly saw a seam that needed mending; in the late summer, thirty-six students received lay ordination on the same day at Zen Center.

Was Suzuki-roshi trying to bind his lay followers to the Precepts?

The Precepts are expressed as prohibitions, but they are meant to encourage right living. (I am indebted to a young Green Gulch resident who articulated the Precepts in memorably simple terms when I asked him to recite them a third time. He also advised me to write them down; it was only the second day of my weeklong stay at Green Gulch, and the young man had other responsibilities.) Buddhists are not supposed to kill, steal, misuse sex, lie, get drunk or high, talk trash about anyone, brag or belittle, be attached or stingy, hope for the worst for someone, or do any harm to the dharma or sangha.

Oh, well; so much for binding people to the Precepts.

Dogen, the thirteenth-century Japanese master, said Zen is one continuous mistake. And it seems clear that Suzuki-roshi ordained Americans to bind them not to the Precepts but to a more ancient matter—the practice. His students do remember him lecturing on the Precepts. Indeed, dozens of his students, and many practitioners who never even met him, like to illustrate his attitude toward the Precepts with one particular exchange he had with a student at Tassajara. (Various second- and third-hand accounts, including a version that was printed in *Wind Bell*, make the same point.) A young man asked Suzuki-roshi about sex; specifically, the young man wanted some guidance on appropriate quantities of sex and sex partners—for instance, was 100 too many?

It is bait that most spiritual teachers could not resist. It's a chance to exercise authority—literally, a chance to author an essential chapter in another person's life. Of course, the question raises another question. Why would a young American man in the late 1960s ask a thrice-married, elderly Japanese man to quantify appropriate sexual behavior for him? Did he actually intend to follow Suzuki-roshi's advice or the advice Suzuki-roshi might have inherited from a bunch of wise men who'd lived in India a couple of thousand years earlier? If a young man did follow such advice, would he ever get a date?

What Suzuki-roshi seems to have heard in the young man's question was the confusion and sadness that lay behind it. He didn't relieve the young man's confusion about sex. He didn't assuage his sorrows. Suzuki-roshi gave it all back to him. He said sex might be like brushing your teeth—a good idea, but not something you're supposed to do constantly. And he thought it was probably okay to have had a lot of partners as long you remembered each one's name.

Of course, it is easy to misconstrue this teaching—if what you want to do is misconstrue this teaching. (This may explain why most religious leaders are so fond of explicit sex policies. They suspect people are always looking for a loophole. The Pope, for instance, is famous for itemizing sexual taboos for Catholics, and the Dalai Lama refers Buddhists to a list of twelfth-century proscriptions against the use of the mouth, masturbation, and "the other hole.") Exactly what did Suzuki-roshi say? What did he mean? Exegesis of Suzuki-roshi's collected and edited lectures is the business of scholars and theologians and linguists. But when you talk to the men and women who knew him, the spirit of his teachings seems perfectly clear. This makes sense; he was talking to them. And even when he was lucky enough to be surrounded by students who had begun to know and love him, Suzuki-roshi always knew he was always speaking to beginners. His message was simple: Don't get attached to my ideas or your ideas about the Precepts. Don't ask me to count your lovers. Don't reduce your former lovers to a head count. Now just sit down. Practice.

In simple historical terms, the Precepts followed from the Buddha's practice. Practice makes precepts.

The famous story of the time the young man asked Suzuki-roshi about sex has been so often passed along that it is threadbare. That's how myths are made. That's the Transmission material. It preserves one mythic moment when Suzuki-roshi shrugged off the authority invested in him by a student. He did so constantly. He gave some to his son Hoitsu; he saddled Richard with a lot of it; he dumped some on Dan; he let a lot fall Yvonne's way, too. He was often surrounded by people who were eager to hand over their authority, but he never held onto it. And when he noticed that it was piling up at the end, he ordained many priests and many laypeople. He turned Zen Center over to his longtime students. He gave Richard Transmission, told Richard to pass it on to Bill Kwong, and told a lot of other students to expect Transmission soon. Maybe Suzuki-roshi figured Richard would do with the authority what he himself had always done with it. Suzuki-roshi shrugged it off. That's what the Buddha did. The Buddha shrugged off his authority. He ditched his palace and his place in a royal lineage. Then he patched together a robe of rags. That's the mythic moment. That's the moment when everything is nothing. And that's the real material.

"My first time sitting at Zen Center was on Bush Street, at Sokoji," remembers Linda Cutts, who became the eighth Abbot in the year 2000. "It was September of 1968. I was about to have a junior year abroad. I was at the University of Minnesota, and I'd met Reb while he was in grad school there. He'd left to go to Zen Center. Since I'd entered college, I'd been miserable, mostly because in 1966 I had become pregnant and given up a child for adoption when I was eighteen. My whole life was going in a false way. I spent a week as a guest student at Zen Center before I left for Italy." She stayed in Italy for two years, transferred to Berkeley, and moved into Page Street while she finished her degree. What made her want to return? "The first time I was in the zendo, I suddenly noticed there was this little face next to mine. It was Suzuki-roshi. I understood that I was seen. And I understood something else, too—it mattered that I was there." Linda says that she "didn't understand one single word he said in lectures all week. Probably he was saying wonderful things. It didn't matter. I do remember that I saw a senior student chopping an onion in the kitchen. I had never seen people take care of doing one thing the way people did at Sokoji. It hit me: This is what I want."

Something about Zen Center didn't survive the move from Sokoji. Leslie James, who became President of Zen Center in the mid-eighties, first sat with the community soon after the move to Page Street. "It was 1971. The feeling at City Center was not the same feeling people found at Sokoji. [The residential building on Page Street] was a very cold place, and anonymous. It was unfriendly in those days, but I didn't really mind. I wasn't sure I wanted anything to do with the Zen Center, and it seemed to have the same idea about me."

Suzuki-roshi had staked everything on heart-to-heart teaching and practice, but by 1969, people were a little confused about exactly what constituted practice, who was responsible for it, and even who was practicing. After the move to 300 Page Street in November 1969, they had to deal with making beds and breakfast and much more money. Was that practice? If so, what did it mean *not* to be a resident? Many people did not live in the building; anyone could drop in for morning and evening zazen and services, but the residents were making more than meals and beds— they were making a common way of life, and it was easy for others to feel left out.

And there were neighborhood confusions. At Sokoji, the students had Japantown as a background for their practice, and this seemed to soften the peculiarity they felt about their appropriation of Japanese habits and manners. (How kind of the Japanese Americans who lived in the vicinity of Bush Street to make a bunch of bald, bowing, barefooted hippies feel at home.) In a roundtable discussion published in the 1970–71 *Wind Bell*, Zen Center's discomfort with its new Page and Laguna Street neighbors is explicit. Crime, fear of crime, and nosey neighborhood kids led them to reverse their policy and lock the front door all day long. And although City Center was almost always operating at full capacity, it was rarely filled with fully familiar faces. It was a remarkably unstable community. Three-quarters of the first Zen students to occupy Page Street were not living there one and a half years later; some were at Tassajara for practice period, others had moved into nearby apartments and group homes, and others had just left. In an attempt to make sure City Center was full of people who really wanted to practice, newcomers were soon required to sit for three months before they were allowed to move in, and then they were expected to practice for an additional six months before being sent to Tassajara. Still, only one of every five people who joined the practice at Page Street would be practicing a year later.

But the most dramatic difference between Sokoji and City Center was one-to-one time with Suzuki-roshi.

Lucy Calhoun remembers sitting at Page Street in 1969, before she moved into the building. "It was clear to me immediately that Suzuki-roshi had senior students to care for him and to care for. He was not really available to the rest of us."

Teah Strozer had met Suzuki-roshi in Los Angeles in 1968. She did not join the community until the mid-seventies. "I came to City Center to sit sesshins, though, and for dokusan [private interviews] with Suzuki-roshi. It was an austere place. The whole operation gave off a feeling of coldness, and I was made very aware of the protectiveness around Suzuki-roshi. When I would call to see him, I would almost inevitably be told he was busy. It was difficult just to talk to him or to be there, and I had a close relationship with him."

In the 1970–71 *Wind Bell* roundtable, Reb Anderson explained that "people don't see much of [Suzuki-roshi]. Most students deal with other students all the time. Some are even afraid of him." Reb made it clear that this was Suzuki-roshi's explicit wish. Taking care of novices was now practice for older students. "I must say, though, I don't know exactly what he wants us to do or what we are doing."

At this same time, Tatsugami-roshi had temporarily taken over Tassajara and instilled the practice with Eiheiji-style formalism and decorum. "He did everything exactly the way Suzuki-roshi had never done it," says Ed Brown. And as if there were not enough loose ends and strained seams, Richard was in Japan. "A lot was happening, and Dick was not there," remembers Lew. "Suzuki-roshi remained accessible to those of us who knew him, but he wasn't talking even to us about his specific plans for Dick, and he definitely didn't want to listen to criticisms of Dick from anyone. To his way of thinking, Dick's commitment was at another level, so the rest of us simply were not in a position to criticize him."

Apparently simple matters started to seem arcane. Was seniority a matter of length of stay or intensity of practice? Was seniority a spiritual or an administrative status? Reb, for instance, had arrived at Zen Center from Minnesota in 1967 and immediately impressed everyone, especially Suzuki-roshi, with the rigor and sincerity of his meditation practice and his depth of study. He was ordained as a priest in 1970. He was a serious student, but his sense of his status seemed to be at odds with the perceptions of others.

Paul Discoe, Zen Center's great carpenter whom Suzuki-roshi sent to Japan, was ordained with Reb. "In those years, Silas Hoadley[a senior student who helped identify and acquire the Page Street building and left soon after Suzuki-roshi died in December 1971], Yvonne, and myself were the older ones. And Peter Schneider [who left for Japan soon after Richard became Abbot, and never returned], and maybe a couple of others. Before I went to Japan, we'd have meetings about Reb, wondering what we were going to do with all the girls who were after him. He was just a newcomer. The rest of us, we were the main people who formulated how things would happen."

Yvonne remembers one of those meetings, which took place at Sokoji. "Reb cares what people think about him. I remember a Board meeting on Bush Street, and what came up was that no one in the room could say, 'I trust you.' What we did say was, 'I don't trust you.' Reb was devastated. Undone. It mattered to him to be trusted."

"Reb came to Zen Center wanting something," says David Chadwick, Suzuki-roshi's biographer. He doesn't think Reb ever wanted to run the place, but from the beginning, David felt it was clear that "Reb wanted to be King of the Mountain."

In a rare instance of agreement, Richard agrees—with all of the above. "Reb has this sense of a real connection with Zen Center from the time he was there with Suzuki-roshi, but when I came back from Japan, Reb was just one of the new people. There were a lot of new people. Suzuki-roshi had a certain interest in Reb because there was a commitment to practice, that was clear." Later, Richard adds, "I think all this time, Reb secretly thought he was [Suzuki-roshi's] successor."

And the new people kept coming. In December of 1970, Suzuki-roshi was in Japan, completing Transmission with Richard. Darlene Cohen and Tony Patchell arrived at Zen Center that month.

"How *did* I get to Zen Center?" Darlene is looking out a window at the end of another day in San Francisco. It is 1999. She smiles. "I'd read Alan Watts."

Darlene's husband, Tony, is slouched in a chair on the other side of the large living room. He is twice as big as Darlene, which means nothing, but he is. "I'd read Watts, too, in California. I used to work for the Grateful Dead, so I knew about Zen Center because of the fund-raiser, the 1966 Zenefit concert for Tassajara. But I met Darlene in Cambridge, Massachusetts."

We're in Tony and Darlene's second-story apartment at the intersection of Page and Laguna streets, directly across from City Center. They have practiced at Zen Center for almost thirty years, but they have not lived in the community for the last fifteen. Darlene is looking across Laguna Street. There's a little café on that corner now. From 1975 until the mid-eighties, it was an organic grocery store run by Zen Center students. But when Darlene arrived at this crossroads thirty years ago, the store was a standard little market run by a widow with a shotgun.

Twilight fades fast in the fog, and before anyone says another word, it's dark beneath another starless sky in San Francisco, city of sudden nights. The big, paned windows of Zen Center make an inviting patchwork of soft light. It is easy to see the promise of the place. It easy to imagine being drawn in when you remember that Nixon was in the White House, and there was napalm in the bombs blasting apart villages in Vietnam, and as Stewart Brand, a founding editor of the *Whole Earth Catalog*, says, "most thinking people were starting to figure out that there weren't any shortcuts if you wanted to reinvent civilization. We'd all tried psychedelics, and the most astonishing revelation turned out to be that it was the same damn mystical revelation over and over again. Even hell was familiar."

Darlene smiles at the windows across Page Street. "I personally retreated into Zen Center," she says. "I wanted to retreat into a moral place, a sane place. I wanted a refuge. It's hard for someone from another generation to understand how we thought about the world then. I saw that there were no alternatives for me. I had quit my job as a psychologist because it was funded with a grant from the National Institutes of Mental Health, and it seemed immoral to work for the government. I was active in the Boston Draft Resistance Group. And I was working five-hour shifts on the weekend as a waitress, just to make enough to live. It was 1969. We thought it was the end. We thought it was the end of the world."

Darlene is a small, winning woman with gray hair and a conniving smile, and she has an unnerving way of not quite meeting your gaze when you want her to. I wasted a lot of time looking at what Darlene was looking at—her wrists, her forearms, the odd angle of her hand against her thigh—just because her gaze is compelling. Finally, I noticed that her joints didn't work right; she shoved a plate of cookies my way without grasping it, as if she were wearing mittens. Later I learned that Darlene had been diagnosed with rheumatoid arthritis in 1977, a lifelong opportunity to just sit there and suffer. This diagnosis accounts for her recalcitrant joints but not her ready sense of humor.

"While another waitress and I were standing by the door one evening, this completely outrageous hippie from California came in dripping with blond hair and buckskin and beads." Darlene sticks out her tongue. "Now, that's sex." That was Tony. "He came to my station, so I gave him a free beer. He left me a tip—a joint rolled in a napkin with a drawing of me on it—with a tear coming down my face. And I thought, Oh, no. Now I'm in love."

Tony nods. "It works every time."

Darlene nods. "That, and the fact that I allowed him to deal grass and acid in the kitchen."

"I was a hippie early on and did lots of drugs, and a lot of it was genuine searching," says Tony. He sips his tea. In the mid-sixties, Tony spent his time in California "working construction, dealing, and tooling around in my friend's Mercedes listening to Jimi Hendrix. And then another friend came back from a tour with the Marines in Vietnam, and I saw in him what was happening to us all. He was a stone-cold killer. He carried a pistol in his boot, purposefully grew his hair long and dressed like a hippie, and he told me—me—he told me he was waiting for one of those motherfucking hippies to pull something on him. It was only a few months later, in September of '69, that I was driving back to Marin from San Francisco, smoking a joint. Ahead of me was a truck with a chain across its open rear end. Like a cattle car. It was full of prisoners being transported to San Quentin, all black guys, and I felt ashamed of myself. They were going away, and I wasn't. And then one of them flipped me the peace sign. When I turned off the freeway, I stopped to pick up a young girl hitching with her bedroll. I thought she was crying. The whites of her eyes were red. But she was fleeing—fleeing Berkeley! She'd been caught in the riots at People's Park, and the tear gas was the same stuff they'd used in Vietnam, which embeds itself into wet tissue and festers. I dropped her off, drove to the house, got my pistol, and figured I had to go to Berkeley. And I knew if I didn't sit down soon, I'd end up in some kind of institution, or I'd kill myself. Instead, [my friend] and I got a bunch of dope, some acid and mescaline, and he loaded up his pistols. We drove right across the country. It was a nightmare trip. Finally, we went our separate ways in Pennsylvania, and I went to see some friends in Cambridge."

Darlene says, "One night, a customer left a copy of Philip Kapleau's book on a table."

"That was it," says Tony. "*The Three Pillars of Zen*. That was it. It was the first book I'd read about Zen that said, Here's what you do."

"To get *enlightened*." Darlene gives the word a rapturous, illicit spin. "Of course, that's heresy here at Zen Center—seeking to be enlightened— but we didn't know that yet. We were taking tons of acid, of course, and the question was, How do you permanently have this state of mind? Tony was the first man I ever knew to use the word cosmic in a sentence—the spiritual side of acid that I didn't know about. I was an atheist. I never dreamed the answer was in the spiritual realm until Tony started showing me Sanskrit words in books he had. That was the first real hook for me—a language about states of mind. On acid trips, I went up into the hallucinations, and when I peaked, it was like ordinary life, but it was wonderful. I was famous for cleaning my apartment during trips, and baking bread. So when I read in Kapleau's *Three Pillars* that Zen was just ordinary life—you know, *Chop wood. Carry water*—it resonated with my trips. So we wrote to Kapleau in New York. And he wrote back a typewritten letter. It's embarrassing now, but all we thought at the time was, He used a typewriter? A typewriter? What kind of technological creep is this?"

Tony shrugs. "We went back to reading *The Whole Earth Catalog*."

The *Whole Earth Catalog* was the Home Shopping Club for the hip. "We didn't sell anything, though," says founder Stewart Brand, who was a frequent guest at Zen Center and a member of the Outside Financial Advisory Board in the 1970s. "We pointed." The *Whole Earth Catalog* was where you went to find out where you could find a yurt or the blueprints for a build-your-own geodesic dome, durable overalls and undyed cotton bedding, the best rolling papers and a field guide to mushrooms. It was also a *Reader's Digest* for the Left and those out in left field, with testimonials from early ecotourists passing through Nepal and Guatemala, debates among eminent scientists and economists about water-management strategies or defense-related scientific research, and recipes for making meals of roadkill. And it was a forum for readers, who could speak to like-minded people across the country by writing to the editor and publisher, Stewart Brand, who was the webmaster of this ink-and-paper Internet.

In the *Whole Earth Catalog*, Darlene and Tony came across a letter to Stewart from Peter Schneider, then President of Zen Center. "It was about ecology, really," says Darlene. "Peter described the ecology of the ory-oki meal. We were sitting in Cambridge, and Tony said, 'Let's go to Zen Center.'"

They had sat zazen once, for half an hour. "We wrote to Peter Schnei-der," says Tony, "and he wrote back—a handwritten letter. That's why, in December of 1970, we came here, right here to this corner. Darlene walked right in. It was a Friday night."

The first time Darlene walked into City Center, she asked the first person she saw if there was anything going on. "The woman at the desk said there was nothing but a five-day sesshin, and when I looked interested, she looked a little worried and told me to talk to Reb, who was the *Ino*, director of the meditation hall. Reb asked if we had any experience sitting, and I said, No, and Reb said, Okay. Our VW bus was parked right out here, at Page and Laguna, in front of what would be the Zen Center Green Gro-cers. Then, though, it was a tiny little tiny store with a vicious German shepherd out front. A little Asian woman ran it. Her husband had been killed by robbers. She had shot three robbers. This was a tough neighbor-hood. Bullets flew.

"We went to the first night introductory meeting, looked at the sched-ule on the bulletin board, and it said zazen, zazen, zazen, zazen, zazen, zazen all the way from four in the morning until nine at night. I started having second thoughts. Tony said, 'Oh, my god,' and I said, 'Look, there's this other thing in between. It says *kinhin*. It won't be so bad.' I didn't know what kinhin was, but I was convinced it was rest periods."

Kinhin is standing-up zazen; you move at the rate of one half-step every eight or ten seconds.

"We had one sitting before we went to bed. It was forty minutes. And I thought I was going to die," remembers Darlene. "Here I was looking at five solid days as we went and got into our bus. We woke up at three-thirty, and I cried my way through that day. At some point—was there a work period, maybe?—I skipped out and went to the bus to lie down, aching everywhere and bored out of my mind. Tony came, too. I said, 'I can't do this. I have to leave.' To his credit, Tony said, 'Ever since I've known you, you've complained that you can't make a go of life, that you suffer existentially. Here's your chance to suffer physically. And all you have to do is sit there.' And I thought, Oh shit. It was true. I complained constantly that I could never engage myself. So on Sunday, I went back and cried through the rest of the day. But the real heartbreak came after the three morning periods. I don't even remember how I got through them. I guess it was just the thought that I would be able to stand, walk upstairs, and sit down and eat breakfast. And finally the third painful period was over, and the bell rang—Breakfast! At last! I walked toward the stairs, and much to my horror I saw people taking trays. A bunch of us didn't get bowls—we weren't regulars, so we wouldn't be having oryoki, but we were heading right back into the zendo. I took that tray and cried and cried and cried. I remember the two women across from me; they were looking at me with such pity that they could hardly eat. And then it was back to the bus."

This was practice. Day after day. And when the weeklong sesshin was done, the normal schedule resumed: Everyone sat for two hours in the morning and two more in the evening, and if you were working in the building, you attended a midday sitting and service. And if you weren't working in the building, you often had to figure out how to get someone to cover for you at your job—or you just quit your job—so you could sit the daylong and weeklong sesshins and go to Tassajara for three months.

"The six-dollars-a-night guest fee was beyond us," says Tony. "We had to sleep in the VW. Sunday night, as I was getting in the bus, two black teenagers stopped, and one of them pointed a gun at me. He said, 'Give me your money.' And I guess because I'd spent fifteen hours sitting in total pain, everything was happening in a kind of slow motion. I said, 'Okay. I'll give you my money, but I want to keep my driver's license.' I had fifteen dollars. I had a couple of money orders, too, but I figured that wasn't real money. As he turned to walk away, I put my hands in my pockets, and I felt a quarter, so I said, 'Hey!' He turned around, and I flipped it at him and said, 'You didn't get it all.'"

"He caught it," Darlene says, and suddenly she turns my way, looking a little skeptical, as if to say, Are you catching this?

Tony says, "He didn't quite know what my attitude was—and I didn't either. Was I insulting him? Being generous? Or completing a transaction? I could see this going through his head."

Darlene says, "I did hope the kid wouldn't kill Tony."

"He slipped the quarter into his pocket and walked off."

"The next morning, I went to tell Reb," says Darlene, laughing, "and I was trying to tell him from the point of view of what sitting had done for us, and he wasn't interested in that, he just wanted us to get into the zendo and sit down. So we went in and sat down. But, that night, they did let us stay inside. They let us stay inside for free for the rest of the time."

And people kept coming. Word was out. In 1970, *Zen Mind, Beginner's Mind,* Suzuki-roshi's edited lectures, became Weatherhill's best-selling title; in 1971, Ed's *Tassajara Bread Book* appeared, and two years later 150,000 copies had been sold. Tassajara and Zen Center had been featured in underground and national newspapers and magazines, including *Time* magazine. By 1971, thousands of people had spent a few summer days or weeks at the hot springs resort, getting a taste of Zen life and Ed's bread.

And Suzuki-roshi was so sick he often could not stand. He leaned on Yvonne, his longtime assistant, who was with him almost daily, and he leaned on his wife, and he leaned on all of his senior students. The care and comfort of Suzuki-roshi became the foremost concern and the principal practice for most of Zen Center's ordained priests. And they wondered what was about to happen to them.

"When Suzuki-roshi was dying, I was seriously examining the possibility of leaving," says Dan Welch. "I was committed to practice, and I didn't know whether I could take [Richard] Baker on as my teacher. I needed someone older, wiser. He is only five years older than I am. Could I take him on unconditionally? It was a watershed for all of us. Once Richard took over, if you stayed on, you were practicing with him. I should say, with *HIM!* But just as I opened the door to see what else might be out there for me, Suzuki-roshi nailed my foot to the floor. My parents were visiting just before he died, and he invited the three of us up to his room. And he took the opportunity to announce to my parents that I was staying on at Zen Center to help Dick be the Abbot. It was news to me," says Dan, "but it didn't shock me. *Help Dick be the Abbot.* What a perfectly undefined, undefinable role. Just the sort of job that might make me stay."

"I have no idea of coming back to Zen Center as Chief Priest," Richard wrote from Japan in response to questions from the Board early in 1971. He thought it would take time for him and for Zen Center to figure out if that "makes sense, feels right, and is natural." He seemed to be wearing his new Transmission status very lightly. The Board asked him to identify and recruit Japanese priests who could be invited to America to help Suzuki-roshi, but Richard shrugged off that authority. "I no longer know enough about Zen Center to play the role of inviter or recommender," he wrote. "Perhaps my practice isn't the same as Zen Center." In Japan, he had acquired the habit of wearing Rinzai robes to express his antisectarian posture. "I just want to continue practicing Buddhism in a way that seems authentic to me."

A few months later, Richard was the Abbot, and a few weeks after that, in December of 1971, Suzuki-roshi was dead.

In March of 1972, Richard pressed his colleagues to purchase Green Gulch Farm from George Wheelwright for $325,000, which he estimated as "about one-fifth its value" and "basically a gift." Richard was always generous in his estimation of the value of property and donations he received on Zen Center's behalf. There were a couple of big useful buildings on the farm that could serve as dormitories, as well as a barn and a trailer, and there was a house for the Abbot and his family.

Did the purchase make sense? Did it feel right? Was it natural? Since he'd returned from Japan, Richard wasn't asking these questions aloud.

"This is how Zen Center became, irreversibly, a residential community. Dick put the deal together and pushed it through, over my objections," says Lew Richmond, who was Treasurer at the time.

Five students moved up to Green Gulch almost immediately, and within a year, twenty-five to thirty Zen students were living on the farm, nineteen miles north of City Center. Richard invited Alan Chadwick, the eminent organic gardener, to design and install the initial plantings. Chadwick had been working with Richard's friend Paul Lee at the University of California at Santa Cruz. He also set up a chicken coop, and submitted a projected first-year materials budget to Lew for $10,000. Chadwick also mentioned that Zen Center would soon have to purchase a tractor or a team of horses and a plough.

According to Richard's estimate, in his first few months, Chadwick transplanted "$100,000 to $200,000" worth of garden stock and seed from his university gardens—which is a grand gesture, 100 or 200 times over. This is a signal estimate; scrutiny of this detail does not yield certainty. Was it leastways accurate as an estimate of the value of those plants and seeds? This is unclear. Richard and his financial staff put this generous estimate on the record in a big way; it was printed in *Wind Bell* articles, letters to donors, and the *Congressional Record*.

Wide-ranging estimates typically make the lower figure look reasonable. Why does it matter what Richard said the seeds were worth? He was not taking the credit. He credited Alan Chadwick. And Chadwick was a friend and colleague of Paul Lee, Richard's friend at UC Santa Cruz. As Richard explains, he had made and maintained many friendships. Some of his friends became famous or powerful. Moreover, as Suzuki-roshi's successor, he'd been welcomed into a lot of fine homes, where he forged more friendships. It is hard to fault him for bringing Zen Center to the attention of his friends, new and old. These were people with money and influence to spare. And Richard was consistently generous in his public thanks to contributors. So, when practitioners began to begrudge him an antique brocade robe, or dinners prepared and served in silence for him and his guests, or etched-glass doors in his city residence, or a BMW, they sounded like ingrates. After all, even the price of that damn car was a quarter—maybe an eighth—of the value of just the initial planting done at Green Gulch during his first few months as Abbot.

The purchase of Green Gulch also made Zen Center a partner with the Nature Conservancy, which had received hundreds of adjoining acres from Wheelwright and was patching them together with other land, which was to become the Golden Gate National Recreation Area. In his testimony before a U.S. Senate subcommittee in September of 1972, Richard explained that "Zen Center was the only organization that [the

Nature Conservancy] could locate that had the organizational stability and ecological responsibility and the extensive financial and manpower resources necessary to maintain the [115-acre farm] valley." It was made true by assertion. There was some supporting evidence: Zen Center was so stable that the eminent Alan Chadwick had invested $100,000 to $200,000 of his personal seed and stock in their land.

Lew says, "You might call the whole thing a rapidly created creative alternative economic structure. It was sold to donors and students as beneficial. And it was fun for a lot of people, and I think they genuinely experienced it as beneficial, but it was designed and carried out principally for the benefit of one person."

"Maybe there are many ways of saying this," says Dan. "Dick was not around during the last years of Suzuki-roshi's life in a day-to-day way, as others of us had the great fortune to be. Our approach to taking care was markedly different than how Dick took Zen Center under his wing when he came back from Japan."

Steve Allen arrived at Zen Center in 1971 and sat one sesshin with Suzuki-roshi. "Then Richard took over. Many of the people who came just after I did and during the next two or three years had read *Zen Mind, Beginner's Mind* and didn't know Suzuki-roshi was dead until they showed up. We heard stories about a few of the original students—the old guard—but they had been cleared out," remembers Steve. "The seventy or eighty people who arrived just after Suzuki-roshi died are the people who made Zen Center. We bonded pretty easily and immediately with Richard. He was the dharma heir. We were fascinated by him, and there was a tremendous amount of energy around him. There may have been bad feelings and consternation among the senior students, but nobody who walked into City Center off the street in the early seventies was confused about who was running the place. Everyone understood. And if you stayed, it was clear what that meant—you were prepared to follow Richard."

Linda Cutts was in that cohort. After she returned from studying abroad in Italy and finished her degree at Berkeley, she became one of the first five students to move to the farm. Her future husband, Steve Weintraub, was the director. "At that time," says Linda, "I felt I was living at the cutting edge of the world, both because of the meditation and being at the forefront of everything new—organic gardening, self-sustaining agriculture, community life, and simplified living. Everything I cared about was being realized here." She sounds a little breathless, and a little giddy, like a much younger Linda might have sounded. "We had these little stipends, and maybe it was all just an invention or a dream, but I felt fabulous, and alive. I remember the first summer very well. On Sundays people would come from City Center, and one woman came into the kitchen with her arms full of irises she'd found, and she was smiling, as if to say, Is this heaven or what? I could tell Richard Baker was an unusual person. I remember working in the kitchen one day, and Richard came in with Ram Dass. Both of them had their shirts off, and they had beads on, and it just felt like anybody who was anything in that world was part of Zen Center. And Richard would often say to us that each student had very little, but all of the students partake of this much larger thing, and they could never have it on their own."

Steve Allen became the Treasurer in the midst of the Apocalypse. "I was looking over expenses through the years. I remembered then that Richard's rationale for Green Gulch had been that people needed a place to stay after Tassajara. You entered through Page Street, made it to Tassajara, and went to start a family at Green Gulch. That was the idea. But [the farm] became largely a place for people who wanted to stay in the community and didn't want to work. It developed, but it turned out that farming takes a lot of time. And a lot of people don't want to be farmers. From 1972 through 1982, we poured a million dollars into Green Gulch for housing and another million dollars to support the people there—just to keep it open. So, in 1976 and 1977, when people in the city found themselves working [long] shifts in the new Zen Center businesses, there was a lot of resentment. They felt they were giving up their practice to support a few people who liked life on a farm."

"It reflects Dick's personality," says Dan. "He is big—very big and very generous. In his mind, If you can think it, you can do it. If there's a $25,000-dollar Buddha—no problem. Dot, dot, dot. I knew Suzuki-roshi wanted Green Gulch. We had talked about it while Dick was in Japan.

Householder practice. The notion was not unique to Dick, but he made it his own. He conceived of this multimillion-dollar enterprise, which was really a developer's plan for the place, not a practice plan." It was evident to several people on the Board that the scale of Green Gulch, and the elaborateness of the plan for developing organic growing gardens, orchards, henhouses, and a residential practice temple—not to mention planting and maintaining green space and monitoring the watershed on behalf of the Nature Conservancy—would require "massive fund-raising for the foreseeable future and beyond." It was, in effect, the antithesis of the modest, self-sustaining, help-your-neighbor, take-time-daily-to-meditate idea of householder practice. Dan shrugs. "Richard was willing to go to Congress to petition the Federal Government to make it happen in this really big way. He threatened to resign as Abbot if the Board would not support it. My reservations were met head on repeatedly. Every time I had a question about scale and speed, he had overwhelmingly energetic, creative, worked-out responses. He had a greater vision and a greater hubris than the rest of us. If Zen Center was ever a great place, it was due to his vision that it could be. If it was crushed by its own weight, it was in many ways his fault."

We are still sitting on a couple of rocks on the side of Crestone Mountain, tipped toward that vast valley on a summer afternoon in 1999. Dan has brought me to Crestone Mountain Zen Center. Richard is in Germany, where he has another Zen Center; I won't meet him until February of the following year, when I will drive through a blinding snowstorm and Richard will talk to me about radar.

Sitting with Dan on the side of the mountain, I can't understand what has brought Dan here. He is looking a little too lean and a little too tired, as if he could use another tuna sandwich and a nap. Other than that, it's hard to see what Dan wants or needs, or how Richard figures in his future.

"Richard had inherited something that wasn't perfectly pieced together," says Dan.

It still needs mending.

"Wonderful things were going on at Zen Center, though. It is easy to overlook that now." Dan is smiling, but his eyes are closed. "What did we really have? We had the transmitted dharma. In the hands of Suzuki-roshi, it was an exquisite dynamic, a powerful teaching, a relevant mystery." He sits up and turns to me. He's holding out his hands, palms up. He looks gleeful, as if he might say something funny. "In our hands—and it was in *our* hands—it became a bludgeon of power, a source of competition, jealousy, and paranoia. That's what we made of it." He turns away, puts his elbows on his knees, and leans hard into the hill, like a big bird pressing toward takeoff. "The one thing that seemed unquestionable was Richard's Transmission. Even when we finally started to talk about everything in 1983, we could not talk about it. Ultimately, I could not accept that." He looks my way again. Very, very slowly, Dan says, "In this domain, our expectations and our reverence for Transmission had survived our experience of it. And I didn't have the skill to say, Let's look at that. I didn't make it happen. And that's how I left it in 1984."

Sometimes there is no sound on Crestone Mountain; whoever is running the show just turns the volume down. It is time out of time until an animal has to conduct some business in a nearby bush, and the audio portion of the program is restored. It might be a rattlesnake or a bobcat, but usually it is a chipmunk, as it is this day with Dan. We sit up. We watch a chipmunk do something very quickly, something we don't understand, and then it runs away.

"We had a farm," says Dan, "but in the true sense of nourishment, it was not working."

20.

"I WAS WRITING ALL THE time, of course," says poet Philip Whalen. He was forty-nine when he moved into City Center. "I'd known Richard for a long while." Philip was an established poet before Richard moved to the Bay Area, and he had a long history with Buddhism. He turns up as Warren Coughlin in Kerouac's *Dharma Bums*. Philip also was one of the six poets at the landmark Six Gallery reading in San Francisco, along with his old friend Gary Snyder, Michael McClure, Philip Lamantia (who read work by the late John Hoffman), and Allen Ginsberg, who read *Howl* for the first time on that night in October 1955. Ferlinghetti was in the audience and asked for a copy of Ginsberg's manuscript, which his City Lights bookstore press published the next year.

Whalen lived for a long time in Japan, and overlapped with Richard in the late sixties. "But it was New Year's Day, 1972, when Richard and Ginny came to Bolinas [north of San Francisco] to see somebody," says Philip. "Everybody was living there, and I'd been to too many parties." Richard was talking about his new position at Zen Center, and Philip asked a lot of questions. Richard said, "Call Yvonne," and Philip did, and he went to take a look at the Page Street building, and when he asked Richard when he could move in, Richard said, "Anytime." And Philip moved in. "Baker said, 'Attend zazen, take your meals in the dining room, and do a daily chore.' I found myself living in a terribly clean place with a lot of people who looked very serene. It was a good situation. Everyone had just finished a sesshin, and they were quite enlightened. After a few days, somebody did let me know there was a waiting list of people to get into the building. It was an embarrassment to find out that I'd leapfrogged in."

Philip is a big, square, stone statue of a man. He wears his embarrassment lightly. "By the fall, I was offered lay ordination, and when I asked about going to Tassajara, Richard said, 'There's a truck leaving tomorrow morning.' Again, I was catapulted to the head of the line. After three weeks at Tassajara, Richard asked how I was doing, and I told him I felt overtrained already—it was not unlike the army, and I'd done two years of that already. But over the next ten years, I did ten practice periods and one summer at Tassajara. In classical form, I had my one thousand days in the monastery." And he continued to live at City Center.

This man just made sense to Richard. "Philip Whalen didn't want any success," says Richard. "He didn't want a second home. He didn't care about how much money he had."

Philip had a life as a poet and scholar ("I've always had a feeling for the Chinese roots of Zen," he says), and he was "at least twenty years older than almost everybody else in the building," he remembers. "I didn't ask why Richard was the head of the place. It was simple. It was his. The old man had handed it to him. I didn't expect anything of him. Baker couldn't disappoint me. He had it from Suzuki-roshi. Isn't that why he and I were both there?"

Jane Hirshfield lived at Zen Center from 1974 until 1982. These days, she teaches a poetry course at Tassajara every summer. When she sits zazen, she sits by herself. And she sits on the Lindisfarne Board with Richard and others whom William Thompson has encouraged and supported. ("Lindisfarne gave Crestone to Dick because it was too hard to get to and no one wanted to go there for meetings and conferences," says Philip. "Lindisfarne itself is interesting, and I don't really know what it does. My first impression was that they are crypto-Christian mystics. Some of their stuff about civilization sounds like those crazy theories Yeats started to spin out about gyres and history. But the Lindisfarne fellows are all very learned and charming, and they think about big things.")

Jane wandered up to Tassajara soon after graduating from college and she stayed for three years, "My one thousand days in the monastery," she says. "People complained that it was a patriarchy. Well, of course it was. I was there because I wanted a discipline imposed on me. That was the point of joining an ancient, formal practice. After that, I moved to Green Gulch, worked like everyone else, and eventually, gradually, it was time to leave." It was time to write.

"The people who were most successful at Zen Center had their craft or art and didn't lose touch with it," says Deborah Madison, the founding chef of Greens restaurant who practiced at Zen Center from 1967 until 1984. "Jane has a deep Buddhism and a deep talent. She was devoted, but she did not give herself over. She didn't have to; she knew how to give herself to her poems."

Jane's admission to Tassajara without prior practice was unusual. "Later, I was told I came in as a poet," she says. It was an unofficial but real status at Zen Center. There was always room for the people Richard admired—for a week in summer or a couple of years in the community. "In three years at Tassajara, I wrote one haiku. We were told to do nothing but practice, and I did," says Jane. "It was long after that, at a Lindisfarne meeting, that [Richard] Baker-roshi came up to me, very perturbed, and said, 'I never said stop writing. I meant stop until it comes back organically.' He loves poetry," says Jane, "and I did start to write again in 1979—organically, I guess." Jane lived at Green Gulch until 1982, "rotating through jobs, and writing. I loved sitting, and I loved Baker-roshi's lectures, but I was not one of his closest students. And I never gave him authority over my life. I was mostly just aware of the privilege of being given a place to stay. In 1980, I was also given permission to go to a workshop at Berkeley Extension and—even better—I was allowed to sleep in the next morning. And that led me to participate in the Poetry in the Schools program, which led me back to lay life. I went to have a conversation with Baker-roshi before I left, and he looked quite startled. He said, 'You'll be back.'" Jane is silent for several seconds. "What I love about the Zen tradition is that the idea of leaving is built in. You have an intensive monastic experience, and you take it with you. You really don't have to feel like a failure when you leave."

"My conception of Zen Center worked for artists," says Richard. And it's true; it did work for some artists for some time. "The same for Isaan Tommy Dorsey. Tommy and Philip and I, we had complete understanding, and for us, [it's] almost [as if] the mess didn't happen."

Issan is the ordination name of Tommy Dorsey, a singular figure at Zen

Center, in San Francisco, in the AIDS hospice movement, and in the development of the American ideal of engaged Buddhism. He was a drag queen and a junkie who turned up at Zen Center just before Suzuki-roshi died, and he flourished as a man and as a teacher with Richard's attention and support. (He is memorialized in *Street Zen*, David Schneider's intimate portrait of Issan's life and work.) Until 1979, Issan was moved through the standard rotation of practice and administrative roles along with his colleagues, who speak about him with genuine joy and love as a "funny," "generous," "witty," "bitchy," "self-mocking," "ironic," "dismissive," "comforting," "compelling," and "increasingly serene" man. Richard saw Issan as an artist. Issan was a genuine original, a marvelous and surprising and complicated creation, and that got Richard's attention. And won his heart.

"Issan and I got a feeling way before AIDS was known that something was going on," remembers Richard. "The whole back alley behind us [at City Center] was mostly gay people, and people would get the flu and die [in those houses and apartments]. Without explanation. We realized something was happening in the homosexual community that was horrible. I'm not saying we were the first, but we were sitting here in the gay community knowing something was going on."

Issan also had a lot of friends, junkies and drag queens among them, and late-night visitors who made people at City Center nervous, according to a student who developed a close friendship with Issan. "There was a fearful sense about the neighborhood already, and Issan was not separate from that. And it was disturbing when he took in a lover who was clearly not healthy in any way. There was some residue from his drug days in his manner. Those chemicals had their effect. And here's what strikes me now—there was a denial at that moment in the gay community that was just like the denial inside Zen Center itself about what was wrong." He pauses. "All of this was true, so people often were astonished when [Issan] spoke or did something, and they realized that he was clearly wise."

Issan moved, and was eventually joined by Philip Whalen; in a small house in the Castro district, Issan opened the independent Hartford Street Zen Center, where Philip succeeded him as Abbot. Richard encouraged and nurtured the project, which was a singular example of senior priests doing what senior priests are supposed to do—start their own temples. In 1981, Issan officially launched his Maitri (Sanskrit for *compassionate care*) Hospice in the house next door to his Zen Center. His small-scale, hands-on, in-this-home-you-are-at-home work with the dying was subsumed into the independently funded (and licensed) Maitri hospice project in 1987.

"A lot of people at the Hartford Street center were put off by Issan turning a meditation center into a hospice," says the man who built the altar for Issan's zendo. "It was something Richard absolutely admired." It was socially engaged Buddhism, and it represents a profound and problematic divide in the minds of many practitioners.

Longtime Berkeley Abbot Mel Weitsman says, "Our purpose is to introduce people to Buddhism and to give them a place to practice. Those are great accomplishments. Social outreach is important, but it has to be secondary. If everybody goes to work in a hospice or a hospital, they will be doing good work, but we will lose the practice. It is unique. The practice. It is important to maintain it. That's why we have priests and dharma Transmission—that's what the culture can't provide. That's our offering."

"Issan was not a Zen practitioner, per se," says Willem Malten. "He was a devotee of Bhakti [the theistic Hindu devotional tradition whose practices are based in the Bhagavad Gita]. I was too limited—by my own limits and by the Japanese and Zen traditions—to understand what he was talking about at the time. Issan was not interested in the castle. I was. And he was steadfast in his lovingness for Richard, though he could see all of his flaws. When I complained to him, he'd always say, 'Something will come up. Something will come up.' Now, I really admire his steadfastness."

In 1987, Richard gave both Philip Whalen and Issan dharma Transmission. In November of 1989, he officially installed Issan as Abbot of Hartford Street Zen Center. Issan was fifty-six years old. In photographs, he looks as skinny, and weak, and old as Suzuki-roshi appeared at Richard's installation ceremony. Issan was HIV positive and nearly dead.

"It was one of Richard's best deeds," says Willem. "I admire Richard's ability to recognize Issan for who he was and the teaching he had. And whatever Issan's practice had become, Richard wanted him to have power as a Transmitted teacher. It was what Issan wanted, too." And just before he died, Issan also wanted to spend a week at a crazy, fancy, gay resort in Palm Springs, remembers Willem. "So I went with him. It was ridiculous—manicured lawns and pool boys in the middle of the desert. We had fun. And we went to see his old friend Ann. She'd run the strip club where Issan had danced. Ann was living in a trailer park. Issan lived and soon died [in September of 1990] in a house in a neighborhood he loved with people who loved him."

Several people repeated Issan's last words to Richard. "He looked up at everyone and said, 'Is someone dying around here?'" Richard smiles.

Issan was extraordinary. And exceptional. And Richard acknowledged him.

"The thing is," says Steve Weintraub, who is married to Abbess Linda Cutts, "a lot of people are not artists. Zen is about human life. Human life is about a bunch of jerks—namely, us—running around, and then we keel over. All of us. That is the practice—to understand that this is just human life. Everybody included." In 1973, Steve was ordained by Richard, and after 1983 Steve went back to school. Now, he practices as a psychotherapist. He is not a poet. "Another way to think about it is wisdom and skillful means." Steve is a thin, fair-haired man, and when he blushes, even his hands go red. "Want to hear my poem? It's a very short poem. I'll tell you my poem." His fingertips are crimson by the time he begins. "Wisdom ain't worth a hill of beans unless you've got skillful means." He nods. "That's it. That's the history of Zen Center. It doesn't really mean anything that Richard was brilliant or that he recognized that a couple of other people were, too. It doesn't mean anything unless you develop the skillful means to translate that into ordinary people's ordinary lives."

Richard admires extraordinary things: paintings by Edward Avedisian (an artist whose work Richard collected and championed until their friendship broke up) and Mayumi Oda (whose giant painting of a White Tara devotional figure hangs in the dining room at Crestone); the poems of Gary Snyder and Philip Whalen; a Gandharan Buddha; and a beautiful breakfront (like the one he bought for the Guest House for $2,500 in

1982; Zen Center had just launched a $2 million capital campaign, principally to eliminate its accumulated debts, which totaled $1.3 million). He has developed and refined a remarkable aesthetic sensibility. It is admirable, and it is deeply personal. "I find something like this"—Richard points to a little burnished cabinet of rich, rosy wood exquisitely disfigured by a painterly swirl of blackness—"which is persimmon wood," he says, entirely without pretense or even a hint of pontification in his voice, "with the wood itself forming that brushstroke, meaning *ichi*—one," he explains. "I mean, I couldn't afford it. It's Korean. I saw it in New York. But, I mean, I dream about it for the next year or so—and I wake up anxious: *Someone's bought it.* So I go back and talk the guy into letting me have it, and I get him involved, and I show him pictures of this place [Crestone], and I tell him it's not going to be in a fancy New York apartment"—it's going to be in a fancy Japanese temple with mud-plaster walls on a 14,000-foot-high mountain in Colorado—"it's going to be in a meditation center. He's actually supplied us with a lot of things—that bell, the Chinese scholar's desk on the other side." We get up to look at the desk, and rub the bell, and hold some tea bowls so fragile, they could break your heart and probably your bank if you broke one, and yet Richard wants you to handle them, to touch the persimmon wood, feel the difference in the lip of this ceramic cup (a little thick; not so good) and this one (perfect; porcelain thinned to a mother-of-pearl moment). Somewhere between the bell and a bowl, he hands me another priceless piece of pottery to sweat into, and he is saying something about how much he paid for the persimmon-wood chest, something about $2,500 and half of that but easily four times more, and I really don't remember if it cost $10 or $200,000, and "Have you ever seen one of these?" I don't even have to look; I know I have never seen one of those, whatever it is, though it is immediately apparent when I do look at it that it is one of the most beautiful ones of those anyone will ever see.

Holy shit. This guy has really good stuff.

"I love that brushstroke," he says of the cabinet when we are seated again. "When people take care with the physical objects in the world, it is wonderful."

It is wonderful. It is wonderful to listen to Richard talk about provenance, and the relationship among utilitarian, ritual, and aesthetic creations, and maybe a line from a poem by Ezra Pound that comes suddenly, inexplicably to his mind. It is a wonderful way to talk about things. And when he talked about Zen Center this way, it sounded wonderful. Michael Murphy was not alone in his admiration for *it*. "Like the Greeks had *it*," Michael says. "Zen Center was telling a round truth—wonderful lectures, the ancient practice, the aesthetics, and the social activism. It was one of the great achievements of the time, and it was tragic that it imploded."

But it was not Zen Center's story. It was not a round truth emerging from a chorus. There were hundreds of unheard voices, hundreds of craftsmen and cooks and seamstresses and servants whose names went unspoken, whose work was not acknowledged, whose tastes were not represented. A single narrative line emerged from Zen Center once Richard became the Abbot; a particular and particularly pointed point of view; a bristle-splitting sensibility; an exquisitely refined aesthetic that was razor sharp in its discriminations. It was almost Japanese in its precision and elegance. And it seemed to be antithetical to the efforts of people who were attempting to sit and practice outside of the dualistic framework of judgment and discrimination.

"It was a little scary sometimes," says Ed Brown. "Dick actually didn't know it was all just a matter of taste. He did not know how to include other people's aesthetics because he thought there was only one aesthetic, one standard. For everything. I mean, I seriously wondered, Does this guy know the difference between a person and a painting?"

"By that late seventies, there started to be little acts of rebellion," says Darlene Cohen. "There was a huge painting by one of his coddled artists that no one else liked. And someone hung a gigantic drape over it in the middle of the night, so when we got up the next day, it was covered, and he demanded to know—like a proper schoolteacher—who had done this terrible thing. Nobody revealed the culprits. It was one of the first times he just had to eat it."

In the midst of a 1977 forest fire that threatened to burn Tassajara, Karin Gjording was helping to organize the rescue effort from the Jamesburg house, which Zen Center had purchased in 1973 as a kind of gatehouse, where visitors could park their cars and be shuttled up the long dirt road to Tassajara. "Issan was in charge of Jamesburg at that time," says Karin. "He lived there. He was a heart person. He could be who he was with anybody." Karin is a cool, slim woman with shoulder-length silver hair. Her angular features and her poise are overlaid with an emotional reserve that initially registers as either aristocratic or corporate, but she says it's just Scandinavian. After a while, you realize it's just grace. "The nearest neighbors were rednecks and ranchers. At one point in the chaos, a seventy-year-old rancher called—his name was Lambert. He asked if we had any doctors, and I called out, and nobody said anything. Finally, Issan said, 'What does he want?' The rancher said, 'My wife needs an insulin injection and I can't get her out to the doctor.' And I told Issan. And he shrugged and said, 'Tell him I'll be right down. I used to shoot heroin.' And the rancher said, 'Great.' And Issan went down and gave her the shot." Karin's smile comes slowly, then she says, "Issan was amazing." Her smile widens, and she almost laughs, but instead she shakes her head and says, "And, you know, so was Lambert."

21.

IF YOU PICK UP A SPECK OF DUST, you pick up all the suffering in the world. If you pick up more than a hundred acres of deep-soil farmland, what do you expect?

In 1973, Zen Center's cash budget was $344,000; its receipts were $281,000. And it owed an additional $66,000 in mortgage and loan payments. The operation was about $125,000 short. Three solutions were proposed: cut expenses; generate more income; establish a property fund.

Zen Center did not manage to cut expenses, which rose steadily by about $150,000 every year until they topped $1 million in 1978. Then they really took off. By 1981, Zen Center expenses were nearly $3.5 million, and before Richard left in 1983, budget projections for the year ahead were above $4.5 million.

Zen Center did not establish an enduring endowment until the late 1990s, and although several attempts were made to establish a building fund, and individual construction projects at Green Gulch and Tassajara were designated in fund-raising and donor appeals, by the mid-seventies the real property fund was Zen Center's complicated mortgage- and debt-financing arrangements, which generated cash, if not balanced cash budgets.

From 1973 until 1983, however, Zen Center did generate income. The community launched and staffed several businesses, several of which garnered citywide followings and national attention. "Obviously, Richard had a stunningly creative entrepreneurial side," says Gib Robinson. "In many important ways, it really worked for the organization. He recognized people of exceptional skill—Paul as a carpenter and builder; Karin as a manager; Deborah as a cook—and made inspired matches of those people with difficult and innovative assignments." Today, Zen Center is almost entirely out of the business of business; indeed, most of its businesses closed or were sold off soon after Richard took a walk.

Twenty-five years after the first of these modest-profit, mindfully managed outlets for quality goods and services opened, the Officers and Directors of Zen Center met at Green Gulch Farm to discuss the budget. What was the enduring legacy of the labors of the seventies and early eighties? The budget was balanced in 1997, but it really was not. Zen Center was $100,000 short of funds for approved financial expenditures. The community still held a lot of real estate, but as then-Abbot Norman said, "We have no reserves to fix the roof. This operation is not sustainable for the next twenty-five years without an endowment." They decided to launch a property endowment fund. The other solutions directly echo the solutions proposed in 1973: Reduce the number of staff positions; cut salaries (actually, in 1973, they were cutting stipends, not salaries); extend the time period before students get the benefits of membership; isn't there something we own that we can sell?; publish more books; increase fees for services (sesshins, workshops, conferences); and "make Green Gulch more cost-effective."

Before he bought Green Gulch, Richard had been offered eighty acres of property about fifty miles north of the city by Sterling Bunnell, an influential psychologist and ecologist who had long been a patron of Zen Center. The land was too far away to serve Richard's plan. He asked Bunnell to talk to Bill Kwong. "I wasn't sure," says Bill. Bill had his doubts about Richard's motives, and he still believed he was owed Transmission. While Bill was making up his mind, the price escalated from $100,000 to $170,000. In 1973, it was more than Bill thought he could afford, but it was clear that he could not pass it up. "It's priceless, this place. I understand that now," says Bill, sitting in his own zendo on a height of land fifty miles away from Zen Center.

In 1972, Zen Center had a reliable full-time population of approximately 150 adults, but month to month they were not the same people. The organization could no longer expect to operate without a sizable and stable cohort of experienced, committed leaders. In addition to duties as Board members and officers, the senior members were rotating through full-time management roles every three months. Each of the three Zen Center locations needed six to ten full-time administrative and practice leaders — a head cook, a head of the meditation hall, a head of operations, and, at Tassajara, a head monk for two three-month practice periods each year.

In 1973, Richard ordained eight new priests. Before he left in 1983, he'd ordained more than sixty people, sometimes in batches of a dozen or more. In 1974, he performed the first of many lay ordination ceremonies; he gave Buddhist names and the Precepts to fifty-three practitioners in a single day. He immediately began to shrug off duties and chores and responsibilities, which were obviously too many for one man to handle, but he did not shrug off any authority. Richard was and remained the only teacher for all of the new practitioners, the lay-ordained, and the ordained priests at Zen Center. He gave almost all of the lectures at all three temples. He alone conducted private interviews, or dokusans, with each student. "When I left [in 1983], there were four hundred dokusan students," remembers Richard. "It didn't seem crazy; it was just normal to me," he says. "I felt a real connection with each person."

A long pause; in fact, a day passes. Richard says, "If you think about it, it was just crazy. There were twelve thousand people on our mailing list in the Bay Area alone. Three to four hundred at every Sunday lecture [at Green Gulch]. A waiting list of three times sixty-five [available spots] to get into Tassajara. I just wanted to make it possible for everybody to practice. If I had stopped and said, *These are my students; these are my disciples,* I would have had to think about it differently. They thought of themselves as my students. I thought of them as Zen Center students. And it was a kind of modesty, but it also deflected my responsibility."

A long pause. Another day passes. Richard says, "Sometimes I would do dokusan for eighteen hours." Students typically can request an interview with a master when he is planning to offer private interviews, or they might be told to show up. "Early in the morning I would start, and I'd see one person after another. They were all lined up in the hall, and I would just sit there. Finish at seven in the evening." His tone darkens, "They say I never did it. In fact, I did far more dokusan than Suzuki-roshi ever did. I saw an individual student far more than Suzuki-roshi saw an individual student, and I, of course, saw more students. You were lucky to see Suzuki-roshi for dokusan [during] a sesshin, and to see him for dokusan outside of a sesshin was totally rare. I did dokusan once a week at Zen Center."

In the memories of Richard's students, until 1978 it was not the infrequency of one-on-one interviews that was surprising. It was the fact that the spiritual guidance often turned intimate, and was broadcast on public frequencies. "It's remarkable," says John Bailes, who took a ten-year leave of absence from Harvard to study at Zen Center in 1972. "You went through Dick Baker for your personal shit in dokusan, and then he would regurgitate it back to the Board and management people. So my relationship with management people—well, I didn't trust them. I was there to hang out with a Zen master. When you're a kid—and everybody there was basically a kid—you tend not to share too much with your peers. You're vulnerable. So I learned not to reveal myself to Dick. Not revealing myself—I guess you can call that my enlightenment experience."

"That's absolutely accurate," says Yvonne Rand. "After the explosion in 1983, people came from Japan and tried to tell us that if we were unhappy with the teacher, we should leave, and the teacher should stay. They told us that part of the problem was that we didn't know what to talk about and what not to talk about. And I think that's true. But Dick wanted to know everything. He insisted that before you made any type of life decision, you had to talk to him first. When I started working with a therapist [in the late 1970s], a therapist he knew and had recommended, Dick said to me, 'Don't talk to him about the relationship between you and me unless you talk to me about it first and tell me what you're going to talk about.'"

Richard says, "I was very clear in my own mind that I didn't give psychological advice to people, and dokusan was clearly about dharma practice. But as Suzuki-roshi used to say, 'You come to America, and the flora and fauna of psychological stuff that people present you with is unbelievable.'" Richard remembers the delicate work of trying to separate personal issues from the spiritual concerns. "I tried to confine myself to repeating back to them what I heard them say. In effect, I thought I was saying, *This is not practice right now, and this is not about your zazen, but if I hear you*—I would listen and say—*it sounds to me you have said . . . And if that's what you really mean, you should decide if that's what you mean and what you want to do.* But it ended up being psychological advice. In effect. And then they were psychologically engaged with me. And that was a mistake. I am quite clear about it now."

Darlene Cohen's memory is of an Abbot who was very kind when she was a new student seeking advice in dokusan. "He would let me go on and on about—well, my bullshit." Later, in the late seventies and early eighties, she recalls less finesse. "He was always trying to talk me into leaving Tony."

Tony Patchell nods and says, "Dick called me in a lot for dokusan—to me, it seems wildly inappropriate the way he used to mess around with people's personal relationships and call it dokusan. It was just what he wanted. He'd say, You know, Tony, Darlene will never be a sweet little housewife. She's got too much intelligence and energy to be in this relationship. He never quite said, *You don't deserve her and I do,* but I knew that's what he was saying, and I didn't have the . . ." Tony looks away. "He had my power. I gave it to him. And he took it. And Darlene and I broke up for three years. I left. Dick and other staff told me I wasn't really a practicing Buddhist. I had a back injury, excruciatingly painful for a year with no relief, and because I wasn't sitting regularly, that became *Tony is not a student.* In fact, I was practicing as hard and deeply and intensely as I ever have in thirty years." Tony is a big man, and he doesn't look happy, and when he stands up suddenly, it occurs to me that he might toss the sofa out the window or walk through a wall. Instead, he laughs. "I left. And the day I left, a four-ton rock fell off my shoulders. What had I been doing? Darlene and I found each other again. And Zen Center found itself eventually. We practice here. But we are both independent of it financially, and we say what we have to say to each other." Tony sits. "The day I left, I thought, I'll outlast that son of a bitch. And we did."

Students do remember Richard not showing up for meditation periods and being late for meetings, and they remember it beginning in the mid-seventies and getting worse with every passing year. "People say I was away," says Richard, not smiling. "Almost entirely, the experience that I was away was that I was at Green Gulch or in San Francisco, so [the people at] Tassajara felt I was away." And it is true that the students who became his personal assistants did a lot of driving.

There are two traditional monastic roles in which students serve the Abbot. The *anja* is, essentially, a housekeeper, and Richard designated a student to this devotional domestic role at each of his three residences. The *jisha* is a personal attendant; in America, this became, essentially, an executive secretary.

"Working for Richard—of whom I am rather fond, actually—was . . ." Deborah Madison pauses for a while. She started practicing at Sokoji in 1967, moved into Page Street, married Dan Welch, became the first head chef at Greens restaurant in 1979, left Zen Center with Dan in 1984, now lives in Santa Fe, and has become one of the country's most influential cookbook authors and food writers. She is still in pause mode. She cooked often at Zen Center, in the community kitchens and in Richard's home for his dinner parties with distinguished guests. She is a calm, slim, smart woman whose obvious competence does not diminish her warmth. "Working for Richard was anxiety producing," she says. "I was always tense beyond belief and constantly making mistakes—as he pointed out. Phoning people to say you're running a little late. Phoning them again to say you are just about to leave. Phoning them again to say, Not yet. Taking care of the car—I'd never had a reason or the money to afford a car." She made the mistake of noticing the oil was down a quart and letting the service station talk her into an oil change. "All minor things that you realized you couldn't do. It was painful, really, learning on the job with someone who is extremely demanding. I felt like a klutz the entire time."

Deborah pours us both some wine. "Suzuki-roshi had Yvonne, but there was a point where Richard had three assistants and it was not enough. I mean, just to try to answer the incredible number of phones in the house . . ."

Richard says he has a "multitrack" mind and style. "In my San Francisco house," he says, "I had fourteen telephones and eight lines, at least. One line just for my family, a red phone, a number only my family knew.

Jacques Barzaghi [California Governor Jerry Brown's aide] used to get really pissed. He wanted that number."

Deborah says, "This is how many people live, to be fair. Right? If you were to think of Zen Center as a corporation, and Richard as CEO, all of this would make perfect sense. It's just that some of us were slow to think in those terms. We thought we were outside of the world of corporate life." They thought of Richard as an enlightened Zen master, and so did many people across the country, and a good many people around the world. "People often ask me, Did Zen make you calm?" Deborah pours us more wine. "Those were the most frenetic years of my life. And though we knew we were supposed to have a calm center—the practice—we were often so tired that people regularly fell asleep in the zendo when we were supposed to be sitting zazen."

Willem Malten remembers Richard arriving late to the zendo. "Sometimes he'd show up in the middle of a sesshin. We'd have heard stories about why he wasn't there—some party or a Rolling Stones concert he was attending. He would come in a mess—a total mess—gray and tired. And within three days he was in shape. He was astonishing to watch. Intellectually and yogically amazing. And then his lectures would be lyrical and poetic. He could keep a room of fifty or sixty people in a total spell for a couple of hours. He was impressive."

Richard says, "I almost never was away from Zen Center." But his idea of Zen Center was much bigger, much farther-reaching than even its spread of real estate. Later he says, "I could've done more," though it is probably just as well for him and for everyone else that he didn't, "but the image that I didn't [do dokusan at all] is just nuts. Like I didn't go to the zendo. I did six sesshins a year. I spent hours—thousands of hours [meditating, so] I really find it annoying that people say I was just an administrator, after all of that. And I was never an administrator. I was an organizer. And even then, I was trying to make it possible for people to sit, to make a place for people to sit."

And more and more people needed a place to sit—and to sleep, and to eat, too. Just between March 1973 and May 1974, eight children were born to full-time staff and residential members. And there were more on the way. And more intensive practice schedules were added at both Green Gulch and City Center, with dramatically extended meditation time, which made it almost impossible for anyone to hold an outside job—and these intense practice periods at Green Gulch and City Center were not substitutes for the requisite monastic training that could only be taken during the three-month fall and winter practice periods at Tassajara, during which none of the sixty-five participants earned any money.

It was no way to run a business.

And no one wanted to foot the bill. "Parents did not send their kids to a Buddhist monastery; they sent them to college," says Richard. "I tried to create an economic support system that simultaneously made Zen Center independent of fund-raising and created practice at lay work [so] they could take this experience outside of Zen Center. . . . It was a threefold thing. The businesses were meant to make it possible for people to continue to practice, and learn how to practice in lay life, and earn enough money to practice at Tassajara. It was very clear to me. For a long time, people understood the contract."

Michael Wenger, Dean of Buddhist Studies at Zen Center, says, "Dick had brought in a feudal-society attitude, and there is a lot of wisdom to that in a meditation community. A craftsman-and-apprentice model. When he was the brilliant guy and there were all these new kids on the block who were young and willing, it worked. He could be involved in every detail and aesthetic choice. But by the time people are thirty or thirty-five, and taking a lot more responsibility, the model doesn't work anymore. No matter what the philosophy. The ceiling had to pop. Dick was the ceiling. The nature of the community had profoundly changed, and he had not."

Retrospectively, Richard sees it, too. "After a while, the contract began to loosen because, after a while, you start to think, My friend who I went to college with? I'm now thirty, and he's thirty, and he's got a second home, and they go to Italy for vacation." People age. Their needs and their desires change. It makes sense.

Not enough sense for Lew Richmond, who thinks it was not principally demographics, but another kind of shift that eventually undid the businesses. "The plan to make the residential community viable and self-sustaining was visionary," he says, "but the cash was mostly flowing through the Abbot, though it was never categorized that way."

Richard says he never profited by Zen Center. Or everyone did. "I think some people didn't realize how well they were living, actually," he says. "In terms of friendships, practice, associations—these people are good people—I thought we had created a little paradise."

When I first heard the story of Zen Center, and the work done by its members to sustain each other and the community, it did raise the possibility of a paradise lost. We do lose stories, and we lose important historical material rather readily when it does not conform to the fabric of our favorite myths—the indomitable individual and the singular genius of American pioneers, inventors, and entrepreneurs. In particular, the creation, staffing, and management of distinctive and distinguished retail and service enterprises at Zen Center in the seventies recalled the work of the American Shakers. The two-hundred-year Shaker story is still treated as a footnote to American social history, and most people do not know the Shakers from the Quakers from the Amish from any of those queer congregations of people who seem intent on getting along with each other.

The Shakers organized themselves into a series of villages, and supported themselves as builders, bakers, farmers, and purveyors of the first packaged garden seeds. They rotated administrative roles and chores among themselves without regard to gender, pigmentation, or age. They produced patented inventions (the circular saw, the automatic washing machine) and practical technologies (the wooden clothespin, the flat broom), as well as the most beautiful chairs, tables, and buildings any American ever made. Profits were shared among members equally; individuals did not sign or otherwise claim the things they invented or designed or baked. The Shaker idea of simplicity was simple—work is a gift to, not from, the one who works.

I didn't think Zen Center was a lost Shaker Village, but I did think that Zen Center had undertaken a radical reconstruction of the idea of work and its relationship to spiritual and devotional practice, and this was suggestively coherent with the practice of the Shakers. The similarities between the spare, utilitarian Shaker designs and architecture and the aesthetics of formal Japanese minimalism have been highlighted in museum and gallery exhibitions. Moreover, Richard, several of his students, and his associates in the human-potential movement locate themselves in the spiritual and philosophical lineage of the American Transcendentalists, and Emerson and his devotees were well aware of the Shaker experiment. The Shaker–Zen Center connection didn't seem far-fetched. And, frankly, I'd had my head turned by the Shakers more than once—first as a kid, who admired and envied the way every detail of ordinary life had been reconsidered and improved in their hands, including rocking chairs with abbreviated runners that didn't mar walls and chandeliers on pulleys that could be drawn up when the Sisters and Brothers wanted to dance. In its attention to ordinary life, Zen Center had turned my head, too.

In response to my initial request for an interview, in which I explicitly drew the Zen Center–Shaker connection, one longtime lay practitioner said, "The Shakers were celibate, weren't they?"

Most of the Zen Center practitioners to whom I spoke were intrigued and dubious whenever I mentioned the apparent similarities. "I've never been called a Shaker before," said a woman who practiced at Zen Center and worked at the community's bakery for a short time before she moved to Vermont to practice with a group of Tibetan Buddhists. "I do remember that some people at the bakery used to call each other Zen slaves."

"The idea of bringing work-practice into Zen Center in the form of businesses was mine from the beginning," says Richard, "but it was happening naturally."

Indeed, work-practice had been happening in China and Japan for centuries, though on a more intimate scale. The Japanese word *samu* translates as work service; it is an important aspect of training in traditional Zen monasteries. The idea is simple. Many Zen Center students attribute their understanding to Gary Snyder's expression that Zen is zazen and cleaning the temple.

"We started baking bread," says Richard. "We all felt good about it, as far as I knew. It was also the [ethos of the] sixties, and the middle of the commune movement, and self-sustaining [enterprises]. Maybe by the eighties that élan was gone. But it just seemed natural. I didn't have to convince anybody."

The Work Company was funded in 1972 by a grant from the Point Foundation. It was the first formal initiative to put people to work at Zen Center in a practicable way. Essentially, it was a loose crew of students who performed odd jobs in people's homes and yards. This work didn't necessarily interfere with practice; students could take short-term assignments as they became available. It didn't last, but it confirmed the possibility of organizing students to do the kinds of work they were already doing at Zen Center, and to make it profitable.

Right from the start, in 1959, Betty Warren and Della Goertz and other women had stuffed cotton batting into squares and rounds of black fabric to make meditation cushions. And by the seventies, many more people than the many people who sat at Zen Center needed something to sit on. Dan Welch's sister, Jeannie Campbell, had taken on the task of making meditation cushions—and futons and some clothing—in the late sixties, and she called her self-supporting business the Alaya Stitchery.

Lynn Hennelly arrived at Zen Center in 1970. "I couldn't sew. Jeannie said, 'You can sew.' I wanted to make enough money to go to Tassajara. I did eventually learn to sew, and I learned pretty quickly about Jeannie's affair with Richard, too. It was long over, but Jeannie still sometimes felt humiliated, I think. I remember that she made Richard a quilt—by then she had a new boyfriend and was getting on with things, and Richard took the opportunity to call her on her [emotional] stuff. He must have known she was troubled. I sensed that she was. And she was sweet."

Jeannie killed herself in 1973. "I can understand why people would put these things together," says Dan. "But Jeannie had her own life, and her own death. That's one fact. And a second fact: My sister's affair with Richard—and my discovering that in 1983—did not fuel the fire that was mine. My fire is a personal fire."

In accordance with Jeannie's wishes, Zen Center created a dedicated space for Alaya on Page Street, and the stitchery was staffed by a couple of students. For a while, Lynn managed the little factory and retail business. "I felt very supported, plus I brought in machines—Jeannie had been doing most of her work by hand." Alaya was the only source for "fat pants," the loose-fitting cotton slacks that had been made and copied for several years by several Zen Center seamstresses, and had a long run as a fashion fad outside of Zen Center. Soon, a whole line of plain, sturdy, comfortable Alaya clothing was available to customers, who knew the store primarily through its beautiful black-and-white catalog. The business was moved across Page Street to make way for a proper City Center library, and by the mid-seventies, an Alaya workshop and retail store were opened on Cole Street, about a mile from Zen Center. The stitchery was a high-volume, low-profit business; as with all Zen Center businesses, a conscious effort was made to keep prices below comparable market rates. This was possible principally because the students who worked at Alaya and the other businesses earned monthly stipends instead of wages, and "earned" room, board, and "tuition," including practice periods at Tassajara.

Net annual profits from the stitchery only once exceeded $10,000, and often it lost money month to month, though its deficits went unnoticed for several years. "I got the job of going to work at Alaya and assess it because it wasn't doing well at all in 1982," says Karin Gjording, who had arrived at Zen Center in 1974 and managed several of the businesses. "It was clear pretty fast that it was not a business Zen Center should be doing. The idea of having people work in the businesses was to create community. Alaya had three people. Nobody wanted to work there. And it had evolved into a clothing store with futons on the side. Most Zen students weren't particularly interested in clothing, of course." Karin left Zen Center soon after the Apocalypse. Since then, she has owned and run the fashionable, popular Alaya women's clothing boutique. "It's funny," says Karin, looking amused, "because I'm not particularly interested in clothing, either. But I am interested in service, so I like it. At Zen Center, though, a job at Alaya was the last job anyone wanted. Of course, we were not making the clothing at this point. The pants were being made in a sweatshop in San Francisco."

Karin had arrived at City Center in 1974 to visit a friend, "and—this is amazing to me because it is so unlike me—I walked in the door and I thought, Oh, my God. This is what I'm looking for. And it never would have occurred to me to go there. I'd worked at an inn in Carmel Valley where people talked fondly of the monks at Tassajara. I was glad somebody did it, but I couldn't imagine being a monk. Then, after that one visit, I got a job in San Francisco, and after a few months of practice, I moved in. And one evening, I just got involved in a task at the Bakers' house next door." Zen Center had bought the three-unit Victorian townhouse next to City Center; Katagiri-roshi had lived in one of the apartments before he went to start his own Zen center in Minnesota in 1973. Because Suzuki-roshi's widow retained their rooms in the City Center building, Richard made his city home in one of the apartments next door—and a few years later, he moved the other tenants out of the Victorian townhouse and restored, remodeled, and took over the whole house.

"The Bakers were having dinner guests that night," remembers Karin. "Zen Center was extremely hierarchical in those days. For a person who'd been practicing only for five months to be in the Abbot's home was unheard of. I looked competent, I guess. As a result of how I served dinner or something, Richard—then Baker-roshi to everyone—noticed me, and I ended up working for him almost immediately. The whole time I was at Zen Center, I worked only for him. And he'd tell me what my job was." Karin stops talking. After a moment, it becomes apparent she is making sense of some facial expression I didn't mean to make. "I sometimes think the whole community was almost in a trance during those years," she says. "Richard is charismatic. He was an incredibly good speaker. He made Buddhism clear and accessible—something that we could bring into our lives easily. He was amazing," she says, "and here I was in his house. I worked for him—all the time. Drove him everywhere, answered phones, typed letters—and he made me the manager of several of the businesses."

Karin was so often on special assignment from the Abbot that she did not go to Tassajara for a practice period for almost eight years. "Ostensibly, assignments were made for the benefit of the person's practice and the benefit of Zen Center," she says. "I think Richard often did not do it for that reason. He had a vision," says Karin, and her tone of voice reveals nothing more, "and he was manipulative, and he had his own agenda. At the time, I didn't feel this way. But many of the senior priests thought he made a huge mistake with me—I had no chance to practice and leave my competence behind. Competence was always my trading card." Given what was being offered to other students for trade, it might have been a bargain. "I don't know what it's like to have those years of practice," says Karin, "but I think I was lucky. I got great business experience."

Karin believes that Zen Center was not smart about these businesses. "The funds to and from each one went through the general Zen Center account—where the money accumulated and was spent long before any reports were made and distributed—so money from somewhere else was constantly funneled to Alaya to pay its bills, and no one seemed to notice that we were essentially paying to sell those clothes. It made no sense. It was carried for years. It could have easily made money. It could've been a place people wanted to work. It was a shame—this place had the first futon business in the country, and it was a real event, and that should've meant something for Alaya and for the people who worked there." That achievement, though, was treated like the money; it went somewhere else. "Rusa, who is married to Reb, had never had a Zen Center job," recalls Karin, "but she was asked to manage Alaya in 1982. She really wanted to be a yoga teacher, but she tried it part-time. She is remarkably smart, and we worked very well together, but there was no support for her." Rusa is now a psychotherapist. "One day, Rusa said to me, 'The reason this business doesn't work is that it reflects the way Baker-roshi treats women.' And that was true. It was all women's work. Rusa and I spent a lot of time thinking about what Alaya could have meant to Zen Center, but our recommendation was, Close it." They prepared a presentation for the Board, and Rusa took the lead. Karin remembers the meeting well. "Rusa was not a student of Richard Baker, and she said, 'The reason it doesn't work is because you treat women as second-class citizens and no one holds you accountable for that.'" Karin looks impressed twenty years later. "At that meeting, several people on the Board told him problems they saw with his leadership style. As far as I know, it had not happened before. It was, I think, the beginning of the end for him."

In 1972, when the work-practice vision was being launched, Zen Center had a deeper experience in business than was immediately apparent even to its members. Since 1967, the students and priests had operated the Tassajara guest season—a full-service summer resort. Despite the fantastically expensive improvements and additions made over the years, Tassajara was profitable in the late seventies, and after 1978, it reliably produced a net profit of more than $100,000 a year. No one liked to think of it as a business, but Richard could see that it was a business, and a good one. Similarly, in 1973, Ed Brown published a second collection of recipes, *Tassajara Cooking,* which quickly sold more than 100,000 copies. Work-practice. Ed's books made more money for Zen Center than its short-lived foray into the retail printing and graphics business, a custom cabinetry operation at the Green Gulch carpenter's shop (which was never not busy making new buildings), an in-house publishing company, or a few other inventory-intensive operations. The best work-practice businesses, as Richard says, were happening naturally.

In theory, the business of these businesses was not to make money. They were meant to bring Zen into the world in a material way and to support students who could not afford to practice intensively. Richard was not unwilling to seize opportunities as they arose (the printing and graphics company, and its inventory of paper, inks, processing chemicals, and equipment, had been sold to Zen Center by the owners on a pay-back-from-profits basis), but he was mindful of his teacher's ideas about moneymaking enterprises. In the late sixties, Richard remembers, "one of the first things we wanted was to start a bookstore. I only saw Suzuki-roshi angry two or three times. He got angry and said, 'Support the local bookstore. Don't start a bookstore to compete with someone else.'" Richard pauses. "That was a strong message."

In July of 1976, *New Age* magazine commissioned a survey of the 100 San Francisco businesses that composed the Briarpatch Network, a commerce association for socially responsible, community-minded entrepreneurs. On the corner of Page and Laguna Streets, diagonally across from City Center, the reviewer liked what he found. The following excerpts from his report were reprinted in many fund-raising letters and brochures.

> The Green Gulch Greengrocer is a corner store owned by the Zen Center that is no larger than most suburban living rooms. It does a roaring business from morning to night in fresh produce, coffee, fresh baked bread, white sugar, tofu, shortbread, carob brownies, ramen, kefir, Coca-Cola, Danish book bags,

bamboo steamers, and just about anything you can imagine except meat, tobacco, and alcohol.

Since its inception last year, its success has been nothing short of phenomenal.

If greed does make the world go round, then someone is going to have to explain why the Green Gulch store is so nifty. Its employees make a monthly stipend that just covers their needs, and their clothes are thrift-shop neat. Probably more than any other Briar business I saw, the Green Gulch store gives you a taste of what the open-ended game of the future could be like. The store serves the surrounding community, from downtown professionals, artists, and students, to monks and poor blacks. Some of the finest produce you will ever see from the Green Gulch Farm sells there at ridiculously low prices, and so do Fritos. The people are courteous and exuberant, and prices are lower than Safeway and most food co-ops. It is definitely Br'er Rabbit country—but I doubt if Uncle Remus knew much about Buddhism.

The Greengrocer also sold hot loaves of bread and fresh pastry baked in the ovens at City Center and carried across Page Street every morning. Between ten and twenty students were typically assigned to manage and work at the store, not including the bakers. Until it was sold in 1989, by which time it was being staffed and managed almost entirely without the involvement of Zen Center students or priests, it never failed to break even; from 1978 to 1981, its net annual profits increased from approximately $10,000 to $75,000. On the Greengrocer's opening day, Richard led a robed procession of priests across the street and through the aisles of the store. Philip Whalen and other senior priests paved the way, spreading flower petals and vegetable leaves.

This was the idea.

In 1973, an old apartment building opposite City Center on Page Street was torched by arsonists. A few years later, the empty lot became Koshland Park and playground, thanks to money from the Koshland family and the efforts of The Neighborhood Foundation, which was Richard's first large-scale philanthropic initiative; it was functional for about five years. The Neighborhood Foundation made real contributions to life on the streets around City Center. It eventually owned and operated four neighborhood buildings as rental properties (replacing absentee landlords and giving control to the tenants who lived in the units); it developed and maintained a community garden and an after-school program; and it worked to organize residents of nearby public housing, who participated in the design and construction of Koshland Park. The foundation Board members were almost all Zen students and priests, as were most of the volunteers. Richard especially remembers the contributions of his wife, Ginny; Renée des Tombe, a close friend of Ginny and Richard's who lived with them at Green Gulch for many years; and Michael Murphy's wife, Dulce.

Richard can give you a lecture on the financial, bureaucratic, and inter-agency details of the foundation, which are every bit as Byzantine as anything you've ever heard about the ego or superego. Its focus was improving the quality of life for other people, and that included field trips with neighborhood kids to the farm, and a local track team, for which Esalen's Michael Murphy recruited a former Olympic runner as coach. Most people think of it as a great idea, and Richard had a rather astonishing repertoire of genuinely great ideas, and his close friends and supporters, like him, tended to be more interested in his newest great idea than his last great idea, and his students were sort of busy meditating, working, raising families, and serving the lunches and dinners at which eminent friends of the Abbot helped him flesh out his latest great idea, which typically required a lot of student labor, and by 1980, The Neighborhood Foundation was kaput. In a letter to Zen Center members, Richard later wrote, "The grocery as a neighborhood institution proved more effective than The Neighborhood Foundation across the street, which we started with more obvious altruistic motives."

But the foundation effected other change. It put Richard in a new public role, and while he learned how to organize people to help the neighbors, he also learned the ins and outs of mortgage- and debt-financing. By 1980, Zen Center owned five Victorian townhouses on Page Street and a twenty-unit apartment building. It had acquired a couple of homes about a mile away from Green Gulch and a two-minute walk from Muir Beach. Many other properties and buildings passed through Zen Center's ledgers, including the houseboat in which Alan Watts had lived; of the houseboat, Richard says simply he "bought it for Zen Center; then we got rid of it; another of my fantasies."

The real estate transactions were complex and variable, and included gifts, trusts, estate-tax benefits for donors, and a lot of leveraging of equity from this old house into that old house. They also occasioned some real confusion, which soured into suspicion in 1983 and 1984, when Zen Center tried to dissolve the Board of The Neighborhood Foundation. "I get the sense," wrote Zen Center's own attorney, "that because Zen Center began, helped fund, and has managed" the foundation, "some believe that [foundation] assets belong to Zen Center. I say it's spinach." The attorney notes that the foundation's board "never functioned properly," and advised Zen Center to give up all claims and control.

Several of the buildings Zen Center bought for itself (one housed the grocery store) did generate rental income, but by its own internal analysis, Zen Center was losing more than $10,000 a year on the Page Street properties. But they were invaluable as leverage—economic and social; for example, when Zen Center bought a building to convert to a Guest House in 1978, the Sunday *Examiner & Chronicle* reported, "It will become a hostel for visiting dignitaries—a spot for [Governor] Jerry Brown to lay his head when he comes to town."

"Because of Dick, everyone was meeting everyone else," says Michael Murphy. "Zen Center was the great connector. There were articles in the *Chronicle* accusing Jerry Brown of using Zen Center connections—but it was true."

In the same year he bought the Guest House, Richard attempted to formalize the Shunryu Suzuki Study Center he had organized as a tribute to his teacher. What had begun as a casual arrangement—inviting scholars and translators to stay at Zen Center or Tassajara for a week; sending students across the bay for seminars and lectures at University of California Extension School—had become something much grander. And someone had to pay for it. Richard proposed an initial slate of eight teachers in residence, including the Japanese Tea Ceremony master Nakamura-sensei; Austrian-born Tibetan Lama Govinda; the Buddhist interpreter and translator Thomas Cleary; and poet Philip Whalen. The proposed first-year budget for the program was just over $100,000. The total net profits from Zen Center businesses that year—including the Tassajara guest season and tuition and room-and-board payments from students not on stipends—were well below $250,000.

It was evident that the Zen Center needed to do some more business. Recorded cash contributions to Zen Center topped $300,000 in 1978 but remained at or below that level through 1981. Almost every year, by December, cash reserves fell to $30,000, requiring students to skip a month or two of stipend and forgo bonuses. And in 1978, Gib Robinson remembers, "I was walking down Page Street, and Richard burst out of his house and said, 'We're going to set up a Buddhist college. Will you run it for us?'" Gib nods, as if to say, *I am not making this up.* "I said, 'Sure.' And, you know, it could have happened. He could do that sort of thing. Of course, I didn't trust him, so I never let him co-opt me—I mean, I never gave up my tenured teaching job. But had he come up with his Buddhist college—I mean, he had begun to put together the campus and a faculty, really—and had he actually opened a college, maybe I would have given up my job." Gib lets a few moments pass—or maybe it's opportunity passing. "More important," says Gib, "had I trusted him, I would have been ordained as a priest."

"In 1975, I think I made $25 a month and lived a very frugal life at Zen Center, and that was what I wanted it to be," says Wendy Johnson. "I had a lot of freedom and encouragement from Richard. I felt very supported by him to be experimental and creative on the farm, but I was never even close to the inner circle. I never was his assistant. I knew there was a hierarchy, but that was for the whiz kids." Wendy looks like she's about to say something, and thinks the better of it. "I was at Tassajara when newly elected Governor Brown came down [he took office in 1975], and it was interesting watching that whole experience unfold. We had some good practice sessions with him." Several of Richard's friends and associates had major roles in Brown's administration as documented in the *San*

Francisco Chronicle and *Los Angeles Times;* even such unusual civil servants as Gary Snyder and actor Peter Coyote landed jobs with the Arts Council, and Sym Van der Ryn was appointed State Architect—and he also worked on the design of Greens restaurant, several Green Gulch buildings, and the zendo in Crestone.

"In those years," says Wendy, "student life was not actually connected to worldly news, though, which was hard for me. We were really out of it. I mean, when Jerry Brown knocked on the gate at Tassajara, most people didn't know who he was. He was told, *We're closed.* It was practice period. He said, 'No, I've come a long way, and I would really like a chance to meet with the Abbot.' And someone said, 'Who cares?' And someone else said, 'I'm going to get the Director.' So the Ino [director of the meditation hall] came out and said, 'We're closed.' But someone else had already gone to get David [Chadwick], who knew a few things, and he said, 'You stupid fucking idiots, it's the Governor of California! Let him in.' And David got on the crank phone and called for Richard, who [was en route and] came and met the governor."

The success of the Greengrocer paved the way to the opening of the Tassajara Bread Bakery in 1976. For ten years, summer guests at Tassajara had been buying bread to take home—3,000 loaves during the summer of 1975. The City Center kitchen could not nearly supply the demand for daily bread occasioned by the opening of the Greengrocer.

Zen Center bought an existing bakery on Cole Street, about a mile away from Page Street, expanded into the building next door to create seating capacity, and soon moved Alaya to a storefront on Cole Street, as well. Almost everyone at Zen Center did a stint at the bakery. And from its opening day, it generated goodwill, good press, and good money. By 1980, the longtime head baker, Peter Overton, and his kitchen crew were turning out 500 to 900 loaves of daily bread, in addition to the pastries, cakes, cookies, and other baked goods that made the place famous. In 1980, the bakery contributed more than $200,000 in net profits to Zen Center.

Karin was the first manager. "The man who'd owned it—Nino—was wonderful. And this was a wonderful thing Zen Center did. The bakery had been a one-man operation, and none of Nino's kids wanted to take it over. We became his kids. He stayed on and trained our head baker, Peter. And though we ended up doing whole-grain, no-preservative baking that was very different from what Nino did, Peter would often call Nino, and Nino knew that we knew that it all came from him. It was what he had wanted—his work went on."

Karin particularly remembers the rush to complete the new seating area. "I knew nothing about construction projects. I'd never worked on one before. Ken, a priest, was head of the construction crew—and, of course, we were doing all of this without permits," she says. "We kept a Dumpster in front of Page Street and I'd have to gather people in the morning in trucks and haul the debris from Cole Street. Ken told me to hang paper on the windows, and how to answer questions from people passing by. On the Friday before we opened, we had to replace a plate glass window, and an inspector walked by. He came in, of course; there were wires sticking out of the walls. Ken came over and, with his back to the inspector, he said, 'Go tell Ned the electrician that the inspector is here.' Ned flew out the back door," says Karin. "Ken knew it would be Monday before the papers could be filed to keep us from opening, so we worked around the clock. And when the inspector came back, we were an operating business. He made us correct some mistakes, but we were open."

No one who worked at the bakery or any of the other businesses that predated it remembers Richard as a roll-up-the-robe, hands-on manager. But he was not exactly a hands-off manager, either. "He gave people tremendous amounts of responsibility," says Steve Weintraub, "and no authority. You mostly heard about your work when something went wrong."

Richard acknowledges that he was particular. "I stopped them for about six months making croissants at the bakery. They'd say, 'They're better than the other bakeries.' But it wasn't really a good croissant." Richard pauses. "And they didn't like that." It was a matter of taste. Richard liked good reviews, but he didn't like feature stories on students and their lives, and when a bakery review for *California Living* magazine turned into a story about the daily life of the bread-baking priests, it turned into a lot of trouble—and many pages of mea culpa memos from the staff.

Richard contended than any portrayal of Zen Center by an outsider was limited and, by definition, a misrepresentation. He figured the practice would look strange. "Not many people see the limitations of [their own] culture," he says. He didn't want journalists bringing the practice to people's attention; that was the role of Zen Center itself. "Through practice, you learn to see the limitations and enter the culture."

Darlene's husband, Tony, remembers what it was like to enter the culture through the bakery door. "For about two years, the bakery was hot stuff for the Abbot. It was the first bakery of that kind in the city. We worked like dogs, and Dick liked to show us off to his friends. Here's what they didn't see: I got up at midnight and worked until noon, or two in the afternoon, six days a week. I was not on Dick Baker's A list—or his B or C or D list for that matter. And most people weren't, so maybe it didn't occur to him to ask, How are these people in the bakery finding any time to practice?"

But on the outside, people who loved the idea of Zen Center, and people who loved croissants and cookies, weren't asking that question. The question was, Can it get any better than this? The Tassajara Bread Bakery had a long run as a San Francisco institution. And it might have gone on indefinitely. But there were other pressures on it. It had become the most important source of cash, and it was often pressed to produce more. Five years after its opening, in 1981, the bakery managers estimated that the new equipment and renovations needed to sustain quality and profits would cost nearly $250,000. Two night-shift bakers who were not Zen Center members had been hired that year, as the student labor pool tightened. At this point, there was a decided shift in tone in the memos and in-house conversations about the future of the bakery. The Apocalypse was on the horizon. Work-for-stipend was increasingly unpopular as the Abbot's travels ranged to the Soviet Union under the aegis of his friend Michael Murphy and the Esalen Soviet-American exchange program, and then Richard bought that BMW. The bakery survived the community's 1983 crisis, and the staff who stuck with the bakery provided everyone at Zen Center with operating capital during some very lean years, but it was on its way out.

In 1986, Zen Center founded the Everyday Corporation as a kind of nonprofit holding company. New tax laws had put the entire work-practice experiment out of business; the clear indication was that employers had to pay workers a regular wage, even if the workers were Zen students who had gotten used to working for nothing. The three businesses that had survived the Apocalypse were managed by the Everyday Board, and Zen Center took a cut of the ever smaller pie. In 1987, Tassajara Bread went wholesale. It was a failure. The bakery and the Tassajara brand name were sold off in 1992 to a dessert-and-café franchise, which itself went bust a few years later.

"It was really all over in 1978," says Tony Patchell. "Ask anyone. Dick decided he needed a bigger showplace than the bakery. That's when he got the idea for the restaurant. Greens. And when Greens began, no one who worked at the bakery ever saw Dick Baker. Finally, someone had the sense to ask him why. And he said, 'The bakery is not so interesting.'"

Darlene says, "Baker-roshi said clearly many times, 'If you don't like it, leave. This is not a democracy.'"

Lew Richmond, who was trained as a classical pianist and composer, had thought of leaving when Suzuki-roshi died. "But Dick appointed me Treasurer—a high post—and I was drawn in. Zen Center in those days was Buddhist Central—people in the Buddhist scene in America today aren't yet where Zen Center was fifteen years ago. Dick envisioned that, and he defined it. He had a vision that others are still hoping to have. He saw a chance to integrate Buddhism into Western society through the arts, business, and politics. In that sense, I think his vision and my own are alike." In 1998, Lew was running a lucrative software consulting group he founded. "I see the future of Buddhism integrated into the world, not apart. That's my dharma work. And Dick had that instinct early on. The fact that he also was trying to benefit himself was true, but a lot of visionaries have that flaw, and in the business world, if you don't have that flaw, you're not a good businessperson. Clients who hear about my Buddhist background want to make sure that I'm sufficiently greedy to make them a lot of money. I tell them I am still paying off my son's education."

What did Lew tell himself during the seventies? "Dick was Suzuki-roshi's successor. I don't think any of us understood that he had no clear idea about what it meant to cause no harm—Precept Number One. Dick's escapades were exploitative. Many of them were, of course, deeply held secrets that didn't surface until 1983. They were with students. The derailing of people's careers, and destroying their self-esteem—that is harm, too. And many kinds of harm happened, and some of them were by-products of our experiment, and we're all responsible for that harm. Working in a bakery for nothing didn't serve everyone who did it. We should have seen that. All of us. But how did it get started? When he became Abbot, Dick forgot to clarify harm in his own mind. I think he's still convinced that he didn't really cause harm. And he did. I've sat with some of the people who were harmed." Lew just sits there for a while, then he says, "You know, a lot of smart, good people—a lot of them Buddhists—spent a lot of time at Zen Center. It tells you something that, for many years, they didn't see what was wrong."

"The way it was presented to those of us who were dinner guests was that all of this was practice," says Stewart Brand. He remembers elaborate and delicious dinners cooked and served by silent and unobtrusive Zen Center students in the home of the Abbot. "Richard knew more about practice than we did. I knew something about acting like a servant and not having anything to say—I'd done my time in the Army. So the dinners and the rest of it didn't register as an injustice to students. If anything, the students were to be envied. They were evidently more spiritual than the rest of us."

"Richard has a way of describing a situation that almost creates it," says Lucy Calhoun. "He is extraordinary in many ways." She lets a few seconds tick by, and when she speaks again, she sounds bemused to find herself talking about her youth. "Richard gave the first Zen lecture I'd ever heard. He was at Elsie Mitchell's house—the Cambridge Buddhist Association—he was in his robes, and I was an undergraduate at Harvard, just beginning to fall apart." Lucy remembers that she couldn't concentrate, and her family couldn't help her. "I went to the Health Center, and they gave me Dexrdrine and told me I had spring fever." Richard had talked about Tassajara, says Lucy, "and by the end of my sophomore year, I had declared a major, and I was completely lost and ready to flunk out, and I saw the brochure for Tassajara, and I thought, I will go, I will sit down, and I will wait until I settle myself." It was the late sixties. She had no money, and her family was not eager to fund a trip west that seemed to make no sense. "I married a guy who wanted to do Zen," says Lucy. He also wanted to avoid the draft, so they eventually moved into Zen Center. The marriage didn't last, and from the time Lucy left Harvard, it took her three years to get to Tassajara. "But I recognized something true about sitting, almost immediately—though it did not immediately fix the rest of my life, oddly enough." She especially remembers a sesshin with Suzuki-roshi in the spring of 1971—he died in December. "Of course, he had close disciples, and I didn't take up any of his time," she says, "but I was drinking up every move he made. And he showed me something I'd not seen before. He was kind. Just kind. When he died, I felt it was a kindness of his to have left us on our own so we would have to claim Zen in our own lives." She pauses. "Suzuki-roshi embodied Zen," says Lucy. "I don't think Richard ever presented himself as a replacement for Suzuki-roshi. Richard had a life the rest of us could not emulate. When Richard became the teacher, it was a new time. It was a new way."

During her third intensive practice period, Lucy's administrative assignment was in the Treasurer's office. "I was in heaven to be given a straightforward job," she says. "I would have done well to stay at Tassajara and do the numbers and do the practice." But Richard came to lead the practice period, his first as Abbot. Within three weeks, he was asking Lucy "to do some letters for him," she recalls. "I had seen what it was like to be his assistant. He'd come to Tassajara before with his wife and one of his secretaries, who tagged after him, and I thought that must be the sorriest of jobs. But he kept bumping into me—at breakfast, outside, in the study hall. Every time, I told him I had no time. Finally, he walked through the study hall while I was sewing my rakusu," the patchwork robe students put on after lay ordination. "I said, 'I guess I have time now.'" She began to type letters to East Coast donors. Almost immediately, she was skipping parts of the practice schedule to do things for him, and six weeks later, during a meeting to discuss people's job assignments, "Richard came in and said something about the complexity of life, and he wanted me to be his assistant. I knew to my core that this was not what I wanted," she says. It would mean moving to Green Gulch, and the farm really didn't make sense to Lucy. "I tried to talk to Reb about why it was a bad idea, and I called one of my sisters on that one terrible crank phone at Tassajara and shouted at her about it, but I didn't know what I was trying to say. And then I moved to Green Gulch."

Lucy is no longer a Zen practitioner, though she was ordained by Richard, with whom she had a long sexual relationship. "Everyone has a central weakness," she says, and she adds, unironically, "he made a huge mistake with me. He initiated the sex—the first time, and every time. It was never up to me. This was not a love affair; that would imply parity. I was very much his student. And it took the foundation I'd begun to build right out from under me." Lucy stayed at Zen Center for about eight years, and for more than half of that time, she was living in his house at Green Gulch with his wife and daughter. "Ginny knew," says Lucy. "She often stood up to him for me. But Ginny and I never spoke of it. I never spoke to anyone about it. It was so important a secret that, for all those years, I couldn't really know anybody."

22.

SOMETIMES, WHEN YOU stand back and look at what was going on at Zen Center in any given month in the late seventies, it doesn't seem so crazy that Richard thought of it as "a little paradise." This was the routine: zazen every morning and evening, and services at noon, at all three of the temples; three meals a day; work in the fields or the forests or in a boutique business with your fellow Buddhists; and an agenda of performances and public speakers as rich as the range offered at any major university. You could listen to astronaut Rusty Schweickart* talk about walking in space, or a harpsichord concert, or a Dave Fishberg* performance; take a course with poet Diane DiPrima, translator Thomas Cleary*, or Buddhist scholars Masao Abe* and Robert Thurman*; attend a special dinner meeting of the California Coastal Commission; spend an evening with actor Peter Coyote*; or sign up for a conference at Green Gulch led by Gregory Bateson* on the pathology of mind/body dualism.[1]

"Dick knew from his study of history that this was a traditional function for temples," says Lew Richmond. "He had a vision of how to make Zen Center a neutral space for the culture to learn about itself and about the dharma."

"Here's Jerry [Brown]*," says Richard, still sounding astonished about the backlash he experienced after working for years to establish Zen Center as a forum and facilitator for the progressive agenda in the Bay Area and around the world. "We had meetings about getting rid of capital pun-

1. For many years, students at Tassajara baked fruitcakes, which were sent to Zen Center supporters as year-end gifts. Friends of Richard Baker and major donors also received personalized thank-you notes. An asterisk indicates a recipient of one of the 150 "fruitcakes that Roshi signed."

ishment, closing nuclear plants—[topics] which were too hot for [the governor] to talk about publicly. He talked about [them] at secret meetings at the Zen Center, because we had privacy, no reporters. Some people say I was trying to use the governor for politics—bullshit. I just liked him." And the former governor has been on the record dozens of times saying the same thing. "We were friends, and I tried to protect his privacy," says Richard. "He basically lived at our house for eight years when he was in San Francisco. We had a room for him and ironed his shirts. I thought it was a fantastic opportunity. I tried to pick people who I thought could learn from him to come and help and to be in the background and just be able to observe. But they didn't appreciate it."

Most of them did appreciate a lot of it. "One of the great benefits of being central and not seen was the contact with amazing people," says Yvonne Rand. She also says, "The craziness is in the details."

And sometimes, when you try to total it up, the price of being a Zen student in "paradise" does seem to have been insanely high.

It is not only the unacknowledged work they did that took its toll on students, though it does help to turn over a conference brochure or a poster for a lecture series and add up the hidden costs. For a relatively simple event—one Coastal Commission dinner, for example—just the setup, serving, and cleaning required eight students (six of them ordained priests), who put in an average of nine hours of after-hours work each, and that didn't include the time someone put in to procure groceries (about half from the Greengrocer), bread and desserts from the bakery, and flowers and firewood from Green Gulch Farm.

"Sometimes, you wondered what you were doing, working so hard and getting up so early," says Deborah Madison. "By 1977 or so, it was no longer a life of my immediate choosing." She pauses, and when she speaks again, her voice is soft and sing-songy. "If you have a bakery, you need bakers, and you need people in sales, and then you need delivery people, so you need to buy a van, but that's too expensive, so you need to fundraise, and then you are constantly asking people with a lot of money to support your work, and you are also interfacing with the community—from whom you constantly need money." Deborah pauses. "It was different. It seemed that all these needs and desires kept multiplying. I think it was a time when I just stopped asking the larger questions about my life."

Lew says, "I loved Suzuki-roshi like no other person, and I felt a tremendous responsibility to stick it out." This echoes the sentiments expressed by all of his colleagues. "I felt he was counting on all of us to stick around. And Zen Center was a very exciting place to be—that often kept me going. I was learning a lot. And for a couple of years," says Lew, "it *was* kind of a privilege to be one of the servants in Dick's household." Lew hesitates, and then he says, "Really. You might say it was a way to vicariously experience a higher social class. The way servants gathered around a room where the Duke's guests were drinking port." Lew smiles. "And maybe you'd get to meet Mick Jagger." Or Joan Baez*, poets Michael McClure*, Don Allen*, and Allen Ginsberg*, or est founder Werner Erhard*.

"Dick was really into the whole San Francisco scene, and he could get you in almost anywhere," recalls Paul Lee*, now retired from the philosophy faculty at UC Santa Cruz. "Whenever I was in the city, Dick and I would go to the Fillmore," the auditorium just a few blocks from City Center, where Bill Graham* became the country's most influential rock music impresario. "Richard had introduced me to his best friend, Earl McGrath. And we became a kind of a triangle," says Paul. Richard had met Earl after he dropped out of Harvard and moved to New York. Earl McGrath, an art collector with influential galleries in New York and Los Angeles, was director of publicity for Atlantic Records in the early seventies, and moved up from there to become president of Rolling Stone Records until 1980. Lew and the other Zen Center students never did meet any of the Rolling Stones, but they heard about them.

In his new life at Crestone, says Richard, "if I happen to spend a day with Mick Jagger, which I don't do now, I don't tell everybody at the Center. At Zen Center, I did."

"Zen Center was incredibly hip," says Stewart Brand*. "And Richard was really charismatic—all the time," he adds. "I'd known a lot of charismatic people—Ken Kesey was foremost among them in my mind. When he was on, everything he said seemed useful and amusing and instructive. And Ken could turn it off and blend in as an ordinary guy. Dick could not turn it off." Stewart thinks this "might have trapped Dick." A charismatic fig-ure is admirable in terms of what he is putting out for energy and ideas, says Stewart, but if he never "turns it off," people begin to sense that "charisma is not a gift; it's theft. The charismatic individual is taking your story and making it his story. This can be amazing. You have a role in a big story. But you do not write it. To the extent that you go along with the official version, you are rewarded. But if you don't go along, or the charis-matic author loses interest in you, you are left with the feeling of having no story at all—no history, and no future—and that is an unrelenting loss."

"I was going to Green Gulch Farm to give a lecture once," remembers Richard. "I was playing 'Some Girls,'" the title track on the 1978 Rolling Stones album. "I had an early mix of it," he adds. "I stop and pick up a hitchhiker. We're going along, and I'm singing, and there's a weird chorus that I am grunting along with, and I said to him, 'Where are you going?' He said, 'I am going to Green Gulch Farm. I am going to a lecture there.' And after I drop him, [about] half an hour later, I come out in my robes, and his face—"

"He'd tell us these stories in his dharma talks," says Deborah. "After a while, I thought, Richard is going to a Rolling Stones concert, and he is going to tell us all about it in his lecture. And none of the rest of us is going to the concert. And it is not only because we don't know the head of Rolling Stone Records, whom he does know; it's also because none of the rest of us has enough money to buy a ticket to a concert." Deborah pauses. "Richard was living a life on the outside for the rest of us."

As Abbot of Zen Center, says Richard, "I thought I should just share everything, and be open about everything. So I would come back and say, I did this and this and this." He grimaces. "[The students] want you to tell—they want to own your life—but then when you tell [them about] your life, and it's different from theirs, then they get pissed off [and] jeal-ous." He puffs up his cheeks and pushes out a big, noisy breath. "I knew lots of people," he says. "I don't know why; it's always been the case. To me it's irrelevant whether they're famous. Many of them weren't famous when I met them; they just became famous."

Many of them he met by virtue of his role as Abbot, though this is not a distinction Richard drew. However he happened to connect with an accomplished or innovative or engaging person, Richard was happy to have another place to set at his table. And he nourished an inclusive, eclectic sense of the American Buddhist project that he served up for students and guests alike, and it sustained a tremendous effort on everyone's part. In a September 1977 dharma talk Richard eulogized social economist E. F. Schumacher, who'd been a guest at Green Gulch a few years earlier. Schumacher's *Small Is Beautiful* made a lot of sense to supporters of the Zen Center enterprise, though Schumacher had confounded many of his admirers by converting to Catholicism late in his life. But Richard was ecumenical. In his lectures, his homes, and his temples, there was room for Ram Dass*, His Holiness the Dalai Lama*, The Reverend William Sloane Coffin*, and Swami Chetanananda*.

"Important ideas were in the air at Zen Center," says Stewart Brand. "And real credit redounds to them for the things they did carefully, the real paying attention, like the way they took care of Gregory Bateson." Anthropologist Gregory Bateson, though skeptical about Buddhism, was a frequent guest and constant supporter of Zen Center. During the last six days of his life, he was attended and cared for by Zen Center students at the Guest House, who also provided care and assistance to Bateson's family. (These six days were chronicled by his daughter, Mary Catherine Bateson, in an article published in a 1980 issue of Stewart Brand's *Co-Evolution Quarterly*.)

"You could also run into half of the Brown Administration over there," Stewart Brand recalls, "and the people Jerry Brown was talking to—from [his chief aide] Jacques Barzaghi* (whose wedding Richard performed in 1975) to Ivan Illich*."

Educational philosopher Ivan Illich had come to prominence in the seventies for his theory of deschooling. "He is a kind of a teacher for me," says Richard, adding, "Ivan and I are very close. And he's great. At his seventieth birthday (in 1996), he had me give a speech, and I said, if I'd met him earlier I might be a Catholic today." Richard remembers a night in the late seventies with Ivan at Green Gulch. "Jerry Brown was there. We had a dinner party. We [could] only fit thirteen people [at our table]. Linda Ronstadt* and others [were there], people I would like to bring into it. You've got to have someone who can have a conversation with Ivan." Students were not invited to dine with the Abbot and his guests. "I thought it was a tremendous privilege that someone like Ivan would be at Green Gulch. It was just fantastic. I'm just in awe of being able to hang out with him."

Deborah remembers many such evenings. "I was in a lot of social situations with Richard because I used to cook for him at his various houses," she says. "And I knew the guests by virtue of hanging around Zen Center so long. They knew me. Had we met on the street, we would have said hello and had a conversation. But in Richard's house, I was not supposed to open my mouth or enter into the event. You were a little wooden thing that displayed perfect behavior. You were not an equal. The student should be seen and not heard. It was a bit like a prolonged childhood."

"Class struggle," says Michael Murphy*, nodding. "I've been through this at Esalen." Retrospectively, Michael sees what he calls a "set of projections" that happened in many communities in the seventies. By way of example he says, "I want to practice with Baker-roshi. I start to practice. My parents told me I had to be somebody. But right now, I'm just working here, changing the sheets. Forgetting that when I came here, it was my choice, I didn't have to come. Meanwhile, there's Baker over there, with the governor and some friends. And I'm picking the carrots. Which is why I came. So I start to get a little pissed off about this, and I forget why I'm here." Michael shrugs. "Do you see what I'm saying?"

"It was Zen Versailles," says then-California State Architect Sym Van der Ryn*. "Richard was working like a dog, but he was living like a king." A night in one of Richard's residences, Sym remembers, was "like being in a great restaurant, and being served all night, and it was great. I never felt there was anything inappropriate in his doing things that way, his behavior or lifestyle," says Sym. "Nor did I ever hear it at that time from any Zen students." Of course, they weren't allowed to speak. "Maybe if I was reading the body language more carefully, I would have, but I never did. In fact, the first time I remember that even coming up was when Rose Bird [the late California Supreme Court Chief Justice] was there. We went to dinner at [Richard's residence] on Page Street. She said, 'I am not at all pleased about being served this way.' And I went, 'Ugh! What is she talking about?' I can remember that's how I felt about it."

Abbess Linda Cutts remembers how she explained her role as silent servant to herself. "I told myself it was for the benefit of Buddhism. I was often involved in helping to cook and clean up for the dinners when all these notables would come. [I told myself] if you serve these people well who come into contact with Baker-roshi, it is in service of a greater good." Linda pauses for only a second. "And, I mean, Deborah Madison was cooking his food. The people in his house were cared for very, very well."

Richard is still confounded by the reaction of Zen Center students to these dinners. "They didn't appreciate it. They saw it as status. People would come by the window [of our house at Green Gulch], and they weren't included," says Richard. "I said to people at this time, 'I can easily have these meetings elsewhere. I think it's healthy for the community to have them here and to learn.' And I said, 'If you can't handle being excluded, you can't practice Zen.'"

"Our experience of life was his life," says Karin Gjording, who served a lot of the meals Deborah cooked. "You often heard what you would be doing next by listening to him talk to guests. That was part of his way of getting things to come together," she says. "I can remember serving a meal—How could it be? I was working at the bakery, too—and there were Michael Murphy, his wife Dulce*, and other friends talking about this restaurant, trying to come up with a name for it. That was going to be Greens." Karin would be the manager and Deborah would be the chef.

"After a dinner, we would have a kind of party," says Richard, "and that seemed all right to me. I used to hear that was a problem, [too, as] it was a problem when people walked by the window," and saw that wine was served with some of these meals, "but I still thought I should do it there [at Green Gulch]."

"The heads of the big temples in Japan do not have splendid daily lives," says Gary Snyder. "It may have been so in the old days. But not by the time I was there in the fifties and sixties. Nobody went to expensive restaurants; they wouldn't let themselves be taken out to dinner regularly. The most extravagant thing I saw is traditional Tea Ceremony, and the preparations for that, in Kyoto, say, are very elegant. Otherwise, the heads of the temple and teachers ate as we students did."

Sym Van der Ryn does not consider himself an expert on Buddhist tradition or practice ("I call myself a Buddhist-by-osmosis; I never practiced seriously"), but he did have a relevant way to measure Richard's increasingly splendid existence. "I do remember one time being with Jerry [Brown] down there and thinking to myself, *Richard has more power than the governor has*," says Sym. "The governor was living in an apartment that I was responsible for [as State Architect], and I remembered when he'd had some problems on a weekend. He had no hot water. He called me up. I said, 'I'm sorry, Governor, I can't call General Services on a weekend. Plumbers are off.' He said, 'What the fuck is the matter? I'm the governor.'" Sym smiles. "Then, there we all were at Zen Center, where Richard's got a bevy of fifteen assistants. I do remember being struck by that. That was a dissonance, really. We were [the people running] the government, but *here* was a guy, Richard, who could say, 'Do this,' and it would happen. Who else could do that?"

Dessert, anyone?

In the summer of 1977, wildfires in the Los Padres National Forest surrounded and threatened Tassajara. The bakery had only recently opened. "Richard called me back to work with him for a while," remembers Karin. This was the period during which she "spent three or four weeks in the Jamesburg [gatehouse] with Issan. It was a massive effort. We stopped everything. That was amazing about Richard. He knew how and when to mobilize people. When the fire started, he wasn't about to let Tassajara burn. He called everyone he knew—including Governor Brown, who managed to get a fire crew in there, and he also got people to bring in a pipe for water supply, as well as trucks from every community in the Bay Area. Richard got things moving. He had over a hundred people there." Karin can still be consumed by that fire and the scope of the work done to control it. "It went on for a long time, that fire did," she says. "Volunteers would sit zazen in the morning and crews of us would go help fight the fire or fix food for the real firemen. I don't think anyone else at Zen Center would have had the ability and the wit to get the attention of people the way Richard Baker did. And then it was back to city, and he and I worked on a fund-raising letter" for the $100,000 it had cost Zen Center, including lost guest-season revenues.

The fire burned hundreds of acres of forest on the slopes above Tassajara. In the autumn, students piled 2,500 sandbags around foundations of buildings, and they pulled and cut 200 trees that had fallen into the swelling creek, but these efforts did not prevent flooding and profound structural damage to cabins, the baths, and the water-supply system.

Gib had volunteered to fight the fire—"Tassajara was my future!"—and then stayed for a year of monastic practice. During the 1978 spring practice period, after the floods had subsided and the cleanup and repair work was under way, Gib was present during a question-and-answer period with the Abbot. "We were always attentive to nuance and innuendo when he addressed issues of practice," says Gib, "and then someone at the back of the room said, 'There's fire down here.' We all thought it was a fancy Zen phrase that we didn't understand. But, actually, the zendo was burning. A fire had started in the kitchen, and as a result of the pipe and water-supply problems we'd had, there was no water pressure for the fire hoses. We just watched the zendo burn. It was agonizing." Gib folds his arms and sits back in his chair. "Here's what's worse, really. I was so well trained already, such an obedient Tassajara student, that I knew my role was to let the fire crew do its number and stay out of the way. I could've walked into that zendo and carried out the big drum that was lost and the stone Buddha that I photographed the next day in pieces." The drums and bells and ceremonial objects lost in the fire were valued at $40,000. The 1,700-year-old Buddha was priceless. The initial estimated cost of building a new zendo was $200,000.

"The fruitcakes that had been baked in advance and stored for aging were also burned in the fire," wrote Linda, then Richard's assistant, in a letter to staff and students at Tassajara, whose time was taxed beyond anything they'd ever experienced by the succession of fires and floods. "There had been a feeling that perhaps we would not bake fruitcakes again [to send as holiday presents to friends and donors] because there was so much to do at Tassajara. Baker-roshi, however, felt that we should make the fruitcakes again." Those fruitcakes had to be baked, wrapped, and stored (during the end of practice period or the beginning of guest season); aged for at least six weeks; wrapped and boxed for shipping; addressed to donors and friends from a set of labels approved by Richard; and before they were taped up and trucked off to a carrier for distribution, a printed greeting card, signed personally by Richard, had to be tucked inside the fruitcakes bound for Erik Erikson*, Daniel Ellsberg*, the Fidelity Johnsons*, the Xerox Carlsons*, the Bethlehem Steel Johnstones*, and Laurance Rockefeller*.

The show must go on.

"There was a reciprocal dynamic," says Lew. "We figured, Richard seems more than a little strange for a Zen master, but look at all these important people who are here and listening to him. And I think the important people were thinking, he doesn't act like a Zen master, but look at all the students he has. It was mutually reinforcing, and both of those communities, which were kept rather separate, saw the other half as proof that this was a good thing."

23.

RICHARD WROTE AND GAVE me what he called "a kind of statement" to reflect his thinking about the controversies occasioned by his relationships with women while he was the Abbot of Zen Center. Here it is:

During the 21 years from 1962 until 1983, I had relationships with seven or eight women, relationships related in various ways to the San Francisco Zen Center.

The first, of course, was my wife of twenty years, legally about thirty years.

The second was a woman who was a practitioner at Zen Center. We had known each other as students at Zen Center. Shortly after I became the teacher, we became lovers. At the time, I saw the relationship as similar to, say, when one of two graduate students at a university becomes an Assistant Professor; the two students' relationship remains the same.

I did not have any idea at the time that my becoming the teacher would have such a big impact on people. This I learned.

In addition, while I was well aware of the dictum that psychoanalysts not have sexual relationships with their patients, I did not think that the relationship between a Zen teacher and a practitioner was in any way similar. I saw Zen practitioners as strong, not as weak, and not as patients.

However, within a year or so, I realized that the two relationships we were developing—lovers, and teacher and disciple—were not working for her. And so I ended the relationship with her. It seemed the only responsible thing to do. In addition, I supported her in having other relationships. When at a later time, she wanted to be ordained, I asked her to wait until she was emotionally free of me. And about a year after that, when I thought she was free of an emotional relationship with me, I ordained her.

This relationship showed me that it was unwise and much too complicated for Zen teachers to have sexual relationships with students.

In the early 70s, there was not yet societal awareness of the potentially exploitative character of relationships between persons in authority and those dependent on authority. And there was not yet the general awareness of how often women were victims of men.

The other relationships I had were not with students. Although, some became students after our relationship began.

For example, one was with a woman about my age with whom I had a brief relationship in the mid-Sixties, when I was still a fairly new Zen student. Later she became a central person within Zen center. During the next 15 years, I think we were lovers once.

As she was about my age and our primary relationship was one of friends and co-workers in Zen (as I saw it), our relationship always seemed good to me. I felt good working with her to develop Zen Center. It was inconceivable to me that a peer with whom I talked and spent time nearly every day could feel anything but my equal in all things.

My basic rules of relationships were that there should be no hurt, or as little as possible, and that those immediately involved should know about any relationship. The latter I always followed; the first I thought I followed, but with hindsight it is obvious I caused a lot of hurt.

Talking about all this is unpleasant. And [it is] unthinkable in my present life and marriage. I guess, then, I felt I had several lives.

I see now that I didn't have a feeling of limits appropriate to the world, nor did I have a realistic feeling for others' limits.

I feel like a stinky fish thrown up on the dock when I talk about these things. But swimming in the water of those twenty-two years was mostly very beautiful.

You can draw a line here. *Richard Baker's business.* Leave it alone.

Look again. There's a whole crowd of women on the other side of that line. In 1983, several of them made it their business to make this material public.

"It was in this atmosphere of the early eighties when everything [was] exploitative," says Richard, "every relationship [was] exploitative, and [people] could say anything. I had no chance."

He did have a chance. He was the Abbot. He could have drawn a line. The idea that sexual congress was exploitative is an old one. It was the very reason the Shakers drew a clear and dramatic line, banning sexual relationships among members. Their founder, Ann Lee, had a terrible marriage to a brutish man, and her children died young. She founded the Shakers, and she invented the celibacy rule, which she and her followers believed was the only way to secure gender parity. It was an arbitrary line, and there might have been other ways of achieving the desired end. But of paramount importance to the Shakers was the principle of equality. Celibacy seemed to secure this principle. So, they toed the line.

The defining principle of the Zen Center organization was the singularity and enlightened spiritual status of the Abbot. The only line this required was the demarcation between the enlightened Abbot and everyone else. This line was clearly drawn and obediently observed—until 1983. The Abbot could cross the line at will, or when he saw a teaching opportunity on the other side, but no one was confused about what it meant to be in contact with the Abbot when he stepped over that boundary. Transmission was not a game of tag. You didn't get *it* by touching the teacher's robe or serving him dinner. When he retreated to the other side of the line, he was still the one and the only one with *it*.

It was a marvelously simple design, as elegant as the severe Shaker line. And it worked. It worked because students toed the line, protecting and preserving the ideal of a singular source of enlightened spiritual author-ity. If the Abbot did or said anything really weird, students had two choices. First, sit with it; it was the student's job to intuit the mysteries of enlightenment. If it continued to seem weird, the student had to sit with that, too, unless she or he was willing to leave the community or risk dis-crediting the entire Zen Center project.

Of course, none of this made any sense outside of Zen Center, and that made even more sense. Both the insiders and outsiders had long since stipulated that the outsiders were not enlightened. So, no matter what happened at Zen Center, no one ever had to draw a line.

During the 21 years from 1962 until 1983, I had relationships with seven or eight women, relationships related in various ways to the San Francisco Zen Center.

"Sex was not the thing," says Michael Wenger. "In San Francisco, peo-ple had dealt with sex. But to this day, Dick says things didn't happen that did happen. One example is the number of different times he has said he didn't have sex with people with whom he did."

This assertion that sex was not the problem seems reasonable, and it also seems to reflect the fact that many members of the community were sexually active with multiple partners—some serially, and some in less linear fashion. No one wanted to draw a line limiting sexual behavior. Who does? Gary Snyder says, "I think it is entirely plausible that Dick didn't think it was wrong to have serial affairs. A lot of other people would not think that was wrong. Or that it was anyone's business. One of the things Dick says is that he comes out of a particular place and time. And so do I. I know what life was like in the forties and the fifties in the Bay Area. Man, we were wild. We didn't think it was anybody's business, either."

Michael Murphy agrees. "But that wasn't the view from over there, from the moral majority at Zen Center [in 1983]. American Puritanism reared its—I almost said ugly—head." Well, he did say it.

"If you sit down with the women, or the men—and I've been in meet-ings with men who were hysterically sobbing about relationships with their male teachers—you realize that serious harm was done to these people," says Lew Richmond. "And you have to work backward from there. There is only one precept. Do not harm." Lew pauses. "When people do not have a clear idea of harm—and it is very hard to talk about sex and get it right—they accuse others of being Puritans. This is going on all over Buddhism today." It has been going on for a while. In 1985, Buddhist teacher and psychotherapist Jack Kornfeld published the results of his interviews with Eastern (principally Buddhist and Hindu) spiritual leaders in *Yoga Journal.* Of the fifty-four teachers and gurus Kornfeld interviewed, thirty-four told him they had been sexually involved with students.

Do not harm. It is an ancient line, but a lot of dust had to be cleared away before anyone could see if it had been transgressed.

The first, of course, was my wife of twenty years, legally about thirty years.

Yvonne Rand remembers Richard telling her that his wife knew of his sexual relationships with her and other women, and that Suzuki-roshi knew, as well. Yvonne never confirmed this with either Virginia or Suzuki-roshi. "What Virginia to this day probably does not understand— she felt I turned toward Dick and away from her—I don't think she ever knew how much fear was at the base of my behavior, and especially my fear of Richard. In subtle but persistent ways he left me with the sense that I better not talk to Virginia about anything." Yvonne looks at her feet. "And I went along with that. It's not behavior I am happy about," she says. "Virginia used to say, 'You know, Yvonne, Dick is crazy.' And just in the way I didn't believe him when he said, 'I don't know how to teach,' I didn't believe her. That was a mistake."

If you'd believed the Abbot was crazy, you would have had to leave Zen Center.

The second was a woman who was a practitioner at Zen Center.

This is not a chronological list. This second woman is Lucy Calhoun.

We had known each other as students at Zen Center.

Lucy went to Zen Center because she felt she was lost, as she had told Richard.

In retrospect, Yvonne says, "Dick's persistent moving on women who were confused in a way that leads to disintegration was a pattern." This was true before and after Lucy showed up at Zen Center, says Yvonne, in a tone of voice that works like a leash on her words, restraining emotion. "One example. I know this from my experience, the experience of Lucy, Anna Hawken's experience, the experience of Dick's secretary at UC Berkeley, and from the experience of Jeannie Campbell. You walk along Page Street, or up the hill at Green Gulch Farm, or up the road at Tassajara, and all of a sudden he bumps you with his hip. It's a very physical contact. And then, if there isn't a lot of negative energy from you, he bumps you again, and if you're scared or confused, he bumps you again."

This is no way to treat a Raku bowl.

But Richard says he really did not understand the fragility of women. He had a very strong mother. "The idea that women could be victims was totally anathema to her. So, I don't know, I had no idea of victims."

"He was physically finding out if you were going to oppose him," says Yvonne. "It's the way he initiated his seduction any number of times. And there was a pattern to his answers—all of us who were his students asked, What about your wife?"

No one drew the line there.

"And there was a consistent articulation from him," says Yvonne. "'What I want matters more than what I do to anyone else.' The language was exactly the same."

This was the articulated spiritual program; if you stay, you submit to the Abbot. Dan Welch says, "In truth, I didn't think of Richard in a heart sense as my teacher, but he was the only teacher. This came to a crisis. In 1975, I was going through a marriage breakup and it caused a lot of upheaval. My role in the community took quite a fall. Dick suggested that I take a leave of absence—maybe a world pilgrimage. The idea was, 'Why don't you take off and test your practice in the world without any net?'" Dan's eyes widen. "I was horrified at the thought. Leave Zen Center? Leave show business? No." Dan makes a face you might make when you see an infant in a crib. "Richard pushed me, and then he said, 'If you're going to stay, you have to take me as your teacher, or you have to go.' I hadn't seen that coming, but I didn't want to leave. Zen Center was thoroughly part of my life, and he was thoroughly part of Zen Center. New Year's Day 1976, I told him I would take him on. He right away asked me to go to Tassajara to be his *anja*—to clean his cabin and make his bed. From one perspective, this was a real step down. But it was a chance to be close to him, and I knew I couldn't approach him intellectually."

Shortly after I became the teacher, [Lucy and I] became lovers.

"We were never lovers," says Lucy. "The sex did not make me feel close to him. Richard got between me and myself, and I was stuck there for many years. I was his assistant. I was his student. I was trying to make everything I did be practice. That didn't work. I was acting out roles, but my heart was not in any of them."

Lucy understood that there was no parity. The Abbot did not.

At the time, I saw the relationship as similar to, say, when one of two graduate students at a university becomes an Assistant Professor; the two students' relationship remains the same.

Richard had dreamed about opening a Buddhist College, but throughout the seventies and early eighties, at this imaginary college, there was only one person on the teaching faculty, and in 1971 he hadn't been named Assistant Professor; he'd become the Dean, President, and Provost.

"I was unable to say no, and that was my problem," says Lucy. "But Richard had the bases loaded. He was my teacher. He was my employer. I was living in his house. I was following his schedule. Was this practice? I didn't know. I do remember reading the *Wind Bell* articles because they explained what we had been doing at Zen Center."

I did not have any idea at the time that my becoming the teacher would have such a big impact on people. This I learned.

This is a recurring topic in Richard's conversations, and he seems repeatedly and genuinely surprised by the authority invested by students in him as their teacher. "Impact," he says. "I began to understand it was a problem. And then all this social and political stuff began to happen about teachers taking advantage of women and men, and I was quite concerned about one teacher in America who was totally irresponsible. Someone would come into dokusan [with him], and if she was pretty or a model or something, he'd jump her. He was just nuts."

Richard speculates that some of the confusion Zen teachers in America began to experience was a cultural confusion, a difference between Japanese and American sensibilities and ethics. "The basic ethic in Japan is, Men and women, if they're alone, fuck. And so, to be out in public is not sexual," he says. "Even in a public bath. To be alone in a room—that's sexual. So for a Japanese man to be alone with a young woman—you put your hand down there, and who cares?"

Maybe the woman?

Well, maybe. But Richard says repeatedly that he was taking his cues from his own mother, whom he sees as an early feminist; thus, he has always believed that women can take care of themselves. "If some teacher hit on [one of my daughters] in high school, I might not like the teacher, but I'd say, 'You take care of yourself. You don't let some teacher hit on you.'"

And it almost makes sense because at some point you forget that this is all by way of analogy. You forget that Richard was not the father of a student being harassed by her teacher but the teacher who was sleeping with his student. And he was not teaching algebra; he was teaching Zen Buddhism. And it was not a high school; it was the first Buddhist monastery established outside of Asia in the history of the world. And he was not Japanese, and neither were his students.

"Richard tried once to be my teacher," remembers Stewart Brand. "He had invited me down to Tassajara during practice period. There were supposedly no guests during that time, and I felt awkward. Then he went into this whole routine of *What are you doing? Why are you here?* And I said, 'Because you invited me.' And I felt weird. It made me very uncomfortable."

In addition, while I was well aware of the dictum that psychoanalysts not have sexual relationships with their patients, I did not think that the relationship between a Zen teacher and a practitioner was in any way similar.
Dokusan.

I saw Zen practitioners as strong, not as weak, and not as patients.

"As the heir and the Abbot, Richard was the ultimate authority on everything," says Steve Weintraub. "That speaks to my being an undeveloped person at the time. I needed someone bigger than life in whose glow I could be me. He was involved in every detail of my life. And at the time, I thought, Well, why not? He's a Zen master. Zen pervades all realms." Steve looks dubious. "It is hard to believe, isn't it? Was this Zen? The question never arose." Steve was Treasurer of Zen Center for several years. "It might help to have an example of what it meant to have Zen pervade your life. After a meeting [with people outside of Zen Center], I said to him, 'You really were very strategic in there.' I was complimenting him. He said, 'No, I never act strategically.'" Steve points into the middle distance. "There it was. Another thing I did not understand. In other words, he was saying, 'I always act from pure motives; I never worry about the world.' And I remember thinking, He's the teacher, so what he says is the truth, but my experience was different. And the gap between those two had to be filled. I filled it with the idea that my practice was bad. The reason I thought he was strategic is that I am no good." Steve is still staring into that moment when he says, "Because it was a fact of being there [at Zen Center] that Richard was better than good. He was right. And that became a damaging dynamic." Steve lets some time drift by. "To say that I had no thought about leaving Zen Center is to understate it. There was one world, one place, one thing. This was it."

However, within a year or so, I realized that the two relationships [Lucy and I] were developing—lovers, and teacher and disciple—were not working for her.

"When he was angry," remembers Lucy, "he would threaten to fire me, wondering aloud if maybe I shouldn't be his assistant anymore. I didn't want to be fired; I wanted to graduate. I told him I wanted to resign from the Board and just sit."

And so I ended the relationship with her. It seemed the only responsible thing to do.

"He made me the head of the kitchen at Green Gulch," says Lucy. "I was, in fact, bulimic."

In addition, I supported her in having other relationships.

"The situation," says Lucy, "created many problems that are close to the problems of incest—of a daughter who cannot trust that she is separate from her father, and so she tries to get to know the world through the father."

When at a later time, [Lucy] wanted to be ordained, I asked her to wait until she was emotionally free of me.

"He told me that I could not be ordained because I thought I had a special relationship with my teacher," remembers Lucy. "I had to see that I didn't have a special relationship, that I was less of a student than the other students."

And about a year after that, when I thought she was free of an emotional relationship with me, I ordained her.

Lucy says, "At the end of the ordination ceremony [hers took place in the autumn of 1977] there are these words spoken—'Now everything is your teacher.' I heard those words."

This relationship showed me that it was unwise and much too complicated for Zen teachers to have sexual relationships with students.

Lucy says, "Yvonne is the person who recognized that something was wrong." Lucy feels Yvonne knew her story, though she is certain Yvonne never asked. "I didn't tell her. I don't think anyone had told her," she says. By 1979 or 1980, it was clear even to Lucy that she could not practice at Zen Center anymore, but she didn't know what to do. On Yvonne's advice, she went to a therapist whom Yvonne knew and who knew about Zen Center. "The therapist never tried to elicit this story from me," says Lucy, "but I was clearly miserable. And by the end of the first session, I was expecting the therapist might say something comforting." Lucy laughs. "She said, 'So what are you going to do about all of this?' I was out of Zen Center in two weeks."

In the early 70s, there was not yet societal awareness of the potentially exploitative character of relationships between persons in authority and those dependent on authority.

"Bosses do not have romantic relationships with their employees," says Stewart Brand. "Most people understand this. Even if the two are consenting adults. There is no graceful way to conduct a relationship under those circumstances."

And there was not yet the general awareness of how often women were victims of men.

"Richard was a strong man who didn't fall into line with the feminists," says former California governor Jerry Brown, now Mayor of Oakland, during a telephone conversation that does not yield much more than this about his time at Zen Center—or almost any other complete sentences. Mayor Brown is friendly, and he answers most questions with lists of words and phrases that I fail to patch together in any meaningful way, though he does name thirteen eminent people he remembers seeing at Zen Center. And at one point, he says, "Baker showed us flair, taste, and leadership. He fostered exchange among creative people and people who were really shaping their communities." Later, the mayor says, "global feminism," and "phenomenal world," and "skin the cat," but by then, I don't think either of us really knows why we are trying to talk to each other.

Global feminism?

Yvonne took a trip to Japan in May of 1978. "Richard, Reb, Lew, Ed, and I—Yvonne and the boys. Dick had gone ahead of us, and he'd been there a week or two. He had met [a woman] and had fallen in love with her. Richard's wife had their second daughter that July. She had pleaded with him to stay with her through the pregnancy."

Richard says, "Mayumi and I fell in love. A powerful relationship. It was the one that was hard for Virginia. But for me, it was like going back into Japan, knowing Suzuki-roshi again; it was kind of finding an intimacy with Japan, which I didn't have, so it was an extraordinary thing for me, like entering another culture."

Yvonne remembers that "the five of us [from Zen Center] were going on a pilgrimage trip. [Dick] opted out at the last minute of this three-day trip, and I wondered. The others were going back [after that to the States], and I was supposed to stay on for another two or three weeks to work on a book of Suzuki-roshi's *Wind Bell* lectures. We were in Kyoto, but we were going up to a house the Bakers had on the Japan Sea. Dick left to do an errand for fifteen minutes." Yvonne lets about six silent seconds pass, though it registers as much more time. "Six hours later he came back. And that happened three days in a row. And I was sitting there. And finally I got it. The veils fell from my eyes at that point. I had no problem with him falling in love. What I was upset about was that he acted on it—in the face of having literally beaten some of his students for such behavior. And that he acted on it in the context of his relationship with Virginia—I knew what she meant to him. I thought, if he can do this to Virginia, he can do this to anyone. What matters to him is what he wants, and he wants what he wants when he wants it, and the fallout for other people doesn't matter. And that was when I got it. This is someone with a characterological hole. And you can't be a Zen teacher if you don't have a heart. You can't do it."

The other relationships I had were not with students. Although, some be-came students after our relationship began.

"For a long time," says Lucy, "there was a missing piece of informa-tion." It is something she needed in order to understand what was wrong with her, something she thinks other people need to understand in order to understand what went wrong at Zen Center. "The missing piece of information was *not* that I was a student," she says, or even the implica-tions of that. "It was that I wasn't supposed to connect [the sexual rela-tionship] to anything. It was supposed to have no effect on any reality elsewhere, or even on my relationship to him. That was devastating." It was a relationship that made no sense, says Lucy. "It worked in no con-text."

For example, one [relationship] was with a woman about my age with whom I had a brief relationship in the mid-Sixties, when I was still a fairly new Zen student. Later she became a central person within Zen center. During the next 15 years, I think we were lovers once.

This is Yvonne, who agrees that the relationship was sexualized, "but minimally." She adds, "Dick was much more interested in control than he was in sex. And authority. I immediately felt like an object. It was very grim. But my waking up didn't happen around my own experience. Initially, I began to see harm to other people."

As she was about my age and our primary relationship was one of friends and co-workers in Zen (as I saw it), our relationship always seemed good to me. I felt good working with her to develop Zen Center.

Richard ordained Yvonne as a Zen priest in 1973. "The day I was ordained," says Yvonne, and then she goes quiet for a moment, as if maybe she has forgotten why she was thinking about that day, but she hasn't. She nods. Until Richard became Abbot, ordination garments were imported from Japan. Richard brought a teacher from Japan to Zen Center to teach students the traditional art of sewing a rakusu (the small patchwork robe put on during lay ordination) and the *okesa,* a sheer, white garment that is wrapped around the body and worn beneath the black sitting robe by ordained priests. "The okesa has a rope," says Yvonne, "and after the ordination ceremony I was in the Baker's apartment trying to learn how to put the robe on. Dick came around behind me and held the robe, and he said, 'Here's the rope. You tie it in a knot, and then you wrap the cloth around the rope the way you might wrap a cloth around my penis.'" Yvonne nods. "I was terrified. I split. I just checked out. I encapsulated that moment for a long time and didn't touch it."

More than twenty years later, in a *Wind Bell* article about the Zen Center tradition of sewing, Reb explained that the okesa is the Japanese version of the ancient robe that, in Sanskrit, is the *uttarasangha*—"the robe that covers the sangha [community]," or "the sangha which covers the person."

It was inconceivable to me that a peer with whom I talked and spent time nearly every day could feel anything but my equal in all things.

Michael Wenger says, "The most shocking thing is this: Dick didn't get it at all. I have lots of excuses and reasons for what happened. He doesn't have to supply them. I lived them. I lived through circumstances where people misunderstood him when he was doing the right thing. But when he fucked up, he had no idea about it. No idea. That is shocking."

Yvonne remembers, "There was a Zen Center priests' meeting [in 1982], and Dick went on a diatribe about [Eido-roshi], the teacher at the Zen Studies Center in New York, who has for years been involved sexually with students. Dick ranted about how terrible this guy was, and not having anything to do with him, and how we should support the [New York] students to lock the kitchen door—cut off his finances. And, I thought, *This is crazy*. But there he was, sticking his neck way out there." Yvonne still looks a little stunned by the performance.

My basic rules of relationships were that there should be no hurt, or as little as possible, and that those immediately involved should know about any relationship. The latter I always followed; the first I thought I followed, but with hindsight it is obvious I caused a lot of hurt.

He did not exactly write *I caused a lot of harm*. This probably means nothing; *harm* is not a word he ever used during our conversations. It's just that *Do not harm* was the language used by everyone else at Zen Center to articulate the first Precept.

Lucy traveled to The Shadows resort in northern California in 1997 when a group of former and current practitioners arranged a weekend meeting with Richard. Whether it was a healing session or a confrontation or a failure varies according to the participants. "I was glad for the chance to see Richard," Lucy says. "He is still extraordinary, and I can admire him." Later, she adds, "I had no unfinished business with [Richard]." There were a lot of people Lucy felt she "really never knew at Zen Center," and at The Shadows, "I was able to be open with them. It was wonderful," she says, sounding suddenly young. "They were finally able to meet me, too, and see who I really am. You see, a lot of them had the impression from Richard that I was a little crazy, even though no one ever heard him say so exactly. In fact, they remember that he *didn't* actually say it."

The idea that you had to interpret what the Abbot didn't say and what the Abbot did say was complicated. It infuriates Richard, who believes it cost him his reputation as a teacher for many years. As Richard explains it, "People said, 'He's a mindfucker. You can't believe him.' People would come and talk to me, and we'd have a reasonable conversation, and then they'd go away and they'd be told, 'Oh he can smell anyone coming. Of course, you've just been fooled.' And that went on for years. No one would talk to me because I was too clever or too persuasive."

Many people still won't talk. In 1998 and 1999, several senior priests were reluctant to speak about specific experiences of their own at Zen Center in the seventies—many of them positive—because they were concerned the material would somehow be used to discredit the women and men who spoke publicly in 1983 about being harmed. And almost everyone who was at Zen Center in the 1970s recalls a pervasive and sometimes punitive atmosphere of silence and secrecy. Many students remember that speaking to each other about their intimate relationships was discouraged; at the same time, many students were persuaded to consult with the teacher about proper conduct in this sphere.

Richard says, "One thing I admire Steve [Weintraub, the former Treasurer, who is now a psychotherapist] and Linda [Cutts, now Abbess of Zen Center] for is that they developed their relationship very discreetly at Tassajara." Steve and Linda had fallen in love and were thinking of getting married. "They talked to me."

"It was totally practice then to talk to Richard about your relationships," says Linda. "I only found out much later that many people were not celibate and alone at Tassajara." She smiles. "I know this is hard to believe."

Richard remembers, "They wanted to spend certain nights together. We worked out certain nights they would spend together. I feel a close relationship to them. And they are such fine people. And when they were sure their relationship was clear and going to last, then they announced it."

"Oh, the secrets," says Darlene Cohen. "I started being a member of a subversive group that Gib started a couple of years before the end. We didn't dare call ourselves what we were. We wanted to talk about Baker-roshi, and we met secretly and swore never to tell anyone else. Seven or eight of us. We felt that the basic relationship [that] Richard had with everyone had lost its legitimacy. Then we discovered there was somebody in the group who, if you tried to talk about sex, would say Baker-roshi's affairs with his students are his affairs. The group broke up."

Talking about all this is unpleasant.

"I knew [my story] would cause people to have difficult feelings—but these were feelings they would have had at the time, had they known," says Lucy. This was the story. Lucy was working on a professional degree and was not involved with Zen Center during the Apocalypse. It was hard at that point for her to talk about her experience, "but friends supported me," she says. "I talked to a small group of senior priests. I spoke up because Richard was lying when he said he had never harmed a student. That's why I came forward."

And [it is] unthinkable in my present life and marriage. I guess, then, I felt I had several lives.

"Here's my feeling," says Michael Murphy. "At some level of his being, Dick wanted out. But he was not absolutely clear about it. He did some things. Then he found himself in the crucible, being accused of things he didn't do." Michael remembers the plot unraveling from there like an Arthur Miller play. "Dick freely confessed his shortcomings. But basically, he was accused of being possessed by the devil." He shrugs. "I think it turned out for the best, except that it is too bad that the whole thing couldn't have been resolved with him staying there. But maybe that was impossible. Twenty key people would have had to go through big changes at the same time, and that's asking too much of this human race at this stage. So, he had to reincarnate in another place, free of all of that."

Is it too much to ask if any of the women with whom Richard was involved in a sexual relationship are still practicing at Zen Center? Yvonne shakes her head. No. "Dead or gone," she says. "The community is stunningly unaware psychologically, and that is especially true of the senior leadership." However, Yvonne sees the work done in the nineties to develop articulated policies and standards—even though it involves a lot more administration—as a genuine accomplishment. "When a group of remarkable people at Zen Center was putting together a code of ethics [in the late eighties and early nineties], it struck me that it was the first time I'd had a conversation with people at Zen Center when I felt I was heard and understood. I said at the time that to develop authentic ethical standards for behavior, you have to find a way to want to hear bad news. Historically, Zen Center has not been such an entity; we failed to cultivate seeing and listening without judging."

I see now that I didn't have a feeling of limits appropriate to the world, nor did I have a realistic feeling for others' limits.

"The sexual misconduct was just the tip of it," says Mel Weitsman. "Dick was using the community for his own ends. He was the king, and the community members were the vassals. His community, his people." Mel laughs, as he often does, when something slightly contradictory occurs to him. "But," he says, "the affair at Tassajara [with Anna Hawken] prompted something unprecedented. Things had been building underneath for a long time, but that was the clincher."

Paul Hawken drew a line. And then he hired a lawyer to underline that line.

Paul Lee, sitting in his kitchen in Santa Cruz, waves off much of the reporting about Richard's sexual liaisons as recriminations from embittered women. But later, by the pool, he recalls awkward evenings that he and his wife and other old friends shared with Richard with "someone who wasn't Ginny."

Another line.

"So," says Gary Snyder, "[Dick] walked around at Tassajara hand-in-hand with Anna?" He is thinking of the 1983 Peace Conference with Thich Nhat Hanh and other Buddhist teachers. Gary narrows his gaze. "On another occasion? Maybe okay. Or in another setting? That might have been absolutely okay. Especially in those times. The problem was, the confluence of issues."

This is how sex became everybody's business. Everybody drew a line somewhere.

I feel like a stinky fish thrown up on the dock when I talk about these things.

"I was never sexually involved with Richard Baker," says Karin Gjording. It is a point many of the women to whom I spoke feel it is necessary to address. "And there were no sexual overtones to our relationship. None. It wouldn't have worked with me." Karin spent a lot of time with Lucy; they were both Richard's assistants, and they had traveled together to England with Richard and a Zen Center patron. Lucy had never spoken of her sexual relationship with Richard. "It was long after we'd spent that time together, and we were driving to Green Gulch," remembers Karin, "when Lucy casually said, 'There is something I have to tell you.' It was out of the blue. And I said, 'You had an affair with Baker-roshi.' And Lucy said, 'How did you know?' I said, 'I didn't.' And I didn't, but the words came right out of my mouth. And then she told me about it. And it was awful. Then, when I was at Tassajara, Richard came down with [a woman]," whom several students and friends of Richard knew as his lover, a frequent visitor, and an employee at a Zen Center business. Karin recalls that she was in the pool; the other woman was sitting by the pool. Richard arrived "and put on a towel and started changing his clothes right there." Karin sort of smiles. "This was way weird. It was the summer of 1982. I went to Reb and said, 'Do you know about this stuff? Is he begging to be caught?' It was shocking. At Tassajara—the heart practice."

But swimming in the water of those twenty-two years was mostly very beautiful.

"I remember the first time I went to Richard's house," says Linda. "It was so beautiful—the beautiful paintings on the wall, and the beautiful furniture, and I couldn't believe it. I had my one room. We lived as monks. So I transferred what I saw and made it mean something else. I told myself none of it mattered to him, that it was all in the service of making Buddhism available to the world. And then I was his assistant for two years, and I was in his house all the time, starting in 1978, and when I had any question about things I saw, I told myself I was inventing the problem, or I would accuse myself of discriminating thinking. And all these different women—I had seen them, and translated what it all meant because of my own needs—I owed my life and happiness to the practice, and Richard was central to the practice. I was protecting my perception of enlightenment."

24.

SEVERAL OF THE PRIESTS at Zen Center who were in college in the late fifties and early sixties first tried to meditate while they were undergraduates. They were warned by resident assistants and deans to avoid the practice. Meditation, they were told, was dangerous, and possibly an occult activity.

"You have to try to remember," says Tim Buckley in his office in the Anthropology Department at the University of Massachusetts, "this was the jump of Buddhism from Asia to the West. Now it seems pretty commonplace. But my godmother, to whom I am very close, and my mother, who is now in her late eighties, and all of my family were convinced I was bound up in idolatry. These were thoughtful and educated people. But in 1965, BOOdism, as they called it, was not a religion but a philosophy with graven images invented by Asians, who were not in their world as human beings. And it was mixed up with rebellion against authority, including Christian and Jewish traditions. So, a lot of people simply had nowhere safe to plug this in—no way to make sense of Buddhism but to connect it to the worst they'd heard or dreamed up about cults. Zen Center was not a cult."

Several times, Zen Center has been challenged to prove it.

When a couple of drunken and bothersome tenants were evicted from a Zen Center rental unit in the mid-seventies, they threatened to sue. They claimed the building manager was discriminating against them because they were gay. Theirs was not an airtight case. The building was managed by the openly gay former drag queen Issan. Still, Zen Center did not breathe easy for a while. In their complaint, the evicted tenants referred to Zen Center as a cult. It was not the first or last time the incendiary charge was used to bolster a claim against the center. "Some woman law-yer was hired [by the tenants], and [attorney] Bob Gnaizda defended us," remembers Richard. The tenants were going to bring in a sociologist and her assistant at Berkeley, who had written about cults. Richard recalls the plaintiffs' representatives were told about the respected people who would file affidavits on behalf of Zen Center. Neither Richard nor his lawyer had any doubt but that Zen Center was not a cult, but they both knew that robed people with shaved heads were vulnerable to the charge. Richard was reassured when his lawyer joked, "We are going to start out [by argu-ing that] lawyers are a kind of cult."

Michael Murphy dismisses the idea of Zen Center as a cult, "not sim-ply because Dick is my pal. I sat through the first 350 seminars done at Esalen. And over the years, I've met a lot of dubious and potentially dan-gerous people. I've met them all. I'm sort of the Toots Shor of the Meta-physical Circuit. When Dick was there, the practice at Zen Center was always deeply rooted in that ancient tradition. It was about practice."

Gary Snyder agrees. "Surely what they were doing at Zen Center was Zen Buddhism. They were practicing mindfully. No doubt about that, in my mind. Maybe they were doing a little too much too fast. *No rush,* you know?" Gary sort of smiles, or maybe it was a wink—it's hard to know. "What I felt, in those years, was that Zen Center was too Japanese. I said so to Dick," remembers Gary. "I said, 'You guys are going to set Zen back a hundred years by being so Japanese.'"

This analysis tallies with practitioners' memories of the hierarchical structure of Zen Center, and with the reaction of visitors, who recall Zen Center's meditation and ceremonial routines as profoundly still, spare, formal experiences compared to practice routines at other Buddhist tem-ples and training centers, which were often informal hybrids of various Eastern traditions, ranging from the eclectic to the unruly. And yet people who stayed at Zen Center through the seventies sometimes find them-selves using the word *cult,* or forms of it *(cultic, cultish, cultlike),* or sug-gestive phrases *(he could cast a spell; it was as if we were in a trance; he was so charismatic that he sort of hypnotized you)* when they are looking back and reaching for a justification for having stayed despite their dissat-isfactions.

In 1971, Jim Jones moved his People's Temple to San Francisco. Throughout the ensuing decade, it became difficult for many Americans *not* to see unsettling similarities in the behavior of his followers and the devotees of traditional Hindu sects, or the thousands who attended the "crazy wisdom" lectures and meditation sessions led by the Tibetan Buddhist guru Trungpa Rimpoche. And only a few years before the mass suicide in 1978 of 912 members of his People's Temple, Jim Jones had endeared himself to Bay Area politicians by delivering thousands of votes in his church neighborhood and generously donating his congregation's money and services. Newspapers and columnists reported that Governor Jerry Brown and then–State Assembly Speaker Willie Brown (later mayor of San Francisco) were among the many elected officials who visited the People's Temple, and Mayor Moscone appointed Jim Jones to the city's Housing Authority Commission.

Private debates about the distinction between a cult and a religion, or a benign and a malignant cult, or a cultic figure and a homicidal maniac, were often resolved tragically. Rather than paying the high price for hindsight, many people adopted a precautionary skepticism or a prophylactic suspicion. Others, including Jerry Brown and his staff, publicly disassociated themselves with the practice of Buddhism. "Jerry Brown has never meditated at Zen Center," his aide Jacques Barzhagi assured the *Los Angeles Times* (although the Page One headline for the April 4, 1977 article was "Zen and the Art of Advising Gov. Brown"). "I have never meditated at Zen Center," added Barzhagi, who'd been married there. "I don't know anybody who has ever meditated at Zen Center."

"It wasn't a cult," says Willem Malten matter-of-factly, "but Richard did cultivate blindness in us and in himself." For example, adds Willem, "Richard Baker's own observation that illegitimate sex is a cause for spiritual communities to break down turned out to be true. He told other people to very careful of that. He wasn't careful. But by saying something aloud so clearly and often, he hid his own life more deeply."

"He wasn't straight with his students," says Paul Discoe, Zen Center's longtime head carpenter. "That's why most of the older, you might say out-of-control people who wanted to practice but didn't want to practice with Dick went to Trungpa" in the early seventies. "Trungpa was wild, but he was honest. He fought fire with fire."

Trungpa's first book, *Meditation in Action* (1969), popularized Tibetan Buddhism in the West, opening the gate for the less esoteric, more ritualistic Tantric traditions and Buddhist sects, which preserve the mystical and magical folk traditions and emphasize the role of the teacher as guru. Trungpa's teaching led to the establishment of the Naropa Institute in Colorado and Gompa Abbey in Nova Scotia. Trungpa also set a remarkably low apparent standard for personal behavior—or maybe it was simply not a *standard* standard. Oddly, this became the standard by which many other teachers were judged to be failures, including Richard. "Trungpa [who was married] was a much more humane teacher," says Willem. "If he wanted to have a sexual affair with someone, Trungpa didn't pretend to fall in love. He told the person he wanted to screw her. If the person agreed, that was her karma." Thus, again, sex was not the problem at Zen Center; hypocrisy was the problem. "Richard was not truthful," says Willem.

Bill Kwong remembers that Suzuki-roshi and Trungpa met four times. "It was a real connection between enlightened people," he says. Bill is not unaware of Trungpa's unconventional morality. "He did it all in the open," says Bill. "There was no scandal. He never forced [people] to figure it out for themselves. Of course, Trungpa was deeply realized. He was a real crazy wisdom holder. Other people tried to be like him, but they weren't deeply realized."

The line was not drawn at behavior in the 1970s and early 1980s; it was drawn at enlightenment.

"Tibetans follow in the Indian style that you must have absolute faith in the guru," says Gary Snyder, "you must obey the guru and accept whatever the guru tells you. People spoke that way about Trungpa. I was scolded by one of his disciples for laughing at Trungpa. He was a nut. But they were very offended. Whereas, it is built into Zen practice that the teacher is a person, too."

Gib Robinson had been drawn to Trungpa after he'd become involved with the Tibetan-refugee resettlement efforts in the early seventies. He remembers trying to do "the odd kind of sitting that people did at these events. But then Trungpa showed up drunk as a skunk in the middle of the afternoon on a Saturday, and basically pissed away the weekend. He was brilliant, but there was not a stable practice."

"We [at the Sonoma Mountain Zen Center] were honored to have a close relationship with Trungpa because of Suzuki-roshi," says Bill, who recalls that Trungpa "could be very unnerving. He could hit you just where you needed to be hit. But Trungpa was gentle. We have a *stupa* [commemorative shrine] here for him. He wanted to come and visit the stupa we have for Suzuki-roshi before he went to Nova Scotia, so we raked and got things ready, and then he was sick and could not come." Trungpa was only forty-eight when he died in 1987; whether he did or didn't die as the result of complications related to alcoholism remains a hotly debated topic in Buddhist books and periodicals. "We were sad when he couldn't come," says Bill, "but we went to the stupa, and when we got there, all these red flowers had bloomed on both sides of the path—flowers that never came back again. It's like that with Trungpa. It's really like that."

It was also like this: Before he died, Trungpa chose as his Vajra Regent—his American teaching heir—a man named Osel Tendzin. Osel continued Trungpa's wild ways for a few years, but he failed to tell the disciples with whom he had sexual relations that he had contracted HIV. Osel died of AIDS-related complications in 1990, having transmitted the virus along with the teaching.

"Trungpa," says Gary. "Talk about cultic. He had women bodyguards in black dresses and high heels packing automatics standing in a circle around him while they served sake and invited me over for a chat. It was bizarre."

It really wasn't like that at Zen Center.

Steve Weintraub is a psychotherapist, and unlike amateur shrinks, he avoids diagnostic and categorical terminology. He hadn't used the word *cult*, but even he says, "I don't know if the label *cult* is good. One could have said it was a benign cult. Of course, I wouldn't have even had that thought [in the seventies]. Was I in a cult? I don't think so. The apocalyptic events of 1983 tell me that if it was a cult, we were able to work our way out of it. Today, Zen Center is obviously not a cult."

John Bailes, who at nineteen found Richard invasive and confounding and intriguing, says, "You know, despite all that I am remembering, it was not even a personality cult. There was a lot of pressure not to say things, but every effort wasn't invested in just worshipping Dick. Nor did Dick conceive it to be or let it become cultish. It's funny," says John, "but what I would say now is that he had the authority, but he really didn't have our hearts." The characteristic behavior of senior priests that John remembers was not adulation but a kind of pious sobriety. He fondly recalls skipping breakfast at Page Street to eat noodles and hot sauce with Philip Whalen, "anything not to eat oatmeal with the silent people. They were very serious, and they always seemed to be very concerned about the future of Buddhism in America. I guess maybe we all began to think of ourselves as Buddhists, and we forgot we were human beings."

Gary says, "It goes back to what Suzuki-roshi had said to me, that these young Americans take Japanese customs too seriously. It's not that the Japanese don't do these things, but they know they are not serious. In Japan," he says, "there is always a wink. They make deep prostrations and bows to the teacher, as though he were a god, on one occasion, and then you see them walking along with him and chatting later. Both the teacher and the student have to know when to wink. Dick didn't understand this himself. He clearly had not had enough training to be playful in that way." Gary makes an *Oh, well*, gesture. "It takes time. It's subtle. And even then, that little wink is very hard to notice if you are a literal person." Gary smiles.

Richard was thirty-six when he became Abbot in 1971. He'd spent less than three years in Japan. Surely, these facts are reflected in his relationship to his authority as Suzuki-roshi's dharma heir; maybe he didn't know enough to wink and shrug it off, so many of the most senior priests never learned to call him on his excesses or laugh off his silliest demands. There was never a moment when he was not the Abbot. Thus, having problems with Richard, who was Abbot-for-life, meant you were having problems with Zen—and that was your problem. "Yvonne came to understand this," says Gary. "Sometime in the early eighties, she said to me, 'Dick has reached the point where he isn't getting any feedback about how he looks or what he is doing.'"

"For a number of years, I tried to talk to somebody about what I saw," says Yvonne. "I went to Katagiri-roshi. I went to Reb. And I went to Lew. All three of them would not let me speak. And when I went back to them later [after 1983], each of them acknowledged that he knew whatever I had to say was big trouble. And Reb said, 'I didn't want to hear what you were coming to talk about because I had a sense that Zen Center would blow up and be no more.' Of the three of them, the one who acknowledged that he had blocked me speaking and apologized was Lew."

It was not, for Lew, cultic devotion to Richard as an enlightened being that informed his own behavior. It was just too hard to believe that Richard did not understand what was obvious to everyone else. "I spent my last days with [Richard] trying to help him, one-on-one," says Lew. "During one twelve-hour day at Tassajara, I heard his piece of it, and I have to say, it made no sense to me. I could not connect the dots. How he saw it, and why he did what he did were difficult to understand—particularly his genuine puzzlement about why everyone was so upset."

The pattern almost everyone confirms is Richard's increasing isolation from the community, and his decreasing attention to students and the daily business of Zen Center. "I had heard rumors," says Teah Strozer, "but they weren't happening in my room, and I didn't have much to do with Richard Baker or his household. You had to be invited over there. And," she adds, "I wasn't among the invitees."

Wherever students found themselves in the late seventies and early eighties, Richard often was not there. This is not the profile of a cult leader. Despite the wishes of many of Richard's students, the price of staying at Zen Center was going out every day into the world, and meeting and serving and greeting nonpractitioners. Students' families and friends were regularly invited to Zen Center events. And the Tassajara guest season provided annual, prolonged, often informal interactions with visitors from around the world. This was really no way to run a cult, which thrives on isolation from the larger world and insulation from its ideas and influences.

John has often heard the charge made that underneath the surface of Zen Center was a current of fear; this is an enduring, if indirect, accusation of cultic manipulation. "And I could not figure out why the senior students—who seemed to live in fear of Dick Baker—stayed. If they were really afraid of him, why didn't they leave?"

Some say that their instinctive response to fear was *not* to flee; others believed that the spirit of the practice at Zen Center was to sit with your fears, to face yourself. Ed Brown recalls a conversation he had with Richard during the Thanksgiving holiday in 1978 in the home of Zen Center patron Nancy Wilson Ross, a prominent New York socialite and writer. "I was Nancy's assistant," says Ed. "I had been the head teacher at City Center, President of Zen Center, and Chairman of the Board," he adds. "We sat down to visit, and I said, 'I have a very difficult time talking to you. I feel scared and intimidated, and it is painful.' Dick said, 'Nobody else at Zen Center has that problem, so it must be your problem. Just look at you, you've got your hand over your mouth. Take it away when you try to talk to me.'"

Richard confirmed Ed's fear.

Ed nods. "It took me four years to say, 'I'm not the only one who has these problems,' and then [Richard] said, 'Oh, I meant, you were the only one of the senior people having these problems.'"

"The senior priests never told us they were having problems," says a former Zen Center student who worked in the bakery in the years leading up to the Apocalypse. "I wasn't personally afraid of Richard Baker, but I was afraid that I was the only person who didn't understand what was going on [at Zen Center]. I felt very strongly that what we were working for was not only our own practice but to help establish Buddhism in this country," he says. "Now, if you ask me exactly how I thought I was going to do that by pushing croissants, I don't know. I do know we weren't in it for the money."

John Bailes felt that some of the senior priests were in it for a payoff— Transmission. "My parting thought in 1984 was, You guys need a job," says John, and then he tilts his head and grins. "But the last thing Reb said to me as I got into a cab to go to the airport? Not, I support you going off into the world. Not, Good-bye. He said, 'I give you a year, and then you'll be back.'" John shrugs it off. "He was always coming up with these weird things."

With hindsight, almost everyone who was at Zen Center in the seventies sees that something was being cultivated, but the right word escapes them.

Willem says Richard cultivated blindness. Isn't that how you make a cult?

Willem shakes his head. No. He is sitting across a table in his crowded Cloud Cliff bakery on a hot summer morning in Santa Fe. He watches the cashier ring up a few customers. "In fact, we were not blind," he says. "Many people in the community knew troubling things long before 1983. Some had witnessed sexual harm. Some were aware of the financial problems all along. Some claim to have seen nothing. Every bit of it was playing out under our noses. And we all stayed, so what does that tell you?" The café is a big, bright place with folk art on the walls, and talkative people at the many tables. Willem is smiling. "When I first heard the word *con*," he says, "it was hard for me to translate into Dutch. But since I've been in America, I've been conned a few times. Looking back, in each case, I can see that I wanted to be conned. I wanted *not* to see the inconsistencies." He watches the comings and goings for a little longer, as if every person who turns up is a pleasant surprise, and he is still looking at the open doorway when he says, "If you were confused or worried about something that Richard did, and you asked Reb or Blanche or one of the senior priests about it, they fell back on the mystery of Transmission. The answer was, Richard has Transmission. Suzuki-roshi had invested his spirit, somehow, mystically, into Richard Baker, and attached his spiritual standing to Richard Baker through a mysterious ceremony." Willem stops to gauge my reaction, and then he adds, "They weren't kidding. And this is what people wanted to be told, because [Transmission] is what these people wanted. They were ambitious, and only Richard could give it to them, because he was the only one who had it."

Willem turns toward me, but he looks right up at the ceiling when he says, "I used the Bodhisattva vows [lay ordination] to set myself apart from other people, from ordinary people. When I vowed to save all beings, I didn't understand that everybody is here to save everybody. My parents were doctors. They saved a lot of people. I felt I was more honorable than they were because I had chosen this anonymous life. I was selfless. I was egoless. My father saved people from pain every day and never gave it a second thought. I was expounding on my discovery of compassion and awareness." Willem aims his gaze directly at mine, so I can't really see him, or maybe I can see him as he is seeing himself. "I am ashamed. We were all in on the con. We were not who the visitors and guests thought we were. Publicly, we were saving all beings. Secretly, we had been encouraged to turn our [ordinations] into careers. That's why 1983 was so devastating. Dozens of careers were reduced to shit in a moment. Our careers as Zen masters-in-training and our status as members of the renowned Zen Center and managers of all those Buddhist businesses—it was all going away."

25.

1977. "My dear darling RDB [Richard Dudley Baker]: I sometimes wonder what posterity will make of my passionate styles of address to you. Maybe these letters should be burned in the dark of the moon—particularly in view of your present high status."

Nancy Wilson Ross was seventy-six when she wrote this, one of hundreds of letters she wrote to Richard, Yvonne, and other members of Zen Center in the later years of her life. Born in 1901, in Olympia, Washington, Nancy Wilson married Charles Ross, and they stayed together for almost twenty years. They studied at the Bauhaus in the thirties, and cultivated a bohemian life among artists and performers at Dartington Hall in England, in New York City, and in the state of Washington, where they had a waterfront house on Hood Canal. From 1924 through 1960, Nancy wrote novels and children's books, and throughout her life, her essays and reviews appeared in the *New Yorker*, the *New York Times Book Review*, and other national magazines and journals.

Nancy's second husband was New York publisher and playwright Stanley Young. They married in 1942, and lived in a house in Old Westbury, Long Island, on the Whitney Estate; they kept a place in Vero Beach, Florida; and they spent most summers on Moose Lake in the Adirondacks, in one of the turn-of-the-century cottages, or "camps," whose owners are members of the Adirondack League Club, which includes a sprawling 1894 club house and lodge, 75,000 acres of forested land, a twelve-mile stretch of the Moose River, and many attendant lakes.

When John D. Rockefeller founded the Asia Society in 1956, he asked Nancy to be on the Board, and she served for thirty years. In 1960, Nancy published an anthology, *The World of Zen*, the first of her three books about Buddhism, a lifelong personal and intellectual passion that became her principal literary, social, and philosophical interest until her death in 1986. She met and practiced with Suzuki-roshi at Sokoji and introduced him to her friends and potential patrons on the East Coast. Her public ties to Richard, and her personal friendship with him, his family, and several of his students at Zen Center had been unraveling for several years before her death. She was memorialized with a service at St. John the Divine in February of 1986, with the cathedral dean, and Yvonne Rand, and former Zen Center student John Bailes officiating without Richard's assistance, and a Buddhist Ashes ceremony in the Adirondacks that Richard did not attend, which one student recalls as "a face-off; nobody seemed sure who was representing Richard, who was representing Zen Center, or who was representing Nancy. It was not what it should have been."

In 1972, the University of Texas purchased the personal and literary papers of Nancy and Stanley. This, and Stanley's ill health, occasioned an opportunity. Nancy needed help organizing her archives, caring for Stanley, and managing her daily life. Shortly before Stanley's death in 1975, Nancy began to forward money from the University of Texas to Zen Center, and every six months or so, Richard sent another student or two to live with Nancy and assist her. The students were paid a regular Zen Center stipend (approximately $100 to $150 a month); some of them received a small clothing allowance because life with Nancy sometimes called for a clean shirt or a decent pair of socks; and depending on their aptitudes and Nancy's needs from day to day, the students served as housemaids, cooks, handymen, secretaries, traveling companions, and confidantes.

"Nancy saw her piece of the agreement to teach these people how to translate what they were doing in Zen practice into their own culture base," says Yvonne. Having adopted an ancient version of Japanese manners, the students were now to acquire a set of old-fashioned American manners. "Nancy had the idea that you set a table and sit down with guests with the same attention you bring to your meal in a meditation hall during a retreat. She had an incredibly developed sense of space, place, objects, and care of the attendant environment," says Yvonne. As one of the few prominent women associated with Buddhism in America, Nancy also offered advice and opinions that were not readily available in the Bay Area. In 1973, she urged Yvonne not to have her head shaved at her ordination, as "even Catholic nuns of old and distinguished Orders are giving up their trappings and their head-shaving." The shock of a shaved woman, wrote Nancy, is off-putting, not inviting, and "I don't think the inner meaning is Big enough to make this a necessity. I think all aspects of the outré must be given up," she wrote, "if people are to be reached on a widening level." (Yvonne was shaved, but these days she has hair.)

"I was very close to Nancy," says Yvonne. "She often introduced me as the unacknowledged Abbess of Zen Center. She was a mentor for me. She took me on, and I learned from her." They maintained a telephone and written correspondence, which matured into cross-country visits and a family friendship. "I was the executor of her estate," says Yvonne, whose second husband became Nancy's legal and financial advisor, when Nancy feared that the arrangements made for the disposal of her real estate holdings might leave her without enough money to live out her life.

"When I met Nancy, it was as if I'd found a long-lost godmother," says Renée des Tombe, who was one of the first women Richard sent. Stanley was dying, and Renée remembers long hours in the vast library, at an ironing board, and in the company of Nancy's friends, including the artists and art patrons Anne Morrow Lindbergh and Margot Wilkie and the actress Beatrice Straight, who was born a Whitney in Old Westbury. Renée was not exactly a Zen student. She lived with Richard and Virginia, sat at Zen Center, and worked on projects as needed, including The Neighborhood Foundation. "[Richard and Virginia] made me a part of their family," she says. Her time with Nancy was full and fascinating, "a glimpse into a world that was going away. I was always delighted to be in her company. And I am as happy serving tea as having tea," Renée adds.

The students Richard sent to Nancy after Renée typically had been, or would become, his assistants. Nancy wrote to Richard and to Yvonne about the quality of work each student did, and she frequently included assessments of a student's affect and attitude, often in psychological terms that reflect her interest in Jungian analysis. There were some imperfect matches, but it is clear that Nancy's life was always eased and often tremendously improved by her Zen Center attendants. "Dick helped lots of people," says Lew Richmond. "Whenever you look at anything to criticize, you have to see it, and then see that it had a beneficent partner." The Nancy Wilson Ross exchange yielded many rewards for many people, and a not a few complications. In essence, it was a maid trade, but it was rather easily integrated into the expansive notion of practice at Zen Center, at least until 1981.

It is not clear that being Nancy's assistant reliably deepened or furthered students' Zen practice, but more than a few of them were willing to try on the role. Deborah Madison was Richard's assistant when she was tapped to go. When she first arrived in New York, "I was so happy that I practically fell on the ground and prayed in gratitude that I was there. It rescued me. Suddenly, I was living with a writer in a house full of books. Her practice was not about zazen but about friendliness, and working carefully through a relationship with one particular person at a time. And Nancy showed me something of the world. We had conversations. She was not an easy person to be with, but it was wonderful. I knew from the start that I could be her student because Nancy let you be a person," says Deborah. "When you were in a social situation with her, she did not want you to sit in the corner with your hands on your lap. You were expected to enter the conversation as an acute listener, or preferably, to enter into the give and take. This never felt true with Baker-roshi."

Dan Welch and Deborah, who had been friends since childhood, overlapped at Nancy's. Dan had gone through his divorce and a stint as Richard's assistant. "One of the best calls Richard ever made was to send me to spend the summer with Nancy Wilson Ross," says Dan. "I needed a wider worldview. Richard joked that I was being sent to finishing school. I feel her deeply in my life," says Dan, and he begins to weep. Slowly, quietly, he says, "It was a different kind of training. I was completely ready for it. I loved every moment of working with Nancy."

"I met Dan at the airport," remembers Deborah. "He was much too thin. His pants were falling off. His eyes were bloodshot. He'd stayed up way too late too many nights, drinking green tea. Being Richard's assistant—up all night, awake too early, driving back and forth to Tassajara—was too hard on people. Dan was basically just a skull. I can't believe I fell in love with him."

At Nancy's, Dan worked on masonry projects and the grounds—"and got curious about the larger world," says Deborah, who sat zazen with Dan in the mornings and did secretarial work and housework and cooked. "It was a hardworking and amazing existence," she says, recalling that it was Nancy who referred to them as her Zen slaves. "When I'd first arrived, I also thought, as a Zen student, it was my duty to suggest that Nancy and I do zazen together, at least once a day, like at five-thirty in the evening, maybe. Nancy said, 'That's a wonderful idea. Let's do.' And when it would get to be about five-thirty, she would say, 'What do you think about an Old Fashioned?' Or, 'How about a gin and tonic?' So zazen became cocktail hour, which I grew to appreciate," says Deborah. "I found cocktail hour was just as worthwhile—it was calming. And when Dan came, because he didn't want to drink [alcohol], he drank huge quantities of tonic water so Nancy couldn't see if there was gin. One day she said, 'I cannot figure out why I am suddenly spending so much more money on tonic water than I am on gin.'" Deborah pauses. "That summer, Dan got some color, and he grew some hair, and he gained some weight, and he learned to put some gin in his tonic."

Dan smiles. "My family never drank. Or dressed for dinner, as we did at Nancy's camp. My parents were Quakers and had taken a vow of voluntary poverty after World War II, so they would not have to pay taxes. Nancy's world had a real allure. She was demandingly articulate, and her support was unconditional. She had participated in the Great White Culture, and as I saw it, she was tying up her life impeccably. In her last years, she let these odd Zen people into her life, and she shared something richly matured with us."

What else did Nancy have to share?

Lucy Calhoun's time with Nancy was "time in a familiar world." She and Nancy discovered mutual family friends among their relatives and family business associates. "Of course, I was numb by the time I was sent to her," says Lucy, whose sexual relationship with Richard was not quite over when she arrived, "and I wasn't sure I wanted another personal relationship that carried responsibilities that I wasn't sure I could handle." Lucy is quiet for a while, and then she says, "In hindsight, I see that I was hoping to be sent. Nancy treated me as an equal. It was very good for me." Lucy also remembers that Richard was awed by Nancy and her wide circle of powerful friends. "She could give him trouble in a way no one else could, as a result."

Karin Gjording followed Lucy. "Nancy felt it was her job to teach all of us what she called Western Tea Ceremony—a kind of American version of royal life, really, though she also said, 'That Richard lives like royalty. No one lives the way he does anymore.'" Karin remembers Nancy's generous way of including her in social and personal conversations and events. "Richard preferred to have you wait in the car for him," Karin explains. "The first time I met Wendell Berry was at a Lindisfarne Association meeting on Long Island. Nancy was a fellow, as was Richard. When he showed up, he clearly expected me to be his attendant more than hers. So when we got to the Lindisfarne meeting, my expectation was that I would wait outside. Nancy just looked at me and said, 'Of course, you will come in and spend the time with us.'"

Before she was called back to San Francisco to manage the opening of the bakery, Karin accompanied Nancy to England, where she'd been invited to speak at Dartington Hall, the innovative arts, gardening, and educational Trust created by Leonard Elmhirst and his American wife, Dorothy Whitney Straight, in 1925 on their 1,000-acre estate in Devon. Nancy also invited Lucy along on the trip. Then, Richard and Virginia and Renée joined them, as did poet Robert Duncan. "Lucy and I had our own apartment, and we all seemed to have a great time together except Lucy, who was in terrible shape, and I didn't know why," recalls Karin. "Lucy was crying all the time, which was really odd for her. Much later, she told me that Richard had his last liaisons with her on that trip. That was when she finally cut it off."

Not all students prospered under Nancy's tutelage. "I was still pretty miserable in my own life when I was sent," says Linda Cutts, "and Nancy almost sent me back to Zen Center at one point." But she stayed for six months. "I got very close to her physically. I was a lady's maid, really. I combed her hair. We would talk about Buddhism sometimes, and I learned how to use a finger bowl. That came in handy—with Nancy." Linda doesn't crack a smile. "I think it was a world Richard aspired to, though like so many other things at the time, that was not obvious to me then."

As she aged, Nancy grew increasingly dependent on the physical and emotional assistance she received. Still, for many, her home was a refuge. Ed Brown remembers his time in New York as "the first time I understood it was possible that I might not be crazy, or at least that I wasn't the only crazy one at Zen Center, which had sort of been my reputation."

Therese Fitzgerald stayed with Nancy almost two years, and recalls the time not as a servant but as "a younger woman doing everything she could for an older woman who was doing everything she could for me. I think Nancy really loved Richard," says Therese, "but she was in a position to take the liberty of not falling into absolute adulation."

"Nancy could be controlling, and she was mercurial," says Yvonne, who recalls trouble between Nancy and students, especially in the 1980s. "Many of the students who went to live with her were limited in their experience, and very idealistic. There was a lot of judgment of Nancy, and accusations that she was an alcoholic, and a racist. And there was truth in that—she was a person of her era with unfortunate attitudes about groups of people. But for students involved in a practice of compassion, it was interesting how hard a time they had."

It is true that Zen practitioners are meant to cultivate nondiscriminating minds. It is also true that there were a lot of people in the Page Street neighborhood whose hair they might have combed. But that is a difficult distinction for a Zen student to articulate; it may be impossible without resorting to dualistic thinking to assert that this (poor, sick, homeless) person is more deserving of compassion than that (wealthy, healthy, four-residenced) person.

The definition of practice at Zen Center did not exclude the provision of personal services to Nancy Wilson Ross. No line was drawn there. This may explain the terrible confusion that ensued in 1981, when people tried to identify the subtle line between opportunity and opportunism, which had evidently been crossed.

––––––––––

John Bailes says, "I always knew with Nancy—even when she was totally irrational, which she could be—there was a personal bond, and it would never be broken. With Dick, there was a myth of affection or romance with people. Nancy had guts. She could let you see that she had been hurt."

Yvonne says, "John loved Nancy, and Nancy thrived on that."

"If Nancy had been thirty years younger—whew." After a few seconds, John says, "Well, it was the best it could have been, given who we were." John credits Richard with introducing him to Nancy, and he credits Nancy for "teaching me to experience the complex drives of people that we, at Zen Center, had not allowed ourselves to see or understand. Even with Richard, Nancy would identify and direct him to his faults. I think that really helped him. But I wonder, Where did all that go?"

John saw Nancy's willingness to open her life to him and other students as a critical difference in her and Richard's teaching styles. "It meant she had taken a personal stake in me. That is Buddhism," he says, "not some ancient story, but the facts. *Here we are. We are going to die. I am going to give you what I've got.* That's what I think Transmission is about." It was Nancy who ultimately convinced John to return to Harvard and complete his degree; she gave him some money, as did her old friend philanthropist Paul Mellon, whose gifts to universities and museums from his family's industrial and banking fortunes were estimated at $1 billion when he died in 1991.

"[Nancy] showed me a world I never would have seen," says John, including trips to Antigua on Mellon's private jet, and "dinner with Robert Giroux, George Braziller, Tom Wolfe, and Nancy in Roger Straus's apartment . . ." John hesitates, as if he is reading from the letterhead of the prestigious publishing company Farrar, Straus & Giroux. "And me," he adds, and he still looks a little surprised that he was invited. "Nancy lived in an America that most Americans think doesn't exist anymore. She made it available. Dick wouldn't."

Every student who spent time with Nancy felt clearly her love, admiration, and respect for Richard. Her private correspondence and her public words and actions through 1980 make very clear her gratitude for her personal relationship with Richard, as well her relationship with his family, friends, and students. Time and again, she happily lent her name and reputation, as well as those of her friends, to Zen Center and its many initiatives. "She was a major source of the East Coast power elite support for Zen Center," says Yvonne. In return, "he manipulated her fear of being alone and not being taken care of, and he was seductive with her. And he furthered this with his students."

As Nancy neared eighty, she and Richard seized a couple of additional opportunities. One was the idea of creating an annuity for Nancy, which could be realized if she donated her Hood Canal property in Washington to Zen Center. The other was for Nancy to nominate Richard for membership in the Adirondack League Club, whose wealthy members John describes as "so Republican they were Republican before there were Republicans. These are people whose names most Americans will never know because they have people working for them just to make sure their names are not known."

As the annuity was being presented to Zen Center lawyers in 1981, and made official in mid-1982, Richard was nominated by Nancy for Club membership. Among his references were Laurance Rockefeller, the Fidelity Johnsons, Beatrice Whitney Straight, William Sloane Coffin, Maurice Ash of Dartington Hall, and Governor Edmund G. Brown, Jr. A ceremonious letter was composed by Nancy, which included a reference to the Dalai Lama's recent visit to Zen Center, but concentrated not on Richard's Buddhist credentials but on Richard's Dudley-ness. He was accepted into the Club as a "descendant of the old, honorable English Dudleys."

Lineage. It's just a line someone draws.

Late summer, 1981. "Dearest Yvonne: This is a day when I truly wish you were in the next room," writes Nancy, who has just had a visit from Lucy. "It was great to see her, although I found her worrisomely thin. We sat up to all hours talking and drinking red wine . . . OUT POURED ALL OF IT. I was appalled to be quite honest; not at Lucy's behavior, but at the behavior of You Know Who. I cannot accept it in my heart, not because of the events themselves, but of the false front. I feel I now understand Trungpa's un-shaken power with his followers; he is impossible to admire for his behavior but at least it is all UP FRONT, from drinking to wenching."

"Once Nancy saw that side of Dick," says John, "she recoiled." To Richard's chagrin, Nancy forwarded all of the arrangements for the annuity and her other properties to the Abbot's Council. "And the Adirondack property," says John, "well, she found out that Dick thought it was his."

Richard wrote to Nancy that he felt she had intended to leave him the camp, which was why he'd been helping her by investing money and his family's time visiting the camp every summer for five years instead of establishing a summer routine at an oceanside location. When Yvonne tried to unravel the situation in a letter to Katagiri-roshi, she remembered that "Dick wanted Nancy to give him, personally, her camp in the woods. And he had some thoughts that she might will [to Zen Center] her property in Long Island, which he had thought of using as a base for a center in the New York region."

"When Nancy saw that in him," says John, "it was all over. That he would be so bold as to assume something like inheriting the camp—and then Nancy put that into the context of my being there and others who were sent there, with [the house on the lake] as the ultimate goal . . ." John raises his eyebrows. "She sold it. It wasn't his."

Adirondack League members pay annual dues. "He never paid his dues, and his name was posted on the [Club] bulletin board for being in arrears," remembers Yvonne. For Nancy, this was "an embarrassing dénouement, to say the least."

Of course, you can say it was just a club. But it was also just Nancy's name, and just her word among people with whom she had shared just forty years of her life. In the ceremonious world of America's aspiring aristocracy, it was not nothing.

The Board at Zen Center began to receive notices for the $1,700 in overdue membership fees. Nancy attempted to arrange a resignation "without prejudice" so that the initiation fees paid upon Richard's admission would not be lost, but the Club had drawn its line on membership dues long before Richard had arrived. A membership could not be resigned if the account was in arrears, which is where Richard's was; thus, either Zen Center wrote a check, or the Chief Priest and Abbot of the Corporation Sole would be assessed membership dues for another year in a Club in which he apparently no longer had any interest.

And by the time Richard was walking to Tassajara by way of Disneyland, it was evident that the value of the Hood Canal property had been incorrectly assessed by both Nancy's advisors and Zen Center's independent agent owing to an "imperfect easement," which no one discovered until after the deal had been signed. By this time, Nancy felt she was dependent on the annuity payments. Her canal property was legally "landlocked" and worth one-third less than anticipated. Instead of selling the land and house in a month to fund the annuity, Zen Center spent more than three years working with realtors in Washington State. The property was advertised locally in Washington, and then in the Bay Area, the *Los Angeles Times*, and the *Wall Street Journal;* and then again in a few international publications. When Zen Center found a taker for the property, the arrangement—which had been designed to yield at least $100,000 for Zen Center—resulted in a net loss.

It was not what it should have been.

A couple of years before Nancy died at eighty-five in January 1986, the Treasurer of Zen Center figured out that the differential between the payments made by Nancy and the cost of providing her with assistants between 1978 and 1984 had resulted in a loss to the community of more than $15,000. In cash terms, they were paying to provide Nancy Wilson Ross with servants. At the same time, the Zen Center Board members were writing letters to scholars and translators and teachers to terminate contractual agreements for long-term support. Zen Center could not meet its financial obligations. Nancy was invited to live at Green Gulch, but she declined; several offers and counteroffers were made, as everyone tried to figure out what could be done to resolve the relationship. And until 1985, Nancy was attended by a Zen Center student.

"There is an interesting parallel with [the Austrian-born Tibetan teacher] Lama Govinda and his wife," says Yvonne. "Dick made commitments that the organization had to carry, and after the 1983 explosion, what happens? The resentment of all those years [unraveled]; people began to see that not only did they feel like servants, they were servants—and a lot of [the resentment] got acted out with the dismantling of commitments to Lama Govinda and his wife—then in their eighties—and Nancy. What was unraveling had to do with grief at the smashing of this dream in which people had invested their lives."

Even in the brief history of Zen Center, the intersection of Nancy and Richard and a few dozen students qualifies only as a minor episode. The disposition of her estate and the controversy that ensued about the cost of caring for Nancy—and the cost of not caring for Nancy—played out as a sideshow to the Apocalypse. But it was not nothing. It changed people's lives. It changed the meaning of practice.

Many years after he he bought the BMW, Richard said, "It just didn't occur to me that people were so involved in such things, the status of things." You don't have to disbelieve him to see that everyone he left behind had to make up a story about the meaning of the practice in which they had invested their lives, a practice that now involved acquiring homes and serving the wealthy, and a Club fee of $1,700—just about the total earned in a year by a stipend student. To any passerby on Page Street who peeked in one of the big, bright windows, those unenlightened students who stayed after Richard left must have looked like ordinary Americans, gathered around a table, adding up the numbers, banging their shaved heads together, trying to figure out how to pay the mortgage.

Richard was able to shrug off Nancy's camp house, the Hood Canal property, and even Zen Center itself. That is the fundamental story of Buddhism—almost. In the traditional telling of the tale, the Buddha shrugged off his own palace, not someone else's.

26. THE BEGINNER'S MIND

Temple on Page Street is 150 miles north of Tassajara, and Green Gulch is further north again, but the farm occupies a dreamy, indefinite space between the city and the monastery. It is a not-quite self-sustaining growing and teaching and experimental organic farm, conference and retreat and workshop center, and training temple.

"I had very clear ideas about why we needed Green Gulch," says Richard. It represented the best, and maybe the only opportunity to realize Suzuki-roshi's haunting and indeterminate vision of his students as not quite laypeople and not quite monks.

It was a dream. And the farm was a dream space. It was somewhere between the Japanese traditions and culture and language that informed the monastic practice at Tassajara and the press and pace and profanity of America's capitalist culture that shaped urban life. "Suzuki-roshi would say, 'You don't have any background, so you're very free to practice in a correct way. You don't have corrupt influences,'" remembers Mel Weitsman. "He wanted us to be clean. He hoped that we would help the Japanese reform their way."

Life on the farm promised to be traditional and unprecedented. It promised clean, green air and gainful employment for families on the temple grounds so practitioners with children could attend daily zazen and services; it promised residents that they could often leave their homes and jobs without risk for three months of intense practice to reawaken "the monk within," as the community's frequent visitor and advisor, Benedictine Brother David Steindl-Rast, named the urge to stillness; it promised to be the realization of the fullness of ordinary life.

Dreams have long lives. They are not susceptible to logic; they are dreamed in defiance of reason. And they are immaterial; even as our bodies wither and fail, teaching us the truth of impermanence, our dreams persist, and renew themselves.

The genuine family and lay practice that Suzuki-roshi envisioned has never actually been established, says Mel, and this was evident by the late 1970s. At that point, and several times since, nonresident laypeople who drop by the farm to sit and stay for Sunday lecture, maybe attend weekday zazen or an evening class, began to form their own councils and boards to help Green Gulch residents understand the concerns and needs of ordinary laypeople.

The farm residents are not monks, either, but this makes them just like, say, Darlene Cohen and Tony Patchell, or any of the practitioners at Zen Center. "And there's a big problem with stagnation at Green Gulch," says Darlene. "There are all of these senior students sitting there—they're in their fifties, but it's as if they're waiting to die. They haven't become teachers. They haven't done anything but raise their families there, and now the children are gone, and they're just sitting there." Darlene lived on the farm for a few years, but for almost fifteen years, she and Tony have shared an apartment on Page Street. She has long supported herself by teaching meditation and practice techniques to people with chronic pain, and after thirty years as lay Buddhists and parents, she and Tony were recently ordained as priests.

The farm never became self-sustaining. By 1981, it was a truism among priests and students in the city that they had lived in single rooms, worked in stores and bakeries and restaurants, and solicited funds from donors for ten years not only to support themselves and secure their time at Tassajara but to funnel more than a million dollars into Green Gulch, where fifty or sixty people lived. "The people on the farm are living in one of the most beautiful spots on the planet, and they do their daily tasks, but other people are working to support them," says Tony, who has worked with sick and elderly homeless people and with street kids in San Francisco for many years. "To this day, I feel oppressed when I go there."

Life on the farm is not a dream; the farm is the repository for a dream. It preserves a view of an integrated life—a safer, slower, simpler way than most Americans can afford, a way most people do not choose when it is available. It is to Zen Center what Zen Center is to the wider society—it doesn't pay its share of the taxes, and it requires a lot of generosity from people who do not seem to receive the most generous share of the benefits. But for many people, giving up on Green Gulch, like giving up on Zen Center, would mean giving up.

Darlene recalls a birthday celebration for one of the abbots in the early 1990s. "It was here at Page Street, and people from Green Gulch said, 'It's too dangerous in the city; we can't come.'" Darlene looks out her apartment window toward the lit-up windows of City Center. "I've often called Green Gulch [residents] the Branch Davidians of Zen Center. And the truth is, Richard would have taken care of that problem right away—*Hey, you, move over here.* One result of not having anyone who can tell other people what to do—which we didn't anticipate—is that no one had authority with senior people." Darlene sees this as "the next big question. There is starting to be a voice—we have an Elders' Council, and among peers, [we are asking] how we will have authority with each other and be each other's teacher."

Maybe it all worked best, maybe it almost made sense, when there was just one gentleman farmer to support and sustain. Maybe Richard was to Green Gulch as Green Gulch was to Zen Center as Zen Center was to the wider world. He had a home on the farm, in the city, and at the monastery. If need be, he could spend a morning in waders reviewing the work of the farmhands, dine on farm-fresh vegetables and home-baked bread in the city with friends, and be in Tassajara for a hot spring bath before an early morning in the zendo. A year before Richard invested Suzuki-roshi's dream in a farm, Suzuki-roshi had invested in Richard the deeded rights to that dream.

Richard was expensive, but maybe giving up on Richard meant giving up.

27.

"When are businesses not businesses?" wrote Lew Richmond in a report to the Abbot and Board in 1982. "When they are Zen Center businesses."

In its survey of the best restaurants in America in the year 2000, *Gourmet* magazine praised Greens in San Francisco "for the finesse of its kitchen, its own organic Green Gulch Farm produce, and exceptional wines by the glass. The view of the marina, windsurfers, and the Golden Gate Bridge doesn't hurt either."

Since 1982, Annie Somerville has been supplying the finesse. "It has been an amazing run," says the Executive Chef. Any restaurant that simply survives for more than twenty years is cause for amazement; a vegetarian restaurant that remains a destination for locals and tourists for two decades is almost unthinkable—as was Greens, until Richard had a thought. Until 1979, Greens was one of many empty concrete warehouses on an abandoned, chain-linked pier in San Francisco. The National Park Service had inherited Fort Mason from the Army and was soliciting applications from entrepreneurs and community agencies with ideas for developing the site, which today is a multicultural arts and convention center. "Friends of mine, Stewart Brand and others, got me to be in the first stages of this project of what to do with the Army base," remembers Richard Baker. "I went to a meeting. I said, I'm thinking I want to do a restaurant, but a warehouse is too big." The project director asked him to look inside. The main room was 4,000 square feet of raw space with a ceiling that rose to twenty-six feet. There were four massive bays (ten by eighteen feet each) of opaque, chicken-wired windows, so the place was dark, and the ocean—which could be heard slapping against the pilings underfoot—was nowhere to be seen, not to mention that beautiful bridge.

"Immediately, I saw that if we raised the floor" by twenty-eight inches, says Richard, and replaced the glass, the room would have one of the city's most spectacular views. "And there was parking. I thought, This has got to work."

There were a lot of people who thought Greens would not work. The Parks Service was nervous about a vegetarian restaurant's capacity to draw crowds to the site, and nervous enough about the food to install a meat-sandwich vending machine in Fort Mason for park employees and construction workers. Greens opened in July of 1979, initially serving only lunches Tuesday through Saturday (on Sundays, students were supposed to go to Green Gulch to listen to Richard's lecture), and within a few weeks, the restaurant was serving 200 people a day. And then the reviews appeared—starting with the *San Francisco Chronicle* and covering a lot of column inches before the *International Herald Tribune* printed the three exhortations that had become a sort of User's Guide to Greens: Go for the superb fresh food; do not skip dessert; and get a load of that view.

Diners at Greens are afforded a view of the shimmering, watery world by a false floor. As Richard explains it, building a twenty-eight-inch-high box on the existing floor also created a useful space in which to hide the messy maze of electrical wires and plumbing pipes that were installed during the renovation. The box top formed the false floor—which was simply called *the floor.*

If you lived at Zen Center and worked at Greens—whether you were a carpenter, a busboy, or a chef—you actually didn't work at Greens, of course; you practiced at Greens. This had been true at the other Zen Center businesses, but the restaurant created a big and public platform for this innovative approach to spiritual awakening. Students did not sit zazen at Greens, and ceremonies were spare; shifts and staff meetings began and ended with a group bow ("bowing in" and "bowing out"), and there was a discreet little altar with a bit of incense in a bowl to make everyone mindful of the spirit of the project. The work you did was called *work-practice.* Looking back, almost no one believes it anymore. They believe it was work. But as the *false floor* had become the *floor,* so *work-practice* became *practice,* and for several years that was enough to hide what lay beneath the whole construct.

Annie was managing the Alaya stitchery until 1982, and she started cooking at Greens after the founding chef, Deborah Madison, went to Tassajara to be *shuso,* or head monk. Annie had been a Zen Center student since 1973, and she had cooked at Page Street and Tassajara, but "at the time of the change, I did not feel I had the skills to do what Deborah had done." Annie has short blond hair and a clear-eyed gaze, and she has an offhand, bemused way of talking about her career. "I wasn't very good at working on the line, at first." She laughs; she laughs a lot. "And we weren't the most efficient operation in the world." They didn't have to be.

In 1982, Lew estimated that Zen Center businesses required the equivalent of 110 full-time employees; Greens accounted for thirty-four of these slots. The actual number of people involved was much higher. Staffing memos (pleas for help) from 1982 show that more than fifty people were needed in any given week to work as servers, runners, busboys, dishwashers, wine and beverage tenders, and hosts. Then there was the kitchen crew. "There were really a lot of us in the kitchen," says Annie. "It took a lot of us to do everything." Inefficiency was affordable until the cheap labor pool began to dry up in 1982. Lew estimated that the average wage paid to a Zen Center employee (including stipend students and the increasing number of nonpractitioners) was $2.89 an hour, "and some of our students whom we do not consider our top producers have been able to make thirteen dollars an hour by taking typing jobs" in downtown San Francisco. And then came the Apocalypse.

"By 1983," says former Abbot Mel Weitsman, "work-practice was dead in the water."

Although Greens showed a modest profit for the first time in 1982, the human cost of operating the restaurant had become intolerable. It was the principal focus of almost every meeting of the Outside Financial Advisory Board (OFAB), which repeatedly suggested a merger of the bakery and the restaurant, and other consolidations and labor-saving strategies. But there was a logic to inefficiency. Running the businesses, like managing rental properties, was practice. As long as a year's losses could be vitiated by donations of cash or stock or property, and as long as budget deficits were modest, the labor-intensive businesses were successful because more and more people were able to (work-) practice.

Even after 1983, Zen Center needed income, and though working at Greens was grueling, many people continued to work for the restaurant; however, most of them stopped practicing at Zen Center, including Annie. Even during those rocky years from 1982 through 1986, Annie says, "Greens was a refuge. Page Street was a very dangerous neighborhood still, and here on the other side of town we had open space, and the ocean. I didn't feel betrayed exactly when things got out of control at Zen Center. But I hadn't ever wanted to be ordained, either, and I made a choice to be here, not there. I'd been at Tassajara for the Los Padres National Forest fire, cooking for the crews. And I was there for the flood. And I was there for the zendo fire. So, I'd already had a lot of calamity in my life. I figured I had been trained for disaster-preparedness in the kitchen." Jay Kenyon, who started washing pots at Greens a month after Annie started cooking, also chose the restaurant; today, Jay is the chef, and Annie says they work with longtime general manager Rick Jones as "a real team." Their goals are clear: "to make delicious food, satisfy staff and customers, and keep this place up. Greens is not twenty years old. I like to think we have patina."

The transition from practice-place to business was completed when Zen Center formed the Everyday Corporation, the nonprofit holding company that enables it to own and operate commercial businesses indirectly. Since it has been run as a restaurant by people who have experience working in a restaurant, Greens requires fewer people and makes a much greater profit. Annie's 1993 best-selling *Fields of Greens* cookbook also continues to yield royalties for Everyday Corporation, which manages Zen Center's trademark and licensing agreements. "People still like to ask if Green Gulch grows all of our produce," she says. "No. It never did. They are on the coast, and it's cold and foggy there. They grow what they can for us—potatoes, chard, kale, spinach, a lot of herbs, radicchio, and escarole. And flowers. And a lot of lettuce. Really, a lot of lettuce. But Green Gulch is also a teaching farm, and a meditation center, and a training temple." Greens is just a restaurant.

Annie credits Richard with the vision and vigor that got the restaurant going. Karin Gjording, the restaurant's founding manager and now an Everyday Board member, agrees. "Richard's idea was to establish vegetarian food as a cuisine in its own right. And Greens did that. He knew that it had to be pretty grand. And he found a phenomenal location—that view really helps."

Annie is not certain how many people at Zen Center feel deeply connected to Greens, which is no longer staffed or managed by students. "They might feel they cannot afford to eat here," she says. Although Greens is the only one of the work-practice enterprises launched in the seventies that is still operating, Zen Center's interest in its future is not strictly sentimental. Since 1986, profits from Greens filtered through the Everyday Corporation have typically accounted for 10 to 20 percent of Zen Center's $2 to $3 million annual income. As a regular revenue source, the restaurant ranks second only to the combined guest and visitor fees for all retreats, conferences, and workshops, as well as the annual summer guest season at Tassajara.

"Now, I'm a little embarrassed by how expensive Greens is," says Richard. "The idea of Greens, in part, was to create a common society in San Francisco."

Almost everyone involved with the Greens project remembers it as a community-wide effort. "People wanted us to succeed," says Karin, who managed the building project before she managed the restaurant. "And we were starting from scratch." A local supplier of restaurant equipment helped Karin assemble a basic list of necessary machinery and fixtures, and immediately located a refurbished commercial mixer for $1,800 (versus $6,500 for a new machine) and dishwasher ($800 versus $2,000 new). "We put in an espresso machine," says Karin "and then I realized that the person who'd be working there probably had never drunk an espresso, never mind made one. I asked her to go to North Beach, to [Caffe] Malvina, and watch what they did. And she did—and they even hired her for a couple of weeks, and she learned that skill and brought it back to us."

Paul Discoe, the carpenter in charge of the warehouse renovation, says, "Everyone knew we were trying to save money. Two of our big expenses were tile and glass for those giant windows. Local merchants gave us a lot of breaks. They seemed to understand who we were."

"Everyone was working really hard," says Karin. "People at the Bakery felt bereft. And those of us who commuted from Green Gulch never got a chance to sit." Practice. "I did not feel acknowledged—and I was pretty unaware of what I felt in those days—but I knew that because when we had the grand opening, it was the first and only time I know of that Richard publicly thanked people at Zen Center. He had a big sign made, and my name was not on it. It was an oversight, of course. I may have thought I didn't care about being acknowledged, but when I walked in, it mattered that he'd forgot."

"I designed it [and] conceived of [the restaurant]," says Richard. "Deborah was the cook who really made it work." Richard adds that Greens was, in part, opened as "a platform" for Deborah's cooking. "And Renée [des Tombe, who lived with Richard's wife and family at Green Gulch] was the maître d' who really made the atmosphere of the restaurant work. The place is inconceivable without the three of us."

"Renée was wonderful," says Ed Brown. "Smart, too, and I appreciated working with her. I remember one day when Renée and I were sitting having lunch on the bench [at Greens]. Dick brought over some very important people. He introduced them to Renée as the manager." Ed's dark eyes brighten. "I was her co-manager." Ed nods. "It was not an oversight. I was on the outs."

Many people remember David Chadwick as the maître d' who made Greens memorable. "His job was to be there at nine to answer the phone and take reservations," remembers Karin, "and he'd run in late in dirty work clothes, put all the calls on hold, run outside and smoke a cigarette, and run back in his zories [sandals] with dirty feet. And he was the perfect host. He treated everyone alike. Homeless people and society ladies all knew David."

David Chadwick, a novelist and biographer of Suzuki-roshi, was an ordained priest with ten years of practice when he left Zen Center in the mid-seventies. Richard fired him from his job at the Greengrocers, to which David responded, "I quit." He never lost touch with Zen Center or Richard, and he was called back for duty when the restaurant opened.

David is not tall, but he is big—not a person you'd push around. At Greens, he says, "my job was to say no. And to make sure the critics and reviewers got good seats. And to give [*San Francisco Chronicle* columnist] Herb Caen a free loaf of sesame-millet bread whenever he came—and he did, often; and he put us in his column, too." Caen got the bread "because he was the first Bay Area journalist to write about the threat of nuclear weapons." And David made it his job to resist the pleas of the self-important. "It felt like evening things out to seat a park employee or a local person who'd been saving up to come eat at the restaurant before I gave a table to a bank vice president. I had a guy yelling at me one day, 'Do you know who I am? Do you know who I am?' And I just wouldn't seat him. He said it every time I walked by him, 'Do you know who I am?' Finally, I turned to one of the waiters and said, 'When that guy figures out who the hell he is, let me know, and I'll try to find a place for him to have lunch.'"

Deborah had been tapped to invent a menu and cook the food. "Richard had always supported and encouraged my cooking," she says. "He liked to see me in that situation, he said, because I was competent."

Deborah had never done any line cooking. She'd never worked in a restaurant. She had heard about Alice Waters's Chez Panisse in Berkeley. (*Gourmet* named Chez Panisse the best restaurant in the San Francisco area in 2000. "What more is there to say about the restaurant that changed the way Americans eat?" asked the reviewer, standing in a line behind many critics and diners who believe Chez Panisse has been the best restaurant in America for twenty-nine years.)

"Richard liked to go there, but I couldn't afford it until I met Alice, and after we'd talked about cooking, she was surprised I'd never been to the restaurant. She said, 'Come, and bring a friend or two.'" Deborah ducks her head. "We went the next night. That meal was utterly confirming. This was the way I thought food should be. I came back and it was late, and I went over to Richard's house because I saw the light was on. I rang the bell. It was 11:45. And this is not what Zen students do. I said, 'I have to work there.'" Surely, this is one of the greatest compliments ever given to a cook for a single meal. "Richard said, 'Great. Did Alice mention that you could?' I called Alice the next day, and she said, 'Come tomorrow.'"

Deborah worked at Chez Panisse for a year, then "sold some stuff I still owned" and went to France to teach herself more about formal food preparation, and in July 1979, Greens opened for lunch. "Two hundred people a day, maybe," remembers Deborah. Within three weeks, the *San Francisco Chronicle* ran that rave review, "and we were seating 350 for lunch every day. It was already hard on the floor staff, the host, and the kitchen. This was harder. Chez Panisse had taught me a craft. I didn't know how to do production." And no one in the kitchen had any kitchen experience. Deborah had to teach people to chop vegetables, use a charcoal grill, and make a salad dressing—"often while there was a line of customers at the door. And Greens took off like a rocket," she says. "It was grueling for everybody. It doesn't matter who is on your team—taking an order, putting it together on a plate, and getting it to a table is bloody hard work. At every step along the delivery process, anything can go wrong." Deborah remembers that the stipend she and Dan Welch were splitting worked out to less than $75 a week—which was more than many of her co-workers received. "And we didn't do things then like hire a cleanup crew. We were Zen students. We not only came in early, unpacked the vegetables—which I'd gone down to the field to get—planned the menu, cooked the meal, and supervised people who had never worked in a restaurant, but we cleaned the mats, scrubbed the counters and the kitchen, and I had to do the ordering and do the next day's menu, and make desserts."

Once the restaurant was open and successful, says Deborah, "I never had the feeling that I did anything good at Greens. It was pretty horrible. We were not allowed to accept praise, so there was no reward for the triumph. It is a shame, but people were never told they had done great work." Deborah was often given assistants who had never cooked even for themselves. "What they went through trying to learn on the job, and what they did learn to do, seemed to matter to no one," says Deborah, who recalls Jane Hirshfield, the poet, arriving with no cooking credentials. "She brought an incredible sense of fidelity. And she was steady. I needed that. And she was a good cook, because she really tasted the food."

Work was not work but practice; people did not have to be paid normal wages, and their work did not have to be acknowledged. This was not an oversight, but it represented a profound difference between the view developing among students and the view from the Abbot's Mountain Seat, or teaching seat.

"Karin was the manager," says Deborah, "and that was lucky for all of us. She's really smart and really organized, and she was always right. I remember her telling me several times I needed to get some rolling racks. And I didn't want things like rolling racks in the kitchen. Then, everyone realized, we needed some place to put things and get them out of our way. I was stubborn, and Karin knew things. She was the only one who did."

"Deborah is an artist," says Karin. "Systems, I could figure out."

"Karin was my assistant at the time," says Richard. "I asked Karin to find out about these dishes, to do this, do that. As my assistant, she did a tremendous amount. But, basically, I chose the silverware. I chose the dishes," he says. "I am sorry to say I did, but I did. One of the things I am concerned with, and one of the only things I felt [at] Zen Center that I really kept for my own, were decisions about how things looked," says Richard. "I made sure that I made the decision about how anything that went out looked. Most other decisions—I didn't go to meetings; people made decisions they wanted [to make]. In my experience, I didn't make all the decisions. But because I had the final say, I actually did have the veto on any final decision. People thought I made [decisions], or felt they didn't have their own freedom. And that may be right [that] they didn't, but that wasn't my experience."

Karin says, "It was impressive to watch so many people work so hard. Dan was demoted from being President at one point to being a dish-washer. And Ed, who'd written the bread books and been President—he was demoted, too. For a while he was a busboy." Karin just stops for a second. "Really. Ed became the manager later. But Ed was a busboy. And I have to say, Ed as a busboy and Dan washing dishes—they were real teachers."

"I designed it."

You could say that the Greens project was the culmination of Richard's understanding of his role as Abbot. "Richard had both sides," says Norman Fischer, Zen Center Abbot from 1995 until 2000. "This was a powerful thing for the community. In Zen, the teaching emphasizes that you go out into the roll-up-your-sleeves world and bring the teaching out; the teacher leads the community as it interfaces with the world."

But whose sleeves were rolled up?

Norman says, "If you're suspicious of one another, a lot of beautiful things don't happen." And this makes sense. And it can yield profound confusion. Many students believe that the teaching about work-practice— that there was no distinction between work and practice, despite the evident disparity—effectively altered their relationship to spiritual practice. Many of them no longer practice Zen Buddhism. The confusion was not strictly philosophical or theoretical; sometimes, it was literal. It made it difficult to understand a simple declarative statement, such as, "I designed Greens."

"I was put in charge of the building project," says Karin, "but Paul [Discoe, Zen Center's head carpenter, who had trained for several years in Japan] was really in charge. He was the builder. I felt my job was to make sure Paul could do his."

"It was a lot of smashing concrete and glass," says Paul, whose crew was made up of mostly unskilled student laborers. "There was a fellow who knew something about plumbing, and Ned knew something about electricity, at least from a theoretical angle. Mostly, it was pretty much, *Well, that looks like a good idea; let's try that.*"

Every review of Greens praises the design of the place. *Interiors* magazine ran a photo spread about the "artistic remodeling," in which light, wood, and open space highlight the oversized paintings of Mike Dixon and Edward Avedisian (who also designed the fabrics for the tables and cushions) and J. B. Blunk's "amazing and vast environmental piece in carved wood [that] forms seating and tables at the café' end."

"I did the part I can do," says Richard, who says he "designed and conceived it."

"Joan Larkey was a Zen student who'd managed Alaya and had a lot of theatrical experience," says Annie. "She designed the beautiful lighting," which *Interiors* magazine credited for making the vast space feel intimate, like an art studio.

"I was quite involved," recalls Sym Van der Ryn, who had resigned as

State Architect by 1978 and returned to his teaching post at Berkeley when Richard asked for his help. "Richard has incredible knowledge and taste. It was pro bono work. And personally, Richard was very gracious. I worked with Paul, the Zen Center carpenter. I could do basic drawings, and being a Japanese-style carpenter, Paul would translate them into details. The whole thing was a lot of fun," says Sym, and then he adds, "I did the design, saw the finished project, and had none of the responsibilities or headaches for doing it. And Richard was generous. I could go to Tassajara as often as I wanted. I had an open ticket to Greens. I thought it was a great relationship."

"We had two architects," says Karin.

The first architect worked with Richard on the project before Sym was called in. In 1981, when this original architect was buying a new home, he wrote to ask when he should expect his $10,000 payment from Zen Center. Richard tried to clear up the confusion; he wrote and told the architect he remembered their arrangement as a *We'll try to pay you something if the restaurant ever makes a profit* deal. Steve Weintraub, then Treasurer, wrote a couple of apologetic notes about the 1980 and 1981 deficits at Zen Center, and included a couple of $500 checks, and finally found $5,000 somewhere, which the architect graciously accepted as a final payment for having provided "the design concept and preliminary design drawings for Greens."

"I kept trying to develop Zen Center so these people could stay," says Richard.

"Richard was Super Dad by the time he opened Greens [in 1979]," says Steve Allen. "He had a big family, and he had to support it, and until then, most of us in the community had felt he was representing us well and doing good work. I really believe the grocery and the bakery had shown people something about our way of doing things."

Yvonne Rand, too, considers the period from 1972 until 1977 "a time of enormous fertility and activity and work that was wonderful. I see what led to the building and making of Greens as the beginning of the end," she adds. "At that point, Dick the Empire Builder came to be predominant. The scale of the Greens project was so big that he stopped practicing within Zen Center in most ways. His life was outside. And Zen Center became a much more public institution."

And a much more solicitous one. By early 1979, Zen Center was sending out letters to its members and donors, asking for help with the start-up costs for Greens, which it estimated at $200,000, or half the free-market value of the labor and materials; the final cost of getting the restaurant up and running for two months turned out to be just over $340,000. By mid-1980, Zen Center was conducting a separate $100,000 fund-raising campaign to purchase the Pines, a 160-acre parcel of land near enough to the Tassajara resort to pose a threat to its isolation, should another organization or commercial interest attempt to develop it. Both of these campaigns intersected with the multiyear campaign to build a new zendo at Tassajara ($200,000 initial estimate) and to recover some of the costs associated with the fires and floods that had preceded the zendo fire. And almost incidentally, a $12,000 statue of the female devotional figure Tara had become available and needed a few big sponsors and, as luck would have it, a $20,000 figure of Jizo Bosatsu turned up, and because his great vow was to "save all beings, especially those in the hell realms," he must have seemed like a good investment.

In 1978, the year before Greens opened, Zen Center's income topped $1 million for the first time; it had been less than a quarter of that when Richard became Abbot. By 1980, total income was well over $2 million. By the end of 1982, two-thirds of the way through the fiscal year, the Treasurer was working with an operations budget of more than $4 million (with income lagging behind expenses). Ten years later, in 1991, annual income and expenses were below $2.5 million.

The budget for the Abbot's department almost doubled in the three years 1981–83 to $215,000. Were these necessary expenses? Zen Center did not cease to operate when Richard walked away in 1983. But in July of that year, the Treasurer estimated Richard's absence would save Zen Center $150,000 on that line item alone—or $40,000 more than the record net profits from the Greengrocer in the same year; or $30,000 more than the unrestricted fund-raising total; or more than the estimated annual cost of a health insurance plan for 200 full-time members, which was being debated at the time.

As income topped $4 million, so did the estimated mortgage value of its properties. And deficit spending plagued Zen Center. Restricted funds designated for the ceremonial Tea House at Green Gulch (a project whose costs neared $300,000) had to be transferred to hasten completion of a guest house ($200,000 and rising), which would produce income by attracting conferees and other visitors to the farm. Richard was driving the BMW by 1981, when he wrote yet another letter to donors, alerting them to Zen Center's desperate need for cash reserves. This was the start of a campaign to raise $2 million; Zen Center was carrying a $1.3 million debt, including a "number of shorter term notes and obligations," with unfavorable interest rates.

Since the mid-seventies, Zen Center had been using the accrual system of accounting—standard business practice. Indeed, a donor had designated a gift for this purpose; in 1976 Coopers & Lybrand designed a manual and trained Zen Center's managerial and bookkeeping staff. That was the official view. In its day-to-day practice, however, Zen Center was a checkbook economy; it was run like a household, wrote Lew, "and our so-called 'capital expenditures' are not investments at all but *purchases,* which we have no expectation will produce income any more than a family expects their living room couch to produce income."

Richard says one of his clear motives for the whole operation was to make it possible for many people to stay at Zen Center. And people did stay. Although membership was fluid, and membership categories were often changed, most estimates counted 350 to 400 regular full- and part-time practitioners by the early 1980s. And few ordained and senior priests were leaving the community, which severely limited the influx of new residential students.

But were they staying to practice or practicing in order to stay? In his extensive, unsolicited 1982 analysis of the businesses, Lew wrote that it was more reasonable to call the "practice centers," like Greens and the bakery, "donative theatres" whose "sets, lighting, design, and drama of movement . . . induce a collective willingness to contribute on the part of the community. As theatre," he wrote, "they are certainly a success." On average, an hour worked by a student returned $2.89 to Zen Center. "Are students really *donating,* pure and simple?" Lew proposed a test: Close all of the businesses, send students to get jobs elsewhere, and ask everyone to contribute $2.89 an hour of the wages they earn. "Most would not," he wrote, "of course."

Zen Center could ill afford the experiment. It had become dependent on its own bigness to supply practice leaders and business managers, as well as cheap labor. And as expenses rose—factor in, say, the spiraling price of oil, inflation, and interest rates from 1972 through 1983—it could only afford to get bigger.

As for the student laborers, a former Board member explains, "many of them were now caught." If relatives or friends could not float them loans, typical Zen Center students were, on paper, qualified to work in service-sector jobs and apply for public-housing subsidies. By 1980, most of them were thirty-five to forty-five. Many of them had families. They had no health insurance, no retirement plans, and most had dropped out of the social security system long ago. And an employer with discriminating habits of mind might well ask, did you manage that business or were you just one of the boss's assistants?

Most significant in the long view, through 1982, Zen Center was still supporting only one teacher. A few senior priests, including Bill Kwong, had started sitting groups or small temples outside of San Francisco that were affiliates of Zen Center. Until they received Transmission and became acknowledged teachers in Suzuki-roshi's lineage, however, these priests could not perform ordinations. Thus, although Richard ordained sixty people before he left, almost none of them had become self-supporting in the traditional way of Zen priests. Issan started his own temple, and he was an inspiration to many, but a model for few. Les Kaye, whom Suzuki-roshi had ordained in 1971, had taken the lead at the Los Altos zendo (where the lectures for *Zen Mind, Beginner's Mind* had been recorded), but Les had a career at IBM. "Most of the people at Zen Center weren't interested in what I was doing," says Les. "They believed corporations were destroying the culture and sapping individual creativity. They had consciously opted out. Once Suzuki-roshi died, I really was a pretty distant observer, but [Zen Center] did look a lot like a corporation by the 1980s, with its managers and competition for status, and Richard at the top."

Mel Weitsman was the teacher at the Berkeley Zen Center at the time. He became Abbot of Zen Center in 1988. He might have been a model. He was a regular presence; he had supported himself and his family as a teacher for almost fifteen years; and many students had found their way to Zen Center after practicing with Mel across the bay in Berkeley. "Dick wasn't impressed by the little guys, so neither were the students," says Mel. "Very early on, he stopped listing the affiliates in Zen Center publications and other mailings. It was a clear message to everyone about what was really important. And his time and energy were focused on Greens. People in the community often had to wait six months to see him. And there were all of these people on the outside he was trying to bring in and trying to impress. And people outside of Zen Center saw him as a wizard. They were buying into it. He had a good thing going, but it was going too fast," Mel says, and then he smiles. "And it was going away. Everybody felt used."

"Greens was Richard's showplace," says Steve Allen. "That's all it was."

"This was a good practice place," says Richard.

"Greens was all about image," says Steve Allen. "That's why it wasn't practice."

Steve's strange path has afforded him many views of Richard. He arrived at Zen Center in 1970, sat one sesshin with Suzuki-roshi, and was the Treasurer during the Apocalypse. After Richard left San Francisco, Steve was one of a handful of students who helped him set up a new, short-lived Zen center in Santa Fe ("He was my teacher," says Steve. "It was my obligation"), and then Steve returned to San Francisco to help Issan get the hospice going on Hartford Street. Steve eventually received Transmission from Issan; thus, he is a branch of Richard's lineage. He lives and practices with his wife and occasional visitors in a setting he calls "a hermitage" at the base of Crestone Mountain in Colorado. Steve and Richard have not spoken to each other or practiced together for many years. "I practice in the shadow of the mountain," he says.

Steve Allen's view of Greens, however, is unobstructed. "Things had to be done in the way society wanted them done at Greens. That's why it psychologically threw the whole community out of balance," he says, in his soft, simple, definitive way. "It was alternative—vegetarian—but it was very high end, a premier stop in San Francisco. And Zen students were quite literally servants. This was the community-wide experience of serving dinner to Richard and his guests," says Steve. "You felt undermined. It turned everything around."

This was not only a *work-practice* confusion; it was not just a literal confusion. This was a confusion in the intuitive teaching process. It was hard to see—not because it was subtle, but because it was so deep. It is best illustrated by an account of one student-teacher relationship over the course of several years.

The student spent three years at Tassajara in the early 1970s. Richard remembers him as "a funky guy; unsure of himself; a sweet guy . . . I hardly remember him [at Tassajara]," says Richard. "I knew him, of course. He was one of sixty-five people." Richard remembers "relating to him and observing his practice, but he is just one of the students getting used to it, and I am just paying attention to him. Don't have much relationship with him." After helping to start the grocery store and spending time at Green Gulch, the student was asked to work at Greens. "When he's at Greens, he is working for Renée; he was an assistant," says Richard, and "always having problems at Greens. I kept encouraging Renée: Let's give him a chance; give him a break. He's a sweet guy. Give him a chance to learn these things. From my point of view, that's when I got to know him. I watched him. I talked to Renée about him, and I really was concerned with him. I met his mother. Every time I saw him, I felt this feeling for him." Richard pauses. "He remembers that someone reported to him what the student later said. "When he was at Tassajara, he thought I was the most extraordinary person he had ever met. And it was the most powerful connection he had ever had with a human being. When he was at Greens, he felt so disconnected from me, and so annoyed by me."

What the student says is, "I did feel close to Richard at Tassajara. At Greens, I felt he just didn't care."

Richard shrugs. "This was a revelation to me. I felt more connection to him then. [Greens] was a good practice place, and I was thinking about his practice, and I think it led him to have a major role at Zen Center. But for him?"

For him? "A vision and a sense of moment can work together; a vision can help people to enact the moment," this student says, "unless the vision takes over so completely that people no longer know where they are. When that happens, people are always trying to catch the bus. And then the vision is nothing but a cover story: My life is miserable, but at least I am on the cutting edge of Buddhism."

"Dick was doing well," says Mel. "The only problem was the people."

The stratification of the community was profound by the time Greens opened in July of 1979. There were a few senior priests who were in positions of spiritual leadership at each of the temples, and a few others in positions of institutional leadership, and they were not carrying trays in a converted warehouse or hauling sacks of flour at the bakery. Lew included himself in this small class of "managers, not producers."

"I was in the so-called cream of the community," says Yvonne, who has a knack for not letting herself off the hook. "I was invited to meetings of Invisible College"—a monthly gathering of eminent thinkers and artists and entrepreneurs Richard organized around elaborate lunches or dinners at the Guest House. "It was very exciting," says Yvonne, "until I was no longer invited to things; that was when I slowly began to wake up, and I began to speak out and disagree, slowly not saying Yes to everything. In Richard's world, if you were not completely with him, you were against him."

Sometimes, in Yvonne's careful gaze and her uninflected and heartening way of saying "we were a real team," or her way of talking about the work that they all did together, you catch a sense of the wonder of it all, and you wonder if the worst thing that happened at Zen Center was the singling out of one person for acknowledgment, the *not* seeing that the team was the teacher—the *not* seeing that made them all unable to see what they had been. "Richard was my teacher," says Yvonne. "I made my best effort to take him as a teacher. One of his explanations for his abuse of his authority in our relationship was that I was really a peer and he wasn't really my teacher. That was a two-edged sword because he also insisted that he was my teacher. He ordained me. And it became a source of terrible grief, to see how I was an agent for him." For a long time, says Yvonne, "I was so with him, and so took on whatever his view was—

sometimes instead of having my own views—that I really enabled him, in the language of addictive family systems."

Zen Center, of course, was not a family; nor was it a refuge from family. "I come from an alcoholic family," says Yvonne, who conducted an "informal poll" of people who had been at Zen Center for more than eight years. "Something above ninety percent of us had come from alcoholic families or families that were dysfunctional with the same patterns." After Suzuki-roshi's death, she says, "there was a very high tolerance for covert disagreement, and no tolerance for overt disagreement; secrets—a taboo against speaking about almost anything; a lot of silence and third-party information; and a reliable pattern of not saying directly what you appreciate or dislike about another person."

Yvonne fell out of favor in 1981, but the community survived her crash. "I'm living proof of why you better not speak out," says Yvonne. "The degree to which I was scapegoated publicly was most effective in keeping everyone else quiet."

This was business as usual. It did not much matter what happened to any one student. And whatever their motives, the senior priests at Zen Center continued to insist that restaurant and bakery and grocery-store work was practice, which did work to preserve the enterprise in which they had invested ten or twenty years of their lives. And it certainly seems to have pleased a lot of eaters to think that their spinach timbales or mushroom crêpes were served with a little spiritual dash, spiced with Buddhism.

But Richard was not Abbot of the World. And he could not protect the community from the divisive laws of the economy. Board notes and officers' reports from 1981 and 1982 document the fiscal and morale problems caused by financial inequities among practitioners at Zen Center.

After years of individually negotiating increases and bonuses and loans, there were evident disparities among stipend students. This was complicated by the fact that some students who did not live at Page Street or Green Gulch were paid an hourly wage, as were the increasing number of nonmembers who worked in the businesses; many of these wage earners also lived in apartments whose rent was subsidized by Zen Center.

Wage earners were also subject to state and federal tax laws, unlike stipend students. And at Greens, there were tips to be divided equitably—neither a problem nor a benefit for, say, a grocery store clerk or a baker. The recurring concern was that these divisions and distinctions were arbitrary. The most profound distinction, of course, was the assertion that the businesses were not businesses. Like many churches and religious organizations, Zen Center had never filed business-income tax returns, based on the assertion (in federal tax code terms) that each of its specific business activities was uniquely suited to the performance of religious functions, not simply compatible with those functions. By 1980, the Treasurer, Board, and legal counsel were aware that the Internal Revenue Service had ruled otherwise in cases involving well-established residential monastic communities with less extensive retail and service operations.

Every new analysis uncovered additional divisions and discriminations but failed to unsettle the view that practice was necessary, and work was necessary, and work was practice. So, when the Treasurer alerted the Board to the fact that a single student living in an apartment cost the community $665 a month in 1982, while a student living at City Center only cost the community $375, nothing happened. They couldn't cram any more students into City Center, and the hourly wages paid by the businesses were so low that the students in the apartments couldn't pay any more rent. By 1982, there were twelve children living in San Francisco and fourteen at Green Gulch, and each child not only increased the parents' stipends but demanded to be fed and bathed and clothed, so single people and couples without children were subsidizing the $70,000 annual cost of other people's children.

All of this suddenly began to seem arbitrary.

And in 1980, the Abbot's daughter was applying to college, and didn't qualify for a scholarship "because of [my wife] Ginny's inheritance," explains Richard. "I was in charge, so I could make the decisions, so I said I would like a $10,000 bonus to my salary so that I can give it to Brown [University] every year." Richard remembers that he "was intending to do that for other people—for Yvonne." He pauses. Yvonne did not receive a tuition bonus for her college-bound daughter, and neither did anyone else. You could say it was arbitrary. Richard says, "It's hard to say who you do it for and who you don't. I had a feeling if [my daughter] can get into Brown, this is normal."

"It was not how I imagined it would be," says Steve Weintraub. "It was a really different way of thinking."

Zen Center was so adept in its commercial ventures that it is easy to see its members as entrepreneurs, but this is not how they saw themselves. They were enlightenment seekers, and there was one enlightened teacher among them. "Dick has very strong psychic powers," says Paul Discoe. "He is able to look into people and see what makes them tick, and then either wind them up or unwind them—whatever seems appropriate. And in most cases he does it for their benefit. Often, with women, he does it for his benefit." Paul says he sometimes still seeks out Richard as a teacher. "He has very deep insight into people. I think he had this before he came to Zen. It is something he was born with. And it's a very handy trait for being a teacher. But it can get you into a lot of trouble, too. Once you do that to someone, they think, *He really understands me.*"

Gib Robinson, who did not take ordination from Richard and still holds the tenured teaching post at San Francisco State University that allowed him to practice with the community without becoming financially dependent, is grateful to Richard for opening the door to practice for him, which he is not certain he would otherwise have found. "And another part of my response to the whole enlightenment program was, *Get real.* I mean, as a rhetorician, he was stunning. But the key for me was his ability to make whatever he was saying confluent with the dharma. He was too consistent. I remember sitting at a lecture [Richard gave about his own] post-kensho experience"—literally, post-enlightenment experience. "It struck me as an odd use of teaching power," says Gib. "You don't talk about enlightenment in personal terms. It's a self-canceling exercise. I mean, I thought I had seen a lot of power-tripping, but it was in much more subtle forms. I was stunned by the baldness of what he was willing to do."

This was the legacy—intended or not—of Suzuki-roshi. Richard was hardly alone at Zen Center in his understanding that he was not only

Chief Priest of a Corporation Sole but Chief Priest of the corporation's souls. This was where most Americans parted company with Zen Center.

This was the gap filled by the businesses. Not a lot of Americans were buying kensho, but they were happy to buy a bowl of Deborah Madison's tomato and white bean soup. And as long as work was practice, this apparently indirect support was a direct endorsement.

Ed Brown remembers a summer sesshin at City Center, "and I was in bliss the whole week." Ed had spent many years not sitting still—he sat with involuntary movements, which often drove him out of the zendo, so this was a breakthrough. "There was a lot of light and warmth, and my body would disappear, and I would just sit there," remembers Ed. "So I said something to Dick in dokusan." Ed smiles. "He said, 'Well, can you shoot your energy up your spine?' I said, 'No.' And he dismissed it. No teaching. No advice for me about how to practice with that. No comment about what that was. If I couldn't shoot my energy up my spine, I hadn't done anything yet." Ed nods. *Really.* "I hadn't arrived. That was my experience with him over and over. He was the only one who really knew what was going on. You were too stupid to do anything on your own." Ed sits with that for a while, and then he says, rather mechanically, "Suzuki-roshi died. I stayed at Zen Center. Dick got by for years on being the enlightened successor." Ed exhales three times, as if something is caught in there. "And he used that until his credit ran out."

"I don't know," says Richard, remembering the advice of people who cautioned him about the risks of opening a restaurant. "It just seemed like we could do it."

"Greens?" says Darlene Cohen. "Greens! It just took over. I'd be in the office at Page Street and someone from Greens would come over and round up people in the hallway and cart them over to work an eight-hour shift. These poor people had already done their jobs and just happened to be in the wrong place at the wrong time."

"And then," remembers Deborah, "Richard arranged a dinner with the Dalai Lama and a hundred and fifty people. So, we planned and planned and put together an amazing meal—how could it be otherwise?—and the next morning, I was called in for dokusan, and Richard told me very strictly that people did not like working with me. I was too demanding. And then back to Greens for another twelve-hour day. And when people got interested in Greens, and wanted to interview me, I was told not to care about that stuff, to be a modest Zen student. So I did no interviews." And then Deborah designed and cooked prix-fixe dinners on Friday and Saturday nights, which were typically booked four to six months in advance. "And why had we missed meditation on Sunday morning?" says Deborah.

"Zen Center students find it physically exhausting to do dinners," wrote Renée and Ed in a memo to the Abbot in 1982. The floor crew typically finished after midnight. "Perhaps," they suggested, "this is more exhausting for someone used to getting up at 5:00 AM."

When Deborah left for Tassajara, Annie started cooking at Greens, studied new recipes, and learned how line-cooks worked. For a while, Jim Fallon did most of the rest of what Deborah had done. "He was a terrific chef," says Deborah, "though we weren't allowed to call ourselves chefs." Jim soon left to enter a Catholic monastery. Then, the managers wrote a memo about their decision to divide Deborah's job "among four or five people."

In its third year, the restaurant began to produce modest profits; by mid-1983, Greens was no longer a "work-practice center" but an "autonomous" operation, on its way to a new status as an ordinary business. Before she and Dan left Zen Center in 1984, Deborah began to write the *Greens Cookbook,* which has stayed in print in hardcover since 1987. Ed assisted Deborah as coauthor, and he also published a third collection of Tassajara recipes; 60 percent of the royalties went to Zen Center.

It might not have been practice, but it was working.

It had been work from the start. "I remember asking if some of the high-priest types would come and work at the restaurant," remembers Deborah, "so they could try to understand how hard it was just to get up in the morning. I thought it might help if they experienced the noise and heat and pressure for twelve and fourteen hours at a time. I mean, zazen before dawn is a great idea, but we needed to get through the day." Deborah pauses. In 1982, when she left Greens to lead the practice period at Tassajara, her face broke out in boils. Now, she just shakes her head and shakes it off. "Reb Anderson came in for one day and washed dishes. He thought it was fun." A little more shaking off. "Well, he was right. It is fun for one day."

Great functioning.

"I don't think about the odds or whether it's possible," says Richard, attempting to account for his own optimism about what can be accomplished. "I have a trust that anything *I think* is possible—and that comes from practice. I don't think thoughts that are impossible. So, if I have a thought, I think it is possible. We call it Great Functioning in Buddhism, which means, you are letting some deeper thinking that takes in the whole situation function through you. And when something occurs to me, I try to do it."

What distinguished Richard was his capacity to muster enthusiasm among others for these ideas. "It doesn't feel special," he says. "It's a clear feeling, so I talk about it." Richard pauses. "I feel embarrassed by it. What I think is normal is weird to other people."

It did occur to Richard, in December of 1979, five months after the opening of Greens, that Zen Center was overextended. He opened a meeting of the Outside Financial Advisory Board (OFAB) by stating, "Our businesses have been very successful, but we now have reached our own limits so it is time to emphasize other areas than businesses." This was an idea the OFAB immediately got behind and rode to the end of the meeting. A few months later, however, in early 1980, another good idea occurred to the Abbot, and Stewart Brand was bringing out a new edition of the *Whole Earth Catalog,* and a relatively usable space was available for very little money at Fort Mason, and Stewart had intentionally not patented the Whole Earth trademark, and though Suzuki-roshi had chastened Richard years before about patronizing local merchants and not setting up competing businesses and had specifically singled out a bookstore as a bad idea, Richard had the sense that he could make a "special bookstore," and so he opened a retail Whole Earth Bookstore at Fort Mason with a mail-order business tied to the *Whole Earth Catalog,* featuring Buddhist books and a number of titles related to the human-potential movement, as well as books by thinkers and entrepreneurs Richard admired, and it better than broke even, and then the store had to move and find someplace else to stash its inventory, and by 1982, there were more than ten employees at the store, but it was not making much money, and catalog sales began to fall off precipitously, but Richard and Sym sat down and drew up plans for renovating a much bigger space at Fort Mason for a permanent bookstore, and by the time the Treasurer's estimates of the cost of that renovation project had escalated from $200,000 to $350,000, and Richard had given away a lot of books to friends and visiting dignitaries ("He made you nervous giving you so many books," recalls the American Zen master Robert Aitken. "All of us knew from friends who ran bookstores that the margins were tiny. And, of course, he had beautiful and expensive books"), it was 1983, and the bookstore's doors were bolted, and the inventory was sold off, and the design plans for the new bookstore were rolled up, and Zen Center ceased to function as a breeder of Buddhist businesses.

"The pattern is self-deception," says Yvonne. "I could see that on my part, and other people's parts, and on Dick's part."

It was not until the floor gave way beneath them that most people at Zen Center came to their present view that work-practice ultimately was not good work and was not good practice. "I was one of the leaders, one of the administrative henchmen," says then-Treasurer Steve Weintraub. "I used to see Richard—*Baker-roshi* we used to call him—with some frequency, but it was never about my practice. It was about business. He might have thought my practice was going swimmingly. In fact, it had dried up. But, we were administering a complex corporation, not worrying about primary spiritual values—humility, and kindness, and compassion."

Deborah remembers the relief of being at Tassajara after Greens. "At Tassajara, the feeling of community and practice was clear. Everyone was concentrating, committed to the same one hundred days [of intensive practice]. It was discrete and particular time," she says. "But when you were not at Tassajara, the Zen Center community sometimes felt artificial. As it did at Greens, for instance. I was aware that Chez Panisse always felt like a community. They never talked about practice; they just did the work. There was no rule about not talking during prep [as there was at Greens], and yet the practice of awareness was much richer there."

Leslie James, who became President of Zen Center in the mid-eighties, had not been deeply involved with the city businesses. She moved to Page Street with her husband and two children in 1981, after many years at Tassajara. Even then, "the experiment seemed exciting. Richard had an idea, and he saw a potential. We were experimenting with a new way of living. Greens was the scariest thing—people had to work too hard—but, you know, we were used to crazy finances. For a long time, every year, everyone would take a cut in pay around Christmastime. Christmas bonuses would come out as your [stipend] was going down to twenty-five dollars a month. We'd be waiting for the [next summer's paid reservations for] Tassajara guest season to start coming in."

Steve Weintraub says, "Obviously, there was a conflict that most of us did not recognize." He remembers explaining financial expenditures to the Board and the general community. "I don't know if I dissembled—I'd have to say Yes and No. At the time, I said to people, 'This is the way it has to be. It is necessary to put $60,000 into one room in [the Abbot's residence] and then spend even more on [his house].' And I did not convey the other side of that point of view. I think I probably conveyed a sense of shame. I didn't recognize or articulate even the obvious conflicts. I mean, Zen Center was a multimillion-dollar nonprofit corporation. And its officers and employees were still dependent on MediCal; when we had a medical problem, we went to a poor people's clinic."

"Greens was an idea to make a kind of club that was a restaurant," says Richard.

"Mike Murphy would come in, and [people say now that] I would sit at the VIP table, or the high table." Richard remembers it as any table. "We would talk. I met the woman who founded the Green Party. Dan Ellsberg was a good friend, and wanted me to meet her, so we ate at Greens. Things like that were always happening," he says. "Earl [McGrath] once came, and I had lunch with him, and he asked why I was having dessert and coffee, and I told him I had a lot to do, so I'd had appetizers with one group, lunch with another group, and 'I am having dessert with you.' And Earl said, 'Dick, you are crazy.'" Richard shrugs. "The students often didn't like it." Earl told Richard to cut it out, and "I stopped." As an afterthought, he says, "It's understandable why rich people only know rich people and celebrities know celebrities." Richard then recalls a lunch in a New York restaurant with a movie star, who is the ex-husband of the sister of the wife of one of Richard's friends. "I don't know how all these things happen," Richard says, and he adds, "If you are rich, and you are with people who are not rich, there is always this tension. You have a hundred million dollars, and I have thirty-five." He pauses. "People wanted to see Greens. I didn't want to have a secret life of people I knew—people who actually helped Zen Center a lot. While it lasted, we were having a good time, and I thought everyone was having a good time."

It is a beautiful view.

28.

On the night of November 17, 1979, four months after Zen Center opened Greens restaurant, Steve Allen remembers, "I happened to be walking out of City Center on Page Street as a call came in. Somebody said, 'I think one of your students has been hurt at the corner of Octavia and Haight Streets.' This was just two blocks away.

"I'd called and talked to Darlene," says Mel van Dusen. "I'd seen the body when I was walking down the street, so I'd crossed to the other side. I thought maybe he was a drunk lying in spilled beer or something, but then I crossed back," and took a better look. "It was Chris [Pirsig]." Mel and Chris had arrived at Zen Center at about the same time, four years earlier, and had been roommates at Green Gulch, he says. He pauses. "His eyes—it was clear he was dead. There was no life in them."

Chris Pirsig was twenty-three when he was stabbed and killed. He had been made famous by his father's account of their trip across the country together in *Zen and the Art of Motorcycle Maintenance*. Robert Pirsig's meditative saga became a genuine cultural phenomenon; the troubling father-son journey, with its resolute spirit of inquiry, and its narrator's irresolute heart and mind, came to epitomize Zen Buddhism, especially for people who had never experienced Zen practice.

Chris Pirsig, according to people who met him and practiced with him, was "messed up" when he arrived, "a refugee from the world of the famous." Press reports after the murder made it clear that Chris had begun to stabilize his shaky life after four years at Zen Center. "Chris came to Zen Center hardened by that book," says Mel. "He looked much younger than his age—he was physically immature, as if he didn't want to build himself up, as if he didn't want to be noticed. He certainly never presented himself as a celebrity. He was trying to be an ideal Zen student." After a moment, he adds, "But a lot of us were like that. Zazen can become a mask," he says.

Steve Allen was Ino, director of the meditation hall, at City Center in 1979. Just half an hour before he overheard the telephone call to Darlene, he had a telephone call from his father, who told Steve that his mother had cancer. Steve organized a service for Chris at midnight and, "at 6:30 the next morning I was on a plane to see my mother. It was a powerful time," he says. What he remembers most clearly, though, is running from City Center and kneeling beside Chris, whose body was beside a fire hydrant at the street corner. "I put my hand on his chest. He had just died. I said, 'Chris. Chris. They've taken you away.' Curiously," says Steve, "it turned out to have been a *they* who did it. Although the police found out nothing, we did. Issan knew the neighborhood, and after he talked to neighbors and a few prostitutes, he was able to figure out that Chris had been killed by a couple of pornographers, who were living in a basement nearby."

"They were involved with drugs, too," says Mel. "Drugs and masturbation videos."

"That's the kind of world we live in," says Steve. "It was arbitrary. The attackers might have tried to rob him"—Chris had bought a six-pack of beer to take to a friend's apartment, and his wallet was found near his body—"and when they found he didn't have any money, they killed him. They didn't care. They didn't know who he was, that he was a young man with parents, a Zen student. They just killed him. It meant nothing to them."

29.

IN JANUARY OF 1983, AT Tassajara, Richard Baker and Reb Anderson performed the *Shiho*—literally, "dharma Transmission"—ceremony. Witnesses included Maezumi-roshi, a longtime friend of Zen Center and Abbot of the Los Angeles Zen Center, and Kobun Chino, one of the young Japanese priests who had served as Suzuki-roshi's assistant in the 1960s. "It had happened," says Gib Robinson. "Reb showed up with a brown robe," a distinction reserved for acknowledged teachers.

The timing of the Shiho ceremony was determined by Richard. In part, he says, he had been unwilling to perform Transmission with Reb or, say, Bill Kwong because of his own inexperience and his sense that the rituals and ceremonies had to be translated—not only literally, but culturally—to have meaning in the American context. Most important, says Richard, as Suzuki-roshi had taught him, "Transmission [must] be real; it can't be done just for institutional reasons; it should be done in a real connection to enlightenment, some depth of understanding of enlightenment, and the enlightening practice."

His readiness to acknowledge Reb as his dharma heir in January was a powerful endorsement of Reb's practice. The Shiho is a private, one-to-one ritual, but Reb's elevation was not a surprise to anyone in the community. Reb was widely perceived to be first among the senior students in a clearly delineated spiritual hierarchy. "Now I look back on that as being extremely naive," says Steve Weintraub. "Right now at Zen Center, there are a dozen Transmitted teachers. At that time, though, Richard was way, way, up there, and then there was a long, long, long, long distance, and there were only two people at that next level—Reb and Lew. The rest of us were way down from there." By acknowledging Reb in the intimate Shiho ceremony, Richard had shrugged off his singular spiritual status. Reb was an acknowledged teacher; he was capable of transmitting the dharma.

In the broader arena of work-practice and teaching, Richard remained the undisputed leader, and Richard's teaching responsibilities were increasingly wide-ranging. He and his wife, Virginia, and Renée des Tombe had traveled with Michael Murphy to Russia under the aegis of the Esalen Soviet-American exchange program in 1982, and he was lecturing and leading seminars around the country on the topic of nuclear genocide at conferences sponsored by the UC Berkeley Extension program, Esalen, and other organizations. He had met and befriended the Vietnamese Buddhist monk Thich Nhat Hanh at a conference in New York in 1982 and participated in several events sponsored by the Buddhist Peace Fellowship, an affiliation of teachers and practitioners committed to extending the principles of a peaceful, contemplative life to personal agency and public activism. The Buddhist Peace Fellowship was an ecumenical coalition that emerged from a consensus on economic and social issues ranging from disarmament to the death penalty. Zen master Robert Aitken and his disciple Nelson Foster helped to establish the coalition in 1978, and they were soon joined by Joanna Macy, Gary Snyder, Jack Kornfeld, and other well-known Buddhist teachers and practitioners. For many, this activism represented a genuinely American manifestation of the dharma and the ancient vow to save all beings. Most of the guests invited to join Thich Nhat Hahn at the Peace Conference at Tassajara in March of 1983 were members of the Buddhist Peace Fellowship.

Willem Malten remembers February of 1983. He was participating in the intensive monastic practice period at Tassajara. "It rained a lot," he says. "It rained and rained and rained, and we had difficulties. Part of the road was washed out for a while. There was a landslide down along the creek. Boulders as big as Volkswagens came down the hill and hit the baths." And then the cable for the crank telephone was knocked out—"we still had no electricity in those days"—which made it impossible to place orders with hardware and grocery stores for the upcoming Peace Conference.

After the telephone was repaired, Willem and another student were sent out in a truck to collect "everything from boxes of tomatoes to sheet rock." They left at 3:30 in the morning. Returning in a rainstorm, Willem's passenger warned him that they were about to miss a left turn, so Willem did take a left. "But it was too late," he says. "We could feel the enormous load in the pickup shifting ever so gently but irrevocably." The truck tumbled into a grassy field and came to rest on its side.

The students eventually climbed out through the window of the truck, and "one guy from Jamesburg came by. He was drunk. He told us we had fucked up, and he drove away." Willem pauses. "I didn't like him for a long time after that." It was not until morning that the truck was towed up the hill, the contents packed into other vehicles, and delivered to Tassajara. "It was another sign that things were not going well," says Willem. "People were angry at me, but mostly people resented the infringement [of the conference] on practice period. Instead of sitting, we were basically building another palace for Baker-roshi and his friends. It was asking a lot. Why couldn't these people do with the facilities we made do with?"

It was mid-March "when these important people started arriving," says Willem. "We were exhausted, and there really was no welcoming committee." Still, Anna Hawken's arrival at the beginning of the week of March 14 was memorable. Willem had missed dinner and gone to the dining room to get a snack after cleaning out Tassajara's fresh-water supply system. "The desilting pond had silted up, and by the time I'd cleaned it out, I was wet and exhausted. Very few of us were keeping the [zazen] schedule, of course. We couldn't." The newly elevated dharma heir, Reb, was talking to Dan in the dining room, but "if Reb didn't like you, you just had to stay out of his way. He always knew better or had more insight and wanted to show it." So Willem looked for someone else to join. "My attention drifted to a gorgeous blond woman. It was Anna. She was radiant." Willem remembers that "Anna was one of the first to arrive. [Her husband] Paul Hawken had not arrived yet. She had her children with her. And after that night, almost incessantly, her little slippers were located at Baker-roshi's cabin—a nice cabin that had been Suzuki-roshi's cabin. Baker and Anna never left the cabin. We all noticed."

By the end of the week, Thich Nhat Hanh, Robert Aitken-roshi, Gary

Snyder, and other notables had arrived. "We were going to open the conference," says Willem. "Meanwhile, Baker is acting totally gaga over this woman. We go to the Suzuki-roshi memorial site, up a path that opens on a clearing. It is a walk that takes twenty minutes or so. Baker was in the front. He was completely lost. Lost. He was holding hands with Anna. It was as if they were on Lovers' Lane, [and] no one else was there. The rest of the people were just silent and worried," remembers Willem.

Richard acknowledges that his feelings were impossible to hide, but he says he doesn't think he and Anna held hands in public at Tassajara. Equal numbers of witnesses say that they did see, did not see, and do not remember if they did or did not see any hand holding—the scarlet-letter gesture that is significant, or ambiguous, or, finally, immaterial.

Paul Discoe says, "There are no sins in Buddhism, which most people don't seem to understand."

"Richard was not communicating with the other guests," says Willem. "He was not his generous, public self. He was focused on this woman in front of everybody. He was leading people up this path, out of his mind, chatting away with Anna." Finally, at the Suzuki-roshi memorial site, "Richard declared the conference open," says Willem. "It was something of an anticlimax, after all of that."

Willem was not exactly appalled; he was impressed. Like most students, he doesn't exactly remember the conference—"I don't know if [Richard] had actually figured out how it was supposed to happen. All of these important people were in the zendo, but Baker was almost never there. It was weird. We were all waiting for the bomb to explode."

And then Paul Hawken arrived. He was not immaterial. He was well known to the community by then, and had a distinctive physical presence—slim and fair, with a runner's body and a boyish face. And he was well known for having founded and later sold the Boston-based Erewhon Trading Company, a retail organic food and supplement chain; for his role as an economic advisor to Governor Jerry Brown; and, since 1978, as cofounder of the Smith & Hawken garden tool and accessory company, a catalog supplier of handsome, expensive spades and shovels and galvanized tin flower pots from France.

Paul Hawken had been a presence at Zen Center since the mid-seventies. Several students remember first meeting him at one of the businesses. In 1975, David Chadwick was working at the Greengrocers when a friend of Zen Center's brought Paul in to look at the operation. "I began to talk him up after that," says David. "It was clear this guy could help us. But I didn't start with Richard. It always helped if Richard heard about people or ideas not directly."

Karin Gjording met Paul while she was working to set up the bakery before it opened in 1976. "He knew about business, and I was trying to figure out how to plan the construction job. He was a great help to me. He had new ideas." Karin recalls that she referred to Paul Hawken so many times that "Richard finally erupted one day and said, 'Don't you mention that name Paul Hawken one more time. I don't want to hear about him.'"

In 1976, when Zen Center formed its Outside Financial Advisory Board, Paul was one of the ten original members. "Paul and I remained in touch through the Greens project," says Karin, "and he came to Tassajara [during the early 1980s] with Richard during practice period—typically, there are no guests allowed—and I would get to visit with him." Paul also helped Karin think through her purchase of the Alaya clothing store and considered buying it with her for a time, and "he offered me a job at Smith & Hawken," before the company moved from Palo Alto [near Stanford University, to Mill Valley, a few miles from Green Gulch Farm]. But I said, 'I would come to work with you, but you're not going to be there, are you?' And he said, 'No,'" remembers Karin, who'd already heard that Paul "was thinking about quitting Smith & Hawken and working as Baker's assistant to learn more about community."

In the eyes of the Zen Center community, Paul was a kind of secular Reb—Richard's acknowledged equal, at least in matters of economics and visionary social planning. "And Paul Hawken had written," says Willem. As an entrepreneur, "he had a track record and money. And he was an idealist. He was the first peer on the inside. And he was a peer with Laurance Rockefeller and Michael Murphy." Paul's insider-outsider status also informed the advice he gave Richard and the Board about fund-raising strategies and the unexamined effect of Zen Center's reputation for self-sufficiency and prosperity on potential donors.

The friendship extended beyond the spiritual and economic concerns of Zen Center; it was a political alliance, too, and involved both Paul and Richard in Jerry Brown's 1980 run for the presidency. And it had a purely social aspect. "That's the funny part of it," says architect Sym Van der Ryn, referring to the collapse of this circle of friends after 1983. One of the traits that distinguished Richard from many of these friends, who did not consider him their spiritual teacher, says Sym, was the conduct of his extramarital relationships with women: "Whatever Richard was up to— talk about discreet . . ." In contrast, Sym remembers a lot of public indiscretion among the residents of the houseboats in Sausalito harbor, where both he and Paul Hawken lived in the seventies, and Sym doesn't exempt himself. When Richard's behavior came to light in 1983, says Sym, he and others did not see it as either distinctive or as grounds for banishment.

Few of Richard's former students credit him with discretion. Paul Discoe remembers that Richard's affair with Mayumi Oda, the painter he'd met in Japan in the late seventies, was "as blatant as it could get. I mean, you didn't see them with their clothes off together, but you saw them in public doing ecstatic things together that only lovers would do. You can't get that happy with somebody unless you are deep into a love affair." Paul says he was simply not interested in Richard's affairs.

Other students saw the same behavior or heard others discussing it, and either ignored it or convinced themselves that it was not happening. Many now recall that they were satisfied by second- or third-hand assurances that Richard had denied any sexual misconduct. "Zen practice is about waking up," says Yvonne. For years, though, she adds, "this was a system that was about staying asleep because it was too risky to wake up."

By 1980, Paul and Anna Hawken were residents of Green Gulch Farm. They were not exactly members of the community. "Paul was not a member of the community," says Mel Weitsman, then head teacher at Berkeley Zen Center. "He was a member of Dick's community. Dick had his own community of people who were not practitioners." But the Hawkens were not *not* members of the community, either. "It was a remarkable privilege to get a house on the grounds," says actor Peter Coyote, who was married at the time to a woman who practiced at Zen Center. Peter continues to be an enthusiastic supporter but was never a resident. Yvonne and other senior priests clearly saw Anna as Richard's student by 1983. And it was more complicated than that. "I was living at Green Gulch," says Wendy Johnson. "One of my closest friends was Anna Hawken. And she said to me later, 'You were the only one who didn't know. Everyone else knew.' I think she had tried to tell me—we were really close," says Wendy. But in the aftermath of the Peace Conference, the damage that worried Wendy was not personal, but "the wider unfolding for the community of what [the affair] actually signified in this place, because the Hawken family lived here, and the Baker family lived here. I was upset for the families."

Lay practice.

The Hawkens were not in a sympathetic position at Green Gulch. Prior to their arrival, new housing for residents came in the form of two new trailers. The arrangements Richard made for the Hawkens to make themselves at home on the farm were far more costly for everyone. "Paul Hawken was buying his way into the community," says then head carpenter Paul Discoe. "It was a turning point. It was almost [that] direct," he says. "Other people might have given Zen Center money or property. This was the first time that someone said, I'll give you $60,000, and you build me a house, and I get to live there."

When the Board attempted to untangle the financial arrangement after March of 1983, its members and Paul Hawken agreed in principle that a cash contribution of $25,000 made by the Hawkens would not be refunded; it was approximately the community's cost of providing the family with room, board, and tuition for thirty-two months. However, it was agreed that Zen Center would repay a $20,000 loan with interest, and that 200 shares of Smith & Hawken stock, valued at $24,000 in the early 1980s, would be returned, as well. (Among the hundreds of letters of unsolicited sympathy and advice that arrived at Zen Center after March, there were more than a few exhortations to the Board to hold onto that stock, whose value, it was variously projected, would increase to $100,000 or even $150,000. The Board, however, did not construe the settlement negotiations as an investment strategy.)

Green Gulch got to keep the house, "which nobody could live in for a long time," says Darlene Cohen. Housing was very tight on the farm, and people lived in pretty grim conditions, she says, but "everyone looked at it with hatred. Now Reb and [his wife] live in it. They have countervailing status, but even they couldn't move in for a long time."

Paul Discoe built the house. "Sym started it out, and I finished the design." No one in the community seems ever to have understood what exactly the Hawken house and its financing represented for Zen Center or its future. Many remember that it was discussed as a model for new, efficient, environmentally sound family housing dreamed up by Richard and Paul Hawken. "There was a lot of glitzy talk of that kind of thing—model homes, good for everyone; it was never a reality. For instance," says Paul Discoe, "it was supposed to be a model of solar heating—that was just before the solar-heating concept collapsed. It had solar hot water and circulation and various things—none of which ever functioned."

Cost- and time-overruns plagued the project, which was competing for the carpentry crew's time with the still unfinished guest house and the ceremonial Tea House. "Then the classic moment came," says Paul Discoe. "Paul Hawken had always said—to anyone who would listen—that he wanted to help build his house, which he never did, of course. You could never find him. He was always too busy."

He was busy. In 1983, Paul Hawken published the first of his celebrated books about management and economics. Almost twenty years later, Paul Discoe takes a big breath and delivers a sermon on the economics of home heating: "The main thing that makes a house work, solar or not solar, is insulation. The whole solar craze collapsed when someone figured out that instead of putting $20,000 into all that solar gadgetry, you could put in $800 worth of insulation, and all you had to do was run around the house twice and the house would heat up. Your body heat would be enough. You certainly didn't need all this space-taking equipment that broke and leaked and did weird things to people. Just insulate. So, we were putting the house together. We were starting to put the shingles on the roof, and Paul Hawken finally decided he wanted to help. He got up there on a ladder. We had put on rigid insulation, a foam with a foil on it that is really bright. And it started to bug him because it was shining in his eyes. And then he started to poke at it and he asked us, 'What is this stuff?' Then he said the urea-formaldehyde was going to off-gas poison everybody. So he tore it all out, and then he shingled the roof." Paul Discoe nods. He slaps his hands on his thighs. "So," says Paul Discoe, "it is a building with no insulation in its roof. Of course, it leaks heat like a sieve; this is the worst possible heat-loss problem you could have in a house. Totally absurd. What did he know? I had carefully put down boards, nice boards that showed inside, and then a layer of craft paper, and a layer of Sheetrock, and a layer of tar paper, and the foam on top of that. Any gas that leaked would have had to leak out through the shingles. This sort of thing is not exactly hard to figure out. There was no way any gas could go into the house. But Paul Hawken was the expert."

Thus, says Mel, "It was not [the community's] loyalty to Paul Hawken specifically that roused people," in March of 1983.

Indeed, loyalty to one specific practitioner had never roused Zen Center to challenge the authority of the teacher. The treatment of individual students was the purview of the teacher. This was the traditional model. Whatever happened, you could say it was a teaching.

But no one who had seen Richard and Paul Hawken together, no one who had watched the Hawken house go up, could say that Paul was just another Zen student. Richard had invented Paul Hawken's special status in the community. Unlike the one-of-a-kind, solar-heated home that was built for him and his family at a comfortable remove from the trailers, Paul actually became a model for the community—a supermodel, really, a glamorous vision of the future of lay practice.

Willem saw Paul soon after he arrived at Tassajara for the Peace Conference. "His complexion was gray," says Willem. "I remember him hanging out, his back to the wall of the dining room, staring at the bridge across the river [toward Richard's cabin]. I remember passing him once and bowing. I remember wondering what he was going to do. It was too hard to believe that Richard Baker would destroy his marriage and family. None of us knew exactly what was happening. The only person who really knew everything at that point was Paul Hawken."

What registered almost immediately with most people on the Board and, subsequently, the vast majority of community members was the profound effect the affair between Richard and Anna had on Paul Hawken. Reports from senior male priests in the community, including Reb, Lew, and Dan, about their initial conversations with Paul at and after the Peace Conference made it clear that Paul's distress was intense. "One of the first things that came out," remembers Steve Allen, was concern that Paul might hurt himself. "I remember that was one of the big triggers for all that followed." Willem remembers that he and the other students at Tassajara were told of the affair, the likelihood that Paul Hawken would divest himself of his interests in the community, and, most compelling, the Board's immediate concern for Paul's well-being, which was at risk. And the circumstances of the affair and the effect on Paul were quickly known outside the community. "Paul told people," remembers Peter Coyote, who felt it was clear at the time that "the affair was above and beyond normal," not only because of the emotional crisis it occasioned for Paul "but the lingering question about the whole arrangement: Had this been a setup?"

Speculation about Richard's motives and intentions provide a measure of the peculiar respect and distrust that Richard engendered among friends and students. Had Richard befriended Paul in order to seduce Anna? Had Richard seduced Anna so that she would encourage Paul to join the community? Steve Allen says that two things were clear to him after Paul Hawken met with the Board of Zen Center. First, it was impossible to know the truth of what had happened. Second, he says, "I think that one meeting severed the Board's emotional ties to Richard."

Within days of the calamitous Peace Conference at Tassajara in March of 1983, the years of negotiating or not negotiating a distinction between Zen Center and the world were nothing. It was as if Richard himself had ripped off the roof. Everyone on the inside could see out, and everyone on the outside could see in.

Within the community, Anna Hawken was seen as Richard's student and Paul was seen as Richard's best friend. Thus, the affair was and was not strictly related to Zen practice. The harm done was and was not an issue of spiritual authority. There were two sides to the story, as there were two sides to Richard, and neither side was looking good. And the view from outside the community was provocative, too. Would the most seasoned Zen practitioners in the West endorse the harm done by their teacher to an admired entrepreneurial idealist and his wife and family?

The logic of every question was intensified by the status of the Hawkens. Who was more likely *not* to be financially bamboozled than Paul Hawken? Who was more likely *not* to be emotionally compromised than the wife of the teacher's best friend?

Over the next few weeks, many more stories of sexual and financial and emotional compromise were told, and some of them were shouted from the rafters of Zen Center. Supporters and friends of Richard continue to refer to this behavior as "piling on," a "witch hunt," and "contrary to the ideal of compassion espoused by the community." The most serious of these charges—and the most pious—was the accusation that the community was failing to act compassionately. This, of course, discounts the community's response to Paul Hawken, his family, and others whose experience had been illuminated by his suffering.

You can argue the quality of compassion, or you can stipulate the failure. It's just a point of view. No amount or degree of compassion would have altered the circumstance in which the community found itself. Zen Center no longer enjoyed the luxury of conducting its business as a private affair. Paul Hawken had made it clear to the Board that he was willing to negotiate a settlement and indemnify the institution and its members against any further legal action, but he expressed no willingness to extend the indemnity to Richard. He drew a line. For more than nine months, the community tried to negotiate this hard and clear line. Should the Board risk the institution's future for one man?

On this question, someone at Zen Center had to speak for Zen Center. This meant either one person or many people would speak. Inadvertently, Richard had made of Zen Center a public forum in which his students were left to discuss, interpret, negotiate, and settle complicated historical, spiritual, and moral issues. Reb, Richard's recently acknowledged dharma heir, did not ask students not to speak. Senior priests in the community did not ask students not to speak. If the personal experiences of practitioners were not relevant to this moment, the personal experiences of practitioners were not relevant to the history or future of Zen Center.

You can say they were piling on, or you can say that they were sorting through a twelve-year pile. "People talked to each other," says Mel Weitsman. "The priests started talking to Dick about it, and he was making all kinds of excuses and crazy rationales. We had Board meetings—some with him. It seemed to me like it was three months, though it might have been three weeks, that every day we would have a meeting to discuss Dick's behavior—not just [the Hawken] incident, but everything people had experienced in their relationship with Dick. And it was horrendous."

And unlike Richard, as Willem points out, "Paul Hawken was not going away." Before spring turned to summer in San Francisco, it occurred to Richard to set off on his walk to Tassajara, the beginning of a nine-month paid leave of absence. Despite many exchanges in letters and telephone calls between Richard and members of the Board, often through intermediaries, it was not until mid-summer that Blanche Hartman, one of his ordained disciples, and Marc Alexander, then President of Zen Center, were able to obtain from Richard his spoken consent to allow the Board to function without his oversight and approval.

At the end of September 1983, Richard wrote an open letter to Zen Center, apologizing for his betrayal of his best friend; for the suffering he had caused his family, Yvonne, Lucy, and others; and for endangering the existence of Zen Center. He was writing from France, and had been joined by his wife; they were staying with Thich Nhat Hanh, who wrote a letter a few weeks later endorsing Richard's sincerity, and exhorting the community to assist and support Richard, whom he considered absolutely trustworthy and, potentially, one of the great Buddhist teachers of the age.

Ed Brown was still managing Greens, and he was the Chairman of the Board until the end of the year. "[Swami] Chetanananda also said to me at one point, 'What's with this guy Dick Baker anyway? He says that this woman seduced him, and in Zen we *do* have this tradition that if you are served food, you eat what is on your plate.'" Ed nods. "This is what Buddhists did who went out begging. But as Chetanananda also said, 'You don't usually eat off the other guy's plate.'"

The Board received opinions from its attorney and from state officials clearly stating that its refusal to separate itself from Richard and accept the offer of indemnity made by Paul Hawken constituted a legally action-able failure, as the Board's primary responsibility was to safeguard the community and its assets. The precedent for the Board's legal responsibil-ities was not a matter of arcane case law; it was standard business practice not to insulate "an irresponsible director at the risk of the institution."

Mel says, "Those people who were so loyal to Dick became his adver-saries. His right- and left-hand people, Reb and Lew, were the first to speak to everybody. I don't know about Reb, but I know Lew felt betrayed," says Mel.

Reb, as Willem recalled, took the stage at Tassajara and apologized for his own failure to prevent or interrupt the harm done by his teacher. This was not widely perceived as an act of loyalty to Richard, who had acknowl-edged Reb as his heir only a few months earlier.

But at Zen Center, the quality of acknowledgment had been strained. "I have said that Dick never acknowledged anyone else," says Ed. "I mean something simple by that. I mean, the simplest thing he could have done is to say, 'I have fallen in love with Anna, and I am going to divorce Vir-ginia,' and people could have accepted or not accepted that. Instead, he told people that Anna had seduced him, and what was he supposed to do?" Then the Board heard from Anna and Paul. "Anna thought Dick loved her. She told the Board he came by day after day and gave her cashmere sweaters, and paintings, and statues, and wore her down. She said she'd been more or less happily married. Eventually, she and Paul did get divorced."

Richard says, "I really loved Anna. . . . I waited for her for a long time."

Ed is silent for a while. "The upshot was we decided not to invite Dick back as Abbot."

In early December, Ed capped off nine months of accusations, confessions, negotiations, and the near-fatal splintering of the Zen Center community, by writing a letter to Richard in which he expressed his personal convic-tion that healing for individuals and for the community would be served by Richard's resignation. On December 20, 1983, Richard wrote an open letter to the community, in which he stated that his decision had come after months of reflection on "the vow I made to Suzuki-roshi to continue and to develop a place for his teaching which would endure." Seeing that his role as Abbot was damaging the very sangha he had intended to nurture, and not without deep regret and shame, Richard resigned.

When the Board voted to accept the resignation of the Abbot, the two nay voters asked to have their names recorded. Lew Richmond voted no, and he asked for a leave of absence from Zen Center, and within a few months he had taken a job at Smith & Hawken, where he worked for a couple of years. "The real reason I left," says Lew, "is that I wanted a private life and my artistic location back." Lew was trained as a classical pianist, and he has pursued a life as a software consultant, a composer, and a lay Buddhist. "I only deeply love my wife and my music—they are the passions," he says.

Dan Welch also voted not to accept Richard's resignation. A few weeks before the vote, on the last day of 1983, he and Deborah had moved out of Zen Center. They took jobs at Chez Panisse, but by the end of the summer of 1984, they had accepted a shared position as private cooks in Rome. "I fell into a dismal despair when I couldn't participate in what Zen Center had become—highly prized real estate and struggles for control," says Dan. "I didn't want to be grappling about who had the better understanding of Suzuki-roshi's way. Deborah and I had stuck it out for nine months of the talking wars at Zen Center, and I had tried to talk to Richard many times. He was impermeable to everything I said. He did not ask, but I made it a point to go and talk to him, and it was just pouring my heart out on a steel door."

Dan and I are sitting in his idling truck just outside the gate of the Crestone Mountain Zen Center, staring at the true-blue midday sky. We are headed to a little airfield, where a twin-engine plane will fly me back onto the map. We've driven about 250 feet, and I think we have about twenty miles to go. If anyone but Dan were in the driver's seat, I'd ask why we had stopped.

Over the course of my first short stay at Crestone during the summer of 1999, I've watched Dan lead the residents in work and practice routines while Richard was away in the Black Forest with his German students. Dan says less than anyone else. He looks people right in the eye. When someone asks him a question after a lecture he has given or while preparing dinner in the kitchen, Dan inclines his long body toward the speaker, and he looks hopeful. He's very good at recognizing people, so good that you feel he must have learned it from a master. Unlike most of the ordained priests who were his peers at Zen Center, in 1999, Dan is not a recognized Zen master. He is working on Transmission with Richard. It is a strange sight for many of their former colleagues, many of whom recognized Dan's suffering at Zen Center even before they were able to acknowledge their own.

I ask Dan if he thinks it's true, as several of Richard's friends and supporters allege, that Zen Center has become a kind of cult devoted to the memory of Suzuki-roshi. Is the veneration of Suzuki-roshi—with public ceremonies to mark his birth, publication of his lectures, and sponsored scholarship about his life and teaching—a way of eclipsing the legacy of Richard Baker at Zen Center?

"I don't see any of that in negative terms. We didn't do it for so long," Dan says, "and now that we've had some experience of [practicing] on our own, we are looking at Suzuki-roshi. And we might say, Oh." Dan is looking at the sky. "Eclipses are wonderful events that happen in the phenomenal world, and interesting things happen at those times, in the strange light before and after an eclipse," he says, and then he adds, "but we don't live in a world of perpetual eclipse."

Everything changes.

Deborah and Dan's marriage did not survive their stay in Rome, but their lifelong friendship has endured. "I pushed Deborah beyond the pale," says Dan, who almost never says anything that is not bittersweet. "I could not let it go. I was at her constantly. She wanted to get on with a life. She wanted a career. I had nothing else I wanted to do," he says, "so I continued to sit. I had taken a set of robes and a rakusu [the patchwork robe from lay ordination] and a zafu [sitting cushion]. And some Dogen books. I wanted to practice. I saw that, and I thought, 'Okay, Suzuki-roshi, I have loved you. And I have put you on a pedestal.' My response was to take down everything that was of a pedestal nature," says Dan. "I created a fire in the backyard of the villa, and I carefully and respectfully put in my rakusu, my robes, the zafu, and the Dogen books. I burned it all. I kept burning it until it was just ashes." And then, in Dan's white truck, it is hard to say if it is suddenly really hot or really cold, but something extreme is happening, and when Dan rolls up his window, I follow his lead, and that makes it inexplicably easier to breathe. He shifts the truck into gear, but we don't move off the side of the road. "The burning was a ritual," Dan says. "It was something more than daily life. We were lost in life as usual." Eventually, he turns my way, and he smiles. I have no idea what he is looking for, but I know that this is Dan's way of not saying more than he means. "Sitting is fire," he says. "A fire puts out something. It is beyond words."

30.

"ZEN BUDDHISM IS A religion," says Norman Fischer, Abbot of Zen Center from 1995 to 2000, "though it is a religion in which one of the cardinal points of understanding is that letting go of the idea of Zen as a religion is part of the religion."

Since 1983, Zen Center has let go of a lot. This is the practical truth of impermanence. And it was not only its own institutional history that demanded forfeitures and accommodations. By the mid-1980s, the very idea of Japan had changed radically; its economic hegemony occasioned a renewed Western interest in its imperial and imperialistic history. The post-Hiroshima Japan from which Suzuki-roshi emerged was almost eclipsed by the new dawn of the Rising Sun. At the same time, the moral and political significance of the story of Tibet and its exiled spiritual leaders captured the hearts and imaginations of many Americans. The spiritual traditions and folk rituals of Tibetan Buddhism were brought compellingly to life in the person and teachings of the Dalai Lama. Suddenly, there were many Buddhisms from which to choose.

And lest we forget, Americans are a busy people. Out of this conglomeration of ideas and influences arose the ecumenical "retreat model" of spiritual practice. This took shape at nonsectarian meditation centers with very small permanent staffs—spiritual economies of scale—which offer laypeople access to teachers from various Buddhist, Hindu, Western, and Yoga traditions in weekend or weeklong conference-style programs of seminars and workshops. "This is the model that seems to serve people today," says Lew Richmond. "Teachers travel around the country to give people a chance to retreat and bring that experience back into their ordinary lives." And, says Wendy Johnson, "the issues [at retreat centers] are not primarily issues of community life and its difficulties, which occupy a lot of time and require a lot of care."

The programs at these nondenominational, nonsectarian retreat centers are not unlike populist versions of Richard Baker's Invisible College, or dinner with the Abbot and his invited guests transposed to a cafeteria setting. Zen Center was well positioned to take advantage of the demand for such programs. Richard's determination to develop and improve Green Gulch created a legacy of handsome meeting rooms and guest accommodations. Indeed, revenues from guest and conference programming have overtaken profits from the sale of farm products at Green Gulch. The farm is more profitable as a teaching tool, and a visitor attraction, than as a working farm. The Tassajara guest season, traditionally the single largest source of revenue for the Zen Center community, has emerged as one of the nation's most popular Buddhist retreat programs, offering a comprehensive slate of participatory yoga, cooking, and bird-watching classes, as well as traditional meditation and study classes with Zen masters and teachers from other Buddhist, Jewish, and Christian traditions. As Norman points out, if Zen Center were divided, Tassajara, City Center, and Green Gulch would each rank among the top ten Buddhist meditation and training centers in the country in size and scope of programming.

Millions of Americans have integrated the practices or ideas or rhetoric of Buddhism into their lives as Buddhist institutions have adapted their traditions and styles of teaching to the culture. "We're developing a sense of religion as a phenomenon," says Norman. "In other words, [a person might say] I have a genuine religious impulse, but I'm not a Catholic and I'm not a Protestant and I'm not a Buddhist, but I do Buddhist meditation, and I have an affinity for other rituals." Norman is Jewish and a Buddhist. "You could say [this approach to religion] is dilettantism," says Norman, "but I'm not so sure it's not a kind of fundamental pluralism—something new, something we haven't seen yet. In the past, there was the idea that this is *the* truth; now, everyone's talking to everyone. Each religious condition is a coherent thing. You might say, 'Maybe this part of me fits into this coherence.' I think it's valid and can be serious. One of our roles at Zen Center is to preserve the integrity of one particular tradition."

You could say that this cross-fertilization among cultures and traditions has also produced some Buddhists, but if you really want to know how many Buddhists there are in the United States, start counting. If you want to know how many Buddhists there are in the United States according to journalists and scholars, the answer is:

> 100,000 ("American-born," according to an October 13, 1997 *Time* cover story, though that estimate didn't include "hundreds of thousands" of Buddhist immigrants);

> ten times as many as there were forty years ago (according to "Why Buddhism, Why Now?" in *Civilization* magazine's online January 1, 2000 issue), as well as ten million "Buddhist sympathizers," a category so utterly imprecise that it seems, in this context, the most meaningful;

> three to four million (estimated by Martin Baumann, based on recent surveys for the 1997/Volume 4 issue of the *Journal of Buddhist Ethics*);

> between five and six million (the oft-cited, off-the-cuff estimate broadcast during a 1994 Peter Jennings interview with translator and teacher Robert Thurman);

> more than there are Episcopalians (as posted in 1999 on nlag.net, an Assembly of God parish homepage).

If you want to know who counts as a Buddhist, you are still not getting the point. While almost everyone agrees that there are now more than 1,000 Buddhist meditation and practice centers in North America, you will meet first-time, one-day visitors to Zen Center who self-identify as Buddhists, and ordained monks who do not. One man who has lived at Zen Center since the early 1970s said confidently, "I haven't seen any Buddhists around here for years."

I frequently recall and rethink my first meeting with Norman.

He is wearing khakis and a blue Oxford-cloth shirt, and his head is shaved. His office is a kind of cozy shed that is attached to, and behind, and somehow also below the library at Green Gulch, but I am always confused by the geometry of the central administrative complex—a big, low dining and conference and guest center, which sort of skulks into the hill below the road. Or maybe I skulk when I am there and, thus, lose my way. I was there once for a week as a guest student, and I had a handsome little room somewhere in that big building, and it was only twenty steps from the zendo, where I headed every morning in the dark—and somehow I never made it to the proper entrance in fewer than fifty steps. I never felt confused about where I was going, but I was constantly lost.

Sitting zazen was a lot like just sitting, and I didn't have any insights, though one morning I did remember almost every word of "The Love Song of J. Alfred Prufrock." Two experienced meditators who were beginning an intensive practice period at Green Gulch when I arrived asked me if I had sensed the world dropping away in the zendo. I never did. But I did notice that the world dropped me a couple of times, and that was news. I also slowed the work crew to which I was assigned each morning, and I really did skulk around in the afternoons, wondering if there were any poor boys in the Buddha's neighborhood who watched him as he walked out of that beautiful palace, and thought knowingly to themselves, *Bad move.* And I wondered if bowing nine times and chanting Japanese syllables I did not understand (handy pronunciation guides are handed out to novices) had altered my view of the farm or skewed my sense of direction.

Norman is a teacher who can convey something about the middle way, the not-this-or-thatness of a moment or a life or an institution. He has many students, and he devoted much of his five-year term as Abbot to teaching, to training priests, and to stabilizing Zen Center's financial foundation. And he made several controversial attempts to promote rapprochement with Richard.

In Norman's office there is a chair and futon. A young woman with dark hair makes us tea, and then moves into a little anteroom, where she immediately disappears into a giant pile of paper. I ask Norman about the seventies. This is our first face-to-face conversation. I tell him I've begun to hear some stories.

"I was studying Zen," says Norman, who had many jobs, including a long stint as manager of the farm. "I was getting what I wanted. Remember, it was a voluntary thing. Richard was very concerned about status, and he did see himself standing on top of others, doing his thing," he says. "What did I care? I was using him as much as he was using me." Then

Norman laughs and says, "I still think you should use the teacher—it shouldn't go the other way around. This is where the fact that I was a poet helped me." Norman says he had not come to Zen Center expecting to be handed a life. He has published almost a dozen books of verse and prose. His wife is a schoolteacher. His twin sons recently graduated from college. He started to practice as a graduate student at Berkeley in the early seventies and moved to Green Gulch in 1976.

Norman is a big man and a soft physical presence—especially when he puts on his wire-rimmed spectacles. He has a rabbinical habit of mind and a goofy sense of humor. And he has a way of describing situations that almost makes sense in the same elusive way that *form is emptiness is form is a speck of dust with all the suffering of the phenomenal world packed into an impermanent delusion arising from desire* makes sense, or makes you feel a little silly for trying to make sense of anything. It's worth just listening to him.

"Dick would say things like, 'I'm only hanging around with all these glorious people so Zen will penetrate the world.' It was, in part, true," says Norman. "The thing he didn't say, that he should've said, is, 'I kind of like it, too.' But he didn't say it. So when it turned out he had his egotistical side, his secret life, and we all realized that this guy was doing all of these things because he liked it, it was an eye-opener. I sort of thought, that wasn't my thing. Any fool would have seen it, but if you're sitting in a monastery, these worldly things are surprising. A lot of the people who were major supporters of Zen Center—and are major supporters today— they knew perfectly well what was going on. You could say, *What a bunch of dummies.* You could also say, *What a beautiful faith.* If we're suspicious of one another, a lot of beautiful things don't happen. I think that if you scratch under the bitterness, there's a lot of beauty there. The years people spent here were not wasted years of being duped. They should take credit for the fact that we did it for many years. We should be affirming that. I feel sorry for anybody who's bitter. We did something great. We overlooked things, but maybe that's what it takes to do something great— to create a wonderful institution that still benefits people."

———

It's a great view. Norman's way of talking about it stuck with me. Sometimes, I used his words as a refresher; sometimes I thought I needed a way of seeing that was not mine and not the way of the last person at Zen Center to whom I'd spoken; and sometimes I wanted to argue a point or two.

I would say that persistent sadness is often mistaken for bitterness.

Or, I would say, Does it matter which parts are the true parts of the things that are "in part, true"?

But what I was really saying every time is exactly what I did not want to believe: *You could say anything.*

31.

A FEW WEEKS AFTER THE PEACE
Conference at Tassajara in March of 1983, Richard Baker accepted an invitation to meet with the Zen Center Board, including the members he had previously disinvited to meetings. Yvonne Rand chaired the meeting and floored everyone by insisting—three times—that Richard not sit on the floor in meditation posture but in a chair. And then the Board members began to speak. And that really was the end of a singular and remarkable story, though no one could quite believe it.

"I definitely wanted Richard Baker to stay," says Leslie James, who would soon be elected President. "I wanted him to join us, and not be so separate, not see himself as so perfect that he couldn't relate with us, but still be the teacher here. And many, many people wanted the same thing, at that point," she remembers. "We were his students. That's how we had stayed at Zen Center—as his students."

Gib Robinson remembers "trying to piece together *How could he do this?* There were certain things I thought I could rely on. I trusted that Lew and Yvonne would have central roles in the community." By 1984, Lew Richmond was working for Paul Hawken. By the end of 1985, Yvonne was on her way out. "And I relied on the fact that Richard could not leave the people with whom he had practiced for twenty years," says Gib. "I was dead wrong."

"Here are these people," says Linda Cutts, who would become Chair of the Board in 1985, "all one family—and Richard Baker called me the enemy. And I loved him so much. I didn't think he was the enemy. I thought he should resign. I told him, 'I just want to do what is best.' I felt what was best was for him to do some inner work."

It was not clear to anyone that Richard would never come back. He could have done it differently. He didn't have to give it all up. He could have just stayed put as Eido-roshi had stayed put at the Zen Studies Center in New York even after students brought charges against him. That would have been the more traditional thing, say many former students. Many Japanese priests offered the same solicited and unsolicited advice— the teacher stays; the disaffected students leave. But Richard Baker was not Japanese. A new American story had been framed, but who had the authority to tell such a story?

The belief that Richard could, would, and should return as a humbled teacher or, better yet, a humble Zen student was represented in every splintered faction of the community. This was not only a symptom of their deep faith in the practice, says Michael Wenger, Dean of Buddhist Studies at Zen Center; it was evidence that "the community could not read the story. When you are in the story, you believe you are the central character." Everyone's place in the story had been established as a one-to-one relationship with Richard; he was the authorized storyteller; without him, it was difficult to see what actions and intentions might mean.

"It would have made a difference if Dick had been able to say, 'I can see the consequences of my behavior,'" says Yvonne. "At the time, I didn't know if he would be able to do that."

Steve Allen was Treasurer, and not exactly in line with the Board, and he remembers "another big community meeting with the Board and the lawyer, and I said, 'The Board should all resign.' And the lawyer said to me, 'It's like the boat's on fire and we're trying to take care of it; why aren't you helping?' And I said, 'The boat *is* on fire, so why are you spending all of your time attacking the captain? Why don't you put out the fire?'" As far as Steve could see, it was still Richard's ship. Steve was among the officers whom Richard had disinvited to meetings; Richard thought he was allied with the Board and the Board considered him "one of Richard's flunkies." Steve shakes his head. "It was hysteria."

Whether you saw what was happening at Zen Center as empowerment or pandemonium, it was hard not to be impressed. "We were all taken aback," says Yvonne. "There were people lined up around the block waiting to tell [Richard] what a piece of shit he was. And people who should have left Zen Center for all the right reasons stayed for all the wrong reasons. It was heartbreaking. The sheer scale of that many people beating on him was daunting," she says. "But if his practice had any taproot, he would have understood that you go back to the new-student seat and sit there until you can change something within yourself. But the fact that we didn't all stay in the same room at the same time long enough to come to some understanding of what had happened has crippled Zen Center ever since."

Mel Weitsman is one of several senior priests who advised Richard in mid-1983—directly or through intermediaries—that it was not too late for him to participate in some kind of repentance ritual and take a new role in the community. For the next two years, American Buddhist and Christian teachers consistently urged the Zen Center membership to reconcile with its teacher. Robert Aitken-roshi found "little optimism and much gloom" when he met with the Zen Center community in mid-1984, and he seemed to sense that the separation might be permanent; however, even Aitken-roshi suggested that a ceremony should be performed with Richard to thank him publicly and amicably conclude the relationship.

By then, though, Richard and the Board were haggling over rugs, robes, statues, and paintings that might have been donated to Zen Center and might have been personal gifts to Richard. Even when the stuff was sorted out to the dissatisfaction of almost everyone, both sides still claimed to be in sole possession of the official version of the unfinished story of the San Francisco Zen Center, and because they could not let it go, they invested themselves and a lot of donated resources in their various efforts not to begin again.

"We tend to think that if we *think* it right, everything will *be* all right," says Michael Wenger. "But this is not a mental universe. The mental universe is part of the universe. And the world is vast and wide."

At the moment Richard began his leave of absence in the spring of 1983, Zen Center began to page through its past—and almost every page they picked up crumbled in someone's hands. "One of the surprising things for me," says Leslie James, "was the number of old disagreements I'd had no idea about—old, hidden problems. And people who'd disagreed all those years hadn't found much space. Well, now there was space for disagreements to come out."

Sitting zazen was not a solution—at least, not in this lifetime. "People were hurt, and cocooned for a while," remembers Michael. "And the practice was threatened." At all three temples, practice leaders reported on dwindling and unpredictable numbers in the zendos. Linda says, "The Apocalypse was an internal crisis, as well—*How can I trust myself?*" She whispers the question, and she is quiet for a moment. "I stayed. I sat. Other people felt, *If this is what comes of zazen, let it go.* For me, it seemed just more obvious that there was nothing but the practice."

No one trusted the hierarchical structure of the community, and there was no precedent in the annals of Zen Center—or the history of Zen Buddhism—for representative self-government. The Board—including eight lifetime members resurrected from the rolls of the disinvited—took the lead, as if it were picking up where it had left off, though it had been largely left out of the decision-making process from the start of Richard's abbacy. Almost from the moment the Board began to meet—often weekly—in 1983, calls for its resignation were issued by students loyal to Richard. Not to be outdone, some of Richard's harshest critics in the community, who perceived Yvonne, Reb, Dan, Lew, and several of the elected officers as Richard's longtime coconspirators, also called for the Board to step aside. In just this way, every schism that opened at Zen Center proved almost instantaneously schismatic. "I remember polarization and a lot of pain," says Linda. "It was hard."

More than a dozen senior members of Zen Center have said, almost to the word, *I was the only one who did not take sides during 1983.* But this is not how they were perceived; no senior priest or veteran lay practitioner is remembered by others as an unaligned or disinterested actor. Nor was any actor unemployed. As the ranks thinned, the number of committees and meetings seemed to increase exponentially; the Abbot's Council, officers, and practice committees had ongoing business and new duties during the interregnum, and there were new, ad hoc audit and restructuring committees and a liaison committee with Richard and the Hawkens, as well as designated "small groups" of community members that met every two weeks to discuss the fate of Zen Center, not to mention community-wide workshops and seminars with psychological counselors and man-agement consultants. For dozens of the senior priests, there were also weekly appointments with psychotherapists—many took to the couch for the first time during these years. At least two eventually became psy-chotherapists, setting up their own private practices.

As early as April of 1983, Steve Weintraub was writing memos to the Board to warn that fewer than twenty-five students were in place to work during the Tassajara Guest Season, which usually had a staff of at least forty-five. By December, twenty residents had left or were leaving Green Gulch. So many students with more than five years' standing were leav-ing that a policy was adopted to offer them two months of transitional pay. Staffing positions were eliminated at all three centers, and doubling up gave way to Board "discussions of whether one vice president can do the work of the present three vice presidents" managing the businesses, real estate, and development.

The work of undoing all of their work was undoing them. Income lagged behind projections. Programs were cut, but the profits bled out of fresh, institutional wounds; as support for scholars and translators was withdrawn, the community incurred $140,000 in unbudgeted legal and accounting fees as it attempted to reconcile its own books and settle with its former teacher. A modest increase in stipends ($10 to $20 per month) was paired with a strict new policy requiring applicants for intensive prac-tice at Tassajara to have saved enough money to pay the full tuition for two practice periods without counting on an income during guest season or other work-for-practice arrangements. Zen Center began to overhaul and winnow its stipend and scholarship policies, and within a few years, almost all of the married senior priests and practice leaders had spouses working outside of the community, effectively ending the appealing ambiguity of their status. If they were still neither laypeople nor monks, they were no longer perceptibly distinct from the faculty of a residential boarding school, nor were they distinguishable from most Protestant clergy, except that most of the Zen Center clergy were practicing with each other instead of with small congregations around the country. Their roles were changing, but the script was not altered.

Deep cuts were made in budgets, and one of the first things to go was fruitcake, which cost $7 a loaf and was replaced with a year-end greeting card. Attention then was turned to real estate. Before the end of 1983, Zen Center sold two neighboring houses it owned on a cul-de-sac near Muir Beach, about a mile from Green Gulch. It was the beginning of a long process of de-acquisition. The San Francisco and Marin County real-estate markets were just five or six years shy of a fantastic price explosion; but a legacy of high mortgages and too much short-term borrowing in the early 1980s left Zen Center in desperate need of cash. Both houses needed costly repairs, and after failing to stir up any bids above the asking prices, they were sold to the longtime tenants—Yvonne and her husband; and next door, the Japanese painter Mayumi Oda—at market value minus the standard broker's fee. Soon, the community was contemplating the sale of several buildings in the Page Street neighborhood. It had already raided its small cash reserves to pay year-end bills, and at the end of 1985, all wage and salary employees of Zen Center were asked to take a week off with no pay during the last quarter of the fiscal year.

So, just as it was not *not* about sex, it was also not *not* about money.

After considering advice from the Outside Financial Advisory Board and a lot of armchair fiduciary experts—who recommended severance packages for Richard ranging from *Audit him* to a lifetime salary—in early 1984, the Board acknowledged Richard's resignation as Abbot and settled for one year's salary and rent-free use of the Green Gulch house for the year; asked him to vacate his city residence by mid-1984; sold the BMW and gave him his old Audi; wrote off $30,000 worth of home furnishings; and made it clear he should not expect help with his telephone bills, car repairs, or other previously reimbursable expenses.

"I remember one of the last things Richard said when we were settling on the $35,000 [severance]," says Darlene Cohen. "He was pacing in despair. He said, 'I won't have health insurance.' And I didn't say this, because I was torn, but I thought, *Welcome to the world of Zen Center.* None of us had insurance."

Zen Center didn't have an Abbot, either—another overlooked clue that no amount of rewriting, revising, or refinancing would revive the old story. Across the country, American Buddhists were beginning to see that no ending could justify the means used to sustain the authority of a singular, enlightened spiritual master. Even in the Zen Center community, there was simple and compelling evidence that senior priests had moved beyond their original interpretation of intimate, heart-mind to heart-mind Transmission unsullied by institutional politics or ambition.

In 1984, Mel Weitsman traveled to Japan, spent about six weeks with Suzuki-roshi's son, Hoitsu, at the temple he had inherited from his father, and there received Transmission in the lineage of Suzuki-roshi. Bill Kwong also had received Transmission from Hoitsu. Neither Bill nor Mel had a practice relationship with Hoitsu. Mel recalls that the ceremony was conducted in Japanese, and like most practitioners at Zen Center, Mel was not fluent in Japanese.

Ed Brown remembers going to Mel for Transmission in 1995. Ed was concerned about having dropped out of a long and unfulfilling process with Reb. "Mel said to me, 'That's nothing. I resigned from three dharma Transmissions.'" Ed smiles. "I realized I had found my teacher." (As Ed recalls the complicated sequence, it became evident to Mel in the mid-seventies that Richard would not give him Transmission, so Mel started to work with Bill; that didn't go well, so he worked with Suzuki-roshi's former assistant, Kobun Chino; while that was under way, Richard approached Mel about Transmission, which Mel considered Suzuki-roshi's intention, so he left Kobun Chino and worked with Richard; by then, it was 1983. "The whole mess happened," says Ed, "and then Dick withdrew his offer because Mel wasn't being politically cooperative—you know, if Mel supports Dick with the Zen Center Board, Mel gets Transmission." Mel has said he was willing to support Richard personally, but not in his role as Abbot. "There would be no quid pro quo with Mel," says Ed. So, Mel went to Japan.)

In 1985, Hoitsu visited America to participate in Mel's installation as Abbot of Berkeley Zen Center, and he gave Transmission to Les Kaye, the IBM executive who had served for more than a decade as teacher at the affiliated Zen center down the peninsula where the lectures for *Zen Mind, Beginner's Mind* were recorded. "There will not be any more Transmissions from me," said Hoitsu in a talk reprinted in the August 1985 *Berkeley Zen Center Newsletter.* "Those three people [Bill, Mel, and Les] have sat zazen a lot longer than I have (laughter), and I kind of hesitate almost to be called their teacher or master. . . . Are there any questions?"

He had answered the pressing question: *No more Transmissions from me.* Hoitsu didn't have an Abbot up his sleeve for San Francisco. And on that late summer day in 1985, no one asked what his dharma Transmissions might mean about the singularity of the Reb-Richard-Suzuki-roshi lineup.

At the San Francisco Zen Center, they were sticking to the script. In 1984, in the immediate aftermath of Richard's resignation, the Board had invited Suzuki-roshi's first and most loyal assistant, Dainin Katagiri-roshi, to serve as interim Abbot for one year. Katagiri-roshi was then Abbot of the Minnesota Zen Center, but he clearly expressed his enthusiasm about returning to San Francisco. "He understood, because it would have been done this way in Japan, that being acting Abbot for that year would mean that he would be asked to be the Abbot," says Yvonne, who was a strong advocate for Katagiri. "He understood that he would remain Abbot long enough to work with Reb so Reb could become the Abbot."

According to the old script, as the only acknowledged American disciple of the only acknowledged American disciple of Suzuki-roshi, Reb was, by definition, already the spiritual leader of Zen Center. But not everyone could see it. Wendy Johnson was still considered sympathetic to Richard, and thus not a natural ally of Yvonne; she was one of several Zen Center veterans who had begun to seek out Thich Nhat Hanh as a teacher. "The Katagiri story is sad," she says. "He was willing to work with Richard. I feel very strongly that Reb did not allow that to happen. It was a bitter struggle." It was not only Reb's supporters who opposed Katagiri, says Wendy. "Some of Richard's strongest advocates were concerned with the lineage hocus pocus. Katagiri was not in *the* lineage."

Katagiri had a number of liabilities in a selection process that almost all of the participants now discuss as a political contest. Yvonne remembers opposition on the Board to a Japanese Abbot. "He wasn't an American," says Michael, who advocated for Katagiri, "and there was nothing he could do about it." Michael considered Katagiri's idea of working with Reb "ideal," but he says that "the tremendous influence on not inviting [Katagiri] was the Minnesota Zen Center's anger and resistance to having their Abbot come to Zen Center. For a sangha that was already hurt, that weighed heavily on people here."

That, says Wendy's husband Peter Rudnick, and "Reb basically had a tantrum about becoming Abbot instead of Katagiri. It broke Katagiri's heart. It was a critical event."

On January 12, 1986, three years after Richard began his leave of absence, two years after he resigned as Abbot-for-life, and one year after the entire Zen Center Board of Directors gave up their lifetime appointments to make way for elected representatives, Reb was finally installed in the Mountain Seat as Abbot of the San Francisco Zen Center.

"Reb had started practicing to be Abbot from the moment he came. He was an older student than I was from his first day," says David Chadwick, who was practicing at Zen Center when Reb arrived in 1967. "And Suzuki-roshi loved Reb, and admired his concentration."

Reb was not exactly the only teacher in the community, but he was the only teacher who was the Abbot. Ed says, "A lot of people were drawn to Reb's intensity and his exclusive focus on practice. He has that Zen demeanor, too; he looks the part. I think, to this day, people have an image of the Zen teacher as a stereotype of a Japanese person—stoic, intense, and inward. You don't have to be particularly friendly. And Reb is brilliant, and very articulate." Other students and teachers characterize Reb's teaching style as "penetrating" or "deep," in contrast to Richard's "coalescent" and "inclusive" lectures.

Members of the community were interviewed about their Abbot preferences—a novel approach to the selection process. Admiration for Reb was tempered by doubts about the legacy of his intimate practice with Richard, his youth (Reb was born in 1944, Richard in 1936), and his lack of interest in administration and social outreach. The vast majority of respondents expressed concerns about vesting one man with spiritual and temporal authority over the community. Leslie supported Reb's nomination as sole Abbot, and she believes it was clear that he had not been acknowledged as the sole teacher. "Some people—a lot—would have happily let him be the only teacher. But we said out loud in various meetings that you don't have to have a particular person be your teacher to be at Zen Center. You have to be open to having a teacher," students were told, "and to be ordained you have to have someone who can do it"—and it must be someone who has Transmission—"but it doesn't have to be the Abbot." Leslie remembers that the consensus was "we still wanted one Abbot to hold things together. Reb was the most obvious person to do it, I thought at the time, and I still feel that was right."

At Zen Center, though, one Abbot had never been able to hold it together.

A lot was said aloud in meetings about the abbacy from 1983 through 1986, but a fundamental confusion about the role of the Abbot was evidently not resolved. What did emerge was strikingly consistent language, which is used by several senior priests to explain why they were willing to support Reb as Abbot. They believed, they say, that "the democratic process" and the "psychological work done by the community" after 1983 were "safeguards" that effectively "hemmed in" the Abbot's role. In 1991, when Reb was interviewed by another Zen Center task force, he was asked whether *abbot* and *head teacher* should be understood as separate functional roles. Reb said that, at Zen Center, they had always been the same thing.

In 1985 many people also believed that Reb might not stay at Zen Center were he not given an opportunity to serve as Abbot-for-life. "It was an ambivalent thing," says Michael. "Reb was young and ambitious. And there was some feeling that everyone was hurting, and no one wanted to hurt Reb, and no one wanted to lose such a first-rate person."

Gib had participated in a small men's group that met with Reb before his ascension to the Mountain Seat, and he worried that Reb shared Richard's capacity for "not keeping people in mind. I saw that happening between Reb and men who had fifteen years as leaders in the community." Gib was then elected to a one-year term on the new Board that voted to approve Reb as Abbot. "When the Board made its decision, I said, 'I will go along with this, but I want it to be clear that this is a four-year term [for Reb], and after that, someone else should be Abbot.' The Board agreed to that. And then I left the Board—it was very amicable," says Gib, whose one-year term was up. "And then the Board reversed itself, opening up the possibility of Reb being Abbot in perpetuity." It was the old story. "And that did it for me," says Gib.

Yvonne saw the Board's behavior as "a step into a downhill slide. I was surprised, and I didn't support the decision." But by 1985, Yvonne was being moved to the margins of the community; and then she moved further away, leading retreats in her own developing practice center and teaching around the country, until in the early 1990s, "Norman asked me to leave. I had been teaching at Green Gulch for many years, and when Reb took over it never occurred to me that I wouldn't keep teaching. And it dawned on me rather late that he was the Abbot and I'd never been invited to teach. Norman pushed me about it. So I resigned from everything." Her leadership during the nine months before Richard resigned had not sat well with students loyal to Richard. Although it was Lew and Michael who wrote a brief, controversial *Wind Bell* article outlining the events that led to Richard's resignation, David and other longtime practitioners, and many of Richard's loyal friends outside of Zen Center, say that it was Yvonne who "got on the phone" in 1983 and talked to influential donors and supporters. In 1984, Yvonne's advocacy for Katagiri was perceived by others as "a power play" to secure her own status, and it did not endear her to Reb's loyal students. "And I went to India [on a pilgrimage with Robert Thurman], and I didn't come back for Reb's installation," she says. "That was seen as a major slap in the face by Reb and his supporters. And when I later received Transmission from Katagiri-roshi, Reb was really upset. He'd wanted me to receive Transmission from him." Maybe most important, though, the interpretations of history that Yvonne had encouraged the community to consider in the immediate aftermath of the Apocalypse eventually did not serve her. Yvonne had forged personal and teaching relationships with psychologists and psychiatrists interested in family-systems and behavioral-patterning analysis, several of whom she invited to work with members of the Zen Center community. "I was so linked—as the other piece of the leadership—with Richard, that there was a certain, not entirely conscious sense that if he had to go, I had to go, too," she says, smiling. "If the father has to go, so does the mother."

In 1985, Wendy Johnson was elected to a three-year Board term. She was still ambivalent about Reb's role in the Apocalypse. In the early 1980s, Wendy says, "Reb and Lew held the practice together, but they'd also offered a kind of cover for Richard. And then, in 1983, Reb did not stand up for Richard—his teacher." Students remember that Reb apologized for having not stood up *to* his teacher. "And Reb benefited by that," says Wendy. "I voted for not choosing an Abbot, with one other Board member. We didn't know what we were doing. We hadn't cleaned up our mess yet. And if you don't clean up your mess, it just expands out, like a radiating circle."

Zen Center continued to occupy a central position in the American Buddhist stream after the Apocalypse. Everyone seemed to know that Reb's path to the Mountain Seat, where he sat alone as teacher and Abbot in 1986, had been as rocky and rough as the road to Tassajara. There was barely a Buddhist teacher of note whose advice and counsel had not been solicited by the residents of Page Street and Green Gulch Farm. When Rick Fields revised his indispensable history of the century-long effort to establish Buddhism in the West, *How the Swans Came to the Lake,* he included a brief review of the sex and money problems of America's dharma heirs and of their Asian teachers since 1981. The scandals, he wrote, had made Americans suspect that "the meeting of East and West heralded by the heady Sixties and early Seventies had turned into nothing less than a head-on collision. Signs of trouble first appeared publicly in 1983 at the San Francisco Zen Center, long thought of as the very model of a modern Zen center."

It was important, then, that signs of restoration appear first in San Francisco. Reb was the headline: The Story Continues. And in January of 1986, Suzuki-roshi's widow and his son Hoitsu participated in Reb's installation ceremony, as did Suzuki-roshi's former assistant Kobun Chino. Katagiri-roshi, who had served the community as interim Abbot during 1984, did not participate in the ceremony, and he was not among the teachers thanked by Reb in his "appreciatory statement." Neither was Richard. Los Angeles Abbot Maezumi-roshi did participate, and Reb thanked him for "great and steadfast support, especially during the last three years."

Maezumi-roshi brought more than goodwill with him to Reb's installation. His presence was ghosted by public confessions he'd made in 1984 about his alcoholism and his sexual involvement with students, including an affair with his female dharma heir, which had destroyed her marriage and Maezumi-roshi's own marriage. But he went into rehab, stuck with his students, and he remained Abbot until his death. This was not exactly the dawn of a new form of spiritual mastery, but it was the ending Zen Center practitioners said they'd wanted with Richard, because it wasn't an end to it all. Reb and Zen Center were not going away with Richard; they were going with the ongoing story. Spiritual teachers acknowledged through the ancient lineages of dharma Transmission were not yet shrugging off their singular authority in America. And they weren't leaving their palaces. When necessary, they were seeking refuge in the newly assembled, cross-cultural, ecumenical Trinity of confession, counseling, and compassion.

You could say it was one continuous mistake—which is the thirteenth-century Japanese master Dogen's description of Zen.

Actor Peter Coyote and Benedictine Brother David Steindl-Rast offered supportive, congratulatory words to Reb on behalf of far-flung friends and admirers, as did UC Berkeley sociologist Robert Bellah, who called Reb's installation "an important moment in the Americanization of Zen Buddhism," according to the Spring 1986 *Wind Bell.*

Zen Center had survived the Apocalypse. Suzuki-roshi's teaching lineage had survived Transmission from one American teacher to another. "The community has taken charge of itself and acted democratically," said Bellah, and yet "recognized the need for continuity with the forms and structures of the Japanese past." Reb, said Bellah, represented "the middle way," a symbol of "the new leadership that will take the next steps to make Buddhism generally and Zen in particular a part of American cultural and spiritual life."

Just about a year later, Reb would be seeking a refund on a small contribution he made to American culture.

32.

RICHARD BAKER RESIGNED
as Abbot of the San Francisco Zen Center in December of 1983, but it is
not clear that he intended to walk away from the Zen Center story. Indeed, many of his former students suspect that he intended to walk away
with the Zen Center story. Whatever his intentions, Richard seems not to
have been satisfied with the way his role was winding down, and long
before he left San Francisco, he had begun to plot an alternative ending.

By October of 1983, Richard had sent his young Dutch student, Willem
Malten, to live in Santa Fe. Three months before he resigned as Abbot,
Richard had secured a new site for a residential training temple. In fact,
Richard had worked out the arrangement even before he went to France
in the fall of 1983 to visit the Vietnamese teacher Thich Nhat Hanh. Wil-
lem became the caretaker for this modest complex of buildings in Santa
Fe, which included a Tibetan-style memorial shrine, a house, and a small
zendo.

The Santa Fe property was owned by David Padwa, the mathematician
and entrepreneur who had sold his company to Xerox and introduced
then-chairman Chester Carlson to Richard and Suzuki-roshi in the late
1960s. In the early summer of 1983, sometime after he set out on his walk
to Tassajara, Richard found himself in Los Angeles. While there, he called
David Padwa, and they worked out a deal. Padwa offered to donate the
zendo to Richard, and Richard was able to use this gift as collateral for a
loan ("through friends of mine," he says) to purchase the rest of the property. "And then Laurance [Rockefeller] started giving me money for it,"
he adds. Rockefeller has remained one of his most generous supporters.
Richard recalls that "the contribution at that time was $300,000" over

several years. The house, the zendo, the money—"All of that came out of that walk [to Tassajara]," says Richard.

It's true; whenever Richard gets dusted up, a lot of what shakes out is gold dust. You could say it's karmic. You could say it's opportunistic. You could say, Richard didn't walk to Tassajara; he flew to Los Angeles, crashed in a friend's house, got on the horn with some donors, and while his students were being scolded by Richard's friends for their lack of compassion, Richard was proving that his former students and their daily practice were expendable. He was not going to end up as Abbot of no place.

Willem remembers the secrecy of his first trip with Richard to Santa Fe. He was eager to leave Zen Center and not eager to prolong the student-teacher relationship. After a tour of Padwa's Santa Fe property and neighboring St. John's College, "we drove back to the airport," says Willem, "and Richard said to me, 'Are you going to do it?' I said, 'We have to talk.' I was very attracted to this area—it was about as exotic for a Dutchman as it could be. I was born six feet below sea level, and here I was two thousand meters high in a desert." Willem is enduringly grateful for his time at Tassajara—both for the practice and for the chance to "have a body" better than the skinny, asthmatic one he had before his years of physical labor in Tassajara's dusty but dry air. And he believed his friendship with Richard had survived his disillusionment as a student. "At the same time, I knew Richard," says Willem. "I wasn't going to put my black robes on and pretend nothing had happened." Willem said he would stay only if Richard asked his approval before sending anyone else to live on the property. "I said, 'I don't want to live with a bunch of slaves. And I don't want to re-create Zen Center. I am just as interested in [having] a vision with a Native American guy in the desert as I am in a dharma talk.' So," says Willem, who would live mostly alone in Santa Fe for the next nine months, "we shook hands. There was no problem," he says. "Of course, that's how problems start—with no problem."

Richard incorporated more than a few familiar elements and characters into his story. In February of 1984, two months after Richard resigned as Abbot, Zen Center's first president and one of Suzuki-roshi's first Western students, the Englishman Grahame Petchey moved into Richard's residence on Page Street, next door to City Center. Although he advised Richard to take the humble route back to Zen Center, Grahame also wanted "to make a statement about my support for [Richard] at the time, especially as he was Suzuki-roshi's heir."

Grahame had returned from Japan in the early 1980s, and Richard had introduced him to Paul Hawken. Grahame worked at the Smith & Hawken garden-tool catalog company for six months, he says, "and quickly realized that this relationship was not going to work. Both of us were used to particular entrepreneurial structures—our own! Paul was autocratic, and I was autocratic, and it is not my nature to upset the harmony of a situation that is working very well and working to the benefit of the people who are there."

In 1984, Richard was in the process of forming a new corporation sole, the Dharma Sangha. Grahame was planning a long stay in England, but before he departed, "we had decided we should start a business together," he remembers. "We had a specific idea of doing a mail-order catalog of unusual and hard-to-find items which Dick would select as he traveled. We were working on that idea when I left."

A sort of friendly companion to the Smith & Hawken catalog?

Many of Richard's students who were still at Zen Center or in the neighborhood continued to seek him out. They remember commuting from Green Gulch or City Center to attend weekly meetings with Richard at an apartment in San Francisco's North Beach neighborhood for a few months. Several of them who stayed connected to Richard remember Mel Weitsman, more than Reb or Yvonne, as the person who spoke most forcefully about the state of Zen Center in the wake of the Apocalypse and the need to restore authenticity and integrity to the practice. He roused a number of Richard's students to leave. By mid-1984, a few of them had visited the Santa Fe property, and they were heartened to know that the poet Philip Whalen intended to join Richard there. Philip later received Transmission from Richard, as did Issan, who had his own Hartford Street hospice and Zen center in San Francisco's Castro neighborhood, but visited Santa Fe often.

Steve Allen stayed at Zen Center until mid-1984. Even after he was no longer Treasurer of Zen Center he attended meetings as an observer, attempting to convince the Board to deal with Richard in terms he considered more equitable. "One of the members suggested that now that I wasn't on the Board, I could be on the Outside Financial Advisory Board," he remembers. "I could serve the community that way. But after all the outside observers were gone, I was sitting across from Yvonne and Dan. They said they knew I was a problem. 'You're not going along,' they said." Steve's sudden silence seems ironic; after a few seconds, though, you realize it signals exhaustion, and surrender. "You know," says Steve, "they were right. They were right about a lot. But they had to be entirely right. So I left Zen Center," he says, smiling as he continues, "and I helped Richard set up Santa Fe," and then he just laughs. For about a year, in the fledgling Dharma Sangha's newsletters and correspondence, Steve was listed as Chief Financial Officer. "Can you believe it?" Can he believe it? "You might ask why," says Steve, who then says he didn't entirely understand his motive at the time. "My analysis is that it had all been too glib, and the connecting links between social involvement and practice had broken down, and I recognized Richard was the teacher, and I had to fulfill my obligation." Richard eventually helped Issan complete dharma Transmission with Steve, who now lives at the base of Crestone Mountain and has no contact with Richard. So the several divergent streams of Suzuki-roshi's lineage flow on in their own particular way.

"Richard would call me in Santa Fe every now and then," remembers Willem. "Sometimes, in the spring of 1984, he would stay with me. And I could see how intense his situation was in San Francisco."

Willem's emotional life was "sort of a wreck, and I quickly ran out of money. Many promises had not come true in the past," he says, "so I knew I needed to make a living. I was illegally in the country at the time, and the best job I could get was night work—eleven to eight in the morning at $4.50 an hour. So I started a bread bakery in a garage in the barrio, and I named it Cloud Cliff, which is my Buddhist [lay ordination] name." In a few years, Willem expanded the business and moved the café and bakery to its spacious location near downtown Santa Fe. "In a way, this whole place came out of my Zen Center experience," he says. "Necessity and resource."

When Richard arrived in mid-1984, "the bakery was still a tiny thing," says Willem. "I had paid $5,500 for all of the equipment. I remember drifting around town with Richard. We went to dinner and drank. We drank more, and talked and talked—he is an amazing talker—and it got later and later, and we had more to drink. There was a strange chasm between us, but I thought it was my problem, maybe. We drove back to the house. It was almost two in the morning. I realized, at three-thirty I would have to be back at the bakery. And it was a combination of that depressing thought and how charming and seductive he had been. I realized he was leading to something. And then, there it was—he wanted a forty percent share in the bakery." Willem says several times, *It was tiny.* "And I said I didn't owe him that, and I found myself another place to live," says Willem, who also sent Richard a letter, "to say thank you, but that's it. And I quoted Nietzsche: *A student who remains a student repays his teacher worst.*"

By late 1984, Richard's Dharma Sangha announced its purchase of a former art-school property on Mariposa Street in San Francisco, including a three-story school building, a house and gardens, and a hilltop view of the city. By the end of 1985, although Dharma Sangha had collected almost $600,000 in donations, loans, and pledges, there were few residential students in Santa Fe, and the monthly mortgage payments for the nonresidential practice center in San Francisco were $2,800, and Richard could only afford to be there once a month, so Issan shuttled between his own Hartford Street Zen Center and Richard's new San Francisco center, where Issan was named head of practice.

Richard was also beginning to find himself in Europe more often, and he quickly became aware of its advantages. "One thing that happens in America—it really is a celebrity and media culture," he says. "We know things only through the media, not through immediate contact. In Europe, where people live near their families and have long-term neighbors, people are much more willing to take me at face value. They've heard things, but it doesn't have the same weight. In America, what people have heard has more weight than my standing in front of them." It was several years before Richard established a Dharma Sangha practice center in Germany's Black Forest, but from his earliest appearances at European conferences and seminars, he says, he knew he could trust "that people will go by what they see and hear and feel rather than the rumors. In America, people carry those things like they carry what Clinton had for breakfast, and it is hard to dissolve those impressions."

This almost makes sense. You *can* say that sex and money are nothing, but that doesn't make them poached eggs on toast. Moreover, by analogy, Richard was not in the uncomfortable position of a disgraced former President; he was more like a monarch who had abdicated the throne he had inherited. And by the end of 1984, the story of the San Francisco Zen Center was not a rumor. There were rumors within it, but something had happened; an ancient tradition had been altered. It was not people who did not know Richard, but the people with whom he had practiced intimately who were articulating a public response to his behavior as Abbot. These were the people who'd had immediate—unmediated—contact with him for two decades. As Steve Weintraub sees it, the formal program of spiritual development and administrative restructuring at Zen Center after 1983 "was an attempt to move away from absolute individual spiritual authority. And how do we Americans do it? Bureaucracy. We invented a bureaucratic system."

"Now it's democratic," says Richard, reflecting on the recent history of Zen Center. "Maybe they like it better." But did *they* have the authority to make history?

Richard was the authorized dharma heir of Suzuki-roshi, and in 1984, he did not lack the energy or the will or the property to retell the Zen Center story, but his version relied on the success of the residential program of spiritual training he was establishing in Santa Fe. "I was in England and received newsletters [from Dharma Sangha] and kept in touch with Dick," says Grahame, who visited San Francisco while Richard was still committed to the new school-building site. "Dick brought up the idea of a restaurant in Santa Fe. During that visit, I roughed out the start of a business plan, and a few months later, Dick came to see me in England."

In late 1985, Grahame moved to Santa Fe for a year. Richard soon relinquished the lease on the San Francisco school building and focused singularly on making Santa Fe self-sustaining. "At that time," remembers Willem, "I was very involved in this little bakery, and [Richard's students and associates] couldn't have cared less about me." It was a few months later that Willem and Issan met again and spent time together. In an act of "one-upmanship," says Willem, "right around the corner from the bakery, Richard chose the building to do his vegetarian restaurant."

As Reb was ascending to the Abbot's seat in San Francisco, Richard "designed the restaurant in Santa Fe," he says. "We had this big warehouse space. And what are we going to do?" It was a familiar story. "Basically, when I had finally visualized it in my mind, I took a piece of chalk, and I didn't actually do the plans, but I took a piece of chalk and drew the counters, the kitchen, etc. And then they came and measured it, and they just followed the lines I drew." Richard says, "I can't draw very well," and then he adds, "I can't draw; I can't act; I can't sing. But I am persistent."

"Next," remembers Willem, "he was going to open a bakery right next door. He was going to re-create Greens and the Tassajara Bread Bakery right next to my little garage bakery."

In a January 3, 1987 review of new styles of restaurants in Santa Fe, the *Journal North* described the interior of Richard's Desert Café: "Japanese cabinetwork and Noguchi paper lamps have been inserted into the industrial Sambusco Market building along with wood-burl sculpture, etched glass, abstract murals, and Shaker- and Amish-inspired furniture." The article reserved special praise for "the extravagantly appointed restrooms." For a preview article in the October 8, 1986 edition of the *New Mexican*, Richard told the reporter that he'd decided to open the place "at the urging of friends," thirty of whom put up almost a million dollars, and "spent $450,000 alone on the interior." Among the investors, reported the *New Mexican*, were "a few Rockefellers and California est guru Werner Erhard," who would find himself the subject of a *60 Minutes* investigation just a few years later, during which some of his children and former est associates made public charges about physical and mental cruelty, to which the IRS added a tax lien, all of which inspired Werner to self-actualize as an expatriate. The criminal charges against him were later proved false or recanted (he won a settlement from the IRS), but he continues to reside outside of the country.

Several people warned Grahame that the restaurant was "a crazy idea." He shrugs. "I could only accept Dick's assurances that what he was saying was backed by experience at Greens." Grahame put together a financial model for one year, and agreed to help raise capital, for which he was paid "a professional fee." One of the most significant warnings Grahame received was delivered by the chairman of Boston's Fidelity Investments. "Ned Johnson put it very, very clearly to me when he came to Santa Fe before we had the restaurant open, and when a considerable amount of financing was still needed, and Dick was hoping Ned would participate," remembers Grahame. "I spent the afternoon with Ned. He said he would not invest—not because he didn't have the money. He did not invest in businesses which he felt had a high chance of failing, and [he felt] that Dick did not have the experience required to run the restaurant. Ned said, as far as he could see, Dick has been successful at Greens basically because of slave labor, labor you didn't have to pay, and this was a very different story."

Richard had never seen it that way. He had fifty-three employees when the Desert Café opened in October of 1996.

"It is a business I would never touch again," says Grahame. "On the two opening days, which were by invitation, and free, we filled the restaurant. I was looking at the kitchen, and I saw that we had about twenty people visible in there and, of course, there were others doing the washing up and so on, and I knew that a business would have to be very, very successful with very, very high margins to support that level of personnel. And I knew that the margins weren't there."

Lew Richmond says, "[Richard's] friends weren't so concerned about his personal life, but they didn't like him losing their money."

The Desert Café closed nine months later.

"So much money went through there," says Willem, "and, in the end, it was just like water."

Grahame was "well out of it before it closed." He knows that not everyone was. He remembers that the owner of the building "had invested unwillingly a substantial amount of money in the restaurant. You see," says Grahame, "the bills for the conversion were very substantial, and Dick did not have the funds, and the building owner more or less had to take a slice of that which he didn't intend to. Dick would probably say that from the very beginning [the owner] said he would do so much and backed out and didn't do it." Grahame shrugs. "Both may be true."

Grahame regrets the loss of his friendship with Richard, to whom he has spoken a couple of times, but whom he has not seen. "We were both responsible," says Grahame. "I was one part of the decision-making process, and things in business don't always go the way you wish they would. Toward the end, though, Dick was making all of the decisions without reference to my numbers. And those decisions resulted in exponential increases in expenditure most of the time. And I know that just before or after the closure, the Avedisian paintings" (Avedisian's paintings also were hung in Greens and the Tassajara Bread Bakery) "and other artwork had been removed—which Dick had appropriated, which certainly [the owner of the building] was very displeased about." Grahame adds, "Dick has probably got a justification for having done that."

In an April 15, 1989 feature story, the *New Mexican* reported that the Desert Café was being replaced by an Italian restaurant whose new owners were ripping out the interior, which they considered "too California slick."

Richard says more about the painter than the restaurant that "went bust." His long friendship with Edward Avedisian, whose work he championed at Zen Center, ended. "I've broken with him—some years ago," says Richard. "He just did too many outrageous things." Accusations about who paid for what, and which painting was a gift, and which one was a repayment, figure prominently in Richard's account of the demise of the friendship. Years earlier, in 1984, when Richard was clearing out of Zen Center, the Board tried to establish who had paid for six Avedisian paintings; it was clear the community had paid for at least two. Richard told the liaison to the Board that "Edward would not want any of his paintings to stay at Zen Center," and the Board agreed to give Richard the paintings. "That's okay," says Richard, reflecting on the conclusion of his friendship with the painter. "We were very close for a long time, and he was a very important person in building confidence in myself."

In 1987, Richard reached the end of the old Zen Center story. He finally left San Francisco, and most of his former students did not. He left Santa

Fe, and almost none of his students followed him north to Colorado, though a few former Zen Center students now practice with him and his small community of ten to twenty residents, some of whom are German and Swiss natives and have practiced at his Zen center in the Black Forest. On Crestone Mountain, Richard has the benefit of an inarguably beautiful view, and "No mortgage. Eighty acres. And if it works, we'll get two more big parcels [of land] so there will be nothing above us. The stretch into the wilderness is very important," says Richard. "It's what was so great about Tassajara."

33.

"I REMEMBER HEARING A rumor that one of my professors thought I was losing it, going crazy," says Willem Malten. He was twenty-two, finishing his university studies in Amsterdam, and he had begun to sit zazen—weekly with a small group, and often for hours in his apartment alone or with a friend. "I was knocking on doors that didn't open," he says. "One day, I went on my bike from university to my apartment with a buddy. I told him what I had heard. I mentioned that some people thought I was going crazy. I said, 'What do you think?' He was silent." Willem grins. "I thought, *Uh-oh. Now I have to be careful.*" Willem pauses, then adds, "And that was my motivation to seek out a teacher. I had no context to make my experience real, no idea what one does with these energies. I wondered, *What is the traditional way to deal with all of this?*"

Willem says today that he has no teacher and many teachers. While working with the Tibetan refugee-resettlement project, he traveled to Dharamsala, in northern India, and met with the Dalai Lama, and "in his room, I felt blessed." Cloud Cliff's success, he thinks, was assured when native farmers approached him about working with the cooperative of local growers; they taught him how to bake with native, organically grown grains, which are now featured in his most popular breads. He sees his father's compassionate work as a doctor in a way he could not when he was younger, and he is grateful to Richard Baker, and he sees now that, like a lot of people, "I was on a collision course with my own lyrical sense of Eastern mysticism. The truth was around my neck, of course, as a question. I could say it, but I couldn't see it. What was true?" Willem smiles again. "One of the things Dutch parents like to say to their children is, If

you are normal, you are already crazy enough. Don't press your luck."
Willem nods. "But it was hard to make consistent the things I was reading at university and the practice of zazen—which I felt was going to save
my very being. It was hard to believe that I or anyone I knew could
answer my question." Willem pauses. "I was pressing my luck," he says.
"Of course, I knew then, as I found out later, that truth does not have to
do with propositions. It has to do with authenticity of actions."

In 1984, after Willem moved to Santa Fe, his father visited him for the
first time since he'd left the Netherlands in 1979. They went together to
an evening of Native American storytelling, and Willem heard the Pueblo
residents describe themselves as Cloud People because of the proximity of
their cliff-top homes to the sky. "I was delighted," says Willem. "I told my
father I would call the bakery Cloud Cliff, which was my Buddhist name,
as well." After his father's visit, "I got very involved with opening the
bakery, and when I told Richard about it, he said I should call it Santa Fe
Valley Bakery. He didn't want me to call it Cloud Cliff."

Before his lay ordination, Willem had read the ancient koan and commentaries about the Chinese monk named Cloud Cliff, whose teacher
repeatedly told him that his whole body was hands and eyes—"compassion and awareness," says Willem, who admits that he found the koans
elusive and defeating but "tried to get somewhere with this one. Richard
lectured on it a couple of times, but I never told him about my attempts to
study it."

After sewing his rakusu, the small patchwork robe, for lay ordination
in 1979, Willem gave it to Richard. "Your teacher gives you a name, which
is written on the back. In Japanese, mine said, *Cloud Cliff*. And I thought,
Of course, everything is coming together. This guy knows everything. I
mean, how could he have known?" Willem pauses. "I ascribe to Richard
this power," he says, "and for years, I deal with him that way. That is my
view of him."

Five years later, in March of 1984, Willem heard about a Zen master
who had settled in Taos, just north of Santa Fe. It was Kobun Chino, one
of the Japanese priests who had assisted Suzuki-roshi in the 1960s. Willem
knew Kobun Chino slightly from the latter's visits to Tassajara; through-

out the 1970s and early 1980s, Kobun also assisted Richard with Zen Center ceremonies, including ordinations. "Kobun was gracious and loving, and though he knew I was not looking for a teacher, he and I became good friends. Eventually he asked to see my rakusu," remembers Willem, "and I showed it to him. He looked at it and pointed to my Buddhist name, Cloud Cliff, and he said, 'My handwriting.'" Willem smiles. And then he opens his eyes very wide. "Kobun Chino had divined the names for us. And I had ascribed that power—and so much more—to Richard Baker. It was a perfect ending."

34.

THE END OF REB ANDERSON'S first year as Abbot was also the end of his last year as sole Abbot of Zen Center, but nobody could see that yet. There were signs. Many senior priests and administrative leaders had opted not to take Reb on as their teacher. Darlene Cohen did not support Reb's initial bid to become Abbot, but she saw his strengths. "When I thought of Reb, I thought, *At least he won't crumble under the pressure.* I thought it was clear that he would stay sane through the tough times," she says, widening her gaze for a moment. In 1987, she saw what she saw. "Reb is impervious to criticism—I saw that as a positive thing then, though I see it as less positive now."

After Richard left Zen Center, Reb heralded what he called "a contractive, solidifying period." By 1986, some students and supporters saw an institution in retreat, but many saw a community being shepherded back to its fundamental purpose. The training program for students was formalized for the first time, highlighting fourteen required "sections" that introduced the basics of Buddhist history and doctrines—a word that had not often appeared in the annals of Zen Center before 1986. *Wind Bell* began to publish articles such as "The Home Altar" (a how-to guide by Reb); "Zazen Posture" (a how-to guide by Patricia Phelan, one of Mel's students); and Suzuki-roshi's lecture on "American Precepts," in which he explained the negative side (prohibitions) and the positive side (encouragement) of the Precepts, and he concluded with an exhortation to "concentrate our life on zazen practice, and organize our life so we can sit well."

It was back to basics. The scope of the community's work and its sense of mission narrowed almost immediately. When Reb became Abbot in 1986, the annual budget was over $4.5 million. By the close of the next fiscal year, the remaining businesses had been segregated into Everyday Corporation and a lot of depreciation schedules had been closed out, and the budget was balanced at just under $1.8 million. Annual income and expenses ranged as high as $2.4 million over the next five years as profits from Everyday (especially from Greens) increased; but Zen Center's annual income and expenses have never again approached the heights of the work-practice years.

In the wider view, though, while Reb's teaching and practice and administrative oversight seemed to be leading Zen Center in a traditional direction, his most ardent supporters and students had adopted a broad vision of that tradition, and they often seemed to be moving in a different direction from him. They were not *not* following the Abbot's lead, but they were taking the progressive route. This is especially evident in the emergence of a new lingo, which was not associated with Reb. Thich Nhat Hanh was a regular visitor and the words *mindful* and *mindfulness*— terms deeply associated with his own teaching and the *mindfulness bell* that his followers ring every fifteen or twenty minutes to refocus their awareness—turned up regularly in meeting notes, letters to supporters, and lectures after 1984.

So, too, phrases such as *transference issues, Jungian archetypes, addictive behavior,* and other mainstays of the polyglot psychotherapeutic lexicon were filtering into meetings and correspondence; a simple *Wind Bell* article justified administrative changes by citing "the debilitating effects of psychological projection" at Zen Center. The emerging scholarship and politics of Buddhist women also made a deep impression on the restructuring process and the community's discussions about spiritual authority. In March of 1987, Zen Center hosted a "Celebration of Women in Buddhist Practice," which was "organized entirely as a leaderless event," according to the Spring 1987 *Wind Bell,* in hopes that "such exploration of consensual and horizontal structures will ripple throughout the Buddhist sanghas in America."

This was the empty form that was evolving at Zen Center, a communal superego too vast and complex to be directed by a single ego. Where did that leave the Abbot? "People began to recognize, in a way that I didn't—I still have blind spots—that they couldn't talk to Reb," says one of his ordained disciples. "He had [some of] the same problems Richard Baker had—he was isolated, he liked power, and people could not get through to him."

Reb's run as Abbot continued. Was anyone following his lead?

"He wouldn't stand up and lead," says Paul Discoe, the former head carpenter. "I think Dick knew that about Reb, and that's why he didn't mind having Reb around. Much as Dick was autocratic, [after he left,] Zen Center had become a paralyzing democracy. Everyone had a little power base. We needed leadership." Many community members thought of the new structures as "participatory" and "more horizontal" and "practice-based," representing the integration of Zen into the contemporary American culture. Paul had another view; he was on the Board when the first wave of administrative changes took effect. "Everybody grabbed onto a position, and they are still there," he says. "These jobs were given to people not because of their competence but as growth opportunities. And they are still there." Paul was a staunch supporter of Reb, but he left in 1987 because he felt the Abbot was hopelessly hemmed in by the new bureaucracy. "These people believed they were professional nonprofit [administrators] who should be paid like people at the March of Dimes. Everybody wanted higher salaries and to send their children to private schools. The whole upper-class mystique and aura that Dick worked so hard to develop really caught on with the generation that came after Suzuki-roshi's death. Dick's disciples really got into it. They wanted flashy cars and upscale clothes. I was always fighting against the big raises," says Paul. "So I left. And they are still there."

Zen master Muso Soseki had written about this very conundrum—religious organizations serving secular ambitions—and Thomas and Christopher Cleary's translation of his "Dream Monologues" about this and other issues was printed in the Spring 1987 *Wind Bell*. It was not a new problem; Muso Soseki was writing in the fifteenth century.

But maybe all problems are traditional problems. In the final monologue printed that spring in *Wind Bell*, the medieval Japanese master warned that "people sometimes go mad from doing zazen." By 1987, even by modest estimates, Reb and his peers at Zen Center had 20,000 to 25,000 hours of meditation under their robes.

In late April of 1987, Reb took off his robes, put on his sneakers, and headed out for his daily jog in Golden Gate Park. "He was walking along Page Street to his car in the Zen Center garage when a man came up behind him with a knife and demanded his money," reported the *San Francisco Chronicle* on June 15, 1987, more than six weeks after the incident. "Anderson, wearing jogging clothes, handed over $20." The thief ran away.

You could say it was an involuntary contribution to the neighborhood fund. Reb has never said anything about it publicly outside of the community. The community said nothing about it publicly for six weeks, and then it was only reporters' questions that prompted them to speak.

"This guy approached him with a knife," says then-president Leslie James, and she gamely adds, "Right?" She does not sound entirely enthusiastic about the likelihood of the story making sense. "How Reb describes it is that he had an inflation."

Inflation? It was twenty dollars. Reb had a home in the city—not as splendid as Richard's, which had become administrative offices, but decent digs, nonetheless—and a place to stay on the farm, and a cabin at a hot springs resort.

"He was just back from doing his first practice period [as Abbot] at Tassajara," says Leslie hopefully. "And Tassajara is a powerful place."

The Abbot, "a muscular former boxer," according to the *Chronicle* reporter Paul Liberatore, "hopped into his car and drove around the neighborhood looking for the mugger."

Leslie says, "[Reb] thought he could make this neighborhood safer for all of us. And he was going to show this guy that he couldn't come around in his neighborhood and do that. And I don't believe he ever intended to hurt the guy at all."

He didn't catch up with the guy, but Reb's intentions were not as clear to his neighbors as they were to his students at Zen Center, because before he hopped into his car, as the *Chronicle* noted, Reb "hurried into the garage, [and] grabbed the unloaded pistol from the [storage] trunk." This was the gun that Reb had found after sitting zazen beside a corpse in Golden Gate Park in 1983, four years before he was mugged. Within a few minutes, "Anderson was arrested for brandishing a pistol in a public housing project."

Leslie says, "The gun was never loaded."

Of course, it's often hard to discern this from the barrel end of a gun.

"And Reb knew it wasn't loaded," says Leslie, though this only matters if the only person who matters is Reb.

The neighbors saw an armed and angry bald former boxer heading for the front door. They called the police, who arrived with their own hardware, and for the second time that day, Reb was faced with a weapon and a request to give something up. He dropped the gun.

"I mean," says Leslie, "I also think, *Stupid. Really stupid.* But it makes a kind of human sense to me that he went looking for the guy."

It was Leslie's unenviable job to make it make sense because her spiritual teacher would not speak to reporters. It was a new twist on an old story. The old story was silence. What the Abbot of Zen Center did was nobody's business. It was nobody's business when he discovered the body of a man who had died violently in Golden Gate Park four years earlier; it was nobody's business when he decided to visit the body and the crime scene for four days' running; it was nobody's business when he handled the corpse and stole a loaded gun from the crime scene; it was nobody's business—not the dead man's friends or relatives, not the police investigators, not his teacher in 1983, and not any of his students for the next four years; and it was still nobody's business when he carried the gun to a public housing project.

David Chadwick remembers hearing about Reb's arrest, and he told Reb that the simplest and cleanest solution was to hold a press conference and answer questions immediately; about fifteen minutes later, David remembers, Reb was angry at him for talking to another senior priest about the incident. "The only goal for Reb was Abbot-for-life," says David, "and he'd jeopardized it. That's what mattered."

The *Chronicle* headline on June 15 was an American koan: *Zen Master Gets in Trouble for Pulling Dead Man's Gun.*

The legal case against Harold (Reb's legal name) Anderson was quickly resolved. Within a few days of the news reports, the case was "diverted," and the charges were dismissed, and Reb was ordered to do thirty days of community service; the records of his arrest and the disposition of his case were destroyed during a routine purge of old folders. "He had some good lawyers," says Mel, then Abbot at Berkeley Zen Center. "Lawyers who knew people."

The spiritual defense of Reb assembled by his advocates at Zen Center was even more impressive.

Was anybody reading *Wind Bell*? "There is no means of safeguarding anything in the world," according to Muso Soseki in the first of his fifteenth-century "Dream Monologues" published in *Wind Bell* that spring. "Therefore to make the acquisition and retention of goods or status one's sole aim in life is productive of grief."

"Reb apologized. Dick didn't," says Michael Wenger, succinctly expressing the consensus of Zen Center's many decision-makers. "I don't care about the words either of them used." Richard had apologized in writing and in telephone calls to many of his students, but the value of his words had suffered a deflation during the Apocalypse. As Mel Weitsman says, "There have been a few feeble attempts to apologize [from Richard], but nobody reads them as sincere." By all accounts, Reb told everyone at Zen Center that he did not know why he had done what he had done; but Reb, they felt, was evidently sincere in his remorse. "I am not sure Reb completely understood what he did, but I know he was sorry for it," says Michael. Reb was so sincere that he had even offered to relinquish his status as Abbot, Zen Center told the newspapers in mid-June, but the Board had rejected his resignation. Four years earlier, the Board had devoted nine months to the task of convincing an Abbot to resign.

Linda Cutts was Chair of the Board in 1987. "It was a bizarre story," she says, "although in some ways—hearing [Reb] tell the story, and then questioning him, and trying to focus on what was going on right there— I just feel that, for me, in part because I was so close to him, watching him struggle with it, and watching him struggle in practice, in an odd way, it was very inspiring."

You don't have to doubt the sincerity of Reb's remorse or the sincerity of his students' admiration for his bearing to see the effect. It broadened the view again. Suddenly, there were many authorities speaking on the nature of sincere practice at Zen Center. Leslie was the spokesperson who had to articulate the official teaching on the Golden Gate Park episode. She explained to the *Chronicle* that Reb's "first response was to call the police" when he discovered the dead man in the park in 1983. "But it is our tradition to sit with a dead person for three days," and "it was somehow kinder to leave him undisturbed."

No, it wasn't, says Mel, who holds a more traditional view of tradition. "We cremate people soon after death. The Neptune Society does it all. Sure, when you have a funeral, and you know who the person is, and you have had a relationship—you attend the body." You don't do it in a public park, says Mel, and you don't sit watch for an hour and then leave the body under the bushes for the rest of the day. "To run across the body of somebody you don't even know—you don't even know if he has committed suicide or was murdered—and to not report it, I mean, that is unprecedented."

"You can imagine what people said," says Linda.

Or perhaps you can't.

"At the time," says a recently ordained priest, "I told Reb that I thought he should go away. I didn't mean forever. I meant, Resign. Go away. Study with someone. Get your shit together. Which he didn't do."

Linda later received dharma Transmission from Reb. She remembers that the aftermath of Reb's arrest "was so emotional, and [Reb's] emotions were overpowering, and Reb is a powerful guy. And he is an adept—his presence is profound. So there were power issues around him, and it turned into a feeding frenzy. It was awful. For him to return and stay—having seen someone unwilling to stay for the real feedback—it impressed me."

Leslie says, "He is lucky he didn't get killed, going into a project with a gun."

It also seems lucky for Reb that he was perceived as the potential victim of his own crimes.

"Reb became the Abbot with the gun," says Peter Rudnick. "Phenomenal. I went to a meeting, and I said, 'You know, Reb, I always wanted to fight you, but I don't fight guys who carry guns.'"

Reb was still in the ring, but he was no longer capable of defending his title. In this moment, he was truly Richard's heir. No American would ever replace Suzuki-roshi as Abbot-for-life of the San Francisco Zen Center.

Reb took a six-month leave of absence from the abbacy. Zen Center was becoming accustomed to this nontraditional style of leaderless leadership. By default, the first Buddhist monastery established outside of Asia in the history of the world had become a cradle of democracy. How did the community—this distinctly American sangha—handle the questions this raised about their teaching lineage and the role of a designated spiritual authority?

"Well, that's very interesting," says Mel. "Reb has a lot of supporters and a lot of nonsupporters."

Norman Fischer remembers that "when Reb was about to be reinstated there was a lot of nervousness. At the dramatic last moment— 'Let's get a co-abbot.'"

Mel says, "I remember being at a Board meeting, and saying that I would do it, but [I said] Reb would have to invite me to do it with him, and he felt the pressure to do that, and he did."

It was the first tentative line of a new telling of the ancient story: Reb was not *the* Abbot, but he was not *not* the Abbot.

"It was decided that we would be equal and figure out how to do that," says Mel. "We eventually decided that we wouldn't divide up Zen Center, but freely move about." The unified view of Zen Center was intact— almost. "But then Reb moved to Green Gulch"—the Hawken house was open—"and that became his place. And City Center was, de facto, my place." Mel was still Abbot of the Berkeley Zen Center. "We shared Tassajara."

"Reb has met everyone's response," says Pat Leonetti, a public health nurse and Reb's ordained disciple. "He stayed in the community and worked it all out, and he has a lifetime of karma where this will come up again and again, and this is what he has to sit with." This distinguishes Reb from Richard in Pat's view, and in the view of many with whom she has practiced for the last fifteen years. "I think that you begin to understand that you are everyone's activity," says Pat. "So can you find a place in yourself that could go get a gun and run down the street? If you can't, then you're compassionless."

It is a projective test. But it is not just a question of imagining yourself in a heated moment. First, you have to find a place in yourself where you can visit the body in the public park and steal the gun and throw the bullets away; then you have to find a place in yourself to hide it for four years; then you have to find the housing project and run in with the gun. And the test isn't over yet. If you not only found those spaces in yourself, but found yourself filling the voids with actions, would you choose you as your spiritual teacher for life?

By the end of 1991, the Board was prepared to propose the permanent adoption of the co-Abbot model and term limits—under normal circumstances, no Abbot would serve more than an initial four-year term followed by a three-year term. "I was on the Board in 1991, and Reb's [second] term was coming up," says Peter Rudnick. "Reb's disciples run Zen Center. I think his idea of himself is like a godfather. He doesn't do things directly; he talks to his students and his students do [things]," he says. "I thought it was time for a new Abbot, and it was resolved very well, I thought."

After a long retreat in 1992, the Board adopted the new term limits. A thick book of revised bylaws, policies, and procedures was printed. It had to be amended immediately, according to the cover letter. "Sometime after the retreat," the Secretary noted, "it became obvious that consensus on the resolution had broken down." A series of community-wide meetings was called.

The Board eventually decided that the end of Reb's abbacy was "not a 'normal' situation." Reb's term was extended for another two years; he would receive his Abbot's salary for five years; he and Mel were named "Dharma teachers at Zen Center for life." Of the two, only Reb resides at Zen Center.

"What Reb has managed is to make the high status position [at Zen

Center] the Senior Dharma Teacher," says Yvonne. "The Abbot position is now a training position."

Reb's third term was up in 1994. Norman was getting his public-school teaching credential and planning to leave Zen Center. He was invited to be Abbot. "I didn't want to [do it], and my wife didn't want me to, but it was the first time they were rotating," says Norman. "And a lot of disciples of Reb wanted him to be Abbot-for-life, despite the bylaws. I knew if I walked away, it would be very tough." Norman was installed as Mel's co-Abbot in 1995; at the end of the following year, Mel stepped down, and Blanche Hartman was installed as Norman's co-Abbot.

"We say we put no one on a pedestal, but I do feel Reb has been put on a pedestal," says Wendy. "And I say so to him. The one Transmitted heir. So what? He is the Transmitted heir who has no truck with his teacher. That seems weird."

It gets weirder. Although few people knew it, by 1987, despite the confessions, counseling, and compassion—not to mention a complete reconstruction of the community's spiritual and administrative roles, programs, and policies—the Transmission lines were in a terrible tangle.

The one Transmitted heir (Reb) and the other one Transmitted heir (Richard) happened to meet "by chance," as Richard remembers it, while Richard was still living in Santa Fe, where he completed Transmission with Philip Whalen and Issan. "I met with Mel and Reb," Richard says, "and I said very clearly to Reb, 'Look, I haven't completed Transmission with you. I just assumed we knew that.'"

Reb was mugged again.

Richard says that the incompleteness of his dharma Transmission was not news to Reb. "I had talked with him about it before. And then Mel was there," Richard says, "and Mel had done Transmission with [Hoitsu] in Japan—I really like Mel; he has a down-to-earth way of teaching and understanding that is good—and I'd be happy to give Mel Transmission. At that time [1983], I didn't know how good Mel was. But at that time [at the 1987 meeting with Reb], I said to Mel, 'If you would like to be more directly in Suzuki-roshi's lineage through me [rather] than [Suzuki-roshi's son], or you'd like to just participate in this, I am happy to give Transmission to both of you with the *kirigami*," which is one of the Transmission rituals Richard says Reb never did, "and [we can] work on the ceremony so we develop the ceremony. I'll make the time to do it.' And I said, 'I won't get into a political thing. I'm not going to expect you to like me. I just think it would be healthy to get this done, so you guys feel better, and I feel better, and maybe it's clearer in the world, even if I'm not expecting you to suddenly become my disciples in a real sense.'" Richard pauses, then says, "I was just willing to do it, almost as a formality."

Steve Allen, who received Transmission from Issan, with Richard's assistance, has thought a lot about tradition and lineage while sitting in the shadow of Crestone Mountain in his hermitage. He spent time in Australia in 1999, finding out about aboriginal religion. "One thing they are saying through their ceremonies is that [the religion] is a central part of their lives because it keeps them connected to the dream kingdom—the mind outside of them. These things are crucial," says Steve, "because if you are disconnected from that world, you've lost your wholeness of heart. If a senior person ceases to perform his function, then the group has a right to send out a party to hunt him down and kill him. With Richard, our link to the tradition was broken. We should have killed him. We didn't, because we're civilized."

"You are supposed to do kirigami," says Richard, who is able to represent in plain and compelling language the evolution of ritual, and how it binds mortals to the dream kingdom. The more perplexing problem, however, was how to bind mere mortals to each other.

Richard says that he and Reb completed some parts of the Transmission process but did not ever do two of the most important. "*Kirigami* (cut paper) means that I give you [my disciple] teachings. You write them down. And at some point, you show them to me, and [of] some of them I say, 'Yes, that's right,' and I put my seal on, and sign it, and [of others] I say, 'Oh, no, you don't quite understand that; you give it back to me.'" The exchange leads to a collection that is the equivalent of the traditional oral teachings. The teacher never writes for the student to read. "The oral transmission in an Asian culture is not *In the beginning was the Word*," says Richard. "It is, *In the beginning was the sound*. And the sound in the word is what carries the truth. And the teaching should be oral. But no one has the skills anymore to remember all of this, so you write it down and the form—those documents and your own memory—you pass it to your teacher. But you [the teacher] never show the disciple your documents, so it [the teaching] is cut—it's cut—just for you. It is not creating a literature." It is creating a lineage. "All those kirigami I never did with Reb. None of them. And, in some ways, that is the most essential part of the whole thing."

Richard also remembers that he and Reb did not undertake the standard study of koans and commentaries, and there are a few other gaps, as well. As a result, he says, Reb "can be a kind of ronin Roshi—a masterless samurai. You can be a ronin; some Zen masters didn't have Transmission but were spontaneously recognized. That's all right. That's the final test. Recognition is the key thing."

"What Richard has renounced is his relationship to Reb," says Mel. "He cannot renounce the Transmission."

"Zen masters do sometimes try to take back their Transmission," says Michael. "It happened with Philip Kapleau." The American author of *Three Pillars of Zen* wrote about dokusan conversations between teachers and students, and that was only one reason that "Harada-roshi said he was no longer his disciple. It happened with Eido-roshi" in New York, too.

"I never made it public [at that time]," says Richard. "I never ever said to anyone anything about Reb's Transmission. It was too painful. I offered [to complete Transmission with] Reb, and then [I] didn't make a thing of it." Word got around somehow. "A friend of mine in Santa Fe, whom Reb was going to visit, wanted to tell Reb, 'You should get together with Baker and get this Transmission completed,'" remembers Richard. "And Reb, when he got there, told him, 'I am fully Transmitted.' Well, that's fine," says Richard. "If he feels he is fully Transmitted, fine with me. It is not my business, really. But then he can't say he is my disciple."

In recent years, the controversy has become public. Richard says he did, in the mid-1990s, write an introduction for a collection of Philip Whalen's poems in which he referred to Philip as his first disciple. "That was the first time I ever found myself saying it publicly," says Richard. The next time was at an ecumenical Esalen seminar. After a morning zazen period, Richard recalls, "a tall young man [was] standing there, and he said, 'Hello, Baker-roshi. I'm your grand-disciple.' I said, 'You are? You are Philip's disciple?'" The young man said he was Reb's disciple. "I said, 'You are not my grand-disciple.' It just came out of my mouth," Richard explains. "And I think he began to tell people that I don't accept Reb. And I tried to make it better. I talked to [the young man] at breakfast and said, 'It's okay. He's your teacher. You like him. The fact is, though, what is it about? It's about trust and friendship and mind-to-mind Transmission. Do you see Reb and me talking? Do you see any compatibility? Look with your own eyes.'"

Many practitioners have learned to look at the controversy and wink.

"Reb takes this seriously," says Yvonne. "He's not his own man in this way. Nobody takes this nearly as seriously as Reb and Richard do."

Tony smiles and says, "Richard still says—to this day—that the Transmission is not complete and is invalid."

Darlene nods. "He enters some twilight zone when he says this. Reb is furious."

Wendy shakes her head. "I'm fifty-one. My husband Peter and I met at Tassajara. Richard Baker married us. Reb was the *jisha* [attendant]. It was that kind of time. It was lovely." Now, as she and Peter are leaving their home on Green Gulch Farm, Wendy looks sort of sad. "Richard says Reb didn't have Transmission, that Reb is incomplete, and Reb is a charlatan—well, for God's sake, why did [Richard] have to do that? How does it serve him to do that? I am doggedly committed not to get caught up in this again."

"I don't particularly want to come back to the San Francisco Zen Center," wrote Richard in an open ten-page letter to the Board and community in 1989. "But," he went on in that letter, "that does not change the fact that I feel that I cannot ever resign in a real sense."

Richard wrote this letter after he had been informed that the Zen Cen-

ter Board had decided to sell a number of the community's rental properties. Financial pressures had not eased at Zen Center by 1989. San Francisco's rent-control laws made it impossible for Zen Center to raise rents
only for nonmembers, and tenant relations had deteriorated, as had the
apartments themselves, which were, according to tenants, "neglected"
and "in violation of health codes."

The Board had tried other solutions. An audit of its Guest House revealed that it represented an annual financial loss to the community of
more than $30,000. Instead of simply selling the townhouse to realize
capital gains, Zen Center leased the building to a new nonprofit venture:
The highly regarded Zen Hospice Program, which is independently
incorporated, staffed, and financed, grew out of a five-year plan that
allowed the hospice to secure its financial stability as Zen Center gradually turned over control of the building. As the hospice was launched,
profits from the bakery continued to fall below projections, and there
were major improvements under way at both Tassajara and Green Gulch,
so the Board decided to sell the townhouses it owned across Page Street
from City Center.

Richard saw the sale of the buildings as the dismantling of Suzuki-
roshi's legacy and an underestimation of the enduring value of the work
done in the 1970s to establish a Zen Center campus in the city. Richard
also thought it might be possible for him to be of some help to Zen Center in its time of need. So, in 1989, he wrote a letter and took a trip to San
Francisco. "He came and talked to the Board," remembers Mel. "He also
invited Reb and me up to his rented room in a hotel on Van Ness. He said,
'If you would let me be Abbot, you guys could run Zen Center. I would
come back for a month or so every once in a while.'"

In his ten-page letter to the Board and community, Richard explained
that he had tendered his resignation to benefit people who were suffering
and to test what he considered a promise made in a letter from Ed Brown
that he would be reinstated immediately. (Ed, then Chair of the Board,
had written that resignation "would allow everyone, including yourself
to unite in the work of establishing your successor or successors . . . to
unite in compassionate support of you as an individual . . . rather than
continuing to find fault with your being in the position of Abbot and

Chief Priest.") Finally, Richard explained, he didn't think his letter of resignation was "a legal resignation. I have always been sure that I was probably still Chief Priest of Zen Center."

This was 1989.

"Dick was establishing himself [as a teacher] in Germany," says Mel. "He needed to establish his credibility. His attitude was, *[Zen Center] is my center for my lifetime, and I just need to be recognized. I don't think I did anything wrong.*"

Richard is ongoingly confounded by opposition he encountered then, and the opposition he has encountered since 1989 whenever he has attempted to establish himself as a teacher in the Bay Area. "They didn't want me in San Francisco. And they didn't want me to have anything to enhance my reputation."

Mel says, "People would be happy to help him with his needs," and then he smiles—or, sort of smiles. "He shouldn't help himself. That is what he tried to do in 1989." Mel is over sixty; he is five-foot-seven, and he is stocky, and he shaves his head; he studied art and worked as a painter before he became a priest; he was Jewish before he became a Buddhist; he has lived and practiced for many years in little houses in Berkeley, a city where street vendors often enjoy longer careers than shopkeepers. As a result, Mel often looks a little amused by things, as if he wants to remind you that *you never know.*

"So it was 1989, and Dick was talking to [Reb and me] in his hotel room about the possibility of somehow returning to Zen Center. But he had already gone up to Sacramento with his lawyer." Mel is not smiling. "And because Dick's name was on the incorporation papers as Chief Priest of Zen Center—it was a Corporation Sole—his lawyer filed amendments to invalidate the Board and its decisions." The legal challenge had two elements. The first was simply the assertion that Richard was still Chief Priest of Zen Center because his name had never been removed from the articles of incorporation. Second, the amendments filed by Richard's lawyer proposed to give the Chief Priest (the head of the Corporation Sole) more control over the decision-making process at Zen Center, making it impossible for the Board to act on the sale of real estate without Richard's approval.

Richard says, "There was a lawyer who kept bugging me. He came here to do sesshins. 'Why don't you do this and that?'" Richard pauses. "I am not trying to pretend I am passive."

Like most of Richard's former students, Ed did not see his former teacher as a passive participant. "Dick tried to take over Zen Center again," says Ed.

Richard says his intention was to protect Suzuki-roshi's legacy and lineage. He remembers that "I called up Leslie [James, Zen Center's President] right away," after the amendments to the articles of incorporation had been filed by his lawyer. "I was on my way to Europe. I said, 'I want to prevent the sale of these buildings. This is my card playing.' I said, 'Really, I don't care.' And I wrote her a letter and said, 'You can ignore all of this. I am not going to do anything.'"

He did, however, talk to Don Lattin, religion writer for the *San Francisco Chronicle*, while he was in Europe, for a May 30, 1989 story. "Baker said members of the current Zen Center leadership 'say we live in a Protestant Democratic country, and lineage should have nothing to do with what they're doing,'" wrote the reporter. "'They are denying 2,500 years of how Buddhism was developed and continued,' [Baker] said. 'They're throwing out the baby with the bath water.'" The reporter also mentioned that Baker "does not recognize the credentials of the current abbots," and he quoted Richard's statement that "the healthiest thing would be for me to come back in some way for a month or a year and just participate and make a healthier transition." And it was not just the corporation that was at stake. Richard's lawyer was quoted as saying, "Baker-roshi is the only American dharma lineage successor to Suzuki-roshi."

Mel says, "We had to hire lawyers to go to Sacramento to deal with this. It cost us $35,000 to $40,000. [Richard's] claim was challenged, and he never followed up." Zen Center has since reincorporated itself as a standard nonprofit religious institution with no Chief Priest invested with sole control. "Some people thought what Dick did was very clever. And so did he. But for me," says Mel, still not smiling, "it was the crowning blow. And a lot of people who had been wavering about whether they still had faith in him finally saw what was going on."

Richard remembers discovering the effects of his actions only after he returned from Europe. "They were in a total panic to have me removed from the [incorporation] papers. It seemed to me a tempest in a teapot," he says. "But they see me as so powerful and dangerous. $45,000? I said, 'You wasted your money.' My lawyer was free, and he didn't do anything but file a piece of paper. I clearly told them I wasn't going to pursue it, and I wrote a letter stating that I wasn't going to pursue it."

Six years earlier, he'd written a letter stating that he had resigned.

Zen Center's abbots have always been slow to recognize and formally acknowledge their disciples. For almost thirty years, many students understood it as their role to sit with those abbots; they understood that it was, by tradition and by dint of enlightenment, the role of their chosen teachers to acknowledge or not to acknowledge disciples. You could say that the role of the Abbot was eviscerated by the end of 1992, a decade after the Zen Center Apocalypse. Or, you could say that Zen Center students, one by one, were slowly waking up and seeing that their teachers desperately needed help, even when—or especially when—they could not acknowledge it.

Paul Discoe gradually left Zen Center in 1987–88 and established a private carpentry and contracting business—after he received Transmission from his teacher, Reb. "It felt substantial," Paul says, and then he adds, "Reb did try to pull it back at the last minute, which I could still kick him in the teeth for. He said, 'Maybe you ought to postpone it for a while. Maybe you shouldn't be doing this right now.'" Paul was pretty sure the timing was right. "I said, 'You got me this far, fella, and now you're going all the way; don't even think about backing out.'"

35.

THERE WAS SOME LINGERING confusion about the role of the Abbot at Zen Center. One of the least-concerned concerned onlookers was Betty Warren, one of Suzuki-roshi's first American students and a Zen Center supporter and monthly donor ever since. Betty stopped sitting at Zen Center after about five years of early morning visits to Sokoji on her way to teach school, and she stopped visiting Green Gulch regularly when "it got too big for me, I guess." She thinks, overall, "the place has been well handled, and I am grateful to people who go along with institutional life," which is not Betty's way. She has been aware of the troubles with the Abbots, she says, but they don't worry her.

"Suzuki-roshi's teaching was well planted," says Betty.

Back on the farm, though, the harvest was not metaphorical. Zen Center had a whole crop of ordained priests and Transmitted teachers in storage, and more on the way. There was no distribution system in place, but more important, there were serious questions about their cultivation methods. In June of 1991, thirty years after the community was first incorporated, the four members of the Task Force on the Role of Abbots met with Suzuki-roshi's son Hoitsu to solicit his understanding of the role of the Abbot in Japan, at Zen Center, and in Suzuki-roshi's teaching.

Hoitsu begins by stating that an Abbot is Abbot-for-life, and his view is not altered by any of the hypothetical scenarios he is offered, which finally escalate to the point where an Abbot has done something "horribly bad." In this case, Hoitsu speculates the Abbot might be asked to make a public apology, and "and then probably he'll stay as Abbot."

Everyone agrees that the Japanese are more committed to the Abbot-for-life appointment than are the Americans.

When he is asked directly for an opinion about the principal duties of an abbot at Zen Center, Hoitsu is definitive. "Teaching," he says. The Task Force explains that there are many administrative responsibilities for an Abbot in the integrated American model. "Work is a big part of why [students] are here," say the Americans. "They want a connection with the Abbot." Hoitsu says that someone else can do administrative tasks; the Abbot is there to teach, "which is what this place is for." But, the Americans ask, once you have people with children who need to be assigned housing and jobs, isn't the Abbot involved, de facto, in administration? "In Japan," says Hoitsu, "laypeople have their own families, so they come for spiritual guidance to the temple; for some other problems, they go to other places—if you are sick, go to doctor; for money—go to bank." But, the Americans explain, "part of the way of teaching [here at Zen Center] is in all the things we do together."

Hoitsu says, "That's fine."

"Abbot should not take care of money," says Hoitsu. "The best is that you should not make a situation for Abbot to be tempted by money. So not give a lot of money." In fact, he says, the position should be financially discouraging, "something difficult, not getting good payment." In America, says Hoitsu, "you give a lot of charming situations—power, money, car."

The Task Force reviews the role of various boards and advisors in Japan in making financial decisions, and Hoitsu reminds them that most Japanese temples are the private homes of the Abbots, so it is salaries, cars, and access to money that are restricted. The Americans have a lot of questions about this, and Hoitsu says that the point is the "teacher is the one who has nonattachment to money and all the material attractions." The Task Force speculates on plausible translations of this advice into the Zen Center model, and Hoitsu says, "Abbot should not consider about the finances. That's very important."

After you receive dharma Transmission, says Hoitsu, you should leave, start you own temple, and teach and ordain disciples there. "You don't take a student while your teacher is with you. That is etiquette," says Hoitsu. "You are in somebody else's temple . . . so you don't do that." Going out to teach is "the duty for people who have received Transmission," he says. The Task Force wonders if this is not a necessary difference in American Buddhist practice because there are so few established temples. Hoitsu says, "I don't think it's America, though. I know other temples send [teachers] out and say, 'Do not return.'"

The bigness of Zen Center is a recurring point of discussion. Almost from the start, Hoitsu reminds the Task Force that Zen Center could be much smaller. The Task Force reminds him that Zen Center is already very big. Hoitsu says, "Zen Center still doesn't have to be big."

The Task Force says that Zen Center is not like a small country temple in Japan, but it is like the big training temples. It was common knowledge among American practitioners for more than two decades that the monastery at Tassajara and the resulting administrative hierarchy at Zen Center were modeled on Eiheiji, the 700-year-old monastery in Japan. While trying to use this analogy with Hoitsu, however, members of the Task Force begin to doubt it; they tell each other that the comparison does not seem to make sense.

Hoitsu says, "I don't think you should compare Eiheiji and Tassajara."

Hoitsu asks several times about the possibility of dividing Zen Center into three temples, and the Task Force points out that Zen Center does not see the temples as separate, and Hoitsu says they could be, but the Task Force points out that they aren't, and Hoitsu tries one more time by saying that Zen Center "can be big; sometimes, it can be small" if only some of the teachers would leave so "Zen Center may look like [it doesn't] have many people there, but the foundation is big," and the Task Force points out that there is no place for the teachers to go because "we have no other temples," and Hoitsu says, "You make temples," and besides, he says, "You have three temples," and the Task Force wonders if maybe "having three Abbots is a good idea," and Hoitsu says, "Can't tell," and then he is reminded that there are already two Abbots, which leads to a lot of questions about who exactly is Abbot of which temple, and when Hoitsu apparently begins to see that there are two Abbots, and each one is nominally Abbot of three temples, though each one is actually Abbot of one temple (Reb at Green Gulch and Mel at City Center), and they share Tassajara, someone reminds Hoitsu that Mel has the Berkeley temple, too, which means that "sometimes [Mel] leads two practice periods at the same time," and Hoitsu says, "Impossible."

The Task Force and Hoitsu are not speaking the same language. Literally. The Task Force speaks English; Hoitsu speaks Japanese; the bilingual painter Mayumi Oda serves as a two-way translator for the session.

In the middle of the interview, Hoitsu quite suddenly asks, "What do you mean, *Abbot*?"

A Task Force member replies, "This is what we are trying to find out."

And it becomes apparent that the word *abbot* has no currency in Japan and has no genuine equivalent. After a lot of confusion, and thirty years after the incorporation of Zen Center, they all make one last effort to try to agree on what they mean by the word *abbot*.

Hoitsu: *Do* is Temple, *cho* is Head. Head of Temple.

Task Force: [At your temple], you are *Docho*?

Hoitsu: Yes.

Task Force: Do you have any other title?

Hoitsu: *Jushoku*.

Task Force: Can you distinguish between *Docho* and *Jushoku*?

Hoitsu: Same.

Task Force: At Eiheiji, *Docho* and . . .

Hoitsu: Eiheiji *Docho* is called *Kancho* [spelling standardized] because it's the same.

Task Force: Like what we call Abbot.

Translator: You see, that's our thing; it's very confusing.

Task Force: *Kancho* is Head of all of *Soto Shu*.

Hoitsu: Not *Kancho, Kanshu*.

Task Force: *Kancho* is Head of all of *Soto Shu.*

Hoitsu: Yes. Same as *Docho.*

Task Force: So sometimes Eiheiji *Kanshu* is *Kancho* and sometimes Sojiji [monastery] *Kanshu* is *Kancho.*

Translator: But in this case, each temple has a *Docho*, but this is not so in Zen Center.

The Task Force had run out of time.

Fu Schraeder, a disciple of Reb, asked, "Do you think Buddha had these problems?"

Hoitsu didn't respond.

Blanche Hartman, who in 1996 would become the seventh Abbot, the fourth co-Abbot, and the first Abbess of Zen Center, said, "Buddha didn't provide for all these monks. They just walked around with their begging bowls."

Sitting on her sofa at home, Betty Warren says, "Suzuki-roshi's teaching is clear. He conveyed it to the first people around him, and it has carried through to people who have never known him." Betty smiles. "I want to tell you a story," she says. "I have told it before. It is my most important lesson. It came with Bill Kwong during a sesshin. We were in the little kitchen at Sokoji," Betty says, "Suzuki-roshi's first temple in America. Bill was cook, and I was his helper. He was toasting rice crust. You know, when you make a pot of rice, there's a lot stuck to the pot. You scrape it off and save it. He had been saving the crusts for days. Usually, we had cereal for breakfast, but this morning it was rice crusts. On the cereal we usually had milk, so I asked if I should take out the milk. Bill said, 'No. Hot water.' So I dutifully took pots of hot water to the table. When time came to eat, and everyone sat down, I had rice crusts in a bowl, and I poured hot water in, and I flipped. I broke down with tears—tears of gratitude—that I had hot water to put onto my rice crusts." Betty slaps her knees, and she leans back into her sofa, laughing at herself. "I wept through breakfast. I was oblivious to everyone at the table. It was the deepest experience of gratitude I have ever known. Here, the universe was providing for my sustenance. I can trust."

36.

"Is there an American Zen?" Blanche Hartman doesn't answer the question. She repeats it in a way that makes it seem rhetorical—at first; then she just lets the question hang there for a while, and eventually it begins to look a little silly.

We are slowly eating and not eating lunch. Most of the Zen Center students and priests have long since finished their black beans and soup and salad, and we are almost alone in the big, handsome City Center dining room. Blanche is a straightforward woman in her seventies with a brown robe and short growth of white hair and no enduring interest in what she calls "the whole realm of alpha maleness." She and her husband have been practicing since 1969. Richard ordained her in 1977. In 1996, she became Norman's co-Abbot. Blanche says that a lot of the community's confusion about teachers and Abbots and Enlightenment and practice—a lot of the long, painful, schismatic story—has a root in "a big error, right at the start," when Bill Kwong's Transmission—which was begun by Suzuki-roshi—was not completed. This gave rise to the role of a single authority and teacher, and "Who could fill that role?" The co-abbacy, she says, and the developing sense of common authority are ways of acknowledging "interdependence and accountability, which are part of everyday life." Later, Blanche says, "You, know, it's just normal to have peers."

American Zen? "It's here," says Blanche, as if a person eating lunch in the San Francisco Zen Center might have deduced the answer to that question, "and it is changing. For a long time, it was a mostly a middle-class white crowd here. There's real diversity today."

"Creating a practice that includes everyone is complicated," says Mel Weitsman. Zen is and is not responsive to an individual's sense of identity, as Zen Center does and does not reflect the culture and mores of the city of San Francisco. "A lot of women and gays have come to Zen Center as a result of [our] openness to everyone," explains Mel, who recalls that "there were a number of gay men working in the [Page Street] office," in the late 1980s, while he was co-Abbot. "They developed a kind of gay banter, and they kind of got out of hand because nobody said anything. I didn't like it because this is the face that was being presented to the public." When Mel raised the issue, "about twenty people requested a meeting with me. And it was a great meeting. It seemed to work out well. I do not have a problem with gay people, but in the office, we should be mindful. Are we Zen students first or gay people? If we are all Zen students first, everyone can fit in and practice."

"My sexuality was never a problem or even a question," says an ordained priest who is gay. Many lesbians and gay men hold leadership positions in the community, he points out, "though it is striking that so few of us—especially the men—are in [domestic] relationships. I don't get it," he adds. "Is it that the gay men who are here are not particularly lucky? not particularly skillful?"

Many gay men might consider a home in San Francisco the definition of good luck, and the Page Street temple is only a few blocks from the Castro district, a landmark neighborhood in the gay-liberation movement of the last forty years. Thus, the position of gay men at Zen Center creates an unlikely, almost un-American impression—rather like the picture that emerges from accounts of life in Zen monasteries in Japan, where sex between men has long been both a common practice and a prohibited activity.

The demographics of Zen Center are slowly changing, but the vast majority of longtime practitioners and new students are so-called white Americans, who were raised in nominally Christian and Jewish families in which a college education was a reasonable economic expectation. The small number of Asian-American practitioners at Zen Center reflects a historic divide between so-called ethnic Buddhists (immigrants from Asia and their descendants who practice in temples devoted to the Buddhist tradition and language of their country of origin) and many American converts; this divide was evident at Sokiji, Suzuki-roshi's first temple in

America. The number of African-American and Hispanic members remains troublingly small. "Our Buddhist community does include people from many diverse backgrounds," wrote Mel Weitsman in 1994, in the first *Wind Bell* article devoted to the issue of social and cultural diversity, "but it is obvious that it is dominated by those on the light side of the spectrum."

Ethnic diversity was not traditionally valued in Japanese Zen or in Japanese culture; in fact, so-called racial purity was idealized. This history helps to explain Zen Buddhism's limited appeal to many Americans. Zen practice, of course, emphasizes the habit of seeing "the true nature," not the surface dualities, as was pointed out by Ralph Steele, a teacher trained in the Vipassana tradition at the Spirit Rock meditation center, who was invited to give a dharma talk at Zen Center in 1999. Cultural conditioning prepares us to see and respond to differences, he said; the practice is meant to help us see something more. But, he added, San Francisco "is probably one of the most diverse cities in the nation. And look at this room. Very interesting, huh?" At a glance, it was evident that the population in the meditation hall was not nearly as diverse ethnically or socially as the city. "We need to investigate that," he said. "There is something wrong."

The most evident demographic change since 1980 is the number of women in positions of leadership. "There has been a conscious effort to create equality between men and women in practice," says Mel Weitsman. In the early sixties, at Sokoji, Suzuki-roshi's first temple in America, women were slightly outnumbered, and men and women sat on opposite sides of the zendo during meditation; at Sokoji, as in Japan, women typically worked in supporting roles. Today, women slightly outnumber men. "In the last ten years," says Mel, "the monastery at Tassajara has been run mostly by women." And in the year 2000, the co-Abbots and President and the majority of officers and directors of Zen Center were all women.

"The spirit of the practice is to be aware that I am doing what I have always been doing," says Blanche. "I've never had the notion of practice having to do with transformation—of myself or anyone else." But as an American institution, Zen Center will inevitably change; for instance, says Blanche, in the last twenty years, Zen Center has become much more egalitarian. "If you choose Zen Center as a refuge—from your culture or from yourself—you'll be defeated."

"Maybe people have to suffer for a generation before they learn they're like everyone else," says David Chadwick, former maître d' at Greens, ordained disciple and biographer of Suzuki-roshi, and still a fixture at Zen Center, though he has not lived or practiced at Zen Center for many years. "I never left Zen Center," he says. "I never joined."

Whenever David seems to be on the verge of saying something conclusive, he disrupts the logic with a joke or a contrary observation or he just up and leaves. "Suzuki-roshi wanted people to start their own sitting groups," he says definitively, "which didn't quite happen." It has happened in the last seven or eight years. *Wind Bell* now lists about a dozen affiliated centers led by former Zen Center students, and another dozen weekly sitting groups. David is still talking, but he's walking away, and when I catch up to him, he is saying something else, something about seeing what happened during the 1970s "as a valiant effort. And, we all certainly did figure out what happens when you have too many people sitting too close together for too long."

David talks fast, and is generous about sharing his research, and I spend most of the day in Sebastopol, about sixty miles north of San Francisco, trailing him from lawn chairs in his front yard into a room above the garage in his backyard where he has accumulated big stacks of files and folders in his study, and then back to the sunny front yard, often with a new stack of photocopies, scribbling illegible notes on the run until it is time to pick up his son from school. Then we have a glass of wine, maybe two. Elin, David's wife, returns from her day of teaching school, and while David is describing his first visit to Japan, and his son is telling a story about space travel, Elin, who is the daughter of astronaut Rusty Schweickart, is asking if I eat meat, and then a lot happens fast, and smells very good, and I drop my notebook as we drift toward the kitchen, and Elin hands me a plastic pitcher and says, "Water," and I fill the pitcher while she picks up the lid of a pot full of hot rice, and soon we are eating a fried chicken dinner in a screened-in gazebo in their backyard. We're all a little stunned by the speed of this achievement, and we're hungry, so there's more nodding and chewing than talking until dinner is done.

We're finished eating. It's summer, but it's Northern California, so it might be spring or autumn, too. I'm tired, and I'm thinking it might be the rice and the chicken or it might be the wine. "Does anybody want to take a dunk in the hot tub?" Nobody wants to solve the mystery of the history of Zen Center this evening, though David offers to dig up some more notes. By then, the eastern edge of the big blue sky is bruised with evening. There are a few stars shining through the end of day. It's definitely the wine. I'm thinking I should offer to do the dishes, but no one seems ready to move inside, and there are no takers on the hot tub. Then I notice that the little chicken bones on David's plate are really clean—I mean, museum quality. I only notice because he is cracking the bones of a bare breast, and eating the meat from between each of the fragile ribs. I'm more than a little interested. He takes his son's plate, stacks it on his own, and then he picks up a half-eaten thigh and polishes that off, too. Well, I think, why not? He plucks some meat from underneath, and works his way around the complicated joint, eating every last bit, and now, I'm impressed, but nobody says anything, so I just let it go. David picks up Elin's plate and adds it to his stack. She had a leg, and she didn't eat all of her rice, and for dessert, she ate about a third of an apple, and as David extracts a little nib of meat from the yellow kneecap, I look at my own plate, and I don't know what it all means, but I can see where this is going, and by the end of the evening, all I know is that I'm of no help with the dishes.

It is always arresting when you first see something familiar done in an unfamiliar way. Blanche remembers her initial encounters with zazen, oryoki-style eating, and especially "all that bowing that was going on during services. I thought it was formal nonsense," she says. "And my practice since then has been primarily a faith and devotion practice. There is nothing better than bowing to express it."

Each Abbot brings a personal sense of practice, and Zen Center brings in a new Abbot every three to five years. Norman received dharma Transmission from Mel. He replaced Reb as Mel's co-Abbot in 1995. When he was asked to serve a second term, Norman agreed to serve an additional half-term. In 1996, Blanche, who also received dharma Transmission from Mel, replaced Mel and became Norman's co-Abbot. A few years later, in 2000, Linda, who received Transmission from Reb, replaced Norman.

"This is the part we don't know about," says Norman, reflecting on the future of the term limits. Can the community train a stream of senior teachers sufficient to produce a new Abbot every three years? "I don't think so," he says. "In the generation I came up with, there are enough people. But later on, practically speaking, I think, eventually, people who have been Abbot in the past will be asked again. That's not in the bylaws, but there is nothing in the bylaws restricting it."

Anything can happen, in other words.

Before Norman stepped down from the abbacy, Zen Center had raised the million dollars it needed to build houses for the trailer people at Green Gulch Farm.

Anything can happen.

Blanche invited Richard to attend and to speak at her installation cere-mony, and he did. Norman and Blanche have both visited Richard at Cre-stone; during their co-abbacy, students from Zen Center have studied with Richard and some of Richard's students have studied and practiced at Zen Center. "Norman and Blanche are incorrigible," says Mel. "No one else wants to put Dick in a special position." But each Abbot has time enough to change not only the future of Zen Center but its past. "Nor-man even included him in the *Buddhism at the Millennium's Edge* series," says Mel. "A lot of people didn't like giving Dick a singular role, but Nor-man did it anyway."

In 1999, Richard lectured in San Francisco and led a weekend work-shop at Zen Center; he was one of twelve "of Western Buddhism's most respected teachers and practitioners" whom Zen Center chose to feature in this widely advertised program. Several hundred people attended Richard's lecture, and Norman introduced him as "one of the most impor-tant teachers in my life" and "crucial to the history of Zen Center and the dharma in the West."

Yvonne Rand says, "When I expressed my dismay that Richard was being invited to be a speaker in the series, a Board member said, 'What's wrong with you? Can't you just get on with it?'" Yvonne nods. "I mean, it's a good question, but there is an answer to it."

"I've always been wary about Dick participating," says Mel. "People's memories are short. Little by little, things work themselves out. But try-ing to do something won't work. It's really up to him."

Anything can happen.

It's not a new language they are speaking, but Zen Center has taken a new form, and it changes the meaning of everything. You can hear the story change in time.

It is 1979. Will he recognize Mel, or Reb, or Linda, or Ed? *It's really up to him.*

It is 1999. Will he recognize Mel, or Reb, or Linda, or Ed? *It's really up to him.*

In addition to the personal and practice connections established by individuals over the years, several recent Zen Center initiatives have included Richard. In the late 1990s, many of the students who studied with Suzuki-roshi—"the disciples" and other senior students—attended a conference about his life and work organized by Gil Fronsdal, and then Lew Richmond set up a series of reunions. "People want to repair their relation to Suzuki-roshi," says Michael Wenger, who has devoted much of his time in recent years to preparing uncollected lectures by Suzuki-roshi for publication. "For the disciples [of Suzuki-roshi] this includes mourning the loss of Suzuki-roshi." A lot has been lost. Most of the disciples no longer practice regularly at Zen Center. Several of them attended only one or two of these gatherings.

"I spend too much time away from my wife as it is," says Les Kaye.

"We were just Zen students," says Ed Brown, who leads cooking and practice seminars and workshops around the country and has mixed feelings about formal practice. "I am not interested in the reunion impulse. It is twenty-five years too late."

Yvonne says, "When the disciples get together, it is not okay to talk about what's difficult. At the first meeting, we all talked about our experiences with Suzuki-roshi, and that helped a lot. That was common ground we could stand on with whole-heartedness." She did not attend the retreat with Richard and former students at The Shadows resort in 1997 "because I thought people might speak more freely if I wasn't there." And, she says, "It took me a long time to let go. It was painful. But it was just grief, and I needed to get through it." She feels the loss of an institutional platform for her work, but there are compensations in her country-temple scale zendo, and her garden. "I don't have much visibility, and that cuts both ways." It does free her to take risks as a teacher and in her daily practice, which is traditional and eclectic—not unlike the companionable congregation of noble old fruit trees and robust roses and fragile wands of gaura that droop into your path as you walk with her. "I'm sixty-four," she says. "I have a hip spur. Sometimes I have to take a nap. Here, there is someone with MS, somebody with a disintegrated disc, somebody with debilitating arthritis. And we're finding out how you practice meditation when your body gives out. And we have a five-year-old Tibetan Lama who lives here with his attendant."

Mel saw the meetings of the disciples as a chance to "find a way to be together" after twenty years of isolation—"which distorts everyone's vision," he says. "There is a need for a public reconciliation, but [what that means] depends on what you mean by reconciliation, for one thing. From my perspective, we can socialize with Dick, but Dick has to reconcile with us." Mel's measure of the progress to date is—well, measured: "Richard and Reb and Lew can be in the same room," he says.

The disciples' meetings occasioned Richard's first appearance at a public event at Green Gulch Farm since the Apocalypse. Instead of the traditional dharma lecture following the public zazen period on Sunday morning, on July 18, 1999, several of Suzuki-roshi's disciples assembled to speak about Zen Center's founder as a benefit for the Suzuki-roshi Archive Project.

The big, beautiful zendo-in-the-barn was packed with the committed and the curious. The extreme effort everyone was expending not to appear excited was making for a sweaty stillness, and every entrance was clotted with latecomers and young students trying to slide by with additional folding chairs hanging from their elbows, so from inside it appeared that everyone in the world wanted to be right where you were. Then an agitated woman on a cushion behind me complained that the people who had not attended zazen should not be seated on chairs. "We sat through the meditation, but they get to sit up there and have a clear view?" This is standard Sunday practice, someone told her; as it turned out, she wasn't interested in explanations. She was interested in Richard's appearance, and she must've stood up or somehow levitated above the rest of us when the disciples entered, because she reported that Richard's robe was "absolutely beautiful, and he looks better than most of the rest of them." A very serious student beside me held up his hand like a stop sign, and that worked for a while, so there was no sound but the rustling of robes while the disciples sat and arranged their many layers, but then late word reached us from an unidentified political correspondent that Jerry Brown was in the room.

That quiet, manic moment made it seem like the seventies at Zen Center.

Norman spoke first, and he has a way of making more room in a room, which he did, and the place cooled down when he stood up, as if he were a big open window. It was, Norman acknowledged, a sad and confounding moment for many Americans. John F. Kennedy, Jr., and his wife were missing; their plane had never made it to Martha's Vineyard. Closer to home, Zen Center members and friends were suffering the absence of two disciples. Grahame Petchey was with his son, who had just been involved in the motorcycle wreck that left him in a coma. And Lew Richmond was not in the room. Lew was in a coma, too, induced by viral encephalitis. No one knew then that the former American president's son was dead, or that Lew would wake up and begin to speak again, or that Grahame's son would slowly approach consciousness and maybe more.

Who among the disciples would speak first? The sequence seemed almost arbitrary. It was alphabetical—American, not Buddhist names. Anderson and Baker, Reb and Richard, first and second.

Reb spoke quietly about welcoming difficulties and escaping one's preconceived ideas, and other things he said he'd heard that Suzuki-roshi had said. That's how Reb said it—*so he'd heard Suzuki-roshi had said*—as if it was nothing anyone else couldn't hear. Richard introduced himself and repeated an offhand observation Suzuki-roshi had made about Americans, and the way they do everything with one hand. In time, Richard said, he saw that Suzuki-roshi tended to do things—pick up a cup, pass you the salt—with both hands, from the center of his body. And Ed remembered Suzuki-roshi telling his students *Don't move. Just sit. Don't move.*

The disciples told many stories about their beloved teacher. Each one was a snapshot. You couldn't exactly see Suzuki-roshi, but you could almost see his bent back and bald head as he moved a big rock from the creek bed to a more suitable spot on a sunny day at Tassajara; a small, steady, robed figure at the top of a creaky wooden staircase at Sokoji; a strong hand gently approaching a sitter's saggy shoulders. You could see that he was an elusive man. Near the end, Ed told a story Lew had told about being Suzuki-roshi's attendant in the 1960s. Lew had the flu; nevertheless, he set up Suzuki-roshi's room for a meeting, and set out some snacks. Lew sat beside his teacher during the meeting, and he ate a couple of olives, and put the pits on a napkin. Suzuki-roshi picked up one of Lew's pits and put it in his own mouth. Lew was impressed, and he was concerned about his germs and roshi getting sick, and he didn't say a word. Suzuki-roshi did it again. No one said a word. Lew watched Suzuki-roshi. And soon Lew recognized what Suzuki-roshi had recognized—that Lew hadn't thoroughly eaten the olives.

The first time you see something done thoroughly, it seems a little peculiar. Eating a half-eaten olive or polishing off a chicken leg; attending a public reunion; just sitting. But whether you see it as appealing or appalling, whether or not you admire such thoroughgoing behavior, it will never seem so strange again. That's the power of recognition.

37.

"Everyone who feels hurt has work to do," says Dan Welch. "And our culture barely understands this."

"Sometimes we take tiny little steps, like *kinhin* [walking meditation]. In America, that's called standing still," Dan says. "But we are walking."

"I don't know if there are or are not many lives. The Buddhist record is variable on it," says Dan. "I feel comfortable with the fact that both are true. Look at me. I'm an old man learning how to walk."

"At the disciples' reunions," says Dan, "I feel their questions, but they are not worded." Dan left Zen Center in 1984 with Deborah, went to Rome, and later landed with a friend in Santa Fe. It was 1987 "when I first turned around," 1988 "when I first approached Richard," and 1997 "when I first did a practice period with him." Since Suzuki-roshi's disciples have begun to meet, Dan has moved from his "little mud house in New Mexico" and taken up residence at Crestone Mountain Zen Center, and many of his former colleagues just can't quite see it.

"An integral part of my work with Richard—my vow—is not to perpetuate misapprehensions." Dan hesitates, then says, "Mel casually mentioned that he would like to talk about what has happened to me. But it might unfold more directly. [The disciples] are all sharp enough to know that they can just watch and see what is happening."

Dan and Richard are engaged in the formal work of dharma Transmission.

Dan says, "I don't know if I can make it clear."

A lot of his former colleagues thought he'd made it clear he wanted to kill Richard in the late 1980s. "No," says Dan, and his truck doesn't seem any bigger when, in near perfect monotone, he says, "I wanted to get Richard's attention. I had tried in very civilized ways and failed. Had he failed? I hadn't got his attention." We are parked halfway down Crestone Mountain. This is the second stop we've made since we climbed into his truck. This is Dan's idea of driving me to the airfield to catch a flight.

"I projected this out," he says. "If it requires me to hit him, I will hit him. And if that does not get his clear and undivided attention of this critical nature, then I will hit him again. And I will keep hitting him until I get it. And if right on the verge of death—he still, when he sensed that he would die if he 'made the choice' that, no, he could still not give me his undivided attention, then my sense of it was . . ." Dan snaps his fingers. "Flick."

We're both breathing hard, and that's about the only sign of life in the truck. Finally, Dan says, "Whew," and he laughs a little, but his see-through blue eyes are wet and shiny. "I can see how that can be construed," he says. "But, no." Dan doesn't move. "Stupid, perhaps, but that was the passion I felt. Undivided attention—that is our lineage, and that is human." Everything we see in the wide, flat world below is framed and stained by the windows. "Meaning was gone," says Dan. "[Richard's] words did not carry any meaning. I didn't have the capacity to endow my words with meaning. But deep fury with each other did not exclude deep love. And finally, I couldn't blame Richard for my anger. And I could clearly see that Richard was doing—I can honestly say—his best." Dan looks straight ahead. "I didn't see it at the time." He doesn't move. "A lot of people are still enormously hurt in ways they might never be able to articulate," says Dan. "They were dashed." He says nothing for almost a minute. "What I am talking about, what I am trying to find a way to talk about," says Dan, "is not to forgive or condone. That is Richard's work. But I have my work, too. And I realized that [Richard and I] are deeply connected." Dan shakes his head. "There is something in the middle that is beyond blame and beyond acclaim."

We just don't move from our precarious perch on the nosedive of a road.

"Once a year for fifteen years [Richard] has asked me why I was so angry," says Dan. "I have tried to articulate it, and I have always come away with the sense that he cannot hear it. It does not bother me that he doesn't hear it. He has his life and talents and problems, and I have mine."

Months later, Richard says, "For a long time, Dan and I were very estranged. I was never mad at Dan. I knew Dan; for him, it was a matter of the heart—not a matter of institutions or politics. It was a matter of the heart."

In the truck, on the verge, still not moving, Dan says, "How we touch each other is not verbal, and the deepest level with Suzuki-roshi was not verbal. That's why I could come back and practice with Richard. I found a window in my view of him between his enormous karmic suffering and unfinished business and his enormous intellect, which staggers me—it stifles me. I don't know how I could see it. It caught me by surprise." It's a singular view, and not one that anyone else can get behind and claim. That's the work Dan and Richard are doing. It is private. It is personal. And it is very old. "It's a little window into his guarded heart—the Richard Baker who gets up and practices every day. It includes and embraces his karmic and intellectual realm. It is very similar to what I saw in myself with Suzuki-roshi, that seemingly tiny window was where we could be together." Dan pauses. "I could hear and feel and see that he did it. He got up and sat."

And in that last moment, I really couldn't say if Dan was talking about Suzuki-roshi or Richard, and I could see, with Dan, the distinction is immaterial.

38.

THE BUDDHA HALL AT CITY Center is a gracious, turn-of-the-century parlor with high ceilings and big windows. It is Sunday, February 13, 2000, and at least 200 people are jammed onto cushions and chairs to watch the installation of Linda Cutts as the eighth Abbot, the fifth co-Abbot, and the second Abbess of the San Francisco Zen Center. Norman stepped down the day before and out into the world and the Worldwide Web, where his new Everyday Zen Foundation resides. There are another 200 people, at least, in the dining room, watching a live video transmission of Linda, freshly shaved, holding her teaching staff, high upon a satin-wrapped platform, the Mountain Seat behind her. She started down the block on Page Street and made her way in and through the Beginner's Mind Temple, accompanied by ringing bells and recitative verses and bowing at the many altars and shrines. Linda's husband, Steve Weintraub, will speak soon, as will Linda and Steve's daughter, and Reb, Linda's teacher, is lined up with the many attendant priests. Linda seems both nearer to us all and farther away as she step-by-ancient-step is raised up by the sangha to her ceremonious place above the rest. She is standing for the questions that will test her mettle and her teaching for the first time in the role of Abbess.

There are videotape and audiotape records of what happens next, but no American who was in the Buddha Hall that day will forget the lesson, or the empty old form in which the lesson was memorably transmitted. You could say it was a joke.

Up the aisle toward the Abbess walks Darlene Cohen. She is sort of smiling, sort of squinting. Linda is not *not* smiling. Darlene talks about why she likes her friends. It's for ordinary pleasures—lipstick and movie sorts of things. The room is so still you can feel people's eyeballs darting back and forth; it's hard to gauge where this might be going, and Darlene seems to be a person known for not going just there. Everyone can see what is happening. Darlene is recognizing Linda. It's enlightening. Linda is not *not* the Abbess, but she's *not* not a woman in the world, and a mother, and a wife, and another woman's friend. And Darlene says she likes her friends to tell her jokes. Darlene is standing still. She says she wants to tell a Knock, Knock joke with the Abbess.

The Abbess gamely agrees.

Darlene has one more trick up her capacious priest's sleeve. Darlene says, "You start."

"I start?" Linda's voice is a little higher than it was before.

"Yes," says Darlene.

And the Buddha Hall is still with expectation.

The Abbess agrees. "Knock, knock," says Linda, sort of laughing already.

Darlene looks really happy and pretty interested when she says, "Who's there?"

"It's Darlene," says Linda.

39.

"ONE MORNING, MAYBE IN 1960 or so, about four or five of us turned up for zazen. This was at Sokoji, on Bush Street," says Betty Warren from the other end of her cozy sofa. Her house in the hills of Sausalito high above the harbor full of houseboats seems even more like a nest since she told me she is leaving it soon. The yard is too much work, she says, and she's been here for more than fifty years, and she talks about it lightly, as if it is just a change of season. "Suzuki-roshi's bedroom was right above the front door on Bush Street," she says, smiling, eager to get to the good part. "We would knock on the door, and usually he would stick his head out and throw us the key. This time, he stuck his head out and said, 'Go away!' Then he closed his window. We didn't know what to do. We were all confounded. We decided he must have a headache, and we all went away. We returned the next day, and we knocked, and he threw us the key." Betty pauses, and her smile widens. "He was teaching us," she says with genuine delight. "He was teaching us the unpredictability of things. You can't even count on your master. And you can count on him. It's all changeable. The lesson you have to learn if you want to count on anything is that you can't count on anything."